Free Will

Other Titles from
HACKETT READINGS

Certainty
Equality
The Good Life
The Idea of Race
Justice
Life and Death
Materialism and the Mind-Body Problem
Reality
Time

Free Will

Second Edition

Edited, with Introduction, by
Derk Pereboom

Hackett Publishing Company, Inc.
Indianapolis/Cambridge

Printed in the United States of America

14 13 12 11 10 09 1 2 3 4 5 6

For further information, please address

Hackett Publishing Company, Inc.
P.O. Box 44937
Indianapolis, IN 46244-0937

www.hackettpublishing.com

Text design by Dan Kirklin

Composition by Agnew's, Inc.

Printed at Edwards Brothers, Inc.

Library of Congress Cataloging-in-Publication Data

Free will / edited, with introduction, by Derk Pereboom. — 2nd ed.
p. cm.
Includes bibliographical references (p.).
ISBN 978-1-60384-129-0 (pbk.) — ISBN 978-1-60384-130-6 (cloth)
1. Free will and determinism. I. Pereboom, Derk, 1957–
BJ1461.F75 2009
123′.5—dc22

2009037563

Contents

Introduction

The problem of free will, which has exercised philosophers from antiquity to the present day, arises from a conflict between two considerations, each of which makes a powerful appeal to our self-understanding. On the one hand, we experience ourselves as agents who are the sources of our actions and thus control how we act; on the other, we have reason to believe that we live in a world in which we are generally subject to forces beyond our control.

So first, we human beings typically suppose that we are the source of our actions in a particularly strong sense, one very different from the sense in which a machine is the source of what it produces. Many of us believe that this is manifest in our ability to control an action so that at the moment of choice we can make it happen or else refrain from making it happen—when we are deliberating, either option is available to us. This difference is reflected in our judgments about blameworthiness and praiseworthiness when their object is a human being rather than a machine. Although we may sometimes blame a photocopier when it malfunctions, we generally consider this response inappropriate. When a normal and mature human being does something wrong, however, we believe that he has the ability to control his actions in a way that justifies our considering him blameworthy. Traditionally, the control over action required to warrant judgments of blameworthiness and praiseworthiness is called *free will,* or, more explicitly, *the sort of free will required for moral responsibility.*

But second, we have reasons for regarding human beings as more like machines than we ordinarily suppose. These reasons stem from scientific views that consider human beings to be parts of nature and therefore governed by natural laws, or from theological perspectives that require every action to be causally determined by God. For many contemporary philosophers, the first of these is especially powerful, and as a result, they accept determinism or claims about the universe that are equally threatening to moral responsibility.

There are three types of reaction to this dilemma. William of Ockham and Thomas Reid maintain that determinism is not compatible with the free will required for moral responsibility—they are *incompatibilists*—but they resist the reasons for holding determinism and embrace free will. Their position is called *libertarianism.* Benedict Spinoza and Joseph Priestley, *hard determinists,* are also incompatibilists, but they accept determinism and deny that we have the sort of free will required for moral responsibility. Gottfried Leibniz and David Hume are *compatibilists,* arguing that it is legitimate to accept determinism and at the same time affirm that we have free will in the sense required for moral responsibility.

According to libertarianism, we can choose to act without being causally determined by factors beyond our control, and we can therefore be morally responsible for our actions. Two versions of libertarianism have been developed. In *agent-causal libertarianism,* freedom of the sort required for moral responsibility is accounted for by the existence of agents who, as substances, possess a causal power to make choices without being causally determined to do so. On one version of agent-causal theory, when such an agent acts freely, she can be inclined but not causally determined to act by factors such as reasons, desires, and beliefs. In this collection, agent-causal libertarianism is represented by Immanuel Kant, Thomas Reid, Roderick Chisholm, Randolph Clarke, and Timothy O'Connor. In *event-causal libertarianism,* only causation among events (or, on a related view, property-instances) and no causation that is fundamentally by substances, is admitted, and indeterminacy in the production of appropriate events is considered sufficient to allow for moral responsibility. The Epicurean philosopher Lucretius provides a rudimentary version of such a view when he claims that free actions are accounted for by undetermined swerves in the downward paths of atoms; the relevant excerpts from *De Rerum Natura (On the Nature of Things)* are included. Robert Kane develops a detailed contemporary version of this position, and he provides an account of this position for this collection.

Critics of libertarianism often contend that indeterministically free-willed action cannot be squared with certain provisions in action theory that libertarians themselves want to endorse. Specifically, they claim that action that is freely willed in the libertarian sense cannot at the same time be morally responsible action, that it cannot meet certain plausible general conditions for explaining such action, and that it cannot be rational. In addition, critics argue that the sort of free will libertarianism espouses cannot harmonize with the empirical evidence. Our choices produce physical events in the brain and in the rest of the body, and these events seem to be governed by physical laws. In response, the libertarian position must make it credible that our actions can be freely willed, in the sense libertarianism advocates, given the evidence we have about these physical laws.

Many philosophers aspire to retain the legitimacy of our ordinary attitudes toward human action and at the same time to regard the world as deterministic or in a way that appears equally responsibility-threatening.

As a result, compatibilism is a commonly held position. Three types of routes to compatibilism can be differentiated. The first, developed by Peter Strawson, argues that contrary to what incompatibilists assume, the truth of determinism is irrelevant to questions of moral responsibility. According to this view, the basis of moral responsibility is found in reactive attitudes such as indignation, resentment, guilt, and gratitude. For example, the fact that agents are typically resented for certain kinds of actions constitutes their being blameworthy for performing such actions. As a result, justification for claims of blameworthiness and praiseworthiness ends in the system of human reactive attitudes. Because moral responsibility has this type of basis, the truth or falsity of determinism is immaterial to whether we are justified in holding agents to be morally responsible.

The second type of route, like the first, objects to a widespread and central incompatibilist assumption. The claim that this second route challenges is that, for an agent to be morally responsible for an action, she must have been able to do otherwise. Harry Frankfurt, in "Alternate Possibilities and Moral Responsibility," provides a powerful argument against this presupposition, and compatibilists such as John Martin Fischer use Frankfurt's argument to attempt to undermine incompatibilism. If it is false that one must have been able to do otherwise to be morally responsible, Fischer argues, then the claim that determinism is incompatible with moral responsibility becomes implausible.

The third and most common type of route to compatibilism tries to distinguish causal circumstances of actions that exclude moral responsibility from those that do not. What underlies this approach is the conviction that moral responsibility requires some type of causal integration between the agent's psychology and her action, while it does not demand the absence of causal determination. This route to compatibilism is typically explored by monitoring our reactions concerning blameworthiness and praiseworthiness in specific cases—cases involving, for example, coercion, addiction, mental illness, hypnotism, and brainwashing. These reactions are used to discover the metaphysical conditions on which moral responsibility depends, conditions which are held to consist in some type of causal integration between the agent's psychology and her action. In this volume, the third type of route is developed by Aristotle, by Augustine, arguably (but controversially) by Aquinas, and by Hume, Ayer, Frankfurt, and Fischer and, with respect to praiseworthiness, by Susan Wolf.

Hard determinism—the incompatibilist endorsement of determinism and rejection of the free will required for moral responsibility—is less frequently defended than either libertarianism or compatibilism. Spinoza is one exception, and the parts of the *Ethics* in which he articulates this position are included here. Philosophers have expressed many concerns about this position. For example, hard determinism would imperil our self-conception as deliberative agents; it would render unjustified our efforts to resist crime and injustice; morality itself would turn out to be incoherent; and the reactive attitudes that lie at the core of human interpersonal relationships would be threatened.

The standard interpretation of quantum mechanics—our best theory about elementary physical stuff—denies that determinism is true. But philosophers have often argued that the kind of indeterminacy affirmed by this interpretation will not undergird the kind of free will required for moral responsibility. In his essay, Galen Strawson argues for the claim that moral responsibility is impossible whether or not determinism is true. In my own view, our best theories about the nature of the physical world seriously threaten morally responsibility. But I also believe that many of the reasons against denying that we are morally responsible are not as compelling as they might at first seem. Disavowing moral responsibility does not imperil our self-conception as deliberative agents, it does not undermine moral principles and values, and it leaves the possibility of good interpersonal relationships intact. Indeed, maintaining a position of this sort might actually prove advantageous by giving pause to the anger and resentment that are so often destructive to human happiness.

Aristotle, from the *Nicomachean Ethics*

Aristotle (384–322 B.C.) was born in Macedonia and practiced philosophy in Athens. His emphasis on the natural sciences distinguishes him from his teacher, Plato. In this excerpt from his Nicomachean Ethics *he develops a compatibilist account of free will, according to which an action can be legitimately subject to praise or blame only if it is voluntary. Actions are voluntary only if, in ways that Aristotle is careful to spell out, they are not forced or done from ignorance. His account of the conditions under which agents are morally responsible serves as a model for the debate, and this view has been very influential among compatibilists.*

Book III

Virtue, then, is about feelings and actions. These receive praise or blame when they are voluntary, but pardon, sometimes even pity, when they are involuntary. Hence, presumably, in examining virtue we must define the voluntary and the involuntary. This is also useful to legislators, both for honours and for corrective treatments.

What comes about by force or because of ignorance seems to be involuntary. What is forced has an external origin, the sort of origin in which the agent or victim contributes nothing—if, e.g., a wind or human beings who control him were to carry him off.

But now consider actions done because of fear of greater evils, or because of something fine. Suppose, e.g., a tyrant tells you to do something shameful, when he has control over your parents and children, and if you do it, they will live, but if not, they will die. These cases raise dispute about whether they are voluntary or involuntary.

However, the same sort of thing also happens with throwing cargo overboard in storms; for no one willingly throws cargo overboard, unconditionally, but anyone with any sense throws it overboard [under some conditions] to save himself and the others.

These sorts of actions, then, are mixed. But they would seem to be more like voluntary actions. For at the time they are done they are choiceworthy, and the goal of an action reflects the occasion; hence also we should call the action voluntary or involuntary with reference to the time when he does it. Now in fact he does it willingly; for in these sorts of actions he has within him the origin of the movement of the limbs that are the instruments [of the action], and when the origin of the actions is in him, it is also up to him to do them or not to do them. Hence actions of this sort are voluntary, though presumably the actions without [the appropriate] condition are involuntary, since no one would choose any action of this sort in itself.

For such [mixed] actions people are sometimes actually praised, whenever they endure something shameful or painful as the price of great and fine results; and if they do the reverse, they are blamed, since it is a base person who endures what is most shameful for nothing fine or for only some moderately fine result.

In some cases there is no praise, but there is pardon, whenever someone does a wrong action because of conditions of a sort that overstrain human nature, and that no one would endure. But presumably there are some things we cannot be compelled to do, and rather than do them we should suffer the most terrible consequences and accept death; for the things that [allegedly] compelled Euripides' Alcmaeon to kill his mother appear ridiculous.

It is sometimes hard, however, to judge what [goods] should be chosen at the price of what [evils], and what [evils] should be endured as the price of what [goods]. And it is even harder to abide by our judgment, since the results we expect [when we endure] are usually painful, and the actions we are compelled [to endure, when we choose] are usually shameful. That is why those who have been compelled or not compelled receive praise and blame.

What sorts of things, then, should we say are forced? Perhaps we should say that something is forced unconditionally whenever its cause is external and the agent contributes nothing. Other things are involuntary in themselves, but choiceworthy on this occasion and as the price of these [goods], and their origin is in the agent. These are involuntary in themselves, but, on this occasion and as the price of these [goods], voluntary. Still, they would seem to be more like voluntary actions, since actions involve particular [conditions], and [in mixed actions] these [conditions] are voluntary. But what sort of thing should be chosen as the price of what [good] is not easy to answer, since there are many differences in particular [conditions].

But suppose someone says that pleasant things and fine things force us, since they are outside us and compel us. It will follow that for him everything is forced, since everyone in every action aims at something fine or pleasant.

Moreover, if we are forced and unwilling to act, we find it painful; but if something pleasant or fine is its cause, we do it with pleasure.

It is ridiculous, then, for [our opponent] to ascribe responsibility to external [causes] and not to himself, when he is easily snared by such things; and ridiculous to take responsibility for fine actions himself, but to hold pleasant things responsible for his shameful actions.

What is forced, then, would seem to be what has its origin outside the person forced, who contributes nothing.

Everything caused by ignorance is non-voluntary, but what is involuntary also causes pain and regret. For if someone's action was caused by ignorance, but he now has no objection to the action, he has done it neither willingly, since he did not know what it was, nor unwillingly, since he now feels no pain. Hence, among those who act because of ignorance, the agent who now regrets his action seems to be unwilling, while the agent with no regrets may be called non-willing, since he is another case—for since he is different, it is better if he has his own special name.

Further, action caused by ignorance would seem to be different from action done in ignorance. For if the agent is drunk or angry, his action seems to be caused by drunkenness or anger, not by ignorance, though it is done in ignorance, not in knowledge.

[This ignorance does not make an action involuntary.] Certainly every vicious person is ignorant of the actions he must do or avoid, and this sort of error makes people unjust, and in general bad. But talk of involuntary action is not meant to apply to [this] ignorance of what is beneficial.

For the cause of involuntary action is not [this] ignorance in the decision, which causes vice; it is not [in other words] ignorance of the universal, since that is a cause for blame. Rather, the cause is ignorance of the particulars which the action consists in and is concerned with; for these allow both pity and pardon, since an agent acts involuntarily if he is ignorant of one of these particulars.

Presumably, then, it is not a bad idea to define these particulars, and say what they are, and how many. They are: (1) who is doing it; (2) what he is doing; (3) about what or to what he is doing it; (4) sometimes also what he is doing it with, e.g., the instrument; (5) for what result, e.g., safety; (6) in what way, e.g., gently or hard.

Now certainly someone could not be ignorant of *all* of these unless he were mad. Nor, clearly, (1) could he be ignorant of who is doing it, since he could hardly be ignorant of himself. But (2) he might be ignorant of what he is doing, as when someone says that [the secret] slipped out while he was speaking, or, as Aeschylus said about the mysteries, that he did not know it was forbidden to reveal it; or, like the person with the catapult, that he let it go when he [only] wanted to demonstrate it. (3) Again, he might think that his son is an enemy, as Merope did; or (4) that the barbed spear has a button on it, or that the stone is pumice-stone. (5) By giving someone a drink to save his life we might kill him; (6) and wanting to touch someone, as they do in sparring, we might wound him.

There is ignorance about all of these [particulars] that the action consists in. Hence someone who was ignorant of one of these seems to have done an action unwillingly, especially when he was ignorant of the most important of them; these seem to be (2) what he is doing, and (5) the result for which he does it.

Hence it is action called involuntary with reference to *this* sort of ignorance [that we meant when we said that] the agent must, in addition, feel pain and regret for his action.

Since, then, what is involuntary is what is forced or is caused by ignorance, what is voluntary seems to be what has its origin in the agent himself when he knows the particulars that the action consists in.

[Our definition is sound.] For, presumably, it is not correct to say that action caused by emotion or appetite is involuntary.

For, first of all, on this view none of the other animals will ever act voluntarily; nor will children. [But clearly they do.]

Next, among all the actions caused by appetite or emotion do we do none of them voluntarily? Or do we do the fine actions voluntarily and the shameful involuntarily? Surely [the second answer] is ridiculous when one and the same thing [i.e., appetite or emotion] causes [both fine and shameful actions]. And presumably it is also absurd to say [as the first answer implies] that things we ought to desire are involuntary; and in fact we ought both to be angry at some things and to have an appetite for some things, e.g., for health and learning.

Again, what is involuntary seems to be painful, whereas what expresses our appetite seems to be pleasant.

Moreover, how are errors that express emotion any less voluntary than those that express rational calculation? For both sorts of errors are to be avoided; and since nonrational feelings seem to be no less human [than rational calculation], actions resulting from emotion or appetite are also proper to a human being; it is absurd, then, to regard them as involuntary.

2

The Stoics, from various sources

Stoicism was a prominent school of philosophy founded in Athens around 300 B.C. Its first leader was Zeno of Citium (c. 336–c. 265 B.C.), the second was Cleanthes (c. 331–232), and the third Chrysippus (c. 279–206). The Stoics were determinists, arguing that everything that happens is determined by the will of God or, equivalently, by the laws of nature. But they also believed that we can have the sort of control over our actions that allows for moral responsibility, and hence they were compatibilists. Very little of the actual writings of these early Stoics are available, and our access to them consists largely of reports by other authors who were familiar with their views. The following selections are examples of such reports.

Epictetus *Discourses* 2.19.1–5

1. The Master Argument [of Diodorus Cronos] seems to be based on premisses of this sort. There is a general conflict among these three statements: [1] everything past and true is necessary; [2] the impossible does not follow from the possible; [3] there is something possible which neither is nor will be true. Seeing this conflict, Diodorus used the plausibility of the first two statements to establish that only that which is or will be true is possible. 2. But from among the [consistent] pairs [of statements] one man will retain these: [3] that there is something possible which neither is nor will be true and [2] that the impossible does not follow from the possible; but [he would not concede] that [1] everything past and true is necessary. This seems to be the position of Cleanthes and his followers, and Antipater generally agreed with it. 3. Others [will accept] the other two, [3] that there is something possible which neither is nor will be true and [1] that everything past and true is necessary; [and they will concede] that the impossible follows from the possible. 4. But it is impossible to retain all three of those statements because of their general conflict

with each other. 5. So if someone asks me, "which pair do you retain?", I will answer him by saying that I do not know. I have learned from research that Diodorus retained one pair, the followers of Panthoides and Cleanthes another, and the followers of Chrysippus another.

Pseudo-Plutarch *On Fate* 547ef

(547e) According to the opposing argument, the first and most important point would seem to be that nothing happens uncaused, but according to prior causes. Second, that this cosmos, which is itself coordinated and sympathetic with itself, is administered by nature. Third, which would seem rather to be additional evidence, is the fact that divination is in good repute with all men because it really does exist, with divine cooperation, and second that wise men are contented in the face of events, (547f) since all of them occur according to [divine] allotment; and third, the much-discussed point, that every proposition is true or false.

Theodoretus *Graecarum Affectionum Cura* 6.14

And Chrysippus the Stoic said that what is necessitated is no different from what is fated, and that fate is an eternal, continuous and ordered motion [or change]. Zeno of Citium called fate a power capable of moving matter and gave to the same [force] the names providence and nature. His successors said that fate was a rational principle for the things administered by providence within the cosmos, and again in other treatises they called fate a string of causes.

Aetius 1.28.4

The Stoics say it is a string of causes, i.e., an ordering and connection which is inescapable.

Alexander *De Anima Mantissa*

But it is conceded that all things which happen by fate occur in a certain order and sequence and have an element of logical consequence in them. . . . Anyway, they say that fate is a string of causes.

Plutarch *Stoic Self-Contradictions* 34, 1049f–1050d

(1049f) But nevertheless one will have not just one or two occasions, but thousands, to address to Chrysippus this remark, which is now praised: "You have said the easiest thing, in blaming the gods." For first, in book one of his *Physics* he compares the eternity of motion to a posset[1] which spins and agitates the various things which come to pass in various ways; then he says: (1050a) "Since the organization of the universe proceeds thus, it is necessary for us to be such as we are, in accordance with it, whether we are ill or lame, contrary to our individual nature, or whether we have turned out to be grammarians or musicians." And again, a bit further on: "and on this principle we will say similar things about our virtue and our vice and, in general, about our skills or lack of them, as I have said". And a bit further on, removing all ambiguity: "for it is impossible for any of the parts, even the smallest one, to turn out differently than according to the common nature and its reason". That the common nature and the (1050b) common reason of nature are fate and providence and Zeus, even the Antipodeans know this; for the Stoics prattle on about this everywhere and he says that Homer correctly said[2] "and Zeus' plan was being fulfilled", referring it to fate and the nature of the universe according to which everything is ordered.

How, then, can it be the case at one and the same time that god is not partly responsible for anything shameful and that not even the smallest thing can occur otherwise than according to the common nature and its reason? For in everything which occurs surely there are some shameful things too. And yet, Epicurus twists this way and that and exercises his ingenuity (1050c) in his attempt to free and liberate voluntary action from the eternal motion, so as not to leave vice free of blame, while Chrysippus gives vice blatant freedom to say not only that it is necessary and according to fate but even that it occurs according to god's reason and the best nature. And this too is plain to see, when we provide the following literal quotation: "for since the common nature extends into everything, it will be necessary that everything which occurs in any way in the universe and in any of its parts should occur according to it [the common nature] and its reason, in proper and unhindered fashion, because there is nothing outside it which could hinder its organization nor (1050d) could any of its parts be moved or be in a state otherwise than according to the common nature."

1. A drink composed of a suspension of solid particles in a fluid base.

2. *Iliad* 1.5.

Simplicius *Commentary on Aristotle's Categories* 13a37

Concerning [pairs of] contradictories which bear on the future, the Stoics accept the same principle as they do for other statements. For what is true of [pairs of] contradictories concerning things present and past is also true, they say, for future contradictories themselves and their parts. For either "it will be" or "it will not be" is true if they must be either true or false. For they are fixed by the future events themselves. And if there will be a sea-battle tomorrow, it is true to say that there will be. But if there will not be a sea-battle, it is false to say that there will be. Either there will or there will not be a battle; therefore, each statement is either true or false.

Plutarch *Stoic Self-Contradictions* 1055de

(1055d) . . . Surely his [Chrysippus's] account of possibility is in conflict with his account of fate. (1055e) For if Diodorus's view of the possible as "what either is or will be true" is not right but [Chrysippus's view is], that "everything which permits of occurring even if it is not going to occur is possible", then many things are possible which are not according to fate. . . . ⟨Therefore, either⟩ fate loses its character as unconquerable, unforceable, and victorious over all things, or, if fate is as Chrysippus claims, then "what permits of occurring" will often turn out to be impossible. And everything true will be necessary, being gripped by the most sovereign of necessities; while everything false will be impossible, since the greatest cause opposes its being true.

Cicero *On Fate* 28–33

28. Nor will the so-called "Lazy Argument" stop us. For a certain argument is called the *argos logos* by the philosophers, and if we listened to it, we would never do anything at all in life. For they argue in the following fashion: "if it is fated for you to recover from this illness whether you call the doctor or not, you will recover; 29. similarly, if it is fated for you not to recover from this illness whether you call the doctor or not, you will not recover. And one of the two is fated. Therefore, there is no point in calling the doctor". It is right to call this kind of argument "lazy" and "slothful," because on the same reasoning all action will be abolished from life. One can also change the form of it, so that the word "fate" is not included and still keep the same sense, in this way: "if from eternity this has been true, 'you will recover from that disease whether you call a doctor or not', you will recover; similarly, if from eternity this has been false, 'you will recover

from that disease whether you call the doctor or not' you will not recover. Et cetera."

30. Chrysippus criticizes this argument. "For," he says, "some things are simple, some conjoined. 'Socrates will die on that day' is simple. Whether he does anything or not, the day of death is fixed for him. But if it is fated, 'Oedipus will be born to Laius', it cannot be said, 'whether Laius lies with a woman or not'. For the events are conjoined and co-fated." For that is how he refers to it, since it is fated thus, *both* that Laius will lie with his wife *and* that Oedipus will be produced by her. Just as, if it had been said, "Milo will wrestle at the Olympics" and someone reported "therefore, he will wrestle whether or not he has an opponent", he would be wrong. For "he will wrestle" is conjoined, because there is no wrestling match without an opponent. "Therefore, all the sophistries of that type are refuted in the same way. 'Whether you call a doctor or not, you will recover' is fallacious; for calling the doctor is fated just as much as recovering". Such situations, as I said, he calls co-fated.

31. Carneades [the Academic] did not accept this entire class [co-fated events] and thought that the above argument had been constructed with insufficient care. And so he approached the argument in another way, not using any fallacious reasoning. This was the result: if there are antecedent causes for everything that happens, then everything happens within a closely knit web of natural connections. If this is so, then necessity causes everything. And if this is true there is nothing in our power. There is, however, something in our power. But if everything happens by fate, everything happens as a result of antecedent causes. Therefore, it is not the case that whatever happens happens by fate. 32. This argument cannot be made tighter. For if someone wished to turn the argument around and say: if every future event is true from eternity so that whatever should happen would certainly happen, then everything happens within a closely knit web of natural connections, he would be speaking nonsense. For there is a great difference between a natural cause making future events true from eternity and future events which might be understood to be true, without natural [cause] from eternity. Thus Carneades said that not even Apollo is able to pronounce on any future events unless it were those the causes of which are already contained in nature, so that they would happen necessarily. 33. On what basis could even a god say that Marcellus, who was three times a consul, would die at sea? This was indeed true from eternity, but it did not have efficient causes. Thus [Carneades] was of the opinion that if not even past events of which no trace existed would be known to Apollo, how much less would he know future events, for only if

the efficient causes of any thing were known would it then be possible to know what would happen in the future. Therefore, Apollo could not predict anything regarding Oedipus, there not being the requisite causes in nature owing to which it was necessary that he would kill his father, or anything of this sort.

Aetius 1.29.7

Anaxagoras and the Stoics say that chance is a cause non-evident to human calculation. For some things happen by necessity, some by fate, some by intention, some by chance and some automatically.

Plutarch *On Stoic Self-Contradictions* 1045b–c

(1045b) Some philosophers think that they can free our impulses from being necessitated by external causes if they posit in the leading part of the soul an adventitious motion which becomes particularly evident in cases where things are indistinguishable. For when two things are equivalent and equal in importance and it is necessary to take one of the two, there being no cause which leads us to one or the other since they do not differ from each other, this adventitious cause generates a swerve in the soul all by itself (1045c) and so cuts through the stalemate. Chrysippus argues against them, on the grounds that they are doing violence to nature by [positing] something which is uncaused, and frequently cites dice and scales and many other things which cannot fall or settle in different ways at different times without some cause or difference, either something which is entirely in the things themselves or something which occurs in the external circumstances. For he claims that the uncaused and the automatic are totally non-existent, and that in these adventitious [causes] which some philosophers make up and talk about there are hidden certain non-evident causes, and they draw our impulse in one direction or another without our perceiving it.

Alexander *De Anima Mantissa*

To say that chance is a cause non-evident to human calculation is not the position of men who posit some nature called chance, but of men who say that chance consists in the relational disposition of men to the causes. . . . For if they were to say not that chance is the cause which is non-evident to some men, but the cause which is universally non-evident to all men, they would not be admitting that chance exists at all, although they grant that divination exists and suppose that it is able to make known to other men the things which seemed to be non-evident.

Alexander of Aphrodisias *On Fate* 26, 196.21–197.3 Bruns

Perhaps it would not be a bad idea for us to take in hand and examine how matters stand with the puzzles they put most confidence in; for perhaps they will appear not too difficult to solve. One of these [difficulties] is as follows: If, they say, things are in our power when we can also do the opposite of those things, and it is upon such things that praise and blame and encouragement and discouragement and punishment and honours are bestowed, then it follows that being prudent and virtuous will not be in the power of those who are prudent and virtuous; for [such men] are no longer capable of receiving the vices opposite to their virtues. And the same point applies to the vices of bad men; for it is no longer in the power of such men to cease being bad. But it is absurd to say that the virtues and vices are not in our power, and that they are not the objects of praise and blame. Therefore, "what is in our power" is not like that.

Aulus Gellius 7.2.15

And so Cicero, in his book entitled *On Fate,* when he said that the question was very obscure and complex, says also in these words that even the philosopher Chrysippus did not get clear on the problem: "Chrysippus, sweating and toiling to discover how he might explain that everything happens by fate and yet that there is something in our own power, gets tangled up like this. . . . "

Cicero *On Fate* 39–44

39. Since there were two opinions of the older philosophers, one belonging to those men who believed that everything occurred by fate in such a way that the fate in question brought to bear the force of necessity (this was the view of Democritus, Heraclitus, Empedocles and Aristotle), the other of those who held that there were voluntary motions of the mind without fate, Chrysippus, it seems to me, wanted to strike a middle path, like an informal arbitrator, but attached himself more to the group which wanted the motions of the mind to be free of necessity. But while employing his

own terms he slipped into such difficulties that he wound up unwillingly confirming the necessity of fate.

40. And, if you please, let us see how this occurs in the case of assent, which we discussed at the start of our discourse. For the older philosophers who held that everything occurred by fate said that it occurred by force and necessity. Those who disagreed with them freed assent from fate and denied that if fate applied to assent it could be free of necessity and so they argued thus: "if everything happens by fate, everything occurs by an antecedent cause and if impulse [is caused], then also what follows from impulse [is caused]; therefore, assent too. But if the cause of impulse is not in us then impulse itself is not in our own power; and if this is so, not even what is produced by impulse is in our power; therefore, neither assent nor action is in our power. From which it follows that neither praise nor blame nor honours nor punishments are fair". Since this is wrong, they think that it is a plausible conclusion that it is not the case that whatever happens happens by fate.

41. Chrysippus, however, since he both rejected necessity and wanted that nothing should occur without prior causes, distinguished among the kinds of causes in order both to escape from necessity and to retain fate. "For," he said, "some causes are perfect and principal, while others are auxiliary and proximate. Therefore, when we say that all things occur by fate by antecedent causes, we do not want the following to be understood, viz. that they occur by perfect and principal causes; but we mean this, that they occur by auxiliary and proximate causes". And so his response to the argument which I just made is this: if everything occurs by fate it does indeed follow that everything occurs by antecedent causes, but not by principal and perfect causes. And if these are not themselves in our power it does not follow that not even impulse is in our power. But this would follow if we were saying that everything occurred by perfect and principal causes with the result that, since these causes are not in our power, ⟨not even [impulse] would be in our power⟩. 42. Therefore, those who introduce fate in such a way that they connect necessity to it are subject to the force of that argument; but those who will not say that antecedent causes are perfect and principal will not be subject to the argument at all.

As to the claim that assents occur by antecedent causes, he says that he can easily explain the meaning of this. For although assent cannot occur unless it is stimulated by a presentation, nevertheless, since it has that presentation as its proximate cause and not as its principal cause, it can be explained in the way which we have been discussing for some time now, just as Chrysippus wishes. It is not the case that the assent could occur if it were not stimulated by a force from outside (for it is necessary that an assent should be stimulated by a presentation); but Chrysippus falls back on his cylinder and cone. These cannot begin to move unless they are struck; but when that happens, he thinks that it is by their own natures that the cylinder rolls and the cone turns.

43. "Therefore," he says, "just as he who pushed the cylinder gave it the start of its motion, he did not, however, give it its "rollability", so a presentation which strikes will certainly impress its object and as it were stamp its form on the mind, but our assent will be in our own power and the assent, just as was said in the case of the cylinder, when struck from without, will henceforth be moved by its own force and nature. But if something were produced without an antecedent cause, then it would be false that everything occurs by fate. But if it is probable that a cause precedes all things which occur, what could block the conclusion that all things occur by fate? Let it only be understood what difference and distinction there is among causes."

44. Since Chrysippus has clarified this, if his opponents who say that assents do not occur by fate were nevertheless to concede that they do not occur without a presentation as antecedent [cause]—then that is a different argument; but if they grant that presentations precede and nevertheless that assents do not occur by fate, on the grounds that it is not that proximate and immediate [kind of] cause which moves the assent, note that they are really saying the same thing [as Chrysippus]. For Chrysippus, while granting that there is in the presentation a proximate and immediate cause of assent, will not grant that this cause necessitates assent in such a way that, if all things occur by fate, all things would occur by antecedent and *necessary* causes. And similarly the opponents, who disagree with him while conceding that assents do not occur without prior presentations, will say that, if everything occurs by fate in the sense that nothing occurs without a prior cause, it must be granted that all things occur by fate.

From this it is easy to understand, since both sides get the same result once their opinions are laid out and clarified, that they disagree verbally but not in substance.

Hippolytus *Philosophoumena* 21

They [Zeno and Chrysippus] support the claim that everything happens by fate by using this example. It is as though a dog is tied behind a cart. If he wants to follow, he is both dragged and follows, exercising his autonomy in conjunction with necessity. But if he does not wish to follow, he will nevertheless be forced to. The same thing happens in the case of men. Even if they do not want to follow, they will nevertheless be forced to go along with what has been destined.

Diogenianus in **Eusebius** *Preparatio Evangelica* 6.8, 265d–266d

So in book one of his [Chrysippus'] *On Fate* he used proofs of this nature, and in book two he tries to resolve the absurdities which seem to follow on the thesis that all things are necessitated, which we listed at the beginning: for example, the destruction of our own initiative concerning criticism and praise and encouragement and everything which seems to happen by our own agency.

So, in book two he says that it is obvious that many things occur by our own initiative, but nonetheless these are co-fated with the administration of the universe. And he uses illustrations like these.

The non-destruction of one's coat, he says, is not fated simply, but co-fated with its being taken care of, and someone's being saved from his enemies is co-fated with his fleeing those enemies; and having children is co-fated with being willing to lie with a woman. For just as if, he says, someone says that Hegesarchus the boxer will leave the ring completely untouched, it would be strange for him to think that Hegesarchus should fight with his fists down because it was fated that he should get off untouched (the man who made the assertion saying this because of the fellow's extraordinary protection from being punched), so too the same thing holds in other cases. For many things cannot occur without our being willing and indeed contributing a most strenuous eagerness and zeal for these things, since, he says, it was fated for these things to occur in conjunction with this personal effort. . . . But it will be in our power, he says, with what is in our power being included in fate.

Aulus Gellius 7.2.1–14

1. Chrysippus, the chief Stoic philosopher, defines fate (*heimarmene* in Greek) roughly as follows: "Fate," he says, "is a sempiternal and unchangeable series and chain of things, rolling and unravelling itself through eternal sequences of cause and effect, of which it is composed and compounded". . . .

4. But authors from other schools make this objection to this definition. 5. "If," they say, "Chrysippus thinks that everything is moved and

governed by fate and the sequences and revolutions of fate cannot be turned aside or evaded, then men's sins and misdeeds should not rouse our anger, nor should they be attributed to men and their wills but to a kind of necessity and inevitability which comes from fate, mistress and arbiter of all things, by whose agency all that will be is necessary. And therefore the penalties applied by the law to the guilty are unfair, if men do not turn to misdeeds voluntarily but are dragged by fate."

6. Against this position Chrysippus made many sharp and subtle arguments. But this is the gist of all he said on the topic: 7. although, he said, it is true that by fate all things are forced and linked by a necessary and dominant reason, nevertheless the character of our minds is subject to fate in a manner corresponding to their nature and quality. 8. For if our minds were originally formed by nature in a sound and useful manner, then they pass on all the force of fate which imposes on us from outside in a relatively unobjectionable and more acceptable way. But if, on the other hand, they are rough and untrained and uncouth, supported by no good training, then even if the blows of fated misfortune which strike them are trivial or nonexistent these men will plunge headlong into constant misdeeds and errors because of their own ineptitude and their voluntary impulse. 9. But this state of affairs is itself brought about by that natural and necessary sequence of cause and effect which is called fate. 10. For it is by the very nature of the case fated and determined that bad characters should not be free of misdeeds and errors.

11. He then uses a quite appropriate and clever illustration of this state of affairs. "Just as," he says, "if you throw a cylindrical stone down a steep slope, you are indeed the cause and origin of its descent, nevertheless the stone afterwards rolls down not because you are still doing this, but because such is its nature and the 'rollability' of its form: similarly, the order and reason and necessity of fate sets in motion the general types and starting points of the causes, but each man's own will [or decisions] and the character of his mind govern the impulses of our thoughts and minds and our very actions."

12. He then adds these words, which are consistent with what I have said: "So the Pythagoreans too said, 'You shall know that men have woes which they chose for themselves', since the harm suffered by each man is in his own power and since they err and are harmed voluntarily and by their own plan and decision."

13. Therefore he says that we ought not to tolerate or listen to men who are wicked or lazy and guilty and shameless, who when convicted of misdeeds take refuge in the necessity of fate as in the asylum of a religious

sanctuary and say that their worst misdeeds should be laid at the door, not of their own recklessness, but of fate.

14. And that most wise and ancient poet [Homer] was the first to make this point, in the verses which follow:[3]

> It makes me furious! how mortals blame the gods!
> For they say that their troubles come from us; but they
> incur pains on their own beyond their allotment, because of their wickedness.

3. *Odyssey,* 1.32–4.

3

Lucretius, from *On the Nature of Things*

These short selections are from On the Nature of Things *by Lucretius (c. 99–c. 55 B.C.), a Latin author and advocate of Epicureanism. The Greek philosopher Epicurus (341–271 B.C.) maintained that determinism is false, and this allows for free will. The Epicureans were atomists in the tradition of Democritus, proposing that everything that exists is made of up atoms and the void. Lucretius argues that if the motions of atoms were causally determined they would fall downward (he held that the universe had a determinate orientation). But at times undetermined swerves occur in their paths of motion. The swerves account for interactions among the atoms and for free will. The Epicurean view suggests a version of libertarianism according to which indeterminacy in the production of appropriate events is considered sufficient to allow for free will.*

On the Nature of Things 2.216–293 excerpts

216. On this topic I want you to learn this too, that when the atoms move straight down through the void by their own weight, they deflect a bit in space at a quite uncertain time and in uncertain places, just enough that you could say that their motion had changed. But if they were not in the habit of swerving, they would all fall straight down through the depths of the void, like drops of rain, and no collision would occur, nor would any blow be produced among the atoms. In that case, nature would never have produced anything.

225. And if by chance someone thinks that heavier atoms, in virtue of their more rapid motion straight through the void, could fall from above on the lighter atoms, and that in this way the blows which generate the productive motions could be produced, he has strayed very far from the true account. For everything which falls through water or light air must fall at a speed proportional to their weights, simply because the bulk of the water and the fine nature of the air can hardly delay each thing equally, but

From *Hellenistic Philosophy*, translated and edited by Brad Inwood and L. P. Gerson (Indianapolis: Hackett Publishing Company, 1988).

yield more quickly to the heavier bodies, being overwhelmed by them. But by contrast, at no time and in no place can the empty void resist any thing, but it must, as its nature demands, go on yielding to it. Therefore, everything must move at equal speed through the inactive void, though they are not driven by equal weights. Therefore, heavier atoms can never fall upon lighter atoms from above, nor can they by themselves generate blows which will produce change in the motions through which nature produces things. Again and again, that is why it is necessary that the atoms swerve slightly—but not more than the minimum; otherwise, we would seem to be inventing oblique motions and then the plain facts would refute us. For we see this obviously and apparently, that heavy bodies, insofar as they are heavy bodies, cannot move obliquely, when they fall from above, at least not enough that you could observe it. But who could claim to perceive that none of them swerves at all from a perfectly straight path?

251. Finally, if every motion is always linked to another, and new motions always arise from the old in definite order, and the atoms do not produce by swerving a starting point for motion which can break the bonds of fate and prevent one cause from following another from infinity, where does this free will which living things throughout the world have, where, I say, does this will torn from the grasp of the fates come from? Through this we all go where each one's pleasure[1] leads and swerve from our paths at undetermined times and places, just as our minds incline to do. For it is far from doubtful that everyone's own will provides the starting point for these things and that this is the source of motion in our limbs. . . .

284. That is why it is necessary to admit the same thing for the atoms, namely, that there is another cause of motion besides blows [from collisions] and weight, which is the source of our inborn capability [to act freely], since we see that nothing can come from nothing. For the weight of the atoms prevents it from being the case that everything happens as a result of the blows [of collisions], which are like an external force. But that the mind itself does not have an internal necessity in all its actions, and that it is not forced, as though in chains, to suffer and endure, that is what this tiny swerve of the atoms, occurring at no fixed time or place, accomplishes.

1. 'Will' just above and 'pleasure' here appear in the opposite order in the manuscripts. We follow most editors in reversing them, although some editors defend the transmitted text. In Latin, the two words differ by one letter.

4

Augustine, from *On Free Choice of the Will*

Augustine (354–430 B.C.), a philosopher from northern Africa, was the most prominent philosopher for Christianity in its first millennium. He developed an influential synthesis between Platonism and Christianity. In this excerpt from On Free Choice of the Will, *Augustine argues that although God foresees everything that happens, and that God's foresight is never mistaken, we nevertheless have the sort of free will required for moral responsibility. He also argues that God's goodness is reconcilable with the creation of free beings whom he foreknows will sin, because the existence of beings with free will who sin is better than their nonexistence.*

Book Two

EVODIUS: Now explain to me, if you can, why God gave human beings free choice of the will, since if we had not received it, we would not have been able to sin.

AUGUSTINE: Do you know for certain God gave us this thing that you think should not have been given?

EVODIUS: If I understood Book One correctly, we have free choice of the will and we cannot sin without it.

AUGUSTINE: I too remember that that had become quite clear to us. But what I asked just now was whether you knew that it was *God* who gave us this thing, which we clearly have and by which we sin.

EVODIUS: Who else would it be? For we have our existence from God, and it is from him that we deserve punishment for doing wrong and reward for doing good.

AUGUSTINE: Here again I want to know whether you know this for certain, or whether you willingly believe it on the urging of some authority, without actually knowing it.

EVODIUS: I admit that at first I believed this on authority. But what could be truer than that everything good comes from God, that everything just is good, and that it is just for sinners to be punished and the good rewarded? From this I conclude that it is God who afflicts sinners with unhappiness and confers happiness on the good.

AUGUSTINE: I make no objection. But I do have one further question: How do you know that we have our existence from God? You did not explain that; you showed only that it is from him that we deserve punishment or reward.

EVODIUS: That is an obvious consequence of the fact that God, as the source of all justice, punishes sins. It may be that goodness confers benefits on those not committed to its charge, but justice does not punish those not in its jurisdiction. So it is obvious that we belong to God, because he is not only most generous in conferring benefits but also most just in punishing.

Furthermore, I claimed, and you agreed, that everything good is from God. From this we can understand that human beings too are from God. For human beings as such are good things, since they can live rightly if they so will.

AUGUSTINE: If all of this is true, the question you posed has clearly been answered. If human beings are good things, and they cannot do right unless they so will, then they ought to have a free will, without which they cannot do right. True, they can also use free will to sin, but we should not therefore believe that God gave them free will so that they would be able to sin. The fact that human beings could not live rightly without it was sufficient reason for God to give it. The very fact that anyone who uses free will to sin is divinely punished shows that free will was given to enable human beings to live rightly, for such punishment would be unjust if free will had been given both for living rightly and for sinning. After all, how could someone justly be punished for using the will for the very purpose for which it was given? When God punishes a sinner, don't you think he is saying, "Why didn't you use your free will for the purpose for which I gave it to you?"—that is, for living rightly?

And as for the goodness that we so admired in God's justice—his punishing sins and rewarding good deeds—how could it even exist if human beings lacked the free choice of the will? No action would be either a sin or a good deed if it were not performed by the will, and so both punishment and reward would be unjust if human beings had no free will. But it was right for there to be justice in both reward and punishment, since this is one of the goods that come from God. Therefore, it was right for God to give free will to human beings.

EVODIUS: I concede that point now. But don't you think that if free will was given to us for living rightly, we ought not to have been able to pervert it and use it for sinning? It should have been like justice, which w given to human beings to enable them to live well. No one can use to live wickedly. In the same way, it ought to be the case that no one could use the will to sin, if indeed the will was given for acting rightly.

AUGUSTINE: God will, I hope, enable me to reply to you—or rather, he will enable you to reply to yourself, as Truth, the greatest teacher of all, teaches you within. But first I want you to tell me this. I asked whether you knew for certain that God gave us free will, and you said that you did. So now that we have agreed that he gave us free will, should we presume to say that it should not have been given? If there is some doubt whether it was God who gave it, it is appropriate for us to ask whether it was a good gift; and if we find that it was, then we have also found that it was given by God, from whom the soul has all good gifts. But if we find that it was not a good gift, we will understand that it was not given by God, whom it is impious to blame. But if it is quite certain that God gave us free will, then we must admit that it ought to have been given, and in exactly the way that it was given; for God gave it, and his deeds are utterly beyond reproach.

EVODIUS: Although I hold these things with unshaken faith, let's investigate them as if they were all uncertain, since I do not yet *know* them. It is uncertain whether free will was given for doing right, since we can also use it to sin; consequently, it is also uncertain whether it ought to have been given. For if it is uncertain whether it was given for doing right, then it is also uncertain whether it ought to have been given. This means in turn that it is doubtful whether it was given by God. For if it is doubtful whether it ought to have been given, then it is also doubtful whether it was given by God, since it is impious to believe that God gave something that should not have been given. . . .

EVODIUS: I confess that I am quite convinced that this is the way to prove that God exists—as well as it can be proven in this life among people like us. And I am also convinced that all good things come from God, since everything that exists—whether that which has understanding, life, and existence, or that which has only life and existence, or that which has existence alone—is from God. Now let's take a look at the third question and see whether it can be resolved: should free will be included among those good things? Once that has been shown, I will concede without hesitation that God gave it to us, and that he was right to do so.

AUGUSTINE: You have done a good job of remembering what we set out to do, and you have most astutely realized that the second question has now been answered. But you ought to have seen that the third question too has already been answered. You had said that it seemed that God should not have given us free choice of the will, because whoever sins does so by free choice. I said in reply that no one can act rightly except by that same free choice of the will, and I affirmed that God gave us free choice in order to enable us to act rightly. You replied that free will should have been given to us in the same way that justice is given; no one can use justice wrongly. That reply of yours drove us into a roundabout path of discussion; along the way we showed that there is nothing good, however great or small, that is not from God. But that fact could not be shown clearly enough until we had first challenged the irreligious stupidity of the fool who "said in his heart, 'There is no God'."[1] by attempting to find some evident truth to the contrary, going as far as our reason can take us in such an important matter, with God helping us along this precarious path. But these two facts—I mean that God exists and that every good thing is from him—which of course we believed quite confidently even before this discussion, have now been so thoroughly considered that this third fact seems altogether obvious: free will should indeed be counted as a good thing.

For earlier in our discussion it had become clear, and we had agreed, that the nature of the body is at a lower level than the nature of the soul, and so the soul is a greater good than the body. But even when we find good things in the body that we can use wrongly, we do not say that they ought not to have been given to the body, for we admit that they are in fact good. So why should it be surprising that there are also good things in the soul that we can use wrongly, but which, since they are in fact good, can only have been given by him from whom all good things come?

Consider what a great good a body is missing if it has no hands. And yet people use their hands wrongly in committing violent or shameful acts. If you see someone who has no feet, you admit that his physical well-being is impaired by the absence of so great a good, and yet you would not deny that someone who uses his feet to harm someone else or to disgrace himself is using them wrongly. By our eyes we see light and we distinguish the forms of material objects. They are the most beautiful thing in our bodies, so they were put into the place of greatest dignity; and we use them to preserve our safety and to secure many other good things in life. Nonetheless, many people use their eyes to do many evil things and press them into the service of inordinate desire; and yet you realize what a great good is missing in a face that has no eyes. But when they are present, who gave them, if not God, the generous giver of all good things? So just as you approve of these good things in the body and praise the one who gave

1. Psalm 14:1; 53:1

them, disregarding those who use them wrongly, you should admit that free will, without which no one can live rightly, is a good and divine gift. You should condemn those who misuse this good rather than saying that he who gave it should not have given it.

Evodius: But first I would like for you to prove that free will is a good thing, and then I will concede that God gave it to us, since I admit that all good things come from God.

Augustine: But didn't I just go to a great deal of trouble to prove that in our earlier discussion, when you admitted that every species and form of every material object subsists from the highest form of all things, that is, from truth, and when you conceded that they are good? The truth itself tells us in the gospel that the very hairs of our head are numbered.[2] Have you forgotten what we said about the supremacy of number, and its power reaching from end to end? What perversity, then, to number the hairs of our head among the good things, though of course among the least and most trivial goods, and to attribute them to God, the creator of all good things—for both the greatest and the least goods come from him from whom all good things come—and yet to have doubts about free will, when even those who lead the worst lives admit that no one can live rightly without it! Tell me now, which is better: something without which we *can* live rightly, or something without which we *cannot* live rightly?

Evodius: Please, stop; I am ashamed of my blindness. Who could doubt that something without which no one lives rightly is far superior?

Augustine: Would you deny that a one-eyed man can live rightly?

Evodius: That would be crazy.

Augustine: But you admit that an eye is something good in the body, even though losing it does not interfere with living rightly. So don't you think that free will is a good, since no one can live rightly without it? Look at justice, which no one uses wrongly. Justice, and indeed all the virtues of the soul, are counted among the highest goods that are in human beings, because they constitute an upright and worthy life. For no one uses prudence or fortitude or temperance wrongly; right reason, without which they would not even be virtues, prevails in all of them, just as it does in justice, which you mentioned. And no one can use right reason wrongly.

Therefore, these virtues are great goods. But you must remember that even the lowest goods can exist only from him from whom all good things come, that is, from God. For that was the conclusion of our previous discussion, which you so gladly assented to many times. Thus, the virtues,

2. Cf. Matthew 10:30

by which one lives rightly, are great goods; the beauty of various material objects, without which one can live rightly, are the lowest goods; and the powers of the soul, without which one cannot live rightly, are intermediate goods. No one uses the virtues wrongly, but the other goods, both the lowest and the intermediate, can be used either rightly or wrongly. The virtues cannot be used wrongly precisely because it is their function to make the right use of things that can also be used wrongly, and no one uses something wrongly by using it rightly. So the abundant generosity of the goodness of God has bestowed not only the great goods, but also the lowest and intermediate goods. His goodness deserves more praise for the great goods than for the intermediate goods, and more for the intermediate goods than for the lowest goods; but it deserves more praise for creating all of them than it would deserve for creating only some of them.

EVODIUS: I agree. But there is one thing that concerns me. We see that it is free will that uses other things either rightly or wrongly. So how can free will itself be included among the things that we use?

AUGUSTINE: In the same way that we know by reason everything that we know, and yet reason itself is included among the things that we know by reason. Or have you forgotten that when we were asking what we know by reason, you admitted that we know reason itself by means of reason? So don't be surprised that, even though we use other things by free will, we also use free will itself by means of free will, so that the will that uses other things also uses itself, just as the reason that knows other things also knows itself. Similarly, memory not only grasps everything else that we remember, but also somehow retains itself in us, since we do not forget that we have a memory. It remembers not only other things but also itself; or rather, through memory we remember not only other things, but also memory itself.

Therefore, when the will, which is an intermediate good, cleaves to the unchangeable good that is common, not private—namely, the truth, of which we have said much, but nothing adequate—then one has a happy life. And the happy life, that is, the disposition of a soul that cleaves to the unchangeable good, is the proper and principal good for a human being. It contains all the virtues, which no one can use wrongly. Now the virtues, although they are great and indeed the foremost things in human beings, are not sufficiently common, since they belong exclusively to the individual human being who possesses them. But truth and wisdom are common to all, and all who are wise and happy become so by cleaving to truth and wisdom. No one becomes happy by someone else's happiness; even if you pattern yourself after someone else in order to become happy, your desire is to attain happiness from the same source as the other person, that is, from the unchangeable truth that is common to you both. No one becomes prudent by someone else's prudence, or resolute by someone else's fortitude, or temperate by someone else's temperance, or just by someone else's justice. Instead, you regulate your soul by those unchangeable rules and lights of the virtues that dwell incorruptibly in the common truth and wisdom, just as the one whose virtue you set out to imitate regulated his soul and fixed it upon those rules.

Therefore, when the will cleaves to the common and unchangeable good, it attains the great and foremost goods for human beings, even though the will itself is only an intermediate good. But when the will turns away from the unchangeable and common good toward its own private good, or toward external or inferior things, it sins. It turns toward its own private good when it wants to be under its own control; it turns toward external things when it is keen on things that belong to others or have nothing to do with itself; it turns toward inferior things when it takes delight in physical pleasure. In this way one becomes proud, meddlesome, and lustful; one is caught up into a life that, by comparison with the higher life, is death. But even that life is governed by divine providence, which places all things in their proper order and gives everyone what he deserves.

Hence, the goods that are pursued by sinners are in no way evil things, and neither is free will itself, which we found is to be counted among the intermediate goods. What is evil is the turning of the will away from the unchangeable good and toward changeable goods. And since this turning is not coerced, but voluntary, it is justly and deservedly punished with misery.

But perhaps you are going to ask what is the source of this movement by which the will turns away from the unchangeable good toward a changeable good. This movement is certainly evil, even though free will itself is to be counted among good things, since no one can live rightly without it. For if that movement, that turning away from the Lord God, is undoubtedly sin, surely we cannot say that God is the cause of sin. So that movement is not from God. But then where does it come from? If I told you that I don't know, you might be disappointed; but that would be the truth. For one cannot know that which is nothing.

You must simply hold with unshaken faith that every good thing that you perceive or understand or in any way know is from God. For any nature you come across is from God. So if you see anything at all that has measure, number, and order, do not hesitate to attribute it to God as craftsman. If you take away all measure, number, and order, there is absolutely nothing left. Even if the rudiments of a form remain, in which you find neither measure nor number nor order—since wherever those things are there is a complete form—you must take that away too, for it seems to be like the material on which the craftsman works. For if the completion of form is a good, then the rudiments of a form are themselves not without goodness. So if you take away everything that is good, you will have absolutely nothing left. But every good thing comes from God, so there is no nature that does not come from God. On the other hand, every defect comes from nothing, and that movement of turning away, which we admit is sin, is a defective movement. So you see where that movement comes from; you may be sure that it does not come from God.

But since that movement is voluntary, it has been placed under our control. If you fear it, do not will it; and if you do not will it, it will not exist. What greater security could there be than to have a life in which nothing can happen to you that you do not will? But since we cannot pick ourselves up voluntarily as we fell voluntarily, let us hold with confident faith the right hand of God—that is, our Lord Jesus Christ—which has been held out to us from on high. Let us await him with resolute hope and desire him with ardent charity. But if you think that we need to discuss the origin of sin more carefully, we must postpone that for another discussion.

EVODIUS: I will bow to your will and postpone this question, for I don't think that we have investigated it thoroughly enough yet.

Book Three

EVODIUS: It has been demonstrated to my satisfaction that free will is to be numbered among good things, and indeed not among the least of them, and therefore that it was given to us by God, who acted rightly in giving it. So now, if you think that this is a good time, I would like you to explain the source of the movement by which the will turns away from the common and unchangeable good toward its own good, or the good of others, or lower goods, all of which are changeable.

AUGUSTINE: Why do we need to know that?

EVODIUS: Because if the will was given to us in such a way that it had this movement naturally, then it turned to changeable goods by necessity, and there is no blame involved when nature and necessity determine an action.

AUGUSTINE: Does this movement please you or displease you?

EVODIUS: It displeases me.

AUGUSTINE: So you find fault with it.

EVODIUS: Of course.

AUGUSTINE: Then you find fault with a blameless movement of the soul.

EVODIUS: No, it's just that I don't know whether there is any blame involved when the soul deserts the unchangeable good and turns toward changeable goods.

AUGUSTINE: Then you find fault with what you don't know.

EVODIUS: Don't quibble over words. In saying, "I don't know whether there is any blame involved," I meant it to be understood that there undoubtedly *is* blame involved. The "I don't know" implied that it was ridiculous to have doubts about such an obvious fact.

AUGUSTINE: Then pay close attention to this most certain truth, which has caused you to forget so quickly what you just said. If that movement existed by nature or necessity, it could in no way be blameworthy. But you are so firmly convinced that this movement is indeed blameworthy that you think it would be ridiculous to entertain doubts about something so certain. Why then did you affirm, or at least tentatively assert, something that now seems to you clearly false? For this is what you said: "If the will was given to us in such a way that it had this movement naturally, then it turned to changeable goods by necessity, and there is no blame involved when nature and necessity determine an action." Since you are sure that this movement was blameworthy, you should have been quite sure that the will was not given to us in such a way.

EVODIUS: I said that this movement was blameworthy and that therefore it displeases me. And I am surely right to find fault with it. But I deny that a soul ought to be blamed when this movement pulls it away from the unchangeable good toward changeable goods, if this movement is so much a part of its nature that it is moved by necessity.

AUGUSTINE: You admit that this movement certainly deserves blame; but *whose* movement is it?

EVODIUS: I see that the movement is in the soul, but I don't know whose it is.

AUGUSTINE: Surely you don't deny that the soul is moved by this movement.

EVODIUS: No.

AUGUSTINE: Do you deny that a movement by which a stone is moved is a movement of the stone? I'm not talking about a movement that is caused by us or some other force, as when it is thrown into the air, but the movement that occurs when it falls to the earth by its own weight.

EVODIUS: I don't deny that this movement, by which the stone seeks the lowest place, is a movement of the stone. But it is a natural movement. If that's the sort of movement the soul has, then the soul's movement is also natural. And if it is moved naturally, it cannot justly be blamed; even if it is moved toward something evil, it is compelled by its own nature. But since we don't doubt that this movement is blameworthy, we must absolutely deny that it is natural, and so it is not similar to the natural movement of a stone.

AUGUSTINE: Did we accomplish anything in our first two discussions?

EVODIUS: Of course we did.

AUGUSTINE: I'm sure you recall that in Book One we agreed that nothing can make the mind a slave to inordinate desire except its own will. For the will cannot be forced into such iniquity by anything superior or equal to it, since that would be unjust; or by anything inferior to it, since that is impossible. Only one possibility remains: the movement by which the will turns from enjoying the Creator to enjoying his creatures belongs to the will itself. So if that movement deserves blame (and you said it was ridiculous to entertain doubts on that score), then it is not natural, but voluntary.

This movement of the will is similar to the downward movement of a stone in that it belongs to the will just as that downward movement belongs to the stone. But the two movements are dissimilar in this respect: the stone has no power to check its downward movement, but the soul is not moved to abandon higher things and love inferior things unless it wills to do so. And so the movement of the stone is natural, but the movement of the soul is voluntary. If someone were to say that a stone is sinning because its weight carries it downward, I would not merely say that he was more senseless than the stone itself; I would consider him completely insane. But we accuse a soul of sin when we are convinced that it has abandoned higher things and chosen to enjoy inferior things. Now we admit that this movement belongs to the will alone, and that it is voluntary and therefore blameworthy; and the only useful teaching on this topic is that which condemns and checks this movement and thus serves to rescue our wills from their fall into temporal goods and turn them toward the enjoyment of the eternal good. Therefore, what need is there to ask about the source of the movement by which the will turns away from the unchangeable good toward changeable good?

Evodius: I see that what you are saying is true, and in a way I understand it. There is nothing I feel so firmly and so intimately as that I have a will by which I am moved to enjoy something. If the will by which I choose or refuse things is not mine, then I don't know what I can call mine. So if I use my will to do something evil, whom can I hold responsible but myself? For a good God made me, and I can do nothing good except through my will; therefore, it is quite clear that the will was given to me by a good God so that I might do good. If the movement of the will by which it turns this way or that were not voluntary and under its own control, a person would not deserve praise for turning to higher things or blame for turning to lower things, as if swinging on the hinge of the will. Furthermore, there would be no point in admonishing people to forget about lower things and strive for what is eternal, so that they might refuse to live badly but instead will to live rightly. And anyone who does not think that we ought to admonish people in this way deserves to be banished from the human race.

Since these things are true, I very much wonder how God can have foreknowledge of everything in the future, and yet we do not sin by necessity. It would be an irreligious and completely insane attack on God's foreknowledge to say that something could happen otherwise than as God foreknew. So suppose that God foreknew that the first human being was going to sin. Anyone who admits, as I do, that God foreknows everything in the future will have to grant me that. Now I won't say that God would not have made him—for God made him good, and no sin of his can harm God, who not only made him good but showed His own goodness by creating him, as He also shows His justice by punishing him and His mercy by redeeming him—but I will say this: since God foreknew that he was going to sin, his sin necessarily had to happen. How, then, is the will free when such inescapable necessity is found in it?

Augustine: You have knocked powerfully on the door of God's mercy; may it be present and open the door to those who knock. Nevertheless, I think the only reason that most people are tormented by this question is that they do not ask it piously; they are more eager to excuse than to confess their sins. Some people gladly believe that there is no divine providence in charge of human affairs. They put their bodies and their souls at the mercy of chance and give themselves up to be beaten and mangled by inordinate desires. They disbelieve divine judgments and evade human judgments, thinking that fortune will defend them from those who accuse them. They depict this "fortune" as blind, implying either that they are better than fortune, by which they think they are ruled, or that they themselves suffer from the same blindness. It is perfectly reasonable to admit that such people do everything by chance, since in whatever they do, they fall.[3] But we said enough in Book Two to combat this opinion, which is full of the most foolish and insane error.

Others, however, are not impertinent enough to deny that the providence of God rules over human life; but they prefer the wicked error of believing that it is weak, or unjust, or evil, rather than confessing their sins with humble supplication. If only they would let themselves be convinced that, when they think of what is best and most just and most powerful, the goodness and justice and power of God are far greater and far higher than anything they can conceive; if only they would consider themselves and understand that they would owe thanks to God even if he had willed to make them lower than they are. Then the very bone and marrow of their conscience would cry out, "I said, 'O Lord, have mercy upon me; heal my soul, for I have sinned against you'."[4] Thus they would be led in the secure paths of divine mercy along the road to wisdom, not becoming conceited when they made new discoveries or disheartened when they failed to do so. Their new knowledge would simply prepare them to see more, and their ignorance would make them more patient in seeking the truth. Of course I'm sure that you already believe this. But you will see how easily I can answer your difficult question once I have answered a few preliminary questions.

Surely this is the problem that is disturbing and puzzling you. How is it that these two propositions are not contradictory and inconsistent: (1) God has foreknowledge of everything in the future; and (2) We sin by the will, not by necessity? For, you say, if God foreknows that someone is going to sin, then it is necessary that he sin. But if it is necessary, the will has no choice about whether to sin; there is an inescapable and fixed necessity. And so you fear that this argument forces us into one of two positions: either we draw the heretical conclusion that God does not foreknow everything in the future; or, if we cannot accept this conclusion, we must admit that sin happens by necessity and not by will. Isn't that what is bothering you?

EVODIUS: That's it exactly.

AUGUSTINE: So you think that anything that God foreknows happens by necessity and not by will.

EVODIUS: Precisely.

3. The Latin word for 'chance' (*casus*) is derived from the verb 'to fall' (*cado*).

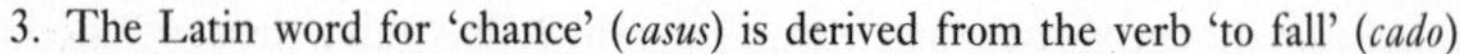

4. Psalm 41:4

AUGUSTINE: Now pay close attention. Look inside yourself for a little while, and tell me, if you can, what sort of will you are going to have tomorrow: a will to do right or a will to sin?

EVODIUS: I don't know.

AUGUSTINE: Do you think that God doesn't know either?

EVODIUS: Not at all—God certainly does know.

AUGUSTINE: Well then, if God knows what you are going to will tomorrow, and foresees the future wills of every human being, both those who exist now and those who will exist in the future, he surely foresees how he is going to treat the just and the irreligious.

EVODIUS: Clearly, if I say that God foreknows all of my actions, I can much more confidently say that he foreknows his own actions and foresees with absolute certainty what he is going to do.

AUGUSTINE: Then aren't you worried that someone might object that God himself will act out of necessity rather than by his will in everything that he is going to do? After all, you said that whatever God foreknows happens by necessity, not by will.

EVODIUS: When I said that, I was thinking only of what happens in his creation and not of what happens within himself. For those things do not come into being; they are eternal.

AUGUSTINE: So God does nothing in his creation.

EVODIUS: He has already established, once for all, the ways in which the universe that he created is to be governed; he does not administer anything by a new act of will.

AUGUSTINE: Doesn't he make anyone happy?

EVODIUS: Of course he does.

AUGUSTINE: And he does this when that person is made happy.

EVODIUS: Right.

AUGUSTINE: Then suppose, for example, that you are going to be happy a year from now. That means that a year from now God is going to make you happy.

EVODIUS: That's right too.

AUGUSTINE: And God knows today what he is going to do a year from now.

EVODIUS: He has always foreknown this, so I admit that he foreknows it now, if indeed it is really going to happen.

AUGUSTINE: Then surely you are not God's creature, or else your happiness does not take place in you.

EVODIUS: But I am God's creature, and my happiness does take place in me.

AUGUSTINE: Then the happiness that God gives you takes place by necessity and not by will.

EVODIUS: His will *is* my necessity.

AUGUSTINE: And so you will be happy against your will.

EVODIUS: If I had the power to be happy, I would be happy right now. Even now I will to be happy, but I'm not, since it is God who makes me happy. I cannot do it for myself.

AUGUSTINE: How clearly the truth speaks through you! You could not help thinking that the only thing that is within our power is that which we do when we will it. Therefore, nothing is so much within our power as the will itself, for it is near at hand the very moment that we will. So we can rightly say, "We grow old by necessity, not by will"; or "We become feeble by necessity, not by will"; or "We die by necessity, not by will," and other such things. But who would be crazy enough to say "We do not will by the will"? Therefore, although God foreknows what we are going to will in the future, it does not follow that we do not will by the will.

When you said that you cannot make yourself happy, you said it as if I had denied it. Not at all; I am merely saying that when you do become happy, it will be in accordance with your will, not against your will. Simply because God foreknows your future happiness—and nothing can happen except as God foreknows it, since otherwise it would not be foreknowledge—it does not follow that you will be happy against your will. That would be completely absurd and far from the truth. So God's foreknowledge, which is certain even today of your future happiness, does not take away your will for happiness once you have begun to be happy; and in the same way, your blameworthy will (if indeed you are going to have such a will) does not cease to be a will simply because God foreknows that you are going to have it.

Just notice how imperceptive someone would have to be to argue thus: "If God has foreknown my future will, it is necessary that I will what he has foreknown, since nothing can happen otherwise than as he has foreknown it. But if it is necessary, then one must concede that I will it by necessity and not by will." What extraordinary foolishness! If God foreknew a future will that turned out not to be a will at all, things would indeed happen otherwise than as God foreknew them. And I will overlook this objector's equally monstrous statement that "it is necessary that I will," for by assuming necessity he tries to abolish will. For if his willing is necessary, how does he will, since there is no will?

Suppose he expressed it in another way and said that, since his willing is necessary, his will is not in his own power. This would run up against the same problem that you had when I asked whether you were going to be happy against your will. You replied that you would already be happy if you had the power; you said that you have the will but not the power. I answered that the truth had spoken through you. For we can deny that something is in our power only if it is not present even when we will it; but if we will, and yet the will remains absent, then we are not really willing at all. Now if it is impossible for us not to will when we are willing, then the will is present to those who will; and if something is present when we will it, then it is in our power. So our will would not be a will if it were not in our power. And since it is in our power, we are free with respect to it. But we are not free with respect to anything that we do not have in our power, and anything that we have cannot be nothing.

Thus, we believe both that God has foreknowledge of everything in the future and that nonetheless we will whatever we will. Since God foreknows our will, the very will that he foreknows will be what comes about. Therefore, it will be a will, since it is a will that he foreknows. And it could not be a will unless it were in our power. Therefore, he also foreknows this power. It follows, then, that his foreknowledge does not take away my power; in fact, it is all the more certain that I will have that power, since he whose foreknowledge never errs foreknows that I will have it.

EVODIUS: I agree now that it is necessary that whatever God has foreknown will happen, and that he foreknows our sins in such a way that our wills remain free and are within our power. . . .

5

Aquinas, from the *Summa Theologica*

PART ONE

Thomas Aquinas (1225–1274) was an Italian philosopher who developed a synthesis of Aristotelianism and Christianity. In these two groups of selections from his Summa Theologica, *Aquinas presents an account of free will in the Aristotelian tradition. In the first group of selections Aquinas argues that human beings have free choice because first, we act from the judgment that something should be avoided or sought, and this judgment is not a function of natural instinct, as in the case of the brute animals, but comes "from some act of comparison in the reason." Aquinas then develops his view about the precise nature of free choice. In the second group of selections he argues that we are capable of voluntary actions, and he develops the Aristotelian view about the nature of the voluntary. An agent performs a voluntary action when she is moved of herself and is moved for the sake of an end. Furthermore, if an agent is moved for the sake of an end, she must have some knowledge of that end. Aquinas then goes on to argue that violence (i.e., force or compulsion) rules out voluntariness but that fear and concupiscence do not. Ignorance may or may not rule out voluntariness depending on what sort of ignorance is at issue.*

Question LXXXIII
FREE CHOICE
(*In Four Articles*)

We now inquire concerning free choice. Under this head there are four points of inquiry: (1) Whether man has free choice? (2) What is free choice—a power, an act, or a habit? (3) If it is a power, is it appetitive or cognitive? (4) If it is appetitive, is it the same power as the will, or distinct?

From Aquinas, *Basic Writings of Saint Thomas Aquinas,* edited by Anton C. Pegis (New York: Random House, 1945. Reissued by Hackett Publishing Company, 1997). Reprinted by permission of Hackett Publishing Company.

First Article

WHETHER MAN HAS FREE CHOICE?

We proceed thus to the First Article:—

Objection 1. It would seem that man has not free choice. For whoever has free choice does what he wills. But man does not what he wills, for it is written (*Rom.* vii. 19): *For the good which I will I do not, but the evil which I will not, that I do.* Therefore man has not free choice.

Obj. 2. Further, whoever has free choice has in his power to will or not to will, to do or not to do. But this is not in man's power, for it is written (*Rom.* ix. 16): *It is not of him that willeth*—namely, to will—*nor of him that runneth*—namely, to run. Therefore man has not free choice.

Obj. 3. Further, he is free who is his own master, as the Philosopher says.[1] Therefore what is moved by another is not free. But God moves the will, for it is written (*Prov.* xxi. 1): *The heart of the king is in the hand of the Lord; whithersoever He will He shall turn it;* and (*Phil.* ii. 13): *It is God Who worketh in you both to will and to accomplish.* Therefore man has not free choice.

Obj. 4. Further, whoever has free choice is master of his own actions. But man is not master of his own actions, for it is written (*Jeremiah* x. 23): *The way of a man is not his, neither is it in a man to walk.* Therefore man has not free choice.

Obj. 5. Further, the Philosopher says: *According as each one is, such does the end seem to him.*[2] But it is not in our power to be such as we are, for this comes to us from nature. Therefore it is natural to us to follow some particular end, and therefore we are not free in so doing.

On the contrary, It is written (*Ecclesiastes* xv. 14): *God made man from the beginning, and left him in the hand of his own counsel;* and the *Gloss* adds: *That is, in the liberty of choice.*

I answer that, Man has free choice, or otherwise counsels, exhortations, commands, prohibitions, rewards, and punishments would be in vain. In order to make this evident, we must observe that some things act without judgment, as a stone moves downwards; and in like manner all things which lack knowledge. And some act from judgment, but not a free judgment; as brute animals. For the sheep, seeing the wolf, judges it a thing to be shunned, from a natural and not a free judgment; because it judges, not from deliberation, but from natural instinct. And the same thing is to be said of any judgment in brute animals. But man acts from

1. Aristotle, *Metaphysics,* I, 2 (982b26).
2. *Nicomachean Ethics,* III, 5 (1114a32).

judgment, because by his apprehensive power he judges that something should be avoided or sought. But because this judgment, in the case of some particular act, is not from a natural instinct, but from some act of comparison in the reason, therefore he acts from free judgment and retains the power of being inclined to various things. For reason in contingent matters may follow opposite courses, as we see in dialectical syllogisms and rhetorical arguments. Now particular operations are contingent, and therefore in such matters the judgment of reason may follow opposite courses, and is not determinate to one. And in that man is rational, it is necessary that he have free choice.

Reply Obj. 1. As we have said above, the sensitive appetite, though it obeys the reason, yet in a given case can resist by desiring what the reason forbids.[3] This is therefore the good which man does not when he wishes—namely, *not to desire against reason,* as Augustine says.

Reply Obj. 2. Those words of the Apostle are not to be taken as though man does not wish or does not run of his free choice, but because free choice is not sufficient thereto unless it be moved and helped by God.

Reply Obj. 3. Free choice is the cause of its own movement, because by his free choice man moves himself to act. But it does not of necessity belong to liberty that what is free should be the first cause of itself, as neither for one thing to be cause of another need it be the first cause. God, therefore, is the first cause, Who moves causes both natural and voluntary. And just as by moving natural causes He does not prevent their actions from being natural, so by moving voluntary causes He does not deprive their actions of being voluntary: but rather is He the cause of this very thing in them, for He operates in each thing according to its own nature.

Reply Obj. 4. *Man's way* is said *not to be his* in the execution of his choice, wherein he may be impeded, whether he will or not. The choice itself, however, is in us, but presupposes the help of God.

Reply Obj. 5. Quality in man is of two kinds: natural and adventitious. Now the natural quality may be in the intellectual part, or in the body and its powers. From the very fact, therefore, that man is such by virtue of a natural quality which is in the intellectual part, he naturally desires his last end, which is happiness. This desire is, indeed, a natural desire, and is not subject to free choice, as is clear from what we have said above.[4] But on the part of the body and its powers, man may be such by virtue of a natural quality, inasmuch as he is of such a temperament or disposition due to any

3. Q. 81, a. 3, and 2.
4. Q. 82, a. 1 and 2.

impression whatever produced by corporeal causes, which cannot affect the intellectual part, since it is not the act of a corporeal organ. And such as a man is by virtue of a corporeal quality, such also does his end seem to him, because from such a disposition a man is inclined to choose or reject something. But these inclinations are subject to the judgment of reason, which the lower appetite obeys, as we have said.[5] Therefore this is in no way prejudicial to free choice.

The adventitious qualities are habits and passions, by virtue of which a man is inclined to one thing rather than to another. And yet even these inclinations are subject to the judgment of reason. Such qualities, too, are subject to reason, as it is in our power either to acquire them, whether by causing them or disposing ourselves to them, or to reject them. And so there is nothing in this that is repugnant to free choice.

Second Article

WHETHER FREE CHOICE IS A POWER?

We proceed thus to the Second Article:—

Objection 1. It would seem that free choice is not a power. For free choice is nothing but a free judgment. But judgment denominates an act, not a power. Therefore free choice is not a power.

Obj. 2. Further, free choice is defined as *the faculty of the will and reason.* But faculty denominates the facility of power, which is due to a habit. Therefore free choice is a habit. Moreover Bernard says that free choice is *the soul's habit of disposing of itself.* Therefore it is not a power.

Obj. 3. Further, no natural power is forfeited through sin. But free choice is forfeited through sin, for Augustine says that *man, by abusing free choice, loses both it and himself.* Therefore free choice is not a power.

On the contrary, Nothing but a power, seemingly, is the subject of a habit. But free choice is the subject of grace, by the help of which it chooses what is good. Therefore free choice is a power.

I answer that, Although *free choice,* in its strict sense, denotes an act, in the common manner of speaking we call free choice that which is the principle of the act by which man judges freely. Now in us the principle of an act is both power and habit; for we say that we know something both by science and by the intellectual power. Therefore free choice must be either a power, or a habit, or a power with a habit. That it is neither a habit nor a power together with a habit can be clearly proved in two ways. First of all, because, if it is a habit, it must be a natural habit; for it is natural to man to

5. Q. 81, a. 3.

have free choice. But there is no natural habit in us with respect to those things which come under free choice, for we are naturally inclined to those things of which we have natural habits, for instance, to assent to first principles. Now those things to which we are naturally inclined are not subject to free choice, as we have said in the case of the desire of happiness.[6] Therefore it is against the very notion of free choice that it should be a natural habit; and that it should be a non-natural habit is against its nature. Therefore in no sense is it a habit.

Secondly, this is clear because habits are defined as that *by reason of which we are well or ill disposed with regard to actions and passions.*[7] For by temperance we are well-disposed as regards concupiscences, and by intemperance ill-disposed; and by science we are well-disposed to the act of the intellect when we know the truth, and by the contrary habit ill-disposed. But free choice is indifferent to choosing well or ill, and therefore it is impossible that it be a habit. Therefore it is a power.

Reply Obj. 1. It is not unusual for a power to be named from its act. And so from this act, which is a free judgment, is named the power which is the principle of this act. Otherwise, if free choice denominated an act, it would not always remain in man.

Reply Obj. 2. *Faculty* sometimes denominates a power ready for operation, and in this sense faculty is used in the definition of free choice. But Bernard takes habit, not as divided against power, but as signifying any aptitude by which a man is somehow disposed to an act. This may be both by a power and by a habit, for by a power man is, as it were, empowered to do the action, and by the habit he is apt to act well or ill.

Reply Obj. 3. Man is said to have lost free choice by falling into sin, not as to natural liberty, which is freedom from coercion, but as regards freedom from fault and unhappiness. Of this we shall treat later in the treatise on Morals in the second part of this work.[8]

Third Article

WHETHER FREE CHOICE IS AN APPETITIVE POWER?

We proceed thus to the Third Article:—

Objection 1. It would seem that free choice is not an appetitive, but a cognitive power. For Damascene says that *free choice straightway accom-*

6. Q. 82, a. I and 2.
7. Aristotle, *Nicomachean Ethics,* II, 5 (1105b 25).
8. *Summa Theologica,* I–II, q. 85; q. 109.

panies the rational power. But reason is a cognitive power. Therefore free choice is a cognitive power.

Obj. 2. Further, free choice is so called as though it were a free judgment. But to judge is an act of a cognitive power. Therefore free choice is a cognitive power.

Obj. 3. Further, the principal function of free choice is election. But election seems to belong to knowledge, because it implies a certain comparison of one thing to another; which belongs to the cognitive power. Therefore free choice is a cognitive power.

On the contrary, The Philosopher says that election is *the desire of those things which are in our power.*[9] But desire is an act of the appetitive power. Therefore election is also. But free choice is that by which we elect. Therefore free choice is an appetitive power.

I answer that, The proper act of free choice is election, for we say that we have a free choice because we can take one thing while refusing another; and this is to elect. Therefore we must consider the nature of free choice by considering the nature of election. Now two things concur in election: one on the part of the cognitive power, the other on the part of the appetitive power. On the part of the cognitive power, counsel is required, by which we judge one thing to be preferred to another; on the part of the appetitive power, it is required that the appetite should accept the judgment of counsel. Therefore Aristotle leaves it in doubt whether election belongs principally to the appetitive or the cognitive power: since he says that election is either *an appetitive intellect or an intellectual appetite.*[10] But he inclines to its being an intellectual appetite when he describes election as *a desire proceeding from counsel.*[11] And the reason of this is because the proper object of election is the means to the end. Now the means, as such, has the nature of that good which is called *useful;* and since the good, as such, is the object of the appetite, it follows that election is principally an act of an appetitive power. And thus free choice is an appetitive power.

Reply Obj. 1. The appetitive powers accompany the apprehensive, and in this sense Damascene says that free choice straightway accompanies the rational power.

Reply Obj. 2. Judgment, as it were, concludes and terminates counsel. Now counsel is terminated, first, by the judgment of reason; secondly, by

9. *Nicomachean Ethics,* III, 3 (1113a 11).

10. *Ibid.,* VI, 2 (1139b 4).

11. *Ibid.,* III, 3 (1113a 11).

the acceptation of the appetite. Hence the Philosopher says that, *having formed a judgment by counsel, we desire in accordance with that counsel.*[12] And in this sense election itself is a judgment from which free choice takes its name.

Reply Obj. 3. This comparison which is implied in the term election belongs to the preceding counsel, which is an act of reason. For though the appetite does not make comparisons, yet inasmuch as it is moved by the apprehensive power which does compare, it has some likeness of comparison, by choosing one in preference to another.

Fourth Article

WHETHER FREE CHOICE IS A POWER DISTINCT FROM THE WILL?

We proceed thus to the Fourth Article:—

Objection 1. It would seem that free choice is a power distinct from the will. For Damascene says that θέκγσιζ is one thing and βούλησις another. But θέλησις is will, while βούλησις seems to be free choice, because βούλησις, according to him, is the will as concerning an object by way of comparison between two things. Therefore it seems that free choice is a power distinct from the will.

Obj. 2. Further, powers are known by their acts. But election, which is the act of free choice, is distinct from the will, because *the will regards the end, whereas choice regards the means to the end.*[13] Therefore free choice is a power distinct from the will.

Obj. 3. Further, the will is the intellectual appetite. But on the part of the intellect there are two powers—agent and possible. Therefore, also on the part of the intellectual appetite there must be another power besides the will. And this, seemingly, can be only free choice. Therefore free choice is a power distinct from the will.

On the contrary, Damascene says free choice is nothing else than the will.

I answer that, The appetitive powers must be proportionate to the apprehensive powers, as we have said above.[14] Now, as on the part of intellectual apprehension we have intellect and reason, so on the part of the intellectual appetite we have will and free choice, which is nothing else but the power of election. And this is clear from their relations to their

12. *Ibid.*

13. Aristotle, *Nicomachean Ethics,* III, 2 (1111b 26).

14. Q. 64, a. 2; q. 80, a. 2.

respective objects and acts. For the act of *understanding* implies the simple acceptation of something, and hence we say that we understand first principles, which are known of themselves without any comparison. But to *reason,* properly speaking, is to come from one thing to the knowledge of another, and so, properly speaking, we reason about conclusions, which are known from the principles. In like manner, on the part of the appetite, to *will* implies the simple appetite for something, and so the will is said to regard the end, which is desired for itself. But to *elect* is to desire something for the sake of obtaining something else, and so, properly speaking, it regards the means to the end. Now in appetitive matters, the end is related to the means, which is desired for the end, in the same way as, in knowledge, principles are related to the conclusion to which we assent because of the principles. Therefore it is evident that as *intellect* is to *reason, so will* is to the *elective power,* which is free choice. But it has been shown above that it belongs to the same power both to understand and to reason,[15] even as it belongs to the same power to be at rest and to be in movement. Hence it belongs also to the same power to will and to elect. And on this account will and the free choice are not two powers, but one.

Reply Obj. 1. βούλησις is distinct from θέλησις because of a distinction, not of powers, but of acts.

Reply Obj. 2. Election and will—that is, the act of willing—are different acts, yet they belong to the same power, as do *to understand* and *to reason,* as we have said.

Reply Obj. 3. The intellect is compared to the will as moving the will. And therefore there is no need to distinguish in the will an *agent* and a *possible* will.

THE SUMMA THEOLOGICA
FIRST PART OF THE SECOND PART
Question VI
ON THE VOLUNTARY AND THE INVOLUNTARY
(*In Eight Articles*)

Since therefore happiness is to be gained by means of certain acts, we must as a consequence consider human acts in order to know by what acts we may obtain happiness, and by what acts we are prevented from obtaining it. But because operations and acts are concerned with what is singular, consequently, all practical knowledge is incomplete unless it take account of things in the particular. The study of Morals, therefore, since it treats of

15. Q. 79, a. 8.

human acts, should consider, first, what is universal; and, secondly, what pertains to the particular.[1]

In treating of what is universal in human acts, the points that offer themselves for our consideration are (1) human acts themselves; (2) their principles.[2] Now of human acts some are proper to man, while others are common to man and animals. And since happiness is man's proper good, those acts which are proper to man have a closer connection with happiness than have those which are common to man and the other animals. First, then, we must consider those acts which are proper to man; secondly, those acts which are common to man and the other animals, and are called passions of the soul.[3] The first of these points offers a twofold consideration: (1) What makes a human act? (2) What distinguishes human acts?[4]

And since those acts are properly called human which are voluntary, because the will is the rational appetite, which is proper to man, we must consider acts in so far as they are voluntary.

First, then, we must consider the voluntary and involuntary in general; secondly, those acts which are voluntary, as being elicited by the will, and as issuing from the will immediately;[5] thirdly, those acts which are voluntary, as being commanded by the will, which issue from the will through the medium of the other powers.[6]

Furthermore, because voluntary acts have certain circumstances, according to which we form our judgment concerning them, we must first consider the voluntary and the involuntary, and afterwards, the circumstances of those acts which are found to be voluntary or involuntary.[7] Under the first head there are eight points of inquiry: (1) Whether there is anything voluntary in human acts? (2) Whether in irrational animals? (3) Whether there can be voluntariness without any act? (4) Whether violence can be done to the will? (5) Whether violence causes involuntariness? (6) Whether fear causes involuntariness? (7) Whether concupiscence causes involuntariness? (8) Whether ignorance causes involuntariness?

1. *Summa Theologica,* II–II.
2. Q. 49.
3. Q. 22.
4. Q. 18.
5. Q. 8.
6. Q. 17.
7. Q. 7.

First Article

WHETHER THERE IS ANYTHING VOLUNTARY IN HUMAN ACTS?

We proceed thus to the First Article:—

Objection 1. It would seem that there is nothing voluntary in human acts. For that is voluntary *which has its principle within itself,* as Gregory of Nyssa, Damascene and Aristotle[8] declare. But the principle of human acts is not in man himself, but outside him, since man's appetite is moved to act by the appetible object which is outside him, and which is as a *mover unmoved.*[9] Therefore there is nothing voluntary in human acts.

Obj. 2. Further, the Philosopher proves that in animals no new movement arises that is not preceded by another and exterior motion.[10] But all human acts are new, since none is eternal. Consequently, the principle of all human acts is from outside man, and therefore there is nothing voluntary in them.

Obj. 3. Further, he that acts voluntarily can act of himself. But this is not true of man, for it is written (*John* xv. 5): *Without Me you can do nothing.* Therefore there is nothing voluntary in human acts.

On the contrary, Damascene says that *the voluntary is an act consisting in a rational operation.* Now such are human acts. Therefore there is something voluntary in human acts.

I answer that, There must needs be something voluntary in human acts. In order to make this clear, we must take note that the principle of some acts is within the agent, or in that which is moved; whereas the principle of some movements or acts is outside. For when a stone is moved upwards, the principle of this movement is outside the stone; whereas, when it is moved downwards, the principle of this movement is in the stone. Now of those things that are moved by an intrinsic principle, some move themselves, some not. For since every agent or thing moved acts or is moved for an end, as was stated above,[11] those are perfectly moved by an intrinsic principle whose intrinsic principle is one not only of movement but of movement for an end. Now in order that a thing be done for an end, some knowledge of the end is necessary. Therefore, whatever so acts or is so moved by an intrinsic principle that it has some knowledge of the end, has within itself the principle of its act, so that it not only acts, but acts for an end. On the other hand, if a thing has no knowledge of the end, even

8. *Nicomachean Ethics,* III, 1 (1111a 23).
9. Aristotle, *De Anima,* III, 10 (433b 11).
10. *Physics,* VIII, 2 (253a 11).
11. Q. 1, a. 2.

though it have an intrinsic principle of action or movement, nevertheless, the principle of acting or being moved for an end is not in that thing, but in something else, by which the principle of its action towards an end is imprinted on it. Therefore such things are not said to move themselves, but to be moved by others. But those things which have a knowledge of the end are said to move themselves because there is in them a principle by which they not only act but also act for an end. And, consequently, since both are from an intrinsic principle, *i.e.*, that they act and that they act for an end, the movements and acts of such things are said to be voluntary; for the term *voluntary* signifies that their movements and acts are from their own inclination. Hence it is that, according to the definitions of Aristotle,[12] Gregory of Nyssa and Damascene, the voluntary is defined not only as having *a principle within* the agent, but also as implying *knowledge*. Therefore, since man especially knows the end of his work, and moves himself, in his acts especially is the voluntary to be found.

Reply Obj. 1. Not every principle is a first principle. Therefore, although it is of the nature of the voluntary act that its principle be within the agent, nevertheless, it is not contrary to the nature of the voluntary act that this intrinsic principle be caused or moved by an extrinsic principle; for it is not of the nature of the voluntary act that its intrinsic principle be a first principle.—Nevertheless, it must be observed that a principle of movement may happen to be first in a genus, but not first absolutely. Thus, in the genus of things subject to alteration, the first principle of alteration is the body of the heavens, which nevertheless is not the first mover absolutely, but is moved locally by a higher mover. And so the intrinsic principle of the voluntary act, *i.e.*, the cognitive and appetitive power, is the first principle in the genus of appetitive movement, although it is moved by an extrinsic principle according to other species of movement.

Reply Obj. 2. New movements in animals are indeed preceded by a motion from without; and this in two respects. First, in so far as by means of an extrinsic motion an animal's senses are confronted with something sensible, which, on being apprehended, moves the appetite. Thus a lion, on seeing the approach of the stag through its movement, begins to be moved towards the stag.—Secondly, in so far as some extrinsic motion produces a physical change in an animal's body, for example, through cold or heat; and when the body is thus affected by the motion of an exterior body, the sensitive appetite likewise, which is the power of a bodily organ, is moved accidentally. Thus, it happens that through some alteration in

12. *Nicomachean Ethics*, III, 1 (1111a 23).

the body the appetite is roused to the desire of something. But this is not contrary to the nature of voluntariness, as was stated above, for such movements caused by an extrinsic principle are of another genus of movement.

Reply Obj. 3. God moves man to act, not only by proposing the appetible to the senses, or by effecting a change in his body, but also by moving the will itself; for every movement both of the will and of nature proceeds from God as the First Mover. And just as it is not incompatible with nature that the movement of nature be from God as the First Mover, inasmuch as nature is an instrument of God moving it, so it is not contrary to the character of a voluntary act that it proceed from God, inasmuch as the will is moved by God. Nevertheless, both natural and voluntary movements have this in common, that it belongs to the nature of both that they should proceed from a principle within the agent.

Second Article

WHETHER THERE IS ANYTHING VOLUNTARY IN IRRATIONAL ANIMALS?

We proceed thus to the Second Article:—

Objection 1. It would seem that there is nothing voluntary in irrational animals. For *voluntary* is so called from *voluntas* [*will*]. Now since the will is in the reason,[13] it cannot be in irrational animals. Therefore neither is there anything voluntary in them.

Obj. 2. Further, according as human acts are voluntary, man is said to be master of his actions. But irrational animals are not masters of their actions; for *they act not, but rather are they acted upon,* as Damascene says. Therefore there is no voluntary act in irrational animals.

Obj. 3. Further, Damascene says that *voluntary acts lead to praise and blame.* But neither praise nor blame befits the acts of irrational animals. Therefore such acts are not voluntary.

On the contrary, The Philosopher says that *both children and irrational animals participate in the voluntary.*[14] The same is said by Gregory of Nyssa and Damascene.

I answer that, As was stated above, it is of the nature of a voluntary act that its principle be within the agent, together with some knowledge of the end. Now knowledge of the end is twofold, perfect and imperfect. Perfect

13. Aristotle, *De Anima,* III, 9 (432b 5).

14. *Nicomachean Ethics,* III, 2 (1111b 8).

knowledge of the end consists in not only apprehending the thing which is the end, but also in knowing it under the aspect of end, and the relationship of the means to that end. And such a knowledge of the end belongs to none but the rational nature.—But imperfect knowledge of the end consists in a mere apprehension of the end, without knowing it under the aspect of end, or the relationship of an act to the end. Such a knowledge of the end is exercised by irrational animals, through their senses and their natural estimative power.

Consequently, perfect knowledge of the end is accompanied by the voluntary in its perfect nature, inasmuch as, having apprehended the end, a man can, from deliberating about the end and the means thereto, be moved, or not, to gain that end.—But imperfect knowledge of the end is accompanied by the voluntary in its imperfect nature, inasmuch as the agent apprehends the end, but does not deliberate, and is moved to the end at once. Therefore the voluntary in its perfection belongs to none but the rational nature, whereas the imperfect voluntary belongs also to irrational animals.

Reply Obj. 1. The will is the name of the rational appetite, and consequently it cannot be in beings devoid of reason. But the term *voluntary* is derived from *voluntas* [*will*], and can be extended to those things in which there is some participation of will, by way of likeness thereto. It is thus that voluntary action is attributed to irrational animals, in so far as they are moved to an end, through some kind of knowledge.

Reply Obj. 2. The fact that man is master of his actions is due to his being able to deliberate about them; for since the deliberating reason is indifferently disposed to opposites, the will can proceed to either. But it is not thus that voluntariness is in irrational animals, as was stated above.

Reply Obj. 3. Praise and blame attach to the voluntary act according to the perfect notion of the voluntary, which is not to be found in irrational animals.

Third Article

WHETHER THERE CAN BE VOLUNTARINESS WITHOUT ANY ACT?

We proceed thus to the Third Article:—

Objection 1. It would seem that voluntariness cannot be without any act. For that is voluntary which proceeds from the will. But nothing can proceed from the will, except through some act, at least an act of the will itself. Therefore there cannot be voluntariness without act.

Obj. 2. Further, just as one is said to will by an act of the will, so when the act of the will ceases, one is said not to will. But not to will causes involuntariness, which is contrary to voluntariness. Therefore there can be nothing voluntary when the act of the will ceases.

Obj. 3. Further, knowledge is part of the nature of the voluntary, as was stated above. But knowledge involves an act. Therefore voluntariness cannot be without some act.

On the contrary, The term *voluntary* is applied to that of which we are masters. Now we are masters in respect of to act and not to act, to will and not to will. Therefore, just as to act and to will are voluntary, so also are not to act and not to will.

I answer that, Voluntary is what proceeds from the will. Now one thing proceeds from another in two ways. First, directly, in which sense something proceeds from another inasmuch as this other acts: *e.g.*, heating from heat. Secondly, indirectly, in which sense something proceeds from another through the fact that this other does not act. Thus the sinking of a ship is attributed to the helmsman, from his having ceased to steer.—But we must take note that the cause of what follows from the failure to act is not always the agent as not acting, but only when the agent can and ought to act. For if the helmsman were unable to steer the ship, or if the ship's helm were not entrusted to him, the sinking of the ship would not be attributed to him, although it might be due to his absence from the helm.

Since, then, by willing and acting, the will is able, and sometimes ought, to hinder not-willing and not-acting, this not-willing and not-acting is imputed to the will as though proceeding from it. And thus it is that we can have the voluntary without an act, and this sometimes without an outward act, but with an interior act, for instance, when one wills not to act, and sometimes without even an interior act, as when one does not will to act.

Reply Obj. 1. We apply the term *voluntary* not only to that which proceeds from the will directly, as from its agent, but also to that which proceeds from it indirectly as from its non-agent.

Reply Obj. 2. *Not to will* is said in two senses. First, as though it were one word, and the infinitive of *I-do-not-will.* Consequently, just as when I say *I do not will to read,* the sense is, *I will not to read,* so *not to will to read* is the same as *to will not to read;* and in this sense *not to will* causes involuntariness.—Secondly it is taken as a sentence, and then no act of the will is affirmed. And in this sense *not to will* does not cause involuntariness.

Reply Obj. 3. Voluntariness requires an act of knowledge in the same way as it requires an act of will, namely, in order that it be in one's power to consider, to will and to act. And then, just as not to will and not to act, when it is time to will and to act, is voluntary, so is it voluntary not to consider.

Fourth Article

WHETHER VIOLENCE CAN BE DONE TO THE WILL?

We proceed thus to the Fourth Article:—

Objection 1. It would seem that violence can be done to the will. For everything can be compelled by that which is more powerful. But there is something, namely, God, that is more powerful than the human will. Therefore it can be compelled, at least by Him.

Obj. 2. Further, every passive subject is compelled by its active principle, when it is changed by it. But the will is a passive power, for it is a *moved mover.*[15] Therefore, since it is sometimes moved by its active principle, it seems that it is sometimes compelled.

Obj. 3. Further, violent movement is that which is contrary to nature. But the movement of the will is sometimes contrary to nature, as is clear of the will's movement to sin, which is contrary to nature, as Damascene says. Therefore the movement of the will can be compelled.

On the contrary, Augustine says that what is done voluntarily is not done of necessity. Now whatever is done under compulsion is done of necessity, and consequently what is done by the will cannot be compelled. Therefore the will cannot be compelled to act.

I answer that, The act of the will is twofold: one is its immediate act, as it were, elicited by it, namely, *to will;* the other is an act of the will commanded by it, and put into execution by means of some other power: *e.g., to walk* and *to speak,* which are commanded by the will to be executed by means of the power of locomotion.

As regards the commanded acts of the will, then, the will can suffer violence, in so far as violence can prevent the exterior members from executing the will's command. But as to the will's own proper act, violence cannot be done to the will. The reason for this is that the act of the will is nothing else than an inclination proceeding from an interior knowing principle, just as the natural appetite is an inclination proceeding from an interior principle without knowledge. Now what is compelled or violent is from an exterior principle. Consequently, it is contrary to the nature of the will's own act that it should be subject to compulsion or violence; just as it is also contrary to the nature of the natural inclination or the movement of a stone to be moved upwards. For a stone may have an upward movement

15. Aristotle, *De Anima,* III, 10 (433a 9; b 16).

from violence, but that this violent movement be from its natural inclination is impossible. In like manner, a man may be dragged by force, but it is contrary to the very notion of violence that he be thus dragged of his own will.

Reply Obj. 1. God, Who is more powerful than the human will, can move the will of man, according to *Proverbs* xxi. 1: *The heart of the king is in the hand of the Lord; whithersoever He will He shall turn it.* But if this were by compulsion, it would no longer be by an act of the will, nor would the will itself be moved, but something else against the will.

Reply Obj. 2. It is not always a violent movement when a passive subject is moved by its active principle, but only then when this is done against the interior inclination of the passive subject. Otherwise, every alteration and generation of simple bodies would be unnatural and violent; whereas they are natural by reason of the natural interior aptitude of the matter or subject to such a disposition. In like manner, when the will is moved, according to its own inclination, by the appetible object, this movement is not violent but voluntary.

Reply Obj. 3. That to which the will tends by sinning, although in reality it is evil and contrary to the rational nature, is nevertheless apprehended as something good and suitable to nature, in so far as it is suitable to man by reason of some pleasurable sensation or some vicious habit.

Fifth Article

WHETHER VIOLENCE CAUSES INVOLUNTARINESS?

We proceed thus to the Fifth Article:—

Objection 1. It would seem that violence does not cause involuntariness. For we speak of voluntariness and involuntariness in terms of the will. But violence cannot be done to the will, as was shown above. Therefore violence cannot cause involuntariness.

Obj. 2. Further, that which is done involuntarily is done with grief, as Damascene and the Philosopher[16] say. But sometimes a man suffers compulsion without being grieved thereby. Therefore violence does not cause involuntariness.

Obj. 3. Further, what is from the will cannot be involuntary. But some violent actions proceed from the will, for instance, when a man with a heavy body goes upwards, or when a man contorts his members in a way

16. *Nicomachean Ethics*, III, 1 (1111a 20).

contrary to their natural flexibility. Therefore violence does not cause involuntariness.

On the contrary, The Philosopher[17] and Damascene say that *things done under compulsion are involuntary.*

I answer that, Violence is directly opposed to the voluntary, as likewise to the natural. For the voluntary and the natural have this in common, that both are from an intrinsic principle, whereas the violent is from an extrinsic principle. And for this reason, just as in things devoid of knowledge violence effects something against nature, so in things endowed with knowledge it effects something against the will. Now that which is against nature is said to be *unnatural,* and, in like manner, that which is against the will is said to be *involuntary.* Therefore violence causes involuntariness.

Reply Obj. 1. The involuntary is opposed to the voluntary. Now it has been said that not only the act which proceeds immediately from the will is called voluntary, but also the act commanded by the will. Consequently, as to the act which proceeds immediately from the will, violence cannot be done to the will, as was stated above. But as to the commanded act, the will can suffer violence, and consequently in this respect violence causes involuntariness.

Reply Obj. 2. Just as that is said to be natural which is according to the inclination of nature, so that is said to be voluntary which is according to the inclination of the will. Now a thing is said to be natural in two ways. First, because it is from nature as from an active principle: *e.g.,* it is natural for fire to produce heat. Secondly, according to a passive principle, because, namely, there is in nature an inclination to receive an action from an extrinsic principle. Thus, the movement of the heavens is said to be natural by reason of the natural aptitude in the body of the heavens to receive such movement, although the cause of that movement is a voluntary agent. In like manner, an act is said to be voluntary in two ways. First, in regard to action, for instance, when one wills to act; secondly, in regard to passion, as when one wills to receive an action from another. Hence, when action is inflicted by an extrinsic agent, as long as the will to suffer that action remains in the passive subject, this is not violent absolutely; for although the patient does nothing by way of action, he does something by being willing to suffer. Consequently this cannot be called involuntary.

Reply Obj. 3. As the Philosopher says,[18] the movement of an animal, whereby at times an animal is moved against the natural inclination of the

17. *Ibid.* (1109b 35).

18. *Physics,* VIII, 4 (254b 14).

body, although it is not natural to the body, is nevertheless in a way natural to the animal, to which it is natural to be moved according to its appetite. Accordingly this is violent, not absolutely, but relatively.—The same remark applies in the case of one who contorts his members in a way that is contrary to their natural disposition. For this is violent relatively, *i.e.*, as to that particular member; but not absolutely, *i.e.*, as to the man himself.

Sixth Article
WHETHER FEAR CAUSES WHAT IS INVOLUNTARY ABSOLUTELY?

We proceed thus to the Sixth Article:—

Objection 1. It would seem that fear causes what is involuntary absolutely. For just as violence regards that which is contrary to the will in the present, so fear regards a future evil which is repugnant to the will. But violence causes what is involuntary absolutely. Therefore fear too causes what is involuntary absolutely.

Obj. 2. Further, that which is of itself such, remains such, whatever be added to it. Thus what is of itself hot, as long as it remains, is still hot, whatever be added to it. But that which is done through fear is involuntary in itself. Therefore, even with the addition of fear it is involuntary.

Obj. 3. Further, that which is such, subject to a condition, is such in a certain respect; whereas what is such, without any condition, is such absolutely. Thus, what is necessary, subject to a condition, is necessary in some respect, but what is necessary without qualification is necessary absolutely. But that which is done through fear is involuntary absolutely; and it is not voluntary, save under a condition, namely, in order that the evil feared may be avoided. Therefore that which is done through fear is involuntary absolutely.

On the contrary, Gregory of Nyssa and the Philosopher[19] say that such things as are done through fear are *voluntary rather than involuntary.*

I answer that, As the Philosopher says,[20] and likewise Gregory of Nyssa in his book *On Man,* such things as are done through fear *are of a mixed character,* being partly voluntary and partly involuntary. For that which is done through fear, considered in itself, is not voluntary; but it becomes voluntary in this particular case, in order, namely, to avoid the evil feared.

But if the matter be considered rightly, such things are voluntary rather than involuntary; for they are voluntary absolutely, but involuntary in a

19. *Nicomachean Ethics,* III, 1 (1110a 12).

20. *Ibid.*

certain respect. For a thing is said to be absolutely according as it is in act; but according as it is only in the apprehension, it is not so absolutely, but in a certain respect. Now that which is done through fear is in act in so far as it is done. For, since acts are concerned with singulars, and since the singular, as such, is here and now, that which is done is in act in so far as it is here and now and under other individuating circumstances. Hence that which is done through fear is voluntary, inasmuch as it is here and now, that is to say, in so far as, under the circumstances, it hinders a greater evil which was feared; and thus, the throwing of the cargo into the sea becomes voluntary during the storm, through fear of danger, and so it is clear that it is voluntary absolutely. And hence it is that what is done out of fear has the nature of what is voluntary, because its principle is within.—But if we consider what is done through fear, as outside this particular case, and inasmuch as it is repugnant to the will, this exists only according to our consideration of things; and consequently it is involuntary, considered in that respect, that is to say, outside the actual circumstances of this or that particular case.

Reply Obj. 1. Things done through fear and compulsion differ not only according to present and future time, but also in this, that the will does not consent, but is moved entirely counter to that which is done through compulsion; whereas what is done through fear becomes voluntary because the will is moved towards it, although not for its own sake, but because of something else, that is, in order to avoid an evil which is feared. For the conditions of a voluntary act are satisfied, if it be done because of something else voluntary; since the voluntary is not only what we will for its own sake as an end, but also that we will for the sake of something else as an end. It is clear therefore that in what is done from compulsion, the will does nothing inwardly, whereas in what is done through fear, the will does something. Accordingly, as Gregory of Nyssa says, in order to exclude things done through fear, a violent action is defined not only as one *whose principle is from the outside*, but with the addition, *in which he that suffers violence concurs not at all*; for the will of him that is in fear does concur somewhat in that which he does through fear.

Reply Obj. 2. Things that are such absolutely, remain such, whatever be added to them: *e.g.*, a cold thing, or a white thing; but things that are such relatively vary according as they are compared with different things. For what is big in comparison with one thing is small in comparison with another. Now a thing is said to be voluntary, not only for its own sake, as it were, absolutely; but also for the sake of something else, as it were, relatively. Accordingly, nothing prevents a thing, which was not voluntary in comparison with one thing, from becoming voluntary when compared with another.

Reply Obj. 3. That which is done through fear is voluntary without any condition, that is to say, according as it is actually done; but it is involuntary under a certain condition, that is to say, if such a fear were not threatening. Consequently, this argument proves rather the opposite.

Seventh Article

WHETHER CONCUPISCENCE CAUSES INVOLUNTARINESS?

We proceed thus to the Seventh Article:—

Objection 1. It would seem that concupiscence causes involuntariness. For just as fear is a passion, so is concupiscence. But fear causes involuntariness to a certain extent. Therefore concupiscence does so too.

Obj. 2. Further, just as the timid man through fear acts counter to that which he proposed, so does the incontinent, through concupiscence. But fear causes involuntariness to a certain extent. Therefore concupiscence does so also.

Obj. 3. Further, knowledge is necessary for voluntariness. But concupiscence impairs knowledge, for the Philosopher says that *delight,* or the lust of pleasure, *destroys the judgment of prudence.*[21] Therefore concupiscence causes involuntariness.

On the contrary, Damascene says: *The involuntary act deserves mercy or indulgence, and is done with regret.* But neither of these can be said of that which is done out of concupiscence. Therefore concupiscence does not cause involuntariness.

I answer that, Concupiscence does not cause involuntariness, but, on the contrary, makes something to be voluntary. For a thing is said to be voluntary from the fact that the will is moved to it. Now concupiscence inclines the will to desire the object of concupiscence. Therefore the effect of concupiscence is to make something to be voluntary rather than involuntary.

Reply Obj. 1. Fear has reference to evil, but concupiscence has reference to good. Now evil of itself is counter to the will, whereas good harmonizes with the will. Therefore fear has a greater tendency than concupiscence to cause involuntariness.

Reply Obj. 2. He who acts from fear retains the repugnance of the will to that which he does, considered in itself. But he that acts from concupiscence, *e.g.*, an incontinent man, does not retain his former will whereby he

21. *Nicomachean Ethics,* VI, 5 (1140b 12).

repudiated the object of his concupiscence; rather his will is changed so that he desires that which previously he repudiated. Accordingly, that which is done out of fear is involuntary, to a certain extent, but that which is done from concupiscence is in no way involuntary. For the man who yields to concupiscence acts counter to that which he purposed at first, but not counter to that which he desires now; whereas the timid man acts counter to that which in itself he desires now.

Reply Obj. 3. If concupiscence were to destroy knowledge altogether, as happens with those whom concupiscence has rendered mad, it would follow that concupiscence would take away voluntariness. And yet, properly speaking, it would not make the act involuntary, because in beings bereft of reason there is neither voluntary nor involuntary. But sometimes in those actions which are done from concupiscence, knowledge is not completely destroyed, because the power of knowing is not taken away entirely, but only the actual consideration in some particular possible act. Nevertheless, this itself is voluntary, according as by voluntary we mean that which is in the power of the will, for example, *not to act* or *not to will,* and in like manner *not to consider;* for the will can resist the passion, as we shall state later on.[22]

Eighth Article

WHETHER IGNORANCE CAUSES INVOLUNTARINESS?

We proceed thus to the Eighth Article:—

Objection 1. It would seem that ignorance does not cause involuntariness. For *the involuntary act deserves pardon,* as Damascene says. But sometimes that which is done through ignorance does not deserve pardon, according to *1 Corinthians* xiv. 38: *If any man know not, he shall not be known.* Therefore ignorance does not cause involuntariness.

Obj. 2. Further, every sin implies ignorance, according to *Proverbs* xiv. 22: *They err, that work evil.* If, therefore, ignorance causes involuntariness, it would follow that every sin is involuntary; which is opposed to the saying of Augustine, that *every sin is voluntary.*

Obj. 3. Further, *involuntariness is not without sadness,* as Damascene says. But some things are done out of ignorance, but without sadness. For instance, a man may kill a foe, whom he wishes to kill, thinking at the time that he is killing a stag. Therefore ignorance does not cause involuntariness.

22. Q. 10, a. 3; q. 77, a. 7.

On the contrary, Damascene and the Philosopher[23] say that *what is done through ignorance is involuntary.*

I answer that, If ignorance cause involuntariness, it is in so far as it deprives one of knowledge, which is a necessary condition of voluntariness, as was declared above. But it is not every ignorance that deprives one of this knowledge. Accordingly, we must take note that ignorance has a threefold relationship to the act of the will: in one way, *concomitantly;* in another, *consequently;* in a third way, *antecedently. Concomitantly,* when there is ignorance of what is done, but so that even if it were known, it would be done. For then ignorance does not induce one to will this to be done, but it just happens that a thing is at the same time done and not known. Thus, in the example given, a man did indeed will to kill his foe, but killed him in ignorance, thinking to kill a stag. And ignorance of this kind, as the Philosopher states,[24] does not cause involuntariness, since it is not the cause of anything that is repugnant to the will; but it causes *non-voluntariness,* since that which is unknown cannot be actually willed.

Ignorance is *consequent* to the act of the will, in so far as ignorance itself is voluntary; and this happens in two ways in accordance with the two aforesaid modes of the voluntary. First, because the act of the will is brought to bear on the ignorance, as when a man wills not to know, that he may have an excuse for sin, or that he may not be withheld from sin, according to *Job* xxi. 14: *We desire not the knowledge of Thy ways.* And this is called *affected ignorance.*—Secondly, ignorance is said to be voluntary, when it regards that which one can and ought to know, for in this sense *not to act* and *not to will* are said to be voluntary, as was stated above. And ignorance of this kind happens either when one does not actually consider what one can and ought to consider (this is called *ignorance of evil choice,* and arises from some passion or habit), or when one does not take the trouble to acquire the knowledge which one ought to have; in which sense, ignorance of the general principles of law, which one ought to know, is voluntary, as being due to negligence.

Accordingly, if in either of these ways ignorance is voluntary, it cannot cause what is involuntary absolutely. Nevertheless it causes involuntariness in a certain respect, inasmuch as it precedes the movement of the will towards the act, which movement would not be, if there were knowledge.

Ignorance is *antecedent* to the act of the will when it is not voluntary, and yet is the cause of man's willing what he would not will otherwise. Thus a

23. *Nicomachean Ethics,* III, 1 (1110a 1).

24. *Ibid.* (1110b 25).

man may be ignorant of some circumstance of his act, which he was not bound to know, with the result that he does that which he would not do if he knew of that circumstance. For instance, a man, after taking proper precaution, may not know that someone is coming along the road, so that he shoots an arrow and slays a passer-by. Such ignorance causes what is involuntary absolutely.

From this may be gathered the solution of the objections. For the first objection deals with ignorance of what a man is bound to know. The second, with ignorance of choice, which is voluntary to a certain extent, as was stated above. The third, with that ignorance which is concomitant with the act of the will.

6

Benedict Spinoza, from the *Ethics*

Benedict Spinoza (1632–1677) was a philosopher from the Netherlands raised in the Jewish community of Amsterdam. Spinoza proposed that because causal determinism is true, we lack the free will required for justified praise and blame. The sections of his major work, the Ethics, *in which this view is expressed and defended are included here.*

Part I Concerning God

PROPOSITION 16

*From the necessity of the divine nature there must follow infinite things in infinite ways [*modis*] (that is, everything that can come within the scope of infinite intellect).*

COROLLARY 1 Hence it follows that God is the efficient cause of all things that can come within the scope of the infinite intellect.

COROLLARY 2 Secondly, it follows that God is the cause through himself, not *per accidens.*

COROLLARY 3 Thirdly, it follows that God is absolutely the first cause.

PROPOSITION 17

God acts solely from the laws of his own nature, constrained by none.

PROPOSITION 26

A thing which has been determined to act in a particular way has necessarily been so determined by God; and a thing which has not been determined by God cannot determine itself to act.

PROPOSITION 27

A thing which has been determined by God to act in a particular way cannot render itself undetermined.

PROPOSITION 28

Every individual thing, i.e., anything whatever which is finite and has a determinate existence, cannot exist or be determined to act unless it be determined to exist and to act by another cause which is also finite and has a determinate existence, and this cause again cannot exist or be determined to act unless it be determined to exist and to act by another cause which is also finite and has a determinate existence, and so ad infinitum.

PROPOSITION 29

Nothing in nature is contingent, but all things are from the necessity of the divine nature determined to exist and to act in a definite way.

PROPOSITION 32

Will cannot be called a free cause, but only a necessary cause.

PROOF Will, like intellect, is only a definite mode of thinking, and so (Pr. 28) no single volition can exist or be determined to act unless it is determined by another cause, and this cause again by another, and so ad infinitum. Now if will be supposed infinite, it must also be determined to exist and to act by God, not insofar as he is absolutely infinite substance, but insofar as he possesses an attribute which expresses the infinite and eternal essence of Thought (Pr. 23). Therefore in whatever way will is conceived, whether finite or infinite, it requires a cause by which it is determined to exist and to act; and so (Def. 7) it cannot be said to be a free cause, but only a necessary or constrained cause.

COROLLARY 1 Hence it follows, firstly, that God does not act from freedom of will.

COROLLARY 2 It follows, secondly, that will and intellect bear the same relationship to God's nature as motion-and-rest and, absolutely, as all natural phenomena that must be determined by God (Pr. 29) to exist and to act in a definite way. For will, like all the rest, stands in need of a cause by which it may be determined to exist and to act in a definite manner. And although from a given will or intellect infinite things may follow, God cannot on that account be said to act from freedom of will any more than he can be said to act from freedom of motion-and-rest because of what follows from motion-and-rest (for from this, too, infinite things follow). Therefore, will pertains to God's nature no more than do other natural phenomena. It bears the same relationship to God's nature as does motion-and-rest and everything else that we have shown to follow from the necessity of the divine nature and to be determined by that divine nature to exist and to act in a definite way.

PROPOSITION 33

Things could not have been produced by God in any other way or in any other order than is the case.

PROOF All things have necessarily followed from the nature of God (Pr. 16) and have been determined to exist and to act in a definite way from the necessity of God's nature (Pr. 29). Therefore, if things could have been of a different nature or been determined to act in a different way so that the order of Nature would have been different, then God's nature, too, could have been other than it now is, and therefore (Pr. 11) this different nature, too, would have had to exist, and consequently there would have been two or more Gods, which (Cor. 1, Pr. 14) is absurd. Therefore things could not have been produced by God in any other way or in any other order than is the case.

SCHOLIUM 1 Since I have here shown more clearly than the midday sun that in things there is absolutely nothing by virtue of which they can be said to be "contingent," I now wish to explain briefly what we should understand by "contingent"; but I must first deal with "necessary" and "impossible." A thing is termed "necessary" either by reason of its essence or by reason of its cause. For a thing's existence necessarily follows either from its essence and definition or from a given efficient cause. Again, it is for these same reasons that a thing is termed "impossible"—that is, either because its essence or definition involves a contradiction or because there is no external cause determined to bring it into existence. But a thing is termed "contingent" for no other reason than the deficiency of our knowledge. For if we do not know whether the essence of a thing involves a contradiction, or if, knowing full well that its essence does not involve a contradiction, we still cannot make any certain judgment as to its existence because the chain of causes is hidden from us, then that thing cannot appear to us either as necessary or as impossible. So we term it either "contingent" or "possible."

SCHOLIUM 2 It clearly follows from the above that things have been brought into being by God with supreme perfection, since they have necessarily followed from a most perfect nature. Nor does this imply any imperfection in God, for it is his perfection that has constrained us to make this affirmation. Indeed, from its contrary it would clearly follow (as I have just shown) that God is not supremely perfect, because if things had been brought into being in a different way by God, we should have to attribute to God another nature different from that which consideration of a most perfect Being has made us attribute to him.

However, I doubt not that many will ridicule this view as absurd and will not give their minds to its examination, and for this reason alone, that they are in the habit of attributing to God another kind of freedom very different from that which we (Def. 7) have assigned to him; that is, an absolute will. Yet I do not doubt that if they were willing to think the matter over and carefully reflect on our chain of proofs they would in the end reject the kind of freedom which they now attribute to God not only as nonsensical but as a serious obstacle to science. It is needless for me here to repeat what was said in the Scholium to Proposition 17. Yet for their sake I shall proceed to show that, even if it were to be granted that will pertains to the essence of God, it would nevertheless follow from his perfection that things could not have been created by God in any other way or in any other order. This will readily be shown if we first consider—as they themselves grant—that on God's decree and will alone does it depend that each thing is what it is. For otherwise, God would not be the cause of all things. Further, there is the fact that all God's decrees have been sanctioned by God from eternity, for otherwise he could be accused of imperfection and inconstancy. But since the eternal does not admit of "when" or "before" or "after," it follows merely from God's perfection that God can never decree otherwise nor ever could have decreed otherwise; in other words, God could not have been prior to his decrees nor can he be without them. "But," they will say, "granted the supposition that God had made a different universe, or that from eternity he had made a different decree concerning Nature and her order, no imperfection in God would follow therefrom." But if they say this, they will be granting at the same time that God can change his decrees. For if God's decrees had been different from what in fact he has decreed regarding Nature and her order—that is, if he had willed and conceived differently concerning Nature—he would necessarily have had a different intellect and a different will from that which he now has. And if it is permissible to attribute to God a different intellect and a different will without any change in his essence and perfection, why should he not now be able to change his decrees concerning created things, and nevertheless remain equally perfect? For his intellect and will regarding created things and their order have the same relation to his essence and perfection, in whatever manner it be conceived.

Then again, all philosophers whom I have read grant that in God there is no intellect in potentiality but only intellect in act. Now since all of them also grant that his intellect and will are not distinct from his essence, it therefore follows from this, too, that if God had had a different intellect in act and a different will, his essence too would necessarily have been different. Therefore—as I deduced from the beginning—if things had been brought into being by God so as to be different from what they now are, God's intellect and will—that is (as is granted), God's essence—must have been different, which is absurd. Therefore since things could not have been brought into being by God in any other way or order—and it follows from God's supreme perfection that this is true—surely we can have no sound reason for believing that God did not wish to create all the things that are in his intellect through that very same perfection whereby he understands them.

"But," they will say, "there is in things no perfection or imperfection; that which is in them whereby they are perfect or imperfect, and are called good or bad, depends only on the will of God. Accordingly, if God had so willed it he could have brought it about that that which is now perfection should be utmost imperfection, and vice versa." But what else is this but an open assertion that God, who necessarily understands that which he wills, can by his will bring it about that he should understand things in a way different from the way he understands them—and this, as I have just shown, is utterly absurd. So I can turn their own argument against them, as follows. All things depend on the power of God. For things to be able to be otherwise than as they are, God's will, too, would necessarily have to be different. But God's will cannot be different (as we have just shown most clearly from the consideration of God's perfection). Therefore, neither can things be different.

I admit that this view which subjects everything to some kind of indifferent will of God and asserts that everything depends on his pleasure diverges less from the truth than the view of those who hold that God does everything with the good in mind. For these people seem to posit something external to God that does not depend upon him, to which in acting God looks as if it were a model, or to which he aims, as if it were a fixed target. This is surely to subject God to fate; and no more absurd assertion can be made about God, whom we have shown to be the first and the only free cause of both the essence and the existence of things. So I need not spend any more time in refuting this absurdity.

PROPOSITION 34

God's power is his very essence.

PROOF From the sole necessity of God's essence it follows that God is self-caused (Pr. 11) and the cause of all things (Pr. 16 and Cor.). Therefore, God's power whereby he and all things are and act, is his very essence.

PROPOSITION 35

Whatever we conceive to be within God's power necessarily exists.

PROOF Whatever is within God's power must be so comprehended in his essence (Pr. 34) that it follows necessarily from it, and thus necessarily exists.

PROPOSITION 36

Nothing exists from whose nature an effect does not follow.

PROOF Whatever exists expresses God's nature or essence in a definite and determinate way (Cor. Pr. 25); that is, (Pr. 34) whatever exists expresses God's power, which is the cause of all things, in a definite and determinate way, and so (Pr. 16) some effect must follow from it.

APPENDIX

I have now explained the nature and properties of God: that he necessarily exists, that he is one alone, that he is and acts solely from the necessity of his own nature, that he is the free cause of all things and how so, that all things are in God and are so dependent on him that they can neither be nor be conceived without him, and lastly, that all things have been predetermined by God, not from his free will or absolute pleasure, but from the absolute nature of God, his infinite power. Furthermore, whenever the opportunity arose I have striven to remove prejudices that might hinder the apprehension of my proofs. But since there still remain a considerable number of prejudices, which have been, and still are, an obstacle—indeed, a very great obstacle—to the acceptance of the concatenation of things in the manner which I have expounded, I have thought it proper at this point to bring these prejudices before the bar of reason.

Now all the prejudices which I intend to mention here turn on this one point, the widespread belief among men that all things in Nature are like themselves in acting with an end in view. Indeed, they hold it as certain that God himself directs everything to a fixed end; for they say that God has made everything for man's sake and has made man so that he should worship God. So this is the first point I shall consider, seeking the reason why most people are victims of this prejudice and why all are so naturally disposed to accept it. Secondly, I shall demonstrate its falsity; and lastly I shall show how it has been the source of misconceptions about good and bad, right and wrong, praise and blame, order and confusion, beauty and ugliness, and the like.

However, it is not appropriate here to demonstrate the origin of these misconceptions from the nature of the human mind. It will suffice at this point if I take as my basis what must be universally admitted, that all men are born ignorant of the causes of things, that they all have a desire to seek their own advantage, a desire of which they are conscious. From this it follows, firstly, that men believe that they are free, precisely because they are conscious of their volitions and desires; yet concerning the causes that have determined them to desire and will they do not think, not even dream about, because they are ignorant of them. Secondly, men act always with an end in view, to wit, the advantage that they seek. Hence it happens that they are always looking only for the final causes of things done, and are satisfied when they find them, having, of course, no reason for further doubt. But if they fail to discover them from some external source, they have no recourse but to turn to themselves, and to reflect on what ends would normally determine them to similar actions, and so they necessarily judge other minds by their own. Further, since they find within themselves and outside themselves a considerable number of means very convenient for the pursuit of their own advantage—as, for instance, eyes for seeing, teeth for chewing, cereals and living creatures for food, the sun for giving light, the sea for breeding fish—the result is that they look on all the things of

Nature as means to their own advantage. And realizing that these were found, not produced by them, they come to believe that there is someone else who produced these means for their use. For looking on things as means, they could not believe them to be self-created, but on the analogy of the means which they are accustomed to produce for themselves, they were bound to conclude that there was some governor or governors of Nature, endowed with human freedom, who have attended to all their needs and made everything for their use. And having no information on the subject, they also had to estimate the character of these rulers by their own, and so they asserted that the gods direct everything for man's use so that they may bind men to them and be held in the highest honor by them. So it came about that every individual devised different methods of worshipping God as he thought fit in order that God should love him beyond others and direct the whole of Nature so as to serve his blind cupidity and insatiable greed. Thus it was that this misconception developed into superstition and became deep-rooted in the minds of men, and it was for this reason that every man strove most earnestly to understand and to explain the final causes of all things. But in seeking to show that Nature does nothing in vain—that is, nothing that is not to man's advantage—they seem to have shown only this, that Nature and the gods are as crazy as mankind.

Consider, I pray, what has been the upshot. Among so many of Nature's blessings they were bound to discover quite a number of disasters, such as storms, earthquakes, diseases, and so forth, and they maintained that these occurred because the gods were angry at the wrongs done to them by men, or the faults committed in the course of their worship. And although daily experience cried out against this and showed by any number of examples that blessings and disasters befall the godly and the ungodly alike without discrimination, they did not on that account abandon their ingrained prejudice. For they found it easier to regard this fact as one among other mysteries they could not understand and thus maintain their innate condition of ignorance rather than to demolish in its entirety the theory they had constructed and devise a new one. Hence they made it axiomatic that the judgment of the gods is far beyond man's understanding. Indeed, it is for this reason, and this reason only, that truth might have evaded mankind forever had not Mathematics, which is concerned not with ends but only with the essences and properties of figures, revealed to men a different standard of truth. And there are other causes too—there is no need to mention them here—which could have made men aware of these widespread misconceptions and brought them to a true knowledge of things.

I have thus sufficiently dealt with my first point. There is no need to spend time in going on to show that Nature has no fixed goal and that all final causes are but figments of the human imagination. For I think that this is now quite evident, both from the basic causes from which I have traced the origin of this misconception and from Proposition 16 and the Corollaries to Proposition 32, and in addition from the whole set or proofs I have adduced to show that all things in Nature proceed from all eternal necessity and with supreme perfection. But I will make this additional point, that this doctrine of Final Causes turns Nature completely upside down, for it regards as an effect that which is in fact a cause, and vice versa. Again, it makes that which is by nature first to be last; and finally, that which is highest and most perfect is held to be the most imperfect. Omitting the first two points as self-evident, Propositions 21, 22, and 23 make it clear that that effect is most perfect which is directly produced by God, and an effect is the less perfect in proportion to the number of intermediary causes required for its production. But if the things produced directly by God were brought about to enable him to attain an end, then of necessity the last things for the sake of which the earlier things were brought about would excel all others. Again, this doctrine negates God's perfection; for if God acts with an end in view, he must necessarily be seeking something that he lacks. And although theologians and metaphysicians may draw a distinction between a purpose arising from want and an assimilative purpose, they still admit that God has acted in all things for the sake of himself, and not for the sake of the things to be created. For prior to creation they are not able to point to anything but God as a purpose for God's action. Thus they have to admit that God lacked and desired those things for the procurement of which he willed to create the means—as is self-evident.

I must not fail to mention here that the advocates of this doctrine, eager to display their talent in assigning purpose to things, have introduced a new style of argument to prove their doctrine, i.e., a reduction, not to the impossible, but to ignorance, thus revealing the lack of any other argument in its favor. For example, if a stone falls from the roof on somebody's head and kills him, by this method of arguing they will prove that the stone fell in order to kill the man; for if it had not fallen for this purpose by the will of God, how could so many circumstances (and there are often many coinciding circumstances) have chanced to concur? Perhaps you will reply that the event occurred because the wind was blowing and the man was walking that way. But they will persist in asking why the wind blew at that time and why the man was walking that way at that very time. If you again reply that the wind sprang up at that time because on the previous day the sea had begun to toss after a period of calm and that the man had been invited by a friend, they will again persist—for there is no end to questions—"But why did the sea toss, and why was the man invited for that time?" And so they will go on and on asking the causes of causes, until you take refuge in the will of God—that is, the sanctuary of ignorance. Similarly, when they consider the structure of the human body, they are astonished, and being ignorant of the causes of such skillful work they conclude that it is fashioned not by mechanical art but by divine or supernatural art, and is so arranged that no one part shall injure another.

As a result, he who seeks the true causes of miracles and is eager to understand the works of Nature as a scholar, and not just to gape at them like a fool, is universally considered an impious heretic and denounced by those to whom the common people bow down as interpreters of Nature and the gods. For these people know that the dispelling of ignorance would entail the disappearance of that astonishment, which is the one and only support for their argument and for safeguarding their authority. But I will leave this subject and proceed to the third point that I proposed to deal with.

When men became convinced that everything that is created is created on their behalf, they were bound to consider as the most important quality in every individual thing that which was most useful to them, and to regard as of the highest excellence all those things by which they were most benefited. Hence they came to form these abstract notions to explain the natures of things:—Good, Bad, Order, Confusion, Hot, Cold, Beauty, Ugliness; and since they believed that they are free, the following abstract notions came into being:—Praise, Blame, Right, Wrong. The latter I shall deal with later on after I have treated of human nature; at this point I shall briefly explain the former.

All that conduces to well-being and to the worship of God they call Good, and the contrary, Bad. And since those who do not understand the nature of things, but only imagine things, make no affirmative judgments about things themselves and mistake their imagination for intellect, they are firmly convinced that there is order in things, ignorant as they are of things and of their own nature. For when things are in such arrangement that, being presented to us through our senses, we can readily picture them and thus readily remember them, we say that they are well arranged; if the contrary, we say that they are ill arranged, or confused. And since those things we can readily picture we find pleasing compared with other things, men prefer order to confusion, as though order were something in Nature other than what is relative to our imagination. And they say that God has created all things in an orderly way, without realizing that they are thus attributing human imagination to God—unless perchance they mean that God, out of consideration for the human imagination, arranged all things in the way that men could most easily imagine. And perhaps they will find no obstacle in the fact that there are any number of things that far surpass our imagination, and a considerable number that confuse the imagination because of its weakness.

But I have devoted enough time to this. Other notions, too, are nothing but modes of imagining whereby the imagination is affected in various ways, and yet the ignorant consider them as important attributes of things because they believe—as I have said—that all things were made on their behalf, and they call a thing's nature good or bad, healthy or rotten and corrupt, according to its effect on them. For instance, if the motion communicated to our nervous system by objects presented through our eyes is conducive to our feeling of well-being, the objects which are its cause are said to be beautiful, while the objects which provoke a contrary motion are called ugly. Those things that we sense through the nose are called fragrant or fetid, through the tongue, sweet or bitter, tasty or tasteless, those that we sense by touch are called hard or soft, rough or smooth, and so on. Finally, those that we sense through our ears are said to give forth noise, sound, or harmony, the last of which has driven men to such madness that they used to believe that even God delights in harmony. There are philosophers who have convinced themselves that the motions of the heavens give rise to harmony. All this goes to show that everyone's judgment is a function of the disposition of his brain, or rather, that he mistakes for reality the way his imagination is affected. Hence it is no wonder—as we should note in passing—that we find so many controversies arising among men, resulting finally in skepticism. For although human bodies agree in many respects, there are very many differences, and so one man thinks good what another thinks bad; what to one man is well-ordered, to another is confused; what to one is pleasing, to another is displeasing, and so forth. I say no more here because this is not the place to treat at length of this subject, and also because all are well acquainted with it from experience. Everybody knows those sayings: "So many heads, so many opinions," "everyone is wise in his own sight," "brains differ as much as palates," all of which show clearly that men's judgment is a function of the disposition of the brain, and they are guided by imagination rather than intellect. For if men understood things, all that I have put forward would be found, if not attractive, at any rate convincing, as Mathematics attests.

We see therefore that all the notions whereby the common people are wont to explain Nature are merely modes of imagining, and denote not the nature of anything but only the constitution of the imagination. And because these notions have names as if they were the names of entities existing independently of the imagination I call them "entities of imagination" [*entia imaginationis*] rather than "entities of reason" [*entia ràtionis*]. So all arguments drawn from such notions against me can be easily refuted. For many are wont to argue on the following lines: if everything has followed from the necessity of God's most perfect nature, why does Nature display so many imperfections, such as rottenness to the point of putridity, nauseating ugliness, confusion, evil, sin, and so on? But, as I have just pointed out, they are easily refuted. For the perfection of things should be measured solely from their own nature and power; nor are things more or less perfect to the extent that they please or offend human senses, serve or oppose human interests. As to those who ask why God did not create men in such a way that they should be governed solely by reason, I make only this reply, that he lacked not material for creating all things from the highest to the lowest degree of perfection; or, to speak more accurately, the laws of his nature were so comprehensive as to suffice for the production of everything that can be conceived by an infinite intellect, as I proved in Proposition 16.

These are the misconceptions which I undertook to deal with at this point. Any other misconception of this kind can be corrected by everyone with a little reflection.

PART II Of the Nature and Origin of the Mind

PROPOSITION 48

In the mind there is no absolute, or free, will. The mind is determined to this or that volition by a cause, which is likewise determined by another cause, and this again by another, and so ad infinitum.

PROOF The mind is a definite and determinate mode of thinking (Pr. 11, II), and thus (Cor. 2, Pr. 17, I) it cannot be the free cause of its actions: that is, it cannot possess an absolute faculty of willing and non-willing. It must be determined to will this or that (Pr. 28, I) by a cause, which likewise is determined by another cause, and this again by another, etc.

SCHOLIUM In the same way it is proved that in the mind there is no absolute faculty of understanding, desiring, loving, etc. Hence it follows that these and similar faculties are either entirely fictitious or nothing more than metaphysical entities or universals which we are wont to form from particulars. So intellect and will bear the same relation to this or that idea, this or that volition, as stoniness to this or that stone, or man to Peter and Paul. As to the reason why men think they are free, we explained that in the Appendix to Part I.

But before proceeding further, it should here be noted that by the will I mean the faculty of affirming and denying, and not desire. I mean, I repeat, the faculty whereby the mind affirms or denies what is true or what is false, not the desire whereby the mind seeks things or shuns them. But now that we have proved that these faculties are universal notions which are not distinct from the particulars from which we form them, we must inquire whether volitions themselves are anything more than ideas of things. We must inquire, I say, whether there is in the mind any other affirmation and denial apart from that which the idea, insofar as it is an idea, involves. On this subject see the following proposition and also Def. 3, II, lest thought becomes confused with pictures. For by ideas I do not mean images such as are formed at the back of the eye—or if you like, in the middle of the brain—but conceptions of thought.

PROPOSITION 49

There is in the mind no volition, that is, affirmation and negation, except that which an idea, insofar as it is an idea, involves.

PROOF There is in the mind (preceding Pr.) no absolute faculty of willing and non-willing, but only particular volitions, namely, this or that affirmation, and this or that negation. Let us therefore conceive a particular volition, namely, a mode of thinking whereby the mind affirms that the three angles of a triangle are equal to two right angles. This affirmation involves the conception, or idea, of a triangle; that is, it cannot be conceived without the idea of a triangle. For to say that A must involve the conception of B is the same as to say that A cannot be conceived without B. Again, this affirmation (Ax. 3, II) cannot even be without the idea of a triangle. Therefore, this idea can neither be nor be conceived without the idea of a triangle. Furthermore, this idea of a triangle must involve this same affirmation, namely, that its three angles are equal to two right angles. Therefore, vice versa, this idea of a triangle can neither be nor be conceived without this affirmation, and so (Def. 2, II) this affirmation belongs to the essence of the idea of a triangle, and is nothing more than the essence itself. And what I have said of this volition (for it was arbitrarily selected) must also be said of every volition, namely, that it is nothing but an idea.

COROLLARY Will and intellect are one and the same thing.

PROOF Will and intellect are nothing but the particular volitions and ideas (Pr. 48, II and Sch.). But a particular volition and idea are one and the same thing (preceding Pr.). Therefore, will and intellect are one and the same thing.

SCHOLIUM By this means we have removed the cause to which error is commonly attributed. We have previously shown that falsity consists only in the privation that fragmentary and confused ideas involve. Therefore, a false idea, insofar as it is false, does not involve certainty. So when we say that a man acquiesces in what is false and has no doubt thereof, we are not thereby saying that he is certain, but only that he does not doubt, or that he acquiesces in what is false because there is nothing to cause his imagination to waver. On this point see Sch. Pr. 44, II. So however much we suppose a man to adhere to what is false, we shall never say that he is certain. For by certainty we mean something positive (Pr. 43, II and Sch.), not privation of doubt. But by privation of certainty we mean falsity.

But for a fuller explanation of the preceding proposition some things remain to be said. Then, again, there is the further task of replying to objections that may be raised against this doctrine of ours. Finally, to remove every shred of doubt, I have thought it worthwhile to point out certain advantages of this doctrine. I say certain advantages, for the most important of them will be better understood from what we have to say in Part V.

I begin, then, with the first point, and I urge my readers to make a careful distinction between an idea—i.e., a conception of the mind—and the images of things that we imagine. Again, it is essential to distinguish between ideas and the words we use to signify things. For since these three—images, words, and ideas—have been utterly confused by many, or else they fail to distinguish between them through lack of accuracy, or, finally, through lack of caution, our doctrine of the will, which it is essential to know both for theory and for the wise ordering of life, has never entered their minds. For those who think that ideas consist in images formed in us from the contact of external bodies are convinced that those ideas of things whereof we can form no like image are not ideas, but mere fictions fashioned arbitrarily at will. So they look on ideas as dumb pictures on a tablet, and misled by this preconception they fail to see that an idea, insofar as it is an idea, involves affirmation or negation. Again, those who confuse words with idea, or with the affirmation which an idea involves, think that when they affirm or deny something merely by words contrary to what they feel, they are able to will contrary to what they feel. Now one can easily dispel these misconceptions if one attends to the nature of thought, which is quite removed from the concept of extension. Then one will clearly understand that an idea, being a mode of thinking, consists neither in the image of a thing nor in words. For the essence of words and images is constituted solely by corporeal motions far removed from the concept of thought. With these few words of warning, I turn to the aforementioned objections.

The first of these rests on the confident claim that the will extends more widely than the intellect, and therefore is different from it. The reason for their belief that the will extends more widely than the intellect is that they find—so they say—that they do not need a greater faculty of assent, that is, of affirming and denying, than they already possess, in order to assent to an infinite number of other things that we do not perceive, but that we do need an increased faculty of understanding. Therefore, will is distinct from intellect, the latter being finite and the former infinite.

Second, it may be objected against us that experience appears to tell us most indisputably that we are able to suspend judgment so as not to assent to things that we perceive, and this is also confirmed by the fact that nobody is said to be deceived insofar as he perceives something, but only insofar as he assents or dissents. For instance, he who imagines a winged horse does not thereby grant that there is a winged horse; that is, he is not thereby deceived unless at the same time he grants that there is a winged horse. So experience appears to tell us most indisputably that the will, that is, the faculty of assenting, is free, and different from the faculty of understanding.

Third, it may be objected that one affirmation does not seem to contain more reality than another; that is, we do not seem to need greater power in order to affirm that what is true is true than to affirm that what is false is true. On the other hand, we do perceive that one idea has more reality or perfection than another. For some ideas are more perfect than others in proportion as some objects are superior to others. This, again, is a clear indication that there is a difference between will and intellect.

Fourth, it may be objected that if man does not act from freedom of will, what would happen if he should be in a state of equilibrium like Buridan's ass? Will he perish of hunger and thirst? If I were to grant this, I would appear to be thinking of an ass or a statue, not of a man. If I deny it, then the man will be determining himself, and consequently will possess the faculty of going and doing whatever he wants.

Besides these objections there may possibly be others. But since I am not obliged to quash every objection that can be dreamed up, I shall make it my task to reply to these objections only, and as briefly as possible.

To the first objection I reply that, if by the intellect is meant clear and distinct ideas only, I grant that the will extends more widely than the intellect, but I deny that the will extends more widely than perceptions, that is, the faculty of conceiving. Nor indeed do I see why the faculty of willing should be termed infinite any more than the faculty of sensing. For just as by the same faculty of willing we can affirm an infinite number of things (but in succession, for we cannot affirm an infinite number of things simultaneously), so also we can sense or perceive an infinite number of bodies (in succession) by the same faculty of sensing. If my objectors should say that there are an infinite number of things that we cannot sense, I retort that we cannot grasp them by any amount of thought, and consequently by any amount of willing. But, they say, if God wanted to bring it about that we should perceive these too, he would have had to give us a greater faculty of perceiving, but not a greater faculty of willing than he has already given us. This is the same as saying that if God wishes to bring it about that we should understand an infinite number of other entities, he would have to give us a greater intellect than he already has, so as to encompass these same infinite entities, but not a more universal idea of entity. For we have shown that the will is a universal entity, or the idea whereby we explicate all particular volitions; that is, that which is common to all particular volitions. So if they believe that this common or universal idea of volitions is a faculty, it is not at all surprising that they declare this faculty to extend beyond the limits of the intellect to infinity. For the term "universal" is applied equally to one, to many, and to an infinite number of individuals.

To the second objection I reply by denying that we have free power to suspend judgment. For when we say that someone suspends judgment, we are saying only that he sees that he is not adequately perceiving the thing. So suspension of judgment is really a perception, not free will. To understand this more clearly, let us conceive a boy imagining a winged horse and having no other perception. Since this imagining involves the existence of a horse (Cor. Pr. 17, II), and the boy perceives nothing to annul the existence of the horse, he will regard the horse as present and he will not be able to doubt its existence, although he is not certain of it. We experience this quite commonly in dreams, nor do I believe there is anyone who thinks that while dreaming he has free power to suspend judgment regarding the contents of his dream, and of bringing it about that he should not dream what he dreams that he sees. Nevertheless, it does happen that even in dreams we suspend judgment, to wit, when we dream that we are dreaming. Furthermore, I grant that nobody is deceived insofar as he has a perception; that is, I grant that the imaginings of the mind, considered in themselves, involve no error (see Sch. Pr. 17, II). But I deny that a man makes no affirmation insofar as he has a perception. For what else is perceiving a winged horse than affirming wings of a horse? For if the mind should perceive nothing apart from the winged horse, it would regard the horse as present to it, and would have no cause to doubt its existence nor any faculty of dissenting, unless the imagining of the winged horse were to be connected to an idea which annuls the existence of the said horse, or he perceives that the idea which he has of the winged horse is inadequate. Then he will either necessarily deny the existence of the horse or he will necessarily doubt it.

In the above I think I have also answered the third objection by my assertion that the will is a universal term predicated of all ideas and signifying only what is common to all ideas, namely, affirmation, the adequate essence of which, insofar as it is thus conceived as an abstract term, must be in every single idea, and the same in all in this respect only. But not insofar as it is considered as constituting the essence of the idea, for in that respect particular affirmations differ among themselves as much as do ideas. For example, the affirmation which the idea of a circle involves differs from the affirmation which the idea of a triangle involves as much as the idea of a circle differs from the idea of a triangle. Again, I absolutely deny that we need an equal power of thinking to affirm that what is true is true as to affirm that what is false is true. For these two affirmations, if you look to their meaning and not to the words alone, are related to one another as being to non-being. For there is nothing in ideas that constitutes the form of falsity (see Pr. 35, II with Sch. and Sch. Pr. 47, II). Therefore, it is important to note here how easily we are deceived when we confuse universals with particulars, and mental constructs [*entia rationis*] and abstract terms with the real.

As to the fourth objection, I readily grant that a man placed in such a state of equilibrium (namely, where he feels nothing else but hunger and thirst and perceives nothing but such-and-such food and drink at equal distances from him) will die of hunger and thirst. If they ask me whether such a man is not to be reckoned an ass rather than a man, I reply that I do not know, just as I do not know how one should reckon a man who hangs himself, or how one should reckon babies, fools, and madmen.

My final task is to show what practical advantages accrue from knowledge of this doctrine, and this we shall readily gather from the following points:

1. It teaches that we act only by God's will, and that we share in the divine nature, and all the more as our actions become more perfect and as we understand God more and more. Therefore, this doctrine, apart from giving us complete tranquillity of mind, has the further advantage of teaching us wherein lies our greatest happiness or blessedness, namely, in the knowledge of God alone, as a result of which we are induced only to such actions as are urged on us by love and piety. Hence we clearly understand how far astray from the true estimation of virtue are those who, failing to understand that virtue itself and the service of God are happiness itself and utmost freedom, expect God to bestow on them the highest rewards in return for their virtue and meritorious actions as if in return for the basest slavery.

2. It teaches us what attitude we should adopt regarding fortune, or the things that are not in our power, that is, the things that do not follow from our nature; namely, to expect and to endure with patience both faces of fortune. For all things follow from God's eternal decree by the same necessity as it follows from the essence of a triangle that its three angles are equal to two right angles.

3. This doctrine assists us in our social relations, in that it teaches us to hate no one, despise no one, ridicule no one, be angry with no one, envy no one. Then again, it teaches us that each should be content with what he has and should help his neighbor, not from womanish pity, or favor, or superstition, but from the guidance of reason as occasion and circumstance require. This I shall demonstrate in Part IV.

4. Finally, this doctrine is also of no small advantage to the commonwealth, in that it teaches the manner in which citizens should be governed and led; namely, not so as to be slaves, but so as to do freely what is best.

And thus I have completed the task I undertook in this Scholium, and thereby I bring to an end Part II, in which I think I have explained the nature of the human mind and its properties at sufficient length and as clearly as the difficult subject matter permits, and that from my account can be drawn many excellent lessons, most useful and necessary to know, as will partly be disclosed in what is to follow.

7

David Hume, from *A Treatise of Human Nature*

PART III.

Of the Will and Direct Passions

David Hume (1711–1776) was a Scottish philosopher and an advocate of a demystified, naturalistic conception of the world. In this selection from A Treatise of Human Nature *(1739–1740) he argues that the extent to which natural events are predictable provides us with good reason to believe that they are causally determined. But furthermore, we have exactly as much reason to believe that human actions are determined, because they are predictable to the same degree. Subsequently, Hume attempts to undermine our reasons for believing that we have "liberty," that is, the capacity for undetermined free choice. In addition, he argues that if we were not determined, we could not be morally responsible for our actions, because there could not then be a close enough tie between our character and our action.*

SECTION I.
Of liberty and necessity.

We come now to explain the *direct* passions, or the impressions, which arise immediately from good or evil, from pain or pleasure. Of this kind are, *desire and aversion, grief and joy, hope and fear.*

Of all the immediate effects of pain and pleasure, there is none more remarkable than the WILL; and tho', properly speaking, it be not comprehended among the passions, yet as the full understanding of its nature and properties, is necessary to the explanation of them, we shall here make it the subject of our enquiry. I desire it may be observ'd, that by the *will,* I mean nothing but *the internal impression we feel and are conscious of, when we knowingly give rise to any new motion of our body, or new perception of our mind.* This impression, like the preceding ones of pride and humility, love and hatred, 'tis impossible to define, and needless to describe any farther; for which reason we shall cut off all those definitions and distinctions, with which philosophers are wont to perplex rather than clear up this question; and entering at first upon the subject, shall examine that long disputed question concerning *liberty and necessity;* which occurs so naturally in treating of the will.

'Tis universally acknowledg'd, that the operations of external bodies are necessary, and that in the communication of their motion, in their attraction, and mutual cohesion, there are not the least traces of indifference or liberty. Every object is determin'd by an absolute fate to a certain degree and direction of its motion, and can no more depart from that precise line, in which it moves, than it can convert itself into an angel, or spirit, or any superior substance. The actions, therefore, of matter are to be regarded as instances of necessary actions; and whatever is in this respect on the same footing with matter, must be acknowledg'd to be necessary. That we may know whether this be the case with the actions of the mind, we shall begin with examining matter, and considering on what the idea of a necessity in its operations are founded, and why we conclude one body or action to be the infallible cause of another.

It has been observ'd already, that in no single instance the ultimate connexion of any objects is discoverable, either by our senses or reason, and that we can never penetrate so far into the essence and construction of bodies, as to perceive the principle, on which their mutual influence depends. 'Tis their constant union alone, with which we are acquainted; and 'tis from the constant union the necessity arises. If objects had not an uniform and regular conjunction with each other, we shou'd never arrive at any idea of cause and effect; and even after all, the necessity, which enters into that idea, is nothing but a determination of the mind to pass from one object to its usual attendant, and infer the existence of one from that of the other. Here then are two particulars, which we are to consider as essential to necessity, *viz.* the constant *union* and the *inference* of the mind; and wherever we discover these we must acknowledge a necessity. As the actions of matter have no necessity, but what is deriv'd from these circumstances, and it is not by any insight into the essence of bodies we discover their connexion, the absence of this insight, while the union and inference remain, will never, in any case, remove the necessity. 'Tis the observation of the union, which produces the inference; for which reason it might be thought sufficient, if we prove a constant union in the actions of the mind, in order to establish the inference, along with the necessity of these actions. But that I may bestow a greater force on my reasoning, I shall examine these particulars apart, and shall first prove from experience, that our actions have a constant union with our motives, tempers, and circumstances, before I consider the inferences we draw from it.

To this end a very slight and general view of the common course of human affairs will be sufficient. There is no light, in which we can take them, that does not confirm this principle. Whether we consider mankind according to the difference of sexes, ages, governments, conditions, or methods of education; the same uniformity and regular operation of natural principles are discernible. Like causes still produce like effects; in the same manner as in the mutual action of the elements and powers of nature.

There are different trees, which regularly produce fruit, whose relish is different from each other; and this regularity will be admitted as an instance of necessity and causes in external bodies. But are the products of *Guienne* and of *Champagne* more regularly different than the sentiments, actions, and passions of the two sexes, of which the one are distinguish'd by their force and maturity, the other by their delicacy and softness?

Are the changes of our body from infancy to old age more regular and certain than those of our mind and conduct? And wou'd a man be more ridiculous, who wou'd expect that an infant of four years old will raise a weight of three hundred pound, than one, who from a person of the same age, wou'd look for a philosophical reasoning, or a prudent and well-concerted action?

We must certainly allow, that the cohesion of the parts of matter arises from natural and necessary principles, whatever difficulty we may find in explaining them: And for a like reason we must allow, that human society is founded on like principles; and our reason in the latter case, is better than even that in the former; because we not only observe, that men *always* seek society, but can also explain the principles, on which this universal propensity is founded. For is it more certain, that two flat pieces of marble will unite together, than that two young savages of different sexes will copulate? Do the children arise from this copulation more uniformly, than does the parents care for their safety and preservation? And after they have arriv'd at years of discretion by the care of their parents, are the inconveniencies attending their separation more certain than their foresight of these inconveniencies, and their care of avoiding them by a close union and confederacy?

The skin, pores, muscles, and nerves of a day-labourer are different from those of a man of quality: So are his sentiments, actions and manners. The different stations of life influence the whole fabric, external and internal; and these different stations arise necessarily, because uniformly, from the necessary and uniform principles of human nature. Men cannot live without society, and cannot be associated without government. Government makes a distinction of property, and establishes the different ranks of men. This produces industry, traffic, manufactures, law-suits, war, leagues, alliances, voyages, travels, cities, fleets, ports, and all those other actions and objects, which cause such a diversity, and at the same time maintain such an uniformity in human life.

Shou'd a traveller, returning from a far country, tell us, that he had seen a climate in the fiftieth degree of northern latitude, where all the fruits ripen and come to perfection in the winter, and decay in the summer, after the same manner as in *England* they are produc'd and decay in the contrary seasons, he wou'd find few so credulous as to believe him. I am apt to think a traveller wou'd meet with as little credit, who shou'd inform us of people exactly of the same character with those in *Plato's Republic* on the one hand, or those in *Hobbes's Leviathan* on the other. There is a general course of nature in human actions, as well as in the operations of the sun and the climate. There are also characters peculiar to different nations and particular persons, as well as common to mankind. The knowledge of these characters is founded on the observation of an uniformity in the actions, that flow from them; and this uniformity forms the very essence of necessity.

I can imagine only one way of eluding this argument, which is by denying that uniformity of human actions, on which it is founded. As long as actions have a constant union and connexion with the situation and temper of the agent, however, we may in words refuse to acknowledge the necessity, we really allow the thing. Now some may, perhaps, find a pretext to deny this regular union and connexion. For what is more capricious than human actions? What more inconstant than the desires of man? And what creature departs more widely, not only from right reason, but from his own character and disposition? An hour, a moment is sufficient to make him change from one extreme to another, and overturn what cost the greatest pain and labour to establish. Necessity is regular and certain. Human conduct is irregular and uncertain. The one, therefore, proceeds not from the other.

To this I reply, that in judging of the actions of men we must proceed upon the same maxims, as when we reason concerning external objects. When any phænomena are constantly and invariably conjoin'd together, they acquire such a connexion in the imagination, that it passes from one to the other, without any doubt or hesitation. But below this there are many inferior degrees of evidence and probability, nor does one single contrariety of experiment entirely destroy all our reasoning. The mind ballances the contrary experiments, and deducting the inferior from the superior, proceeds with that degree of assurance or evidence, which remains. Even when these contrary experiments are entirely equal, we remove not the notion of causes and necessity; but supposing that the usual contrariety proceeds from the operation of contrary and conceal'd causes, we conclude, that the chance or indifference lies only in our judgment on account of our imperfect knowledge, not in the things themselves, which are in every case equally necessary, tho' to appearance not equally constant or certain. No union can be more constant and certain, than that of some actions with some motives and characters; and if in other cases the union is uncertain, 'tis no more than what happens in the operations of body, nor can we conclude any thing from the one irregularity, which will not follow equally from the other.

'Tis commonly allow'd that mad-men have no liberty. But were we to judge by their actions, these have less regularity and constancy than the actions of wise-men, and consequently are farther remov'd from necessity. Our way of thinking in this particular is, therefore, absolutely inconsistent; but is a natural consequence of these confus'd ideas and undefin'd terms, which we so commonly make use of in our reasonings, especially on the present subject.

We must now shew, that as the *union* betwixt motives and actions has the same constancy, as that in any natural operations, so its influence on the understanding is also the same, in *determining* us to infer the existence of one from that of another. If this shall appear, there is no known circumstance, that enters into the connexion and production of the actions of matter, that is not to be found in all the operations of the mind; and consequently we cannot, without a manifest absurdity, attribute necessity to the one, and refuse it to the other.

There is no philosopher, whose judgment is so riveted to this fantastical system of liberty, as not to acknowledge the force of *moral evidence,* and both in speculation and practice proceed upon it, as upon a reasonable foundation. Now moral evidence is nothing but a conclusion concerning the actions of men, deriv'd from the consideration of their motives, temper and situation. Thus when we see certain characters or figures describ'd upon paper, we infer that the person, who produc'd them, would affirm such facts, the death of *Cæsar,* the success of *Augustus,* the cruelty of *Nero;* and remembring many other concurrent testimonies we conclude, that those facts were once really existent, and that so many men, without any interest, wou'd never conspire to deceive us; especially since they must, in the attempt, expose themselves to the derision of all their contemporaries, when these facts were asserted to be recent and universally known. The same kind of reasoning runs thro' politics, war, commerce, oeconomy, and indeed mixes itself so entirely in human life, that 'tis impossible to act or subsist a moment without having recourse to it. A prince, who imposes a tax upon his subjects, expects their compliance. A general, who conducts an army, makes account of a certain degree of courage. A merchant looks for fidelity and skill in his factor or supercargo. A man, who gives orders for his dinner, doubts not of the obedience of his servants. In short, as nothing more nearly interests us than our own actions and those of others, the greatest part of our reasonings is employ'd in judgments concerning them. Now I assert, that whoever reasons after this manner, does *ipso facto* believe the actions of the will to arise from necessity, and that he knows not what he means, when he denies it.

All those objects, of which we call the one *cause* and the other *effect*, consider'd in themselves, are as distinct and separate from each other, as any two things in nature, nor can we ever, by the most accurate survey of them, infer the existence of the one from that of the other. 'Tis only from experience and the observation of their constant union, that we are able to form this inference; and even after all, the inference is nothing but the effects of custom on the imagination. We must not here be content with saying, that the idea of cause and effect arises from objects constantly united; but must affirm, that 'tis the very same with the idea of these objects, and that the *necessary connexion* is not discover'd by a conclusion of the understanding, but is merely a perception of the mind. Wherever, therefore, we observe the same union, and wherever the union operates in the same manner upon the belief and opinion, we have the idea of causes and necessity, tho' perhaps we may avoid those expressions. Motion in one body in all past instances, that have fallen under our observation, is follow'd upon impulse by motion in another. 'Tis impossible for the mind to penetrate farther. From this constant union it *forms* the idea of cause and effect, and by its influence *feels* the necessity. As there is the same constancy, and the same influence in what we call moral evidence, I ask no more. What remains can only be a dispute of words.

And indeed, when we consider how aptly *natural* and *moral* evidence cement together, and form only one chain of argument betwixt them, we shall make no scruple to allow, that they are of the same nature, and deriv'd from the same principles. A prisoner, who has neither money nor interest, discovers the impossibility of his escape, as well from the obstinacy of the goaler, as from the walls and bars with which he is surrounded; and in all attempts for his freedom chuses rather to work upon the stone and iron of the one, than upon the inflexible nature of the other. The same prisoner, when conducted to the scaffold, foresees his death as certainly from the constancy and fidelity of his guards as from the operation of the ax or wheel. His mind runs along a certain train of ideas: The refusal of the soldiers to consent to his escape, the action of the executioner; the separation of the head and body; bleeding, convulsive motions, and death. Here is a connected chain of natural causes and voluntary actions; but the mind feels no difference betwixt them in passing from one link to another; nor is less certain of the future event than if it were connected with the present impressions of the memory and senses by a train of causes cemented together by what we are pleas'd to call a *physical necessity.* The same experienc'd union has the same effect on the mind, whether the united objects be motives, volitions and actions; or figure and motion. We may change the names of things; but their nature and their operation on the understanding never change.

I dare be positive no one will ever endeavour to refute these reasonings otherwise than by altering my definitions, and assigning a different meaning to the terms of *cause, and effect, and necessity, and liberty, and chance.* According to my definitions, necessity makes an essential part of causation; and consequently liberty, by removing necessity, removes also causes, and is the very same thing with chance. As chance is commonly thought to imply a contradiction, and is at least directly contrary to experience, there are always the same arguments against liberty or free-will. If any one alters the definitions, I cannot pretend to argue with him, 'till I know the meaning he assigns to these terms.

SECTION II.
The same subject continu'd.

I believe we may assign the three following reasons for the prevalence of the doctrine of liberty, however absurd it may be in one sense, and unintelligible in any other. First, After we have perform'd any action; tho' we confess we were influenc'd by particular views and motives; 'tis difficult for us to perswade ourselves we were govern'd by necessity, and that 'twas utterly impossible for us to have acted otherwise; the idea of necessity seeming to imply something of force, and violence, and constraint, of which we are not sensible. Few are capable of distinguishing betwixt the liberty of *spontaniety,* as it is call'd in the schools, and the liberty of *indifference;* betwixt that which is oppos'd to violence, and that which means a negation of necessity and causes. The first is even the most common sense of the word; and as 'tis only that species of liberty, which it concerns us to preserve, our thoughts have been principally turn'd towards it, and have almost universally confounded it with the other.

Secondly, there is a *false sensation or experience* even of the liberty of indifference; which is regarded as an argument for its real existence. The necessity of any action, whether of matter or of the mind, is not properly a quality in the agent, but in any thinking or intelligent being, who may consider the action, and consists in the determination of his thought to infer its existence from some preceding objects: As liberty or chance, on the other hand, is nothing but the want of that determination, and a certain looseness, which we feel in passing or not passing from the idea of one to that of the other. Now we may observe, that tho' in reflecting on human actions we seldom feel such a looseness or indifference, yet it very commonly happens, that in performing the actions themselves we are sensible of something like it: And as all related or resembling objects are readily taken for each other, this has been employ'd as a demonstrative or even an intuitive proof of human liberty. We feel that our actions are subject to our will on most occasions, and imagine we feel that the will itself is subject to nothing; because when by a denial of it we are provok'd to try, we feel that it moves easily every way, and produces an image of itself even on that side, on which it did not settle. This image or faint motion, we perswade ourselves, cou'd have been compleated into the thing itself; because, shou'd that be deny'd, we find, upon a second trial, that it can.

But these efforts are all in vain; and whatever capricious and irregular actions we may perform; as the desire of showing our liberty is the sole motive of our actions; we can never free ourselves from the bonds of necessity. We may imagine we feel a liberty within ourselves; but a spectator can commonly infer our actions from our motives and character; and even where he cannot, he concludes in general, that he might, were he perfectly acquainted with every circumstance of our situation and temper, and the most secret springs of our complexion and disposition. Now this is the very essence of necessity, according to the foregoing doctrine.

A third reason why the doctrine of liberty has generally been better receiv'd in the world, than its antagonist, proceeds from *religion,* which has been very unnecessarily interested in this question. There is no method of reasoning more common, and yet none more blameable, than in philosophical debates to endeavour to refute any hypothesis by a pretext of its dangerous consequences to religion and morality. When any opinion leads us into absurdities, 'tis certainly false; but 'tis not certain an opinion is false, because 'tis of dangerous consequence. Such topics, therefore, ought entirely to be foreborn, as serving nothing to the discovery of truth, but only to make the person of an antagonist odious. This I observe in general, without pretending to draw any advantage from it. I submit myself frankly to an examination of this kind, and dare venture to affirm, that the doctrine of necessity, according to my explication of it, is not only innocent, but even advantageous to religion and morality.

I define necessity two ways, conformable to the two definitions of *cause,* of which it makes an essential part. I place it either in the constant union and conjunction of like objects, or in the inference of the mind from the one to the other. Now necessity, in both these senses, has universally, tho' tacitely, in the schools, in the pulpit, and in common life, been allow'd to belong to the will of man, and no one has ever pretended to deny, that we can draw inferences concerning human actions, and that those inferences are founded on the experienc'd union of like actions with like motives and circumstances. The only particular in which any one can differ from me, is either, that perhaps he will refuse to call this necessity. But as long as the meaning is understood, I hope the word can do no harm. Or that he will maintain there is something else in the operations of matter. Now whether it be so or not is of no consequence to religion, whatever it may be to natural philosophy. I may be mistaken in asserting, that we have no idea of any other connexion in the actions of body, and shall be glad to be farther instructed on that head: But sure I am, I ascribe nothing to the actions of the mind, but what must readily be allow'd of. Let no one, therefore, put an invidious construction on my words, by saying simply, that I assert the necessity of human actions, and place them on the same footing with the operations of senseless matter. I do not ascribe to the will that unintelligible necessity, which is suppos'd to lie in matter. But I ascribe to matter, that intelligible quality, call it necessity or not, which the most rigorous orthodoxy does or must allow to belong to the will. I change, therefore, nothing in the receiv'd systems, with regard to the will, but only with regard to material objects.

Nay I shall go farther, and assert, that this kind of necessity is so essential to religion and morality, that without it there must ensue an absolute subversion of both, and that every other supposition is entirely destructive to all laws both *divine* and *human.* 'Tis indeed certain, that as all human laws are founded on rewards and punishments, 'tis suppos'd as a fundamental principle, that these motives have an influence on the mind, and both produce the good and prevent the evil actions. We may give to this influence what name we please; but as 'tis usually conjoin'd with the action, common sense requires it shou'd be esteem'd a cause, and be look'd upon as an instance of that necessity, which I wou'd establish.

This reasoning is equally solid, when apply'd to *divine* laws, so far as the deity is consider'd as a legislator, and is suppos'd to inflict punishment and bestow rewards with a design to produce obedience. But I also maintain, that even where he acts not in his magisterial capacity, but is regarded as the avenger of crimes merely on account of their odiousness and deformity, not only 'tis impossible, without the necessary connexion of cause and effect in human actions, that punishments cou'd be inflicted compatible with justice and moral equity; but also that it cou'd ever enter into the thoughts of any reasonable being to inflict them. The constant and universal object of hatred or anger is a person or creature endow'd with thought and consciousness; and when any criminal or injurious actions excite that passion, 'tis only by their relation to the person or connexion with him. But according to the doctrine of liberty or chance, this connexion is reduc'd to nothing, nor are men more accountable for those actions, which are design'd and premeditated, than for such as are the most casual and accidental. Actions are by their very nature temporary and perishing; and where they proceed not from some cause in the characters and disposition of the person, who perform'd them, they infix not themselves upon him, and can neither redound to his honour, if good, nor infamy, if evil. The action itself may be blameable; it may be contrary to all the rules of morality and religion: But the person is not responsible for it; and as it proceeded from nothing in him, that is durable or constant, and leaves nothing of that nature behind it, 'tis impossible he can, upon its account, become the object of punishment or vengeance. According to the hypothesis of liberty, therefore, a man is as pure and untainted, after having committed the most horrid crimes, as at the first moment of his birth, nor is his character any way concern'd in his actions; since they are not deriv'd from it, and the wickedness of the one can never be us'd as a proof of the depravity of the other. 'Tis only upon the principles of necessity, that a person acquires any merit or demerit from his actions, however the common opinion may incline to the contrary.

But so inconsistent are men with themselves, that tho' they often assert, that necessity utterly destroys all merit and demerit either towards mankind or superior powers, yet they continue still to reason upon these very principles of necessity in all their judgments concerning this matter. Men are not blam'd for such evil actions as they perform ignorantly and casually, whatever may be their consequences. Why? but because the causes of these actions are only momentary, and terminate in them alone. Men are less blam'd for such evil actions, as they perform hastily and unpremeditately, than for such as proceed from thought and deliberation. For what reason? but because a hasty temper, tho' a constant cause in the mind, operates only by intervals, and infects not the whole character. Again, repentance wipes off every crime, especially if attended with an evident reformation of life and manners. How is this to be accounted for? But by asserting that actions render a person criminal, merely as they are proofs of criminal passions or principles in the mind; and when by any alteration of these principles they cease to be just proofs, they likewise cease to be criminal. But according to the doctrine of *liberty* or *chance* they never were just proofs, and consequently never were criminal.

Here then I turn to my adversary, and desire him to free his own system from these odious consequences before he charge them upon others. Or if he rather chuses, that this question shou'd be decided by fair arguments before philosophers, than by declamations before the people, let him return to what I have advanc'd to prove that liberty and chance are synonimous; and concerning the nature of moral evidence and the regularity of human actions. Upon a review of these reasonings, I cannot doubt of an entire victory; and therefore having prov'd, that all actions of the will have particular causes, I proceed to explain what these causes are, and how they operate.

8

David Hume, from *An Enquiry Concerning Human Understanding*

In this selection from An Enquiry Concerning Human Understanding *(1748) Hume reiterates the argument developed in the* Treatise *for the causal determination of human action. He also provides a compatibilist account of liberty:* "a power of acting or not acting, according to the determinations of the will; *that is, if we choose to remain at rest we may; if we choose to move, we also may.*" *Here Hume seems to define liberty as a power to do otherwise, where this power is analyzed as the power to do as one chooses. In addition, near the end of the section, in his discussion of the effect of the thesis of divine determinism on the moral sentiments, Hume prefigures the solution to the debate provided by P. F. Strawson.*

SECTION VIII.—*Of Liberty and Necessity.*

PART 1.

It might reasonably be expected, in questions, which have been canvassed and disputed with great eagerness, since the first origin of science and philosophy, that the meaning of all the terms, at least, should have been agreed upon among the disputants; and our enquiries, in the course of two thousand years, been able to pass from words to the true and real subject of the controversy. For how easy may it seem to give exact definitions of the terms employed in reasoning, and make these definitions, not the mere sound of words, the object of future scrutiny and examination? But if we consider the matter more narrowly, we shall be apt to draw a quite opposite conclusion. From this circumstance alone, that a controversy has been long kept on foot, and remains still undecided, we may presume, that there is some ambiguity in the expression, and that the disputants affix different ideas to the terms employed in the controversy. For as the faculties of the mind are supposed to be naturally alike in every individual; otherwise nothing could be more fruitless than to reason or dispute together; it were impossible, if men affix the same ideas to their terms, that they could so long form different opinions of the same subject;

especially when they communicate their views, and each party turn themselves on all sides, in search of arguments, which may give them the victory over their antagonists. It is true; if men attempt the discussion of questions, which lie entirely beyond the reach of human capacity, such as those concerning the origin of worlds, or the economy of the intellectual system or region of spirits, they may long beat the air in their fruitless contests, and never arrive at any determinate conclusion. But if the question regard any subject of common life and experience; nothing, one would think, could preserve the dispute so long undecided, but some ambiguous expressions, which keep the antagonists still at a distance, and hinder them from grappling with each other.

This has been the case in the long disputed question concerning liberty and necessity; and to so remarkable a degree, that, if I be not much mistaken, we shall find, that all mankind, both learned and ignorant, have always been of the same opinion with regard to this subject, and that a few intelligible definitions would immediately have put an end to the whole controversy. I own, that this dispute has been so much canvassed on all hands, and has led philosophers into such a labyrinth of obscure sophistry, that it is no wonder, if a sensible reader indulge his ease so far as to turn a deaf ear to the proposal of such a question, from which he can expect neither instruction nor entertainment. But the state of the argument here proposed may, perhaps, serve to renew his attention; as it has more novelty, promises at least some decision of the controversy, and will not much disturb his ease by any intricate or obscure reasoning.

I hope, therefore, to make it appear, that all men have ever agreed in the doctrine both of necessity and of liberty, according to any reasonable sense, which can be put on these terms; and that the whole controversy has hitherto turned merely upon words. We shall begin with examining the doctrine of necessity.

It is universally allowed, that matter, in all its operations, is actuated by a necessary force, and that every natural effect is so precisely determined by the energy of its cause, that no other effect, in such particular circumstances, could possibly have resulted from it. The degree and direction of every motion is, by the laws of nature, prescribed with such exactness, that a living creature may as soon arise from the shock of two bodies, as motion, in any other degree or direction than what is actually produced by it. Would we, therefore, form a just and precise idea of *necessity*, we must consider whence that idea arises, when we apply it to the operation of bodies.

It seems evident, that, if all the scenes of nature were continually shifted in such a manner, that no two events bore any resemblance to each other, but every object was entirely new, without any similitude to whatever had been seen before, we should never, in that case, have attained the least idea of necessity, or of a connexion among these objects. We might say, upon such a supposition, that one object or event has followed another; not that one was produced by the other. The relation of cause and effect must be utterly unknown to mankind. Inference and reasoning concerning the operations of nature would, from that moment, be at an end; and the memory and senses remain the only canals, by which the knowledge of any real existence could possibly have access to the mind. Our idea, therefore, of necessity and causation arises entirely from the uniformity, observable in the operations of nature; where similar objects are constantly conjoined together, and the mind is determined by custom to infer the one from the appearance of the other. These two circumstances form the whole of that necessity, which we ascribe to matter. Beyond the constant *conjunction* of similar objects, and the consequent *inference* from one to the other, we have no notion of any necessity, or connexion.

If it appear, therefore, that all mankind have ever allowed, without any doubt or hesitation, that these two circumstances take place in the voluntary actions of men, and in the operations of mind; it must follow, that all mankind have ever agreed in the doctrine of necessity, and that they have hitherto disputed, merely for not understanding each other.

As to the first circumstance, the constant and regular conjunction of similar events; we may possibly satisfy ourselves by the following considerations. It is universally acknowledged, that there is a great uniformity among the actions of men, in all nations and ages, and that human nature remains still the same, in its principles and operations. The same motives always produce the same actions: The same events follow from the same causes. Ambition, avarice, self-love, vanity, friendship, generosity, public spirit; these passions, mixed in various degrees, and distributed through society, have been, from the beginning of the world, and still are, the source of all the actions and enterprises, which have ever been observed among mankind. Would you know the sentiments, inclinations, and course of life of the GREEKS and ROMANS? Study well the temper and actions of the FRENCH and ENGLISH: You cannot be much mistaken in transferring to the former *most* of the observations, which you have made with regard to the latter. Mankind are so much the same, in all times and places, that history informs us of nothing new or strange in this particular. Its chief use is only to discover the constant and universal principles of human nature, by showing men in all varieties of circumstances and situations, and furnishing us with materials, from which we may form our

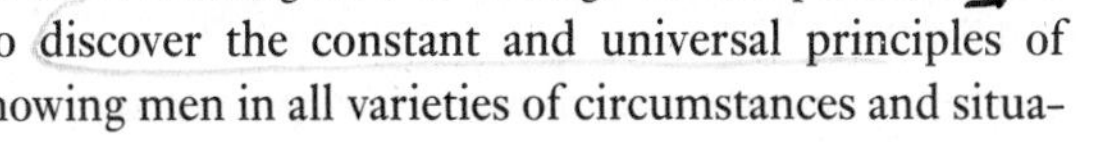

observations, and become acquainted with the regular springs of human action and behaviour. These records of wars, intrigues, factions, and revolutions, are so many collections of experiments, by which the politician or moral philosopher fixes the principles of his science; in the same manner as the physician or natural philosopher becomes acquainted with the nature of plants, minerals, and other external objects, by the experiments, which he forms concerning them. Nor are the earth, water, and other elements, examined by ARISTOTLE, and HIPPOCRATES, more like to those, which at present lie under our observation, than the men, described by POLYBIUS and TACITUS, are to those, who now govern the world.

Should a traveller, returning from a far country, bring us an account of men, wholly different from any, with whom we were ever acquainted; men, who were entirely divested of avarice, ambition, or revenge; who knew no pleasure but friendship, generosity, and public spirit; we should immediately, from these circumstances, detect the falsehood, and prove him a liar, with the same certainty as if he had stuffed his narration with stories of centaurs and dragons, miracles and prodigies. And if we would explode any forgery in history, we cannot make use of a more convincing argument, than to prove, that the actions, ascribed to any person, are directly contrary to the course of nature, and that no human motives, in such circumstances, could ever induce him to such a conduct. The veracity of QUINTUS CURTIUS is as much to be suspected, when he describes the supernatural courage of ALEXANDER, by which he was hurried on singly to attack multitudes, as when he describes his supernatural force and activity, by which he was able to resist them. So readily and universally do we acknowledge a uniformity in human motives and actions as well as in the operations of body.

Hence likewise the benefit of that experience, acquired by long life and a variety of business and company, in order to instruct us in the principles of human nature, and regulate our future conduct, as well as speculation. By means of this guide, we mount up to the knowledge of men's inclinations and motives, from their actions, expressions, and even gestures; and again, descend to the interpretation of their actions from our knowledge of their motives and inclinations. The general observations, treasured up by a course of experience, give us the clue of human nature, and teach us to unravel all its intricacies. Pretexts and appearances no longer deceive us. Public declarations pass for the specious colouring of a cause. And though virtue and honour be allowed their proper weight and authority, that perfect disinterestedness, so often pretended to, is never expected in multitudes and parties; seldom in their leaders; and scarcely even in individuals of any rank or station. But were there no uniformity in human actions, and were every experiment, which we could form of this kind, irregular and anomalous, it were impossible to collect any general observations concerning mankind; and no experience, however accurately digested by reflection, would ever serve to any purpose. Why is the aged husbandman more skilful in his calling than the young beginner, but because there is a certain uniformity in the operation of the sun, rain, and earth, towards the production of vegetables; and experience teaches the old practitioner the rules, by which this operation is governed and directed?

We must not, however, expect, that this uniformity of human actions should be carried to such a length, as that all men, in the same circumstances, will always act precisely in the same manner, without making any allowance for the diversity of characters, prejudices, and opinions. Such a uniformity in every particular, is found in no part of nature. On the contrary, from observing the variety of conduct in different men, we are enabled to form a greater variety of maxims, which still suppose a degree of uniformity and regularity.

Are the manners of men different in different ages and countries? We learn thence the great force of custom and education, which mould the human mind from its infancy, and form it into a fixed and established character. Is the behaviour and conduct of the one sex very unlike that of the other? It is thence we become acquainted with the different characters, which nature has impressed upon the sexes, and which she preserves with constancy and regularity. Are the actions of the same person much diversified in the different periods of his life, from infancy to old age? This affords room for many general observations concerning the gradual change of our sentiments and inclinations, and the different maxims, which prevail in the different ages of human creatures. Even the characters, which are peculiar to each individual, have a uniformity in their influence; otherwise our acquaintance with the persons and our observation of their conduct, could never teach us their dispositions, or serve to direct our behaviour with regard to them.

I grant it possible to find some actions, which seem to have no regular connexion with any known motives, and are exceptions to all the measures of conduct, which have ever been established for the government of men. But if we would willingly know, what judgment should be formed of such irregular and extraordinary actions; we may consider the sentiments, commonly entertained with regard to those irregular events, which appear in the course of nature, and the operations of external objects. All causes are not conjoined to their usual effects, with like uniformity. An artificer, who handles only dead matter, may be disappointed of his aim, as well as the politician, who directs the conduct of sensible and intelligent agents.

The vulgar, who take things according to their first appearance, attribute the uncertainty of events to such an uncertainty in the causes as makes the latter often fail of their usual influence; though they meet with no impediment in their operation. But philosophers, observing, that, almost in every part of nature, there is contained a vast variety of springs and principles, which are hid, by reason of their minuteness or remoteness, find, that it is at least possible the contrariety of events may not proceed from any contingency in the cause, but from the secret operation of contrary causes. This possibility is converted into certainty by farther observation; when they remark, that, upon an exact scrutiny, a contrariety of effects always betrays a contrariety of causes, and proceeds from their mutual opposition. A peasant can give no better reason for the stopping of any clock or watch than to say that it does not commonly go right: But an artist easily perceives, that the same force in the spring or pendulum has always the same influence on the wheels; but fails of its usual effect, perhaps by reason of a grain of dust, which puts a stop to the whole movement. From the observation of several parallel instances, philosophers form a maxim, that the connexion between all causes and effects is equally necessary, and that its seeming uncertainty in some instances proceeds from the secret opposition of contrary causes.

Thus for instance, in the human body, when the usual symptoms of health or sickness disappoint our expectation; when medicines operate not with their wonted powers; when irregular events follow from any particular cause; the philosopher and physician are not surprised at the matter, nor are ever tempted to deny, in general, the necessity and uniformity of those principles, by which the animal economy is conducted. They know, that a human body is a mighty complicated machine: That many secret powers lurk in it, which are altogether beyond our comprehension: That to us it must often appear very uncertain in its operations: And that therefore the irregular events, which outwardly discover themselves, can be no proof, that the laws of nature are not observed with the greatest regularity in its internal operations and government.

The philosopher, if he be consistent, must apply the same reasoning to the actions and volitions of intelligent agents. The most irregular and unexpected resolutions of men may frequently be accounted for by those, who know every particular circumstance of their character and situation. A person of an obliging disposition gives a peevish answer: But he has the

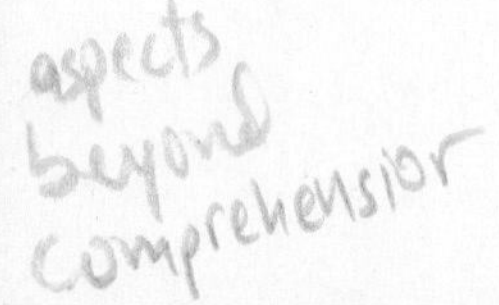

toothache, or has not dined. A stupid fellow discovers an uncommon alacrity in his carriage: But he has met with a sudden piece of good fortune. Or even when an action, as sometimes happens, cannot be particularly accounted for, either by the person himself or by others; we know, in general, that the characters of men are, to a certain degree, inconstant and irregular. This is, in a manner, the constant character of human nature; though it be applicable, in a more particular manner, to some persons, who have no fixed rule for their conduct, but proceed in a continued course of caprice and inconstancy. The internal principles and motives may operate in a uniform manner, notwithstanding these seeming irregularities; in the same manner as the winds, rain, clouds, and other variations of the weather are supposed to be governed by steady principles; though not easily discoverable by human sagacity and enquiry.

Thus it appears, not only that the conjunction between motives and voluntary actions is as regular and uniform, as that between the cause and effect in any part of nature; but also that this regular conjunction has been universally acknowledged among mankind, and has never been the subject of dispute, either in philosophy or common life. Now, as it is from past experience, that we draw all inferences concerning the future, and as we conclude, that objects will always be conjoined together, which we find to have always been conjoined; it may seem superfluous to prove, that this experienced uniformity in human actions is a source, whence we draw *inferences* concerning them. But in order to throw the argument into a greater variety of lights, we shall also insist, though briefly, on this latter topic.

The mutual dependence of men is so great, in all societies, that scarce any human action is entirely complete in itself, or is performed without some reference to the actions of others, which are requisite to make it answer fully the intention of the agent. The poorest artificer, who labours alone, expects at least the protection of the magistrate, to ensure him the enjoyment of the fruits of his labour. He also expects, that, when he carries his goods to market, and offers them at a reasonable price, he shall find purchasers; and shall be able, by the money he acquires, to engage others to supply him with those commodities, which are requisite for his subsistence. In proportion as men extend their dealings, and render their intercourse with others more complicated, they always comprehend, in their schemes of life, a greater variety of voluntary actions, which they expect, from the proper motives, to co-operate with their own. In all these conclusions, they take their measures from past experience, in the same manner as in their reasonings concerning external objects; and firmly believe, that men, as well as all the elements, are to continue, in their operations, the same, that they have ever found them. A manufacturer reckons upon the labour of his servants, for the execution of any work, as much as upon the tools, which he employs, and would be equally surprised, were his expectations disappointed. In short, this experimental

inference and reasoning concerning the actions of others enters so much into human life, that no man, while awake, is ever a moment without employing it. Have we not reason, therefore, to affirm, that all mankind have always agreed in the doctrine of necessity, according to the foregoing definition and explication of it?

Nor have philosophers ever entertained a different opinion from the people in this particular. For not to mention, that almost every action of their life supposes that opinion; there are even few of the speculative parts of learning, to which it is not essential. What would become of *history,* had we not a dependence on the veracity of the historian, according to the experience, which we have had of mankind? How could *politics* be a science, if laws and forms of government had not a uniform influence upon society? Where would be the foundation of *morals,* if particular

characters had no certain or determinate power to produce particular sentiments, and if these sentiments had no constant operation on actions? And with what pretence could we employ our *criticism* upon any poet or polite author, if we could not pronounce the conduct and sentiments of his actors, either natural or unnatural, to such characters, and in such circumstances? It seems almost impossible, therefore, to engage, either in science or action of any kind, without acknowledging the doctrine of necessity, and this *inference* from motives to voluntary actions; from characters to conduct.

And indeed, when we consider how aptly *natural* and *moral* evidence link together, and form only one chain of argument, we shall make no scruple to allow, that they are of the same nature, and derived from the same principles. A prisoner, who has neither money nor interest, discovers the impossibility of his escape, as well when he considers the obstinacy of the gaoler, as the walls and bars, with which he is surrounded; and, in all attempts for his freedom, chooses rather to work upon the stone and iron of the one, than upon the inflexible nature of the other. The same prisoner, when conducted to the scaffold, foresees his death as certainly from the constancy and fidelity of his guards, as from the operation of the ax or wheel. His mind runs along a certain train of ideas: The refusal of the soldiers to consent to his escape; the action of the executioner; the separation of the head and body; bleeding, convulsive motions, and death. Here is a connected chain of natural causes and voluntary actions; but the mind feels no difference between them, in passing from one link to another: Nor is less certain of the future event than if it were connected with the objects present to the memory or senses, by a train of causes, cemented together by what we are pleased to call a *physical* necessity. The same experienced union has the same effect on the mind, whether the united objects be motives, volition, and actions; or figure and motion. We may change the names of things; but their nature and their operation on the understanding never change.

Were a man, whom I know to be honest and opulent, and with whom I live in intimate friendship, to come into my house, where I am surrounded with my servants, I rest assured, that he is not to stab me before he leaves it, in order to rob me of my silver standish; and I no more suspect this event, than the falling of the house itself which is new, and solidly built and founded.—*But he may have been seized with a sudden and unknown frenzy.*—So may a sudden earthquake arise, and shake and tumble my house about my ears. I shall therefore change the suppositions. I shall say, that I know with certainty, that he is not to put his hand into the fire, and hold it there, till it be consumed: And this event, I think I can foretell with the same assurance, as that, if he throw himself out at the window, and meet with no obstruction, he will not remain a moment suspended in the air. No suspicion of an unknown frenzy can give the least possibility to the former event, which is so contrary to all the known principles of human nature. A man who at noon leaves his purse full of gold on the pavement at Charing-Cross, may as well expect that it will fly away like a feather, as that he will find it untouched an hour after. Above one half of human reasonings contain inferences of a similar nature, attended with more or less degrees of certainty, proportioned to our experience of the usual conduct of mankind in such particular situations.

I have frequently considered, what could possibly be the reason, why all mankind, though they have ever, without hesitation, acknowledged the doctrine of necessity, in their whole practice and reasoning, have yet discovered such a reluctance to acknowledge it in words, and have rather shown a propensity, in all ages, to profess the contrary opinion. The matter, I think, may be accounted for, after the following manner. If we examine the operations of body, and the production of effects from their causes, we shall find, that all our faculties can never carry us farther in our knowledge of this relation, than barely to observe, that particular objects are *constantly conjoined* together, and that the mind is carried, by a *customary transition,* from the appearance of one to the belief of the other. But though this conclusion concerning human ignorance be the result of the strictest scrutiny of this subject, men still entertain a strong propensity to believe, that they penetrate farther into the powers of nature, and perceive something like a necessary connexion between the cause and the effect. When again they turn their reflections towards the operations of their own minds, and *feel* no such connexion of the motive and the action; they are thence apt to suppose, that there is a difference between the effects, which result from material force, and those which arise from thought and intelligence. But being once convinced, that we know nothing farther of causation of any kind, than merely the *constant conjunction* of objects, and the consequent *inference* of the mind from one to another, and finding, that these two circumstances are universally allowed to have place in voluntary actions; we may be more easily led to own the same necessity common to all causes. And though this reasoning may contradict the systems of many philosophers, in ascribing necessity to the determinations of the will, we shall find, upon reflection, that they dissent from it in words only, not in their real sentiment. Necessity, according to the sense, in which it is here taken, has never yet been rejected, nor can ever, I think, be rejected by any philosopher. It may only, perhaps, be pretended, that the mind can perceive, in the operations of matter, some farther connexion between the cause and effect; and a connexion that has not place in the voluntary actions of intelligent beings. Now whether it be so or not, can only appear upon examination; and it is incumbent on these philosophers to make good their assertion, by defining or describing that necessity, and pointing it out to us in the operations of material causes.

It would seem, indeed, that men begin at the wrong end of this question concerning liberty and necessity, when they enter upon it by examining the faculties of the soul, the influence of the understanding, and the operations of the will. Let them first discuss a more simple question, namely, the operations of body and of brute unintelligent matter; and try whether they can there form any idea of causation and necessity, except that of a constant conjunction of objects, and subsequent inference of the mind from one to another. If these circumstances form, in reality, the whole of that necessity, which we conceive in matter, and if these circumstances be also universally acknowledged to take place in the operations of the mind, the dispute is at an end; at least, must be owned to be thenceforth merely verbal. But as long as we will rashly suppose, that we have some farther idea of necessity and causation in the operations of external objects; at the same time, that we can find nothing farther, in the voluntary actions of the mind; there is no possibility of bringing the question to any determinate issue, while we proceed upon so erroneous a supposition. The only method of undeceiving us, is, to mount up higher; to examine the narrow extent of science when applied to material causes; and to convince ourselves, that all we know of them, is, the constant conjunction and inference above mentioned. We may, perhaps, find, that it is with difficulty we are induced to fix such narrow limits to human understanding: But we can afterwards find no difficulty when we come to apply this doctrine to the actions of the will. For as it is evident, that these have a regular conjunction with motives and circumstances and characters, and as we always draw inferences from one to the other, we must be obliged to acknowledge in words, that necessity, which we have already avowed, in every deliberation of our lives, and in every step of our conduct and behaviour.[1]

1. The prevalence of the doctrine of liberty may be accounted for, from another cause, *viz.* a false sensation or seeming experience which we have, or may have, of liberty or indifference, in many of our actions. The necessity of any action, whether of matter or of mind, is not, properly speaking, a quality in the agent, but in any thinking or intelligent being, who may consider the action; and it consists chiefly in the determination of his thoughts to infer the existence of that action from some preceding objects; as liberty, when opposed to necessity, is nothing but the want of that determination, and a certain looseness or indifference, which we feel, in passing, or not passing, from the idea of one object to that of any succeeding one. Now we may observe, that, though, in *reflecting* on human actions, we seldom feel such a looseness or indifference, but are commonly able to infer them with considerable certainty from their motives, and from the dispositions of the agent; yet it frequently happens, that, in *performing* the actions themselves, we are sensible of something like it: And as all resembling objects are readily taken for each other, this has been employed as a demonstrative and even intuitive proof of human liberty. We feel, that our actions are subject to our will, on most occasions; and imagine we feel, that the will itself is subject to nothing, because, when by a denial of it we are provoked to try, we feel, that it moves easily every way, and produces an image of itself, (or a *Velleity,* as it is called in the schools) even on that side, on which it did not settle. This image, or faint motion, we persuade ourselves, could, at that time, have been completed into the thing itself; because, should that be denied, we find, upon a second trial, that, at present, it can. We consider not, that the fantastical desire of showing liberty, is here the motive of our actions. And it seems certain, that, however we may imagine we feel a liberty within ourselves, a spectator can commonly infer our actions from our motives and character; and even where he cannot, he concludes in general, that he might, were he perfectly acquainted with every circumstance of our situation and temper, and the most secret springs of our complexion and disposition. Now this is the very essence of necessity, according to the foregoing doctrine.

But to proceed in this reconciling project with regard to the question of liberty and necessity; the most contentious question, of metaphysics, the most contentious science; it will not require many words to prove, that all mankind have ever agreed in the doctrine of liberty as well as in that of necessity, and that the whole dispute, in this respect also, has been hitherto merely verbal. For what is meant by liberty, when applied to voluntary actions? We cannot surely mean, that actions have so little connexion with motives, inclinations, and circumstances, that one does not follow with a certain degree of uniformity from the other, and that one affords no inference by which we can conclude the existence of the other. For these are plain and acknowledged matters of fact. By liberty, then, we can only mean *a power of acting or not acting, according to the determinations of the will;* that is, if we choose to remain at rest, we may; if we choose to move, we also may. Now this hypothetical liberty is universally allowed to belong to every one, who is not a prisoner and in chains. Here then is no subject of dispute.

Whatever definition we may give of liberty, we should be careful to observe two requisite circumstances; *first,* that it be consistent with plain matter of fact; *secondly,* that it be consistent with itself. If we observe these circumstances, and render our definition intelligible, I am persuaded that all mankind will be found of one opinion with regard to it.

It is universally allowed, that nothing exists without a cause of its existence, and that chance, when strictly examined, is a mere negative word, and means not any real power, which has any where, a being in nature. But it is pretended, that some causes are necessary, some not necessary. Here then is the advantage of definitions. Let any one *define* a cause, without comprehending, as a part of the definition, a *necessary connexion* with its effect; and let him show distinctly the origin of the idea, expressed by the definition; and I shall readily give up the whole controversy. But if the foregoing explication of the matter be received, this must be absolutely impracticable. Had not objects a regular conjunction with each other, we should never have entertained any notion of cause and effect; and this regular conjunction produces that inference of the understanding, which is the only connexion, that we can have any comprehension of. Whoever attempts a definition of cause, exclusive of these circumstances, will be obliged, either to employ unintelligible terms, or such as are synonymous to the term, which he endeavours to define.[2] And

2. Thus, if a cause be defined, *that which produces any thing;* it is easy to observe, that *producing* is synonymous to *causing.* In like manner, if a cause be defined, *that*

if the definition above mentioned be admitted; liberty, when opposed to necessity, not to constraint, is the same thing with chance; which is universally allowed to have no existence.

PART II.

There is no method of reasoning more common, and yet none more blameable, than, in philosophical disputes, to endeavour the refutation of any hypothesis, by a pretence of its dangerous consequences to religion and morality. When any opinion leads to absurdities, it is certainly false; but it is not certain than an opinion is false, because it is of dangerous consequence. Such topics, therefore, ought entirely to be forborne; as serving nothing to the discovery of truth, but only to make the person of an antagonist odious. This I observe in general, without pretending to draw any advantage from it. I frankly submit to an examination of this kind, and shall venture to affirm, that the doctrines, both of necessity and of liberty, as above explained, are not only consistent with morality, but are absolutely essential to its support.

Necessity may be defined two ways, conformably to the two definitions of *cause,* of which it makes an essential part. It consists either in the constant conjunction of like objects, or in the inference of the understanding from one object to another. Now necessity, in both these senses, (which, indeed, are, at bottom, the same) has universally, though tacitly, in the schools, in the pulpit, and in common life, been allowed to belong to the will of man; and no one has ever pretended to deny, that we can draw inferences concerning human actions, and that those inferences are founded on the experienced union of like actions, with like motives, inclinations, and circumstances. The only particular, in which any one can differ, is, that either, perhaps, he will refuse to give the name of necessity to this property of human actions: But as long as the meaning is understood, I hope the word can do no harm: Or that he will maintain it possible to discover something farther in the operations of matter. But this, it must be acknowledged, can be of no consequence to morality or religion, whatever it may be to natural philosophy or metaphysics. We may here be mistaken in asserting, that there is no idea of any other necessity or

---

by which anything exists; this is liable to the same objection. For what is meant by these words, *by which?* Had it been said, that a cause is *that* after which *anything constantly exists;* we should have understood the terms. For this is, indeed, all we know of the matter. And this constancy forms the very essence of necessity, nor have we any other idea of it.

connexion in the actions of body: But surely we ascribe nothing to the actions of the mind, but what every one does, and must readily allow of. We change no circumstance in the received orthodox system with regard to the will, but only in that with regard to material objects and causes. Nothing therefore can be more innocent, at least, than this doctrine.

All laws being founded on rewards and punishments, it is supposed as a fundamental principle, that these motives have a regular and uniform influence on the mind, and both produce the good and prevent the evil actions. We may give to this influence what name we please; but, as it is usually conjoined with the action, it must be esteemed a *cause,* and be looked upon as an instance of that necessity, which we would here establish.

The only proper object of hatred or vengeance, is a person or creature, endowed with thought and consciousness; and when any criminal or injurious actions excite that passion, it is only by their relation to the person, or connexion with him. Actions are, by their very nature, temporary and perishing; and where they proceed not from some *cause* in the character and disposition of the person who performed them, they can neither redound to his honour, if good; nor infamy, if evil. The actions themselves may be blameable; they may be contrary to all the rules of morality and religion: But the person is not answerable for them; and as they proceeded from nothing in him, that is durable and constant, and leave nothing of that nature behind them, it is impossible he can, upon their account, become the object of punishment or vengeance. According to the principle, therefore, which denies necessity, and consequently causes, a man is as pure and untainted, after having committed the most horrid crime, as at the first moment of his birth, nor is his character any wise concerned in his actions; since they are not derived from it, and the wickedness of the one can never be used as a proof of the depravity of the other.

Men are not blamed for such actions, as they perform ignorantly and casually, whatever may be the consequences. Why? but because the principles of these actions are only momentary, and terminate in them alone. Men are less blamed for such actions as they perform hastily and unpremeditately, than for such as proceed from deliberation. For what reason? but because a hasty temper, though a constant cause or principle in the mind, operates only by intervals, and infects not the whole character. Again, repentance wipes off every crime, if attended with a reformation of life and manners. How is this to be accounted for? but by asserting, that actions render a person criminal, merely as they are proofs of criminal principles in the mind; and when, by an alteration of these principles, they cease to be just proofs, they likewise cease to be criminal. But, except upon the doctrine of necessity, they never were just proofs, and consequently never were criminal.

It will be equally easy to prove, and from the same arguments, that *liberty,* according to that definition above mentioned, in which all men agree, is also essential to morality, and that no human actions, where it is wanting, are susceptible of any moral qualities, or can be the objects either of approbation or dislike. For as actions are objects of our moral sentiment, so far only as they are indications of the internal character, passions, and affections; it is impossible that they can give rise either to praise or blame, where they proceed not from these principles, but are derived altogether from external violence.

I pretend not to have obviated or removed all objections to this theory, with regard to necessity and liberty. I can foresee other objections, derived from topics, which have not here been treated of. It may be said, for instance, that, if voluntary actions be subjected to the same laws of necessity with the operations of matter, there is a continued chain of necessary causes, pre-ordained and pre-determined, reaching from the original cause of all, to every single volition of every human creature. No contingency any where in the universe; no indifference; no liberty. While we act, we are, at the same time, acted upon. The ultimate Author of all our volitions is the Creator of the world, who first bestowed motion on this immense machine, and, placed all beings in that particular position, whence every subsequent event, by an inevitable necessity, must result. Human actions, therefore, either can have no moral turpitude at all, as proceeding from so good a cause; or if they have any turpitude, they must involve our Creator in the same guilt, while he is acknowledged to be their ultimate cause and author. For as a man, who fired a mine, is answerable for all the consequences whether the train he employed be long or short; so wherever a continued chain of necessary causes is fixed, that Being, either finite or infinite, who produces the first, is likewise the author of all the rest, and must both bear the blame and acquire the praise, which belong to them. Our clear and unalterable ideas of morality establish this rule, upon unquestionable reasons, when we examine the consequences of any human action; and these reasons must still have greater force, when applied to the volitions and intentions of a Being, infinitely wise and powerful. Ignorance or impotence may be pleaded for so limited a creature as man; but those imperfections have no place in our Creator. He foresaw, he ordained, he intended all those actions of men, which we so rashly pronounce criminal. And we must therefore conclude, either that they are not criminal, or that the Deity, not man, is accountable for them. But as either of these positions is absurd and impious; it follows, that the doctrine, from which they are deduced, cannot possibly be true, as being liable to all the same objections. An absurd consequence, if necessary, proves the original doctrine to be absurd; in the same manner as criminal actions render criminal the original cause, if the connexion between them be necessary and inevitable.

This objection consists of two parts, which we shall examine separately; *First,* that, if human actions can be traced up, by a necessary chain, to the Deity, they can never be criminal; on account of the infinite perfection of that Being, from whom they are derived, and who can intend nothing but what is altogether good and laudable. Or, *Secondly,* if they be criminal, we must retract the attribute of perfection, which we ascribe to the Deity, and must acknowledge him to be the ultimate author of guilt and moral turpitude in all his creatures.

The answer to the first objection seems obvious and convincing. There are many philosophers, who, after an exact scrutiny of all the phenomena of nature, conclude, that the WHOLE, considered as one system, is, in every period of its existence, ordered with perfect benevolence; and that the utmost possible happiness will, in the end, result to all created beings, without any mixture of positive or absolute ill and misery. Every physical ill, say they, makes an essential part of this benevolent system, and could not possibly be removed, even by the Deity himself, considered as a wise agent, without giving entrance to greater ill, or excluding greater good, which will result from it. From this theory, some philosophers, and the ancient *Stoics* among the rest, derived a topic of consolation under all afflictions, while they taught their pupils, that those ills, under which they laboured, were, in reality, goods to the universe; and that to an enlarged view, which could comprehend the whole system of nature, every event became an object of joy and exultation. But though this topic be specious and sublime, it was soon found in practice weak and ineffectual. You would surely more irritate, than appease a man, lying under the racking pains of the gout, by preaching up to him the rectitude of those general laws, which produced the malignant humours in his body, and led them through the proper canals, to the sinews and nerves, where they now excite such acute torments. These enlarged views may, for a moment, please the imagination of a speculative man, who is placed in ease and security; but neither can they dwell with constancy on his mind, even though undisturbed by the emotions of pain or passion; much less can they maintain their ground, when attacked by such powerful antagonists. The affections take a narrower and more natural survey of their object; and by an economy, more suitable to the infirmity of human minds, regard alone the beings around us, and are actuated by such events as appear good or ill to the private system.

The case is the same with *moral* as with *physical* ill. It cannot reasonably be supposed, that those remote considerations, which are found of so little efficacy with regard to one, will have a more powerful influence with regard to the other. The mind of man is so formed by nature, that, upon the appearance of certain characters, dispositions, and actions, it immediately feels the sentiment of approbation or blame; nor are there any emotions more essential to its frame and constitution. The characters, which engage our approbation, are chiefly such as contribute to the peace and security of human society; as the characters, which excite blame, are chiefly such as tend to public detriment and disturbance: Whence it may reasonably be presumed, that the moral sentiments arise, either mediately or immediately, from a reflection on these opposite interests. What though philosophical meditations establish a different opinion or conjecture; that every thing is right with regard to the WHOLE, and that the qualities, which disturb society, are, in the main, as beneficial, and are as suitable to the primary intention of nature, as those which more directly promote its happiness and welfare? Are such remote and uncertain speculations able to counterbalance the sentiments, which arise from the natural and immediate view of the objects? A man who is robbed of a considerable sum; does he find his vexation for the loss any wise diminished by these sublime reflections? Why then should his moral resentment against the crime be supposed incompatible with them? Or why should not the acknowledgment of a real distinction between vice and virtue be reconcilable to all speculative systems of philosophy, as well as that of a real distinction between personal beauty and deformity? Both these distinctions are founded in the natural sentiments of the human mind: And these sentiments are not to be controlled or altered by any philosophical theory or speculation whatsoever.

The *second* objection admits not of so easy and satisfactory an answer; nor is it possible to explain distinctly, how the Deity can be the mediate cause of all the actions of men, without being the author of sin and moral turpitude. These are mysteries, which mere natural and unassisted reason is very unfit to handle; and whatever system she embraces, she must find herself involved in inextricable difficulties, and even contradictions, at every step which she takes with regard to such subjects. To reconcile the indifference and contingency of human actions with prescience; or to defend absolute decrees, and yet free the Deity from being the author of sin, has been found hitherto to exceed all the power of philosophy. Happy, if she be thence sensible of her temerity, when she pries into these sublime mysteries; and leaving a scene so full of obscurities and perplexities, return, with suitable modesty, to her true and proper province, the examination of common life; where she will find difficulties enough to employ her enquiries, without launching into so boundless an ocean of doubt, uncertainty, and contradiction!

9

Immanuel Kant, from the *Critique of Pure Reason*

Immanuel Kant (1724–1804) was a German philosopher, whose aims included reconciling morality and religion with the emerging scientific world view. In this selection from his Critique of Pure Reason *(1781), Kant argues that for agents to be morally responsible and subject to moral laws they must have* transcendental freedom, *the power to cause an action without being causally determined to cause it. But he also agrees with Hume that everything that we experience—not only the physical, but the psychological as well—is governed by deterministic causal laws. In Kant's view, if we were free, we would have to be free in a way that is inaccessible to experience. His way of stating the view is that we would have to be free as things in themselves beyond space and time, in an intelligible realm that is beyond our capacity to experience.*

III
SOLUTION OF THE COSMOLOGICAL IDEA OF TOTALITY IN THE DERIVATION OF WORLD EVENTS FROM THEIR CAUSES

Only two kinds of causality can be conceived in regard to what occurs, viz., either a causality according to *nature* or one from *freedom.* The causality according to nature is the connection, in the world of sense, of one state with a previous state upon which the state follows according to a rule. Now the *causality* of appearances rests on conditions of time; and the previous state, if it had always been there, would not have produced an effect that first arises in time. Therefore, the causality of the cause of what occurs or comes about has likewise *come about,* and—according to the principle of understanding—itself requires a cause in turn.

By freedom, on the other hand, in the cosmological sense of the term, I mean the power to begin a state *on one's own.* Thus the causality of freedom is not in turn subject, according to the law of nature, to another cause that determines it as regards time. Freedom, in this meaning of the term, is a pure transcendental idea. This idea, first, contains nothing borrowed from experience. Moreover, second, the object of this idea cannot be given determinately in any experience, because there is a universal law of the very possibility of all experience whereby whatever occurs must have a cause, and whereby, therefore, also the cause's causality which *itself has occurred* or come about must in turn have a cause. And thus the entire realm of experience, however far it may extend, is transformed into a sum of what is mere nature. But since in this way no absolute totality of conditions in the causal relation can be obtained, reason creates for itself the idea of a spontaneity that can, on its own, start to act—without, i.e., needing to be preceded by another cause by means of which it is determined to action in turn, according to the law of causal connection.

Extremely noteworthy is the fact that this *transcendental idea of freedom* is the basis of the practical concept of freedom, and that transcendental freedom is what in practical freedom amounts to the proper moment of the difficulties that have all along surrounded the question of practical freedom's possibility. *Freedom in the practical meaning* of the term is the independence of our power of choice from coercion by impulses of sensibility. For a power of choice is *sensible* sensible insofar as it is *pathologically affected* (i.e., affected by motivating causes of sensibility); it is called animal power of choice (*arbitrium brutum*) if it can be *pathologically necessitated.* The human power of choice, although an *arbitrium sensitivum,* is an *arbitrium* not *brutum* but *liberum;* for its action is not made necessary necessary by sensibility, but the human being has a power to determine himself on his own, independently of coercion by sensible impulses.

We readily see that if all causality in the world of sense were merely nature, then every event would be determined by another event in time and according to necessary laws; and hence, since appearances insofar as they determine the power of choice would have to make every action necessary as their natural result, the annulment of transcendental freedom would simultaneously eliminate all practical freedom. For practical freedom presupposes that although something did not occur, it yet *ought* to have occurred, and that hence the cause of this something in [the realm of] appearance was not completely determinative: not so determinative, viz., that there did not lie in our power of choice a causality for producing, independently of those natural causes and even against their force and influence, something that in the time order is determined according to empirical laws—and hence a causality whereby we can begin a series of events *entirely on our own.*

Hence what happens here—as we find in general in the conflict of a reason that ventures beyond the bounds of possible experience—is that the problem is in fact not *physiological* but *transcendental.* Hence the question of the possibility of freedom does indeed challenge psychology; but since it rests on dialectical arguments of the merely pure reason, it must, along with its solution, engage only transcendental philosophy. Now in order to enable transcendental philosophy to give a satisfactory answer to this problem, which it cannot decline to do, I must first try—by the following remark—to determine more closely the procedure of transcendental philosophy in dealing with this problem.

If appearances were things in themselves, and hence if space and time were forms of the existence of things themselves, then the conditions and the conditioned would always belong, as members, to one and the same series. And from this there would arise, in the present case also, the antinomy that is common to all transcendental ideas: viz., that this series would have to turn out inevitably too large or too small for the understanding. However, the dynamical concepts of reason, with which we are dealing in this and the following subsection, have the following peculiarity. Because these concepts have to do not with an object considered as a magnitude but only with the object's *existence,* we can abstract also from the magnitude of the series of conditions, and what matters in their case is merely the dynamical relation of the condition to the conditioned. Thus in the question concerning nature and freedom we already encounter the difficulty as to whether freedom is even possible at all, and, if it is possible, whether it can coexist with the universality of the natural law of causality. And hence the question arises whether the proposition that every effect in the world must arise *either* from nature *or* from freedom is a correct disjunction, or whether—rather—*both* can, with one and the same event but in different reference, take place simultaneously. As for the principle concerning the thoroughgoing connection of all events in the world of sense according to immutable natural laws, its correctness is already established as a principle of the Transcendental Analytic and tolerates no impairment. Hence the question is only whether, in regard to the same effect that is determined according to nature, freedom can nonetheless also take place, or whether freedom is completely excluded by that inviolable rule. And here the deceptive, although common, presupposition of the *absolute reality* of appearances at once shows its detrimental influence of confusing our reason. For if appearances are things in themselves, then freedom cannot be saved. Nature is then the complete and in itself sufficiently determining cause of every event, and the condition of this cause is always contained only in the series of appearances—which, along with their effect, are necessary under natural law. If, on the other hand, appearances count as nothing more than they in fact are, viz., if they count not as things in themselves but as mere presentations connected according to empirical laws, then they must themselves still have bases that are not appearances. But such an intelligible cause is not, as regards its causality, determined by appearances, although its effects appear and thus can be determined by other appearances. Hence this cause, along with its causality, is outside the series of empirical conditions, whereas its effects are encountered within the series. Hence the effect can be considered as free with regard to its intelligible cause, and yet with regard to appearances be considered simultaneously as resulting from these according to the necessity of nature. This distinction, when set forth in a universal way and quite abstractly, must appear extremely subtle and obscure, but it will become clear in its application. Here I wanted only to make the comment that since the thoroughgoing connection of all appearances in one context of nature is an inexorable law, this law would necessarily have to overturn all freedom if one were to adhere obstinately to the reality of appearances. This is also the reason why those who follow the common opinion in this matter have never succeeded in reconciling nature and freedom with each other.

Possibility of the Causality through Freedom, as Reconciled with the Universal Law of Natural Necessity

What in an object of the senses is not itself appearance I call *intelligible.* Accordingly, if what in the world of sense must be regarded as appearance has, when taken in itself, also a power which is not an object of sensible intuition but through which it can still be the cause of appearances, then the *causality* of this being can be considered from two sides: as *intelligible,* according to its action as that of a thing in itself; and as *sensible,* according to the effects of this causality as those of an appearance in the world of sense. Thus regarding such a subject's power we would frame an empirical as well as an intellectual concept of its causality, these concepts occurring together in one and the same effect. Such a twofold side from which to think the power of an object of the senses contradicts none of the concepts that we have to frame of appearances and of a possible experience. For since these appearances are not in themselves things, they must be based on a transcendental object determining them as mere presentations; and hence nothing prevents us from attributing to this transcendental object, besides the property through which it appears, also a *causality* that is not appearance although its *effect* is nonetheless encountered in appearance. Any efficient cause, however, must have a **character,** i.e., a law of its causality without which it would not be a cause at all. And thus in a subject of the world of sense we would have, first, an *empirical character.* Through this character the subject's actions, as appearances, would according to constant natural laws stand throughout in connection with other appearances and could be derived from these appearances as the actions' conditions; and thus these actions would, in combination with those other appearances, amount to members of a single series of the natural order. Second, one would have to grant to the subject also an *intelligible character.* Through this character the subject is indeed the cause of those actions as appearances, but the character itself is not subject to any conditions of sensibility and is not itself appearance. The first character could also be called the character of such a thing in [the realm of] appearance, the second the character of the thing in itself.

Now according to its intelligible character this acting subject would not stand under any conditions of time; for time is the condition only of appearances and not of things in themselves. In this subject no *action* would *arise* or *pass away.* Hence it would also not be subjected to the law of all time determination and of everything changeable, viz., that everything *that occurs* has its cause *in appearances* (those of the previous state). In a word, the subject's causality, insofar as it is intellectual, would not stand at all in the series of empirical conditions that make the event necessary in the world of sense. We could not, indeed, ever become acquainted with this intelligible character directly, because we cannot perceive anything except insofar as it appears; but we would still have to *think* it in accordance with the empirical character, just as in general we must—in thought—lay a transcendental object at the basis of appearances although we know nothing about this object as to what it is in itself.

Hence according to its empirical character this subject, as appearance, would be subjected to all laws of determination in terms of causal linkage. To this extent the subject would be nothing but a part of the world of sense; and its effects would, like any other appearance, flow from nature unfailingly. Just as outer appearances would influence this subject, and as the subject's empirical character, i.e., the law of its causality, would be cognized through experience, so all its actions would have to be explicable according to natural laws, and all requirements for a complete and necessary determination of these actions would have to be found in a possible experience.

But according to its intelligible character (although we can have nothing more of this character than just the general concept of it) the same subject would nonetheless have to be pronounced free from any influence of sensibility and determination by appearances. For insofar as this subject is *noumenon,* nothing *occurs* in it and there is found in it no change requiring dynamical time determination and hence no connection with appearances as causes. Therefore, this active being would to this extent be independent and free in its actions from all natural necessity, which is found only in the world of sense. Of this subject we would say quite correctly that it begins its effects in the world of sense *on its own,* without the action's beginning *in the subject* itself. And this would be valid without any consequent need for the effects in the world of sense to begin on their own. For in that world they are always predetermined—although only by means of the empirical character (which is merely the appearance of the intelligible character)—by empirical conditions in the previous time, and are possible only as a continuation of the series of natural causes. And thus freedom and nature, each in the complete meaning of its term, would be found in the same actions—according as these are compared with their intelligible or with their sensible cause—simultaneously and without any conflict.

Elucidation of the Cosmological Idea of a Freedom in Combination with the Universal Natural Necessity

I thought it good to start by sketching the outline of the solution to our transcendental problem, in order that we might better survey the course that reason takes in solving the problem. Let us now spell out the moments that are in fact at issue in deciding this solution, and examine each separately.

Consider the natural law that everything that occurs has a cause; that since the causality of this cause, i.e., the *action,* precedes [the effect] in time and—in regard to an effect that has *arisen*—cannot itself always have been there but must have *occurred,* this causality likewise has among appearances its cause whereby it is determined; and that, consequently, all events are determined empirically within a natural order. This law, through which appearances can first amount to a *nature* and yield objects of an experience, is a law of understanding from which we are not permitted on any pretext to deviate, nor exempt any appearance. For otherwise we would posit the appearance outside of all possible experience, but thereby would distinguish it from all objects of possible experience and thus would turn it into a mere thought-entity and chimera.

Thus it looks, here, as if there is only a chain of causes that in the regression to the causes' conditions permits no *absolute totality* at all. Yet this perplexity in no way detains us; for it has already been removed in our general judgment on the antinomy of reason, into which reason falls when in the series of appearances it aims at the unconditioned. If we wish to yield to the delusion of transcendental realism, then we are left with neither nature nor freedom. Here the question is only whether, if in the entire series of all events we acknowledge nothing but natural necessity, it is still possible to regard the same event, which on the one hand is a mere natural effect, as yet being on the other hand an effect arising from freedom, or whether we find between these two kinds of causality a direct contradiction.

Among the causes in [the realm of] appearance there assuredly cannot be anything that could absolutely and on its own begin a series. For here every action, as appearance, insofar as it produces an event, is itself an event or happening that presupposes another state wherein its cause is to be found; and thus everything that occurs is only a continuation of the series, and in this series no beginning that takes place on its own is possible. Hence all the actions of natural causes in the time sequence are themselves in turn effects that likewise presuppose their causes in the time series. An *original* action, through which something occurs that was not there before, is not to be expected from the causal connection of appearances.

But if effects are appearances, is it indeed also necessary that the causality of their cause, which (cause) itself is also appearance, must be solely empirical? And is it not possible, rather, that although every effect in [the realm of] appearance does indeed require a connection with its cause according to laws of empirical causality, yet this empirical causality itself could nonetheless, without in the least interrupting its connection with natural causes, be an effect of a causality that is not empirical but intelligible? I.e., could not the empirical causality itself be an effect of an action, original in regard to appearances, of a cause that in so far is therefore not appearance but—according to this power—intelligible, although otherwise it also must, as a link in the chain of nature, be classed entirely with the world of sense?

The principle of the causality of appearances among one another is required by us in order that for natural events we can seek and indicate natural conditions, i.e., causes in [the realm of] appearance. If this requirement is granted to us and not weakened by any exception, then the understanding—which in its empirical use sees in all happenings nothing but nature and is, moreover, entitled to do so—has all that it can demand,

and physical explanations proceed along their course unhindered. Now in this [task] the understanding is not impaired in the least if one assumes—even supposing that the assumption were, besides, to be merely invented—that among the natural causes there are also some which have a power that is only intelligible, inasmuch as this power's determination to action never rests on empirical conditions but rests on mere bases of understanding—yet rests on these in such a way that this cause's *action in [the realm of] appearance* conforms to all laws of empirical causality. For in this way the acting subject would, as *causa phaenomenon,* be linked up with nature in the unsevered dependence of all this cause's actions; and this subject's phenomenon (with all its causality in [the realm of] appearance) would only contain certain conditions that, if one wants to ascend from the empirical object to the transcendental, would have to be regarded as merely intelligible. For if we only follow the rule of nature in regard to what may be the cause among appearances, then we need not be concerned as to what sort of basis of these appearances and their connection is being thought in the transcendental subject, which is empirically unknown to us. This intelligible basis in no way challenges the empirical questions, but concerns perhaps merely the thinking in pure understanding; and although the effects of this thinking and acting of pure understanding are found in the appearances, yet these appearances must nonetheless be capable of being explained completely, according to natural laws, from their cause in [the realm of] appearance. The appearances must be capable of being explained by pursuing, as the supreme basis of explanation, their merely empirical character, and by entirely bypassing as unknown the intelligible character that is the empirical character's transcendental cause—except insofar as this intelligible character is indicated by the empirical character as the intelligible character's sensible sign. Let us apply this to experience. The human being is one of the appearances in the world of sense, and in so far is also one of the natural causes, the causality of which must be subject to empirical laws. As such a cause he must, accordingly, also have an empirical character, as do all other things of nature. We discern this character through abilities and powers that he manifests in his effects. In inanimate nature, or in animate but merely animal nature, we find no basis for thinking any power as being other than merely sensibly conditioned. Only the human being, who otherwise is acquainted with all of nature solely through his senses, cognizes himself also through mere apperception—viz., in actions and inner determinations that he cannot class at all with any impression of the senses. And thus he is to himself, indeed, on the one hand phenomenon, but on the other hand—viz., in regard to certain powers—a merely intelligible object, because his action cannot be classed at all with the receptivity of sensibility. We call these [specifically human] powers understanding and reason. Reason, above all, is quite particularly and primarily distinguished from all empirically conditioned abilities, because it examines its objects merely according to ideas and according to these ideas determines the understanding, which then makes an empirical use of its own (although likewise pure) concepts.

Now, that this reason has causality, or that we at least conceive such a causality in it, is evident from the *imperatives* which, in all that is practical, we impose as rules on the performative powers. The *ought* expresses a kind of necessity and connection with bases that does not otherwise occur in all of nature. The understanding can cognize regarding nature only *what is,* or has been, or will be. That something in nature *ought to be* other than what in fact it is in all these time relations—this is impossible; indeed, the [term] ought, if we have in mind merely the course of nature, has no meaning whatsoever. We cannot ask at all what ought to happen in nature, any more than what properties a circle ought to have, but can ask only what happens in nature, or what properties the circle has.

Now this *ought* expresses a possible action whose basis is nothing but a mere concept, whereas the basis of a mere action of nature must always be an appearance. Now the [concept-based] action must indeed be possible under natural conditions, if the *ought* is directed to nature; however, these natural conditions concern not the determination itself of the power of choice but only this determination's effect and result in [the realm of] appearance. No matter how many natural bases—how many sensible stimuli—impel me to *will,* they yet cannot produce the *ought;* they can produce only a willing that is far from necessary but is always conditioned, whereas the ought pronounced by reason opposes this conditioned willing with standard and goal—indeed, with prohibition and authority. Whether the object is one of mere sensibility (the agreeable) or even of pure reason (the good), reason does not yield to the empirically given basis and does not follow the order of things as they exhibit themselves in appearance, but with complete spontaneity makes for itself an order of its own according to ideas. Reason adapts the empirical conditions to accord with these ideas, and in conformity with these ideas declares to be necessary even such actions as in fact *have not occurred* and perhaps will not occur, but concerning which reason nonetheless presupposes that it can have causality in reference to them, since otherwise reason would not expect from its ideas effects in experience.

Let us now remain with this point and assume as at least possible that reason actually has causality with regard to appearances. In that case, despite being all reason, it must yet show itself as having an empirical character. For any cause presupposes a rule according to which certain appearances follow as effects; and any rule requires a uniformity of effects that is the basis for the concept of cause (as a power). And this concept, insofar as it must become evident from mere appearances, we may call the power's empirical character. This character is constant, whereas the effects appear in changeable shapes according to the difference in the accompanying and in part limiting conditions.

Thus every human being's power of choice has an empirical character. This character is nothing but a certain causality of his reason insofar as this causality shows in its effects in [the realm of] appearance a rule whereby one can gather, in terms of their kind and degrees, the bases and actions of his reason and thereby judge the subjective principles of his power of choice. Since this empirical character itself must be drawn from appearances, as its effect, and from the rule of these as provided to us by experience, all actions of a human being are determined in appearance on the basis of his empirical character and the other contributing causes according to the order of nature; and if we could explore all appearances of his power of choice down to the bottom, there would not be a single human action that we could not with certainty predict and cognize as necessary from its preceding conditions. In regard to this empirical character, therefore, there is no freedom; and yet only in terms of this character can we consider a human being if we seek merely to **observe** him and, as is done in anthropology, explore physiologically the motivating causes of his actions.

But if we examine the same actions in reference to reason—not, however, speculative reason in order to *explain* them in terms of their origin, but reason solely insofar as it is itself the cause *for producing* them—in a word: if we compare these actions with reason in a *practical* regard, then we find a rule and order quite different from the order of nature. For in that regard perhaps there *ought not to have occurred* all that according to nature's course yet *has occurred* and according to its own empirical bases inevitably had to occur. But sometimes we find, or at least believe that we find, that the ideas of reason have actually proved their causality in regard to human beings' actions considered as appearances, and that these actions

have occurred not because they were determined by empirical causes—no: but because they were determined by bases of reason.

Now supposing one could say that reason has causality in regard to appearance: could reason's action then indeed be called free, when in reason's empirical character (the way of sensing) the action is quite exactly determined and necessary? This empirical character in turn is determined in the intelligible character (the way of thinking). We are not, however, acquainted with the intelligible character but designate it only by appearances, which, properly speaking, allow us to cognize directly only the way of sensing (empirical character).[1] Now insofar as the action is attributable to the way of thinking as its cause, it yet in no way results from this way of thinking according to empirical laws, i.e., in such a way that the conditions of pure reason *precede* the action, but only in such a way that the effects of these in [the realm of] appearance of inner sense precede it. Pure reason, as a merely intelligible power, is not subjected to the form of time, nor consequently to the conditions of temporal succession. The causality of reason in its intelligible character by no means *arises,* or starts at a certain time, in order to produce an effect. For otherwise it would itself be subjected to the natural law of appearances insofar as this law determines causal series with regard to time, and the causality of reason would then be nature, not freedom. Hence we must be entitled to say that if reason can have causality in regard to appearances, then it is a power *through* which the sensible condition of an empirical series of effects first begins. For the condition that lies in reason is not sensible and hence does not itself begin. Accordingly, there takes place here what in all empirical series we were unable to find: viz., that the *condition* of a successive series of events can itself be empirically unconditioned. For here the condition is *outside* the series of appearances (viz., in the intelligible) and hence is subjected to no sensible condition and no time determination by a preceding cause.

Yet in another reference the same cause belongs nonetheless also to the series of appearances. The human being is himself an appearance. His

1. Hence the morality proper of actions (merit and guilt), even the morality of our own conduct, remains entirely hidden to us. Our imputations can be referred only to the empirical character. But no one can fathom how much of this character is a pure effect of freedom, and how much is to be ascribed to mere nature: viz., either to a defect of temperament that one has through no fault of one's own, or to one's temperament's fortunate constitution (*meritum fortunae*). And hence no one can pass judgment in accordance with complete justice.

power of choice has an empirical character that is the (empirical) cause of all his actions. There is no condition determining a human being in accordance with this character which is not contained in the series of natural effects and which does not obey nature's law—the law according to which an unconditioned empirical causality of what occurs in time is not to be found at all. Therefore, no given action (since it can be perceived only as appearance) can begin absolutely on its own. Of reason, however, one cannot say that the state wherein it determines the power of choice is preceded by another state wherein that state itself is determined. For since reason itself is not an appearance and is not subjected to any conditions of sensibility, there takes place in reason, even as concerns its causality, no temporal succession; and hence the dynamical law of nature that determines temporal succession according to rules cannot be applied to reason.

Hence reason is the permanent condition of all the voluntary actions under which the human being appears. Each of these actions, even before it occurs, is predetermined in the human being's empirical character. But in regard to the intelligible character, of which the empirical character is only the sensible schema, no *before* or *after* holds, and every action—regardless of its time relation to other appearances—is the direct effect of the intelligible character of pure reason. Hence pure reason acts freely, i.e., without being dynamically determined in the chain of natural causes by external or internal bases that precede the action as regards time. And this freedom of pure reason can be regarded not only negatively, as independence from empirical conditions (for the power of reason would thus cease to be a cause of appearances). Rather, this freedom can be designated also positively, as a power of reason to begin on its own a series of events. Reason begins the series in such a way that nothing begins in reason itself, but that reason, as unconditioned condition of any voluntary action, permits no conditions above itself that precede the action as regards time—although reason's effect does begin in the series of appearances, but in the series can never amount to an absolutely first beginning.

To illustrate the regulative principle of reason involved here by an example drawn from the principle's empirical use—not to confirm it (for such proofs by example are unsuitable for transcendental assertions)—let us take a voluntary action, e.g., a malicious lie, by means of which a person has brought a certain amount of confusion into society. And suppose that we first investigate his action as to its motivating causes from which it arose, and that thereupon we judge how the action can, along with its consequences, be imputed to him. In pursuing the first aim we search through the agent's empirical character until we come to its sources. We locate these in bad upbringing, evil company, partly also in the wickedness of a natural makeup that is insensitive to shame; and partly we put them to frivolity and rashness. Here, then, we do not ignore the occasioning causes that prompted the action. In all this we proceed as we do in general when we investigate the series of determining causes for a given natural effect. But although we believe the action to be determined by these causes, we nevertheless blame the perpetrator. We blame him not because of his unfortunate natural makeup, nor because of the circumstances influencing him—indeed, not even because of his previous way of life. For we presuppose that we can set aside entirely how this way of life was, and that we can regard the bygone series of conditions as not having occurred, and can regard this deed as entirely unconditioned with respect to the previous state, as if the perpetrator starts with it a series of consequences completely on his own. This blame is based on a law of reason; and reason is regarded in this blaming as a cause that, regardless of all the mentioned empirical conditions, could and ought to have determined the person's conduct differently. And the causality of reason is by no means regarded merely as concurrence; rather, it is regarded as in itself complete, even if the sensible incentives were not at all for this causality but were even against it. The action is imputed to the agent's intelligible character now—at the instant when he is lying—the guilt is entirely his. Hence his reason, regardless of all empirical conditions of the deed, was wholly free, and to its failure is the deed to be imputed entirely.

We can readily see from this imputing judgment that in making it we are thinking that reason is in no way affected by all that sensibility; that reason does not change (although reason's appearances—viz., the way in which reason manifests itself in its effects—do change); that in reason there is no antecedent state determining the subsequent state, and that reason therefore does not belong at all in the series of sensible conditions that make appearances necessary according to natural laws. Reason is present to, and is the same in, all actions of the human being in all circumstances of time. But reason itself is not in time, and by no means gets into a new state in which it previously was not; with regard to this state reason is *determinative,* but not *determinable.* Hence we cannot ask, Why did reason not determine *itself* differently?—but only, Why did reason not determine *appearances* differently through its causality? To this, however, no answer is possible. For a different intelligible character of reason would have given a different empirical character. And when we say that regardless of his entire previous way of life the perpetrator could still have abstained from the lie, this means only that the lie is directly subject to the force of reason, and reason is not subjected in its causality to any conditions of appearance and of the course of time. And it means, moreover, that although the difference of time can make a principal difference for appearances in regard to one another, it can make no difference for the action in reference to reason, because appearances are not things in themselves and hence are also not causes in themselves.

Hence in judging free actions with regard to their causality we can get only as far as the intelligible cause, but not *beyond it.* We can cognize that this cause determines [actions] freely, i.e., independently of sensibility, and that in this way it can be the sensibly unconditioned condition of appearances. But why the intelligible character gives precisely these appearances and this empirical character under the conditions at hand—this question far exceeds all our reason's power to answer it, indeed, all its right even to ask it; it exceeds these as far as if we asked whence it is that the transcendental object of our outer sensible intuition gives us precisely intuition in *space* only, and not some other intuition. However, the problem that we had to solve does not obligate us to answer that question. For that problem was only this: whether freedom conflicts with natural necessity in one and the same action; and this we have answered sufficiently. For we have shown that, because in the case of freedom a reference to a quite different kind of conditions is possible from the kind found in the case of natural necessity, the latter's law does not affect freedom, and hence both can take place independently of, and without interfering with, each other.

It must be noted carefully that by this contemplation we have not sought to establish the *actuality* of freedom as one of the powers containing the cause of the appearances of our world of sense. For not only would this contemplation then not have been a transcendental one at all, which deals merely with concepts, but this [attempt to establish the actuality of such freedom] also could not succeed; for from experience we can never infer something that must not be thought according to laws of experience at all. Furthermore, we have not even sought to prove the *possibility* of freedom; for this [attempt] also would not have succeeded, because in general we cannot from mere a priori concepts cognize the possibility of any real basis and any causality. Freedom is being treated here only as a transcendental idea whereby reason means to start absolutely the series of conditions in [the realm of] appearance by the sensibly unconditioned. In this [attempt], however, reason becomes entangled in an antinomy with its own laws, the laws that it prescribes to the empirical use of understanding. Now, to show that this antinomy rests on a mere illusion and that nature at least does *not conflict* with the causality from freedom—this was the only goal that we were able to accomplish, and it was, moreover, our one and only concern.

10

Immanuel Kant, from the *Critique of Practical Reason*

In this selection from his Critique of Practical Reason *(1788), Kant argues against the "empiricist" solution to the problem of free will and determinism, which can plausibly be taken to be the kind of solution that Hume advocates. Kant argues that if agents were wholly within time, then they would be completely governed by deterministic causal laws. Under such conditions, I could not be free, for "since the past is no longer in my power, every action which I perform is necessary because of determining grounds which are not in my power." In Kant's view the only way to rescue the kind of freedom required for moral responsibility is to think of ourselves as things in themselves that are outside of time and not bound by deterministic laws.*

However, in place of [a] deduction of the supreme principle of pure practical reason, i.e., explanation of the possibility of such an a priori cognition, we were able to adduce nothing more than this: that if one had insight into the possibility of the freedom of an efficient cause, then one would also have insight not merely into the possibility but even into the necessity of the moral law as the supreme practical law of rational beings, to whom one attributes freedom of the causality of their will. For, the two concepts are so inseparably linked that practical freedom could also be defined as independence of the will from anything else except solely the moral law. However, one cannot in any way have insight into the freedom of an efficient cause, above all in the world of sense, as regards this freedom's possibility; fortunate we are!, if we can just be sufficiently assured that there is no proof of its impossibility, and are now—by the moral law, which postulates this freedom—compelled and precisely thereby also entitled to assume it. However, there are still many who continue to believe that they can explain this freedom in terms of empirical principles, like any other natural ability. They regard it as a *psychological* property, the explanation of which hinges solely on a more exact investigation into the *nature of the soul* and into [an] incentive of the will, and not as a *transcendental* predicate of the causality of a being that belongs to the world of sense (although this alone is actually at issue); and thus they annul the splendid disclosure that comes upon us through pure practical reason by means of the moral law, viz., the disclosure of an intelligible world through realization[1] of the otherwise transcendent concept of freedom, and with it they annul the moral law itself, which throughout assumes no empirical determining basis. Therefore it will be necessary to adduce here some further [considerations] in order to guard against this deception and exhibit *empiricism* with its shallowness entirely laid bare.

The concept of causality as *natural necessity,* as distinguished from causality as *freedom,* concerns only the existence of things insofar as it is *determinable in time* and consequently [of things] as appearances, in contrast to their causality as things in themselves. Now if one takes the determinations of the existence of things in time to be determinations of things in themselves (which is the most ordinary way of conceiving[2] [them]), then the necessity in the causal relation can in no way be reconciled with freedom; rather, they are contradictorily opposed to each other. For from that necessity it follows that every event, and consequently also every action that takes place at a point of time, is necessary under the condition of what was in the preceding time. Now, because past time is no longer under my control, every action that I perform must be necessary because of determining bases *that are not under my control,* i.e., at the point of time in which I act I am never free. Indeed, even if I assumed my entire existence as [being] independent of any foreign cause (e.g., God), so that the determining bases of my causality and even of my entire existence are not outside me at all, this would still not in the least convert that natural necessity into freedom. For at every point of time I am still always subject tot he necessity of being determined to action by *what is not under my control,* and the series of events—which is infinite *a parte priori*[3] and which I can always continue only according to an already predetermined order—would nowhere start on its own [but] would be a steady chain of nature, and therefore my causality would never be freedom.

Hence if one wants to attribute freedom to a being whose existence is determined in time, then at least to this extent one cannot exempt this being from the law of the natural necessity of all events in its existence and

1. [I.e., providing with reality (applicability to objects).]
2. [Or 'presenting': *vorstellen.*]
3. [I.e., on the side of what is prior, or antecedent.]

hence also of all its action; for, this would be tantamount to handing the being over to blind chance. However, this law unavoidably concerns all causality of things insofar as their *existence* is determinable *in time;* hence if this were the way in which one had to conceive also the *existence of these things in themselves,* then freedom would have to be repudiated as a null and impossible concept. Consequently, if one still wants to rescue it, no other path remains than to attribute the existence of a thing insofar as it is determinable in time, and hence also the [thing's] causality according to the law of *natural necessity, merely to appearance,* but to attribute *freedom to the same being as a thing in itself.* This is indeed unavoidable if one wants to maintain simultaneously both of these mutually repellent concepts; in application, however, if one wants to explain them as reconciled in one and the same action and hence explain this reconciliation itself, great difficulties emerge that seem to make such a reconciliation unfeasible.

If concerning a human being who commits a theft I say that this deed is, according to the natural law of causality, a necessary result of the determining bases in the preceding time, then it was impossible that the deed could have been left undone. How, then, can the judging according to the moral law make a change in this and presuppose that the deed surely could have been omitted because the law says that it ought to have been omitted? That is, how can that person be called entirely free at the same point of time at which, and in regard to the same action regarding which, he is nonetheless subject to an unavoidable necessity? It is a pitiful expedient to seek to escape from this by merely adapting the *kind* of determining bases of this causality according to natural law to a *comparative* concept of freedom. (According to this concept, now and then something is called free action if its determining natural basis lies in the acting being *internally.* For example, [one says this of] what a projectile performs when it is in free motion, because while it is in flight it is not impelled by anything outside it. Again, we also call the motion of a clock a free motion, because the clock itself moves its hand, which therefore does not need to be pushed externally. In the same way, a human being's actions, although they are necessary through their determining bases that precede in time, are nonetheless called by us free, because we are still dealing with internal presentations produced by our own powers, desires generated thereby according to circumstances occasioning [them], and hence actions brought about at our own discretion.) Some still let themselves be put off with this expedient; and thus they suppose that with a little word-splitting they have found the solution to that difficult problem on which [for] millennia [people] have worked in vain and whose solution therefore is not likely to be found so utterly on the surface. For in the question concerning that freedom on which we must base all moral laws and the imputation conforming to them, it does not matter at all whether the causality determined according to a natural law is necessary through determining bases lying *within* the subject or *outside* him, or, in the first case, through instinct or through determining bases thought by means of reasons. If, as these same men admit, these determining presentations themselves do have bases of their existence in time and moreover in the *previous state,* and this state in turn in a preceding one, etc., then by all means let them—these determinations—be internal, let them have psychological rather than mechanical causality, i.e., produce action through presentations rather than through bodily motion; they are always *determining bases* of the causality of a being insofar as this being's existence is determinable in time and hence under necessitating conditions of past time. Thus these determinations, if the subject is to act, *are no longer under his control;* hence they do carry with them psychological freedom (if indeed one wants to use this term for a concatenation of the soul's presentations that is merely internal) but nonetheless natural necessity. Therefore they leave no *transcendental freedom,* which must be thought as independence from everything empirical and thus from nature as such, whether this nature is regarded as an object of inner sense merely in time, or also of outer sense in both space and time. Without this freedom (in the latter and proper signification), which alone is practical a priori, no moral law is possible and [also] no imputation according to it. Precisely because of this, all necessity of events in time according to the natural law of causality can also be called the *mechanism* of nature even though one does not mean by this that things that are subject to it must be actual material *machines.* One is here taking account only of the necessity of the connection of events in a time series as it develops according to natural law, whether the subject in whom this elapsing occurs is called *automaton materiale* inasmuch as the machinery is driven by matter, or, with Leibniz,[4] [*automaton*] *spirituale* inasmuch as it is driven by presentations; and if the freedom of our will were none other than the latter [kind] (say, psychological and comparative freedom, not simultaneously transcendental, i.e., absolute, freedom), then it would basically be no better than the freedom of a turnspit, which, once it has been wound up, also performs its motions on its own.

4. [Baron Gottfried Wilhelm von Leibniz (1646–1716), a German philosopher, mathematician, and author of numerous works. The rationalism of Leibniz is one of the two major philosophical traditions (the other being empiricism) to which Kant's philosophy responds.]

Now in order to annul, in the case at hand, the seeming contradiction between the mechanism of nature and freedom in one and the same action, one must remember what was said in the *Critique of Pure Reason*[5] or follows therefrom: viz., that the natural necessity that is not consistent with the subject's freedom attaches merely to the determinations of a thing which falls under conditions of time and thus only to the determinations of the acting subject as appearance, and that therefore—to this extent—the determining bases of every action of the subject lie in what belongs to past time and *is no longer under his control* (in this must be included also his already committed deeds and the character, thereby determinable for him, that he as phenomenon has in his own eyes). But the same subject, who on the other hand is also conscious of himself as a thing in itself, also considers his existence *insofar as it does not fall under conditions of time,* and considers himself as determinable only by laws that he on his own gives to himself through reason; and in this existence of his there is for him nothing antecedent to the determination of his existence varying in conformity with inner sense, even the entire sequence of his existence as a being of sense—is in the consciousness of his intelligible existence nothing but a consequence, and is never to be viewed as a determining basis of his causality as a *noumenon.* Now, in this regard the rational being can rightly say concerning every unlawful action which he commits that he could have omitted it, even though as appearance it is sufficiently determine in the past and is to this extent unfailingly necessary; for, this action, with everything past that determines it, belongs to a single phenomenon of his character—the character which he on his own imparts to himself and according to which he on his own imputes to himself, as a cause independent of all sensibility, the causality of those appearances.

The judicial pronouncements of that wondrous power in us that we call conscience are also in perfect agreement with this. Let a human being use what art he wants in order to paint to himself a remembered unlawful behavior as a unintentional oversight—as a mere carelessness, which one can never avoid entirely, and thus as something in which he was carried away by the stream of natural necessity—and to declare himself innocent of it; he nonetheless finds that the lawyer who speaks in his favor can in no way silence the prosecutor in him, if only he is conscious that at the time when he committed the wrong he was in his sense, i.e., had the use of his freedom. He nonetheless *explains* his offense to himself [as arising] from a

5. [Cf. the *Critique of Pure Reason,* A 444–51 = B 472–79, A 488/B 516, A 532–58 = B 560–86.]

certain bad habit brought upon himself by a gradual neglect of attentiveness to himself, [and he does so] to such a degree that he can regard the offense as a natural consequence of this habit, even though this still cannot secure him against the self-censure and the reprimand that he casts upon himself. This is also the basis of the repentance for a deed committed long ago, at every recollection of it. Repentance is a painful sensation which is brought about by a moral attitude and which, to the extent that it cannot serve to undo what has been done, is empty practically. Repentance would even be absurd (indeed, *Priestley*,[6] as a genuine *fatalist* who proceeds consistently, declares it to be absurd, and for this candor he deserves more applause than those who, while asserting the will's mechanism in the deed but its freedom by means of words, still want to be considered as including repentance too in their syncretistic system, though without making the possibility of such an imputation comprehensible), but as pain it is nonetheless entirely legitimate, because reason, when the law of our intelligible existence (the moral law) is at issue, acknowledges no distinction of time and asks only whether the event belongs to me as a deed, but then always connects the same sensation with it morally, whether the deed is being done now or was done long ago. For, the *life of sense* has in regard to the *intelligible* consciousness of one's existence (the consciousness of freedom) [the] absolute unity of a phenomenon that, insofar as it contains merely appearances of the attitude which is of concern to the moral law (appearances of character), must be judged not according to the natural necessity which belongs to it as appearance but according to the natural necessity which belongs to it as appearance but according to the absolute spontaneity of freedom. Hence one can grant that if it were possible for us to have so deep an insight into a human being's way of thinking—as this manifests itself through internal as well as external actions—that we would become acquainted with every incentive to actions, even with the slightest, and likewise with all external promptings affecting these incentives, then we could calculate a human being's conduct for the future with certainty, just like any lunar or solar eclipse, and could nonetheless also assert that the human being is free. For if we were capable also of another view (a view which, to be sure, has not been bestowed upon us at all, but in place of which we have only the rational concept), viz., an intellectual intuition of the same subject, then we would nonetheless become aware that this entire chain of appearances depends, with regard to whatever can

6. [See Joseph Priestley (1733–1804), *The Doctrine of Philosophical Necessity Illustrated.*]

be of concern to the moral law, on the spontaneity of the subject as a thing in itself—a spontaneity for the determination of which no physical explanation can be given at all. In the absence of this intuition, the moral law assures us of this distinction of the reference that our actions as appearances have to our subject's sensible being from that [reference of our actions] whereby this sensible being is itself referred to the intelligible substrate in us. From this point of view, which is natural though inexplicable to our reason, one can justify even judgments which, though made in all conscientiousness, yet seem at first glance to conflict thoroughly with all equity. There are cases where human beings, even with the same upbringing that was simultaneously profitable for others, nevertheless show from childhood such early villainy and increase it so continuously into their years of manhood that they are considered to be born villains and entirely incapable of improvement as far as their way of thinking is concerned; yet they are just as much tried for their doing and refraining, just as much reprimanded as guilty of their crimes, and indeed they (the children) themselves find these reprimands [just] as well-based, as [would be the case] if regardless of the hopeless natural constitution of their minds which is attributed to them they remained just as responsible as any other human being. This could not occur if we did not presuppose that whatever arises from one's power of choice (as every deliberately performed action undoubtedly does) has as its basis a free causality, which from early youth expresses its character in its appearances (the actions). These actions, because of the uniformity of conduct, make recognizable a natural connection; this connection, however, does not render the malicious constitution of the will necessary, but is rather the consequence of the voluntarily assumed and immutable evil principles, which only make the will all the more reprehensible and deserving of punishment.

However, freedom still faces a difficulty insofar as it is to be reconciled with the mechanism of nature in a being that belongs to the world of sense, a difficulty which even after all the foregoing has been consented to, nonetheless threatens freedom with its utter demise. But, in this danger, one circumstance nonetheless also gives us hope for an outcome still favorable to affirming freedom, namely that the same difficulty weights much more heavily (indeed, as we shall soon see, weighs only) upon the system in which the existence determinable in time and space is considered to be the existence of things in themselves; that the difficulty therefore does not compel us to give up our foremost presupposition of the ideality of time as a mere form of sensible intuition and thus as merely a way of presenting which is peculiar to the subject as belonging to the world of sense; and that the difficulty therefore requires only that we reconcile this presupposition with the idea of freedom.

For even if it is conceded to us that the intelligible subject can still be free with regard to a given action even though, as a subject who also belongs to the world of sense, he is mechanically conditioned with regard tot his action, it nonetheless seems that as soon as one assumes that *God* as universal original being is *the cause* also *of the existence of substance* (a proposition that can never be given up without simultaneously also giving up the concept of God as the being of all beings and therewith his all-sufficiency, on which everything in theology hinges), one must then also concede that a human being's actions have their determining basis in *what is entirely beyond his control,* viz., in the causality of a supreme being which is distinct from him and one which the human being's existence and the entire determination of his causality depends utterly. Indeed, if a human being's actions, as far as they belong to his determinations in time, were determinations of him not merely as appearance but as a thing in itself, then freedom could not be rescued. A human being would be a puppet, or a Vaucansonian automaton[7] built and wound up by the supreme master of all artificial devices; and although self-consciousness would turn the automaton into a thinking one, yet the automaton's consciousness of its spontaneity deserves to be called freedom only comparatively. For although the proximate determining causes of the automaton's motion—and a long series of these [determining] causes [extending] upward to their [own] determining causes—are internal, the last and highest one is still found entirely in a foreign hand. Therefore I do not see how those who persist in regarding time and space as determinations belonging to the existence of things in themselves are to avoid here the fatalism of actions. Or, if (like the otherwise acute *Mendelssohn*) they straightforwardly admit time and space to be conditions necessarily belonging only to the existence of finite and derivative beings but not to that of the infinite original being, I do not see how they are to justify whence they get this authority for making such a distinction. I do not even see how they are to evade the contradiction that they perpetrate when they regard existence in

7. [Jacques de Vaucanson (1709–82), a French engineer from Grenoble, completed his sophisticated and celebrated life-size automaton flute-player in 1736 (or, according to some sources, in 1737); it was followed by even more ingenious automata, including a tambourine-player and a duck that could imitate eating, drinking, and quacking. These automata were first exhibited in Paris in 1738. Some materialists pointed to them to support their view that human beings are machines.]

time as a determination attaching necessarily to finite things in themselves, while God is the cause of this existence; for he still cannot be the cause of time (or of space) itself (because time must be presupposed as a necessary a priori condition of the existence of things), and consequently his causality in regard to the existence of these things must itself be conditioned in terms of time; and thus all the contradictions against the concepts of his infinity and independence must unavoidably arise. For us, on the other hand, it is quite easy to make the distinction between the determination of divine existence as independent of all conditions of time and [the determination of] the existence of a being of the world of sense, viz., as that between the *existence of a being in itself* and that of a *thing in appearance.* Hence if that ideality of space and time is not assumed, solely *Spinozism* remains, in which space and time are essential determinations of the original being itself, while the things dependent upon it (hence also we ourselves) are not substances but merely accidents inhering in it; for if these things exist merely as its effects *in time,* which would be the condition of their existence in themselves, then the actions of these beings would also have to be merely his actions performed by him somewhere and sometime. Hence Spinozism, despite the absurdity of its basic idea, does [thereafter] infer far more cogently than can be done on the creation theory when the *beings* assumed to be substances and in themselves *existing in time* are regarded as effects of a supreme cause and yet not also as belonging to him and his action but as substances by themselves.

The difficulty mentioned above is resolved briefly and plausibly in the following manner. If existence *in time* is merely a sensible way of presenting on the part of thinking beings in the world and consequently does not pertain to them as things in themselves, because the concept of creation does not belong to the sensible way of presenting existence and to causality but can be referred only to noumena. Consequently, if I say concerning beings in the world of sense that they are created, then I regard them to that extent as noumena. Just as it would thus be a contradiction to say that God is a creator of appearances, so it is also a contradiction to say that as creator he is the cause of the actions in the world of sense and hence [of these actions] as appearances, even though he is the cause of the existence of the acting beings (as noumena). If, now, it is possible (provided only that we assume existence in time to be something that holds merely of appearances, not of things in themselves) to affirm freedom without detriment to the natural mechanism of actions as appearances, then [the fact] that the acting beings are creatures cannot make the slightest change sin this, because creation concerns their intelligible but not their sensible existence and therefore cannot be regarded as determining basis of appearances; but this would turn out quite differently if the beings of the world existed as things in themselves *in time,* since the creator of substance would then also be the originator of the entire machinery in this substance.

Of such great importance is the separation—performed in the critique of pure speculative reason—of time (as well as space) from the existence of things in themselves.[8]

But, it will be said, the difficulty's solution that has been set forth here does have much difficult [material] in it and is hardly susceptible of a clear exhibition. However, is any other solution that has been attempted, or that may be attempted, indeed easier and more graspable? One might rather say that the dogmatic teachers of metaphysics have shown more shrewdness on their part than sincerity in moving this difficult point as far as possible out of sight, in the hope that if they did not speak of it at all then presumably no one would readily think of it either. If a science is to be promoted, all difficulties must be *uncovered,* and those that may still lie hidden in its way must even be *sought out;* for, every difficulty calls forth a remedy that cannot be found without providing the science with an increase either in range or in determinateness, and thus even obstacles become means for furthering the thoroughness of the science. By contrast, if the difficulties are intentionally covered up, or removed merely through palliatives, then sooner or later they break out in incurable bad [consequences] that bring the science to ruin in a complete skepticism.

8. [Cf. the *Critique of Pure Reason,* A 22–49/B 37–73.]

11

Thomas Reid, from *Essays on the Active Powers of Man*

Thomas Reid (1710–1796) was a Scottish philosopher who was born about the same time as his compatriot David Hume but who outlived him by twenty years. Reid rejects Hume's determinism and compatibilism and argues instead for a version of agent-causal libertarianism. These two chapters from his Essays on the Active Powers of Man *(1788) feature the central claims of his position, although it is expressed and defended in much greater detail in this work.*

ESSAY FOUR / OF THE LIBERTY OF MORAL AGENTS

CHAPTER 1 / THE NOTIONS OF MORAL LIBERTY AND NECESSITY STATED

By the *Liberty of a Moral Agent,* I understand, *a power over the determinations of his own Will.*

If, in any action, he had power to will what he did, or not to will it, in that action he is free. But if, in every voluntary action, the determination of his will be the necessary consequence of something involuntary in the state of his mind, or of something in his external circumstances, he is not free; he has not what I call the Liberty of a Moral Agent, but is subject to Necessity.

This Liberty supposes the agent to have Understanding and Will; for the determinations of the will are the sole object about which this power is employed; and there can be no will without such a degree of understanding, at least, as gives the conception of that which we will.

The liberty of a moral agent implies, not only a *conception* of what he wills, but some degree of practical *judgment* or *reason.*

For, if he has not the judgment to discern one determination to be preferable to another, either in itself or for some purpose which he intends, what can be the use of a power to determine? His determinations must be made perfectly in the dark, without reason, motive, or end. They can neither be right nor wrong, wise nor foolish. Whatever the consequences may be, they cannot be imputed to the agent, who had not the capacity of forseeing them, or of perceiving any reason for acting otherwise than he did.

We may, perhaps, be able to conceive a being endowed with power over the determinations of his will, without any light in his mind to direct that power to some end. But such power would be given in vain. No exercise of it could be either blamed or approved. As nature gives no power in vain, I see no ground to ascribe a power over the determinations of the will to any being who has no judgment to apply it to the direction of his conduct, no discernment of what he ought or ought not to do.

For that reason, in this Essay, I speak only of the Liberty of Moral Agents, who are capable of acting well or ill, wisely or foolishly, and this, for distinction's sake, I shall call *Moral Liberty.*

What kind or what degree of liberty belongs to brute animals, or to our own species, before any use of reason, I do not know. We acknowledge that they have not the power of self-government. Such of their actions as may be called *voluntary* seem to be invariably determined by the passion, or appetite, or affection, or habit, which is strongest at the time.

This seems to be the law of their constitution, to which they yield, as the inanimate creation does, without any conception of the law, or any intention of obedience.

But of civil or moral government, which are addressed to the rational powers, and require a conception of the law and an intentional obedience, they are, in the judgment of all mankind, incapable. Nor do I see what end could be served by giving them a power over the determinations of their own will, unless to make them intractable by discipline, which we see they are not.

The effect of moral liberty is, *That it is in the power of the agent to do well or ill.* This power, like every other gift of God, may be abused. The right use of this gift of God is to do well and wisely, as far as his best judgment can direct him, and thereby merit esteem and approbation. The abuse of it is to act contrary to what he knows or suspects to be his duty and his wisdom, and thereby justly merit disapprobation and blame.

By *Necessity,* I understand the want of that moral liberty which I have above defined.

If there can be a better and a worse in actions on the system of Necessity, let us suppose a man necessarily determined in all cases to will and to do what is best to be done, he would surely be innocent and inculpable. But, as far as I am able to judge, he would not be entitled to the esteem and moral approbation of those who knew and believed this necessity. What was, by an ancient author, said of Cato, might, indeed, be said of him: *He was good because he could not be otherwise.* But this saying, if understood literally and strictly, is not the praise of Cato, but of his constitution, which was no more the work of Cato than his existence.

On the other hand, if a man be necessarily determined to do ill, this case seems to me to move pity, but not disapprobation. He was ill, because he could not be other wise. Who can blame him? Necessity has no law. . . .

Such are my notions of moral liberty and necessity, and of the consequences inseparably connected with both the one and the other.

This moral liberty a man may have, though it do not extend to all his actions, or even to all his voluntary actions. He does many things by instinct, many things by the force of habit, without any thought at all, and consequently without will. In the first part of life, he has not the power of self-government any more than the brutes. That power over the determinations of his own will, which belongs to him in ripe years, is limited, as all his powers are; and it is, perhaps, beyond the reach of his understanding to define its limits with precision. We can only say, in general, that it extends to every action for which he is accountable.

This power is given by his Maker, and at his pleasure whose gift it is it may be enlarged or diminished, continued or withdrawn. No power in the creature can be independent of the Creator. His hook is in its nose; he can give it line as far as he sees fit, and, when he pleases, can restrain it, or turn it whithersoever he will. Let this be always understood when we ascribe liberty to man, or to any created being.

Supposing it therefore to be true, *That man is a free agent,* it may be true, at the same time, that his liberty may be impaired or lost, by disorder of body or mind, as in melancholy, or in madness; it may be impaired or lost by vicious habits; it may, in particular cases, be restrained by divine interposition.

We call man a *free* agent in the same way as we call him a *reasonable* agent. In many things he is not guided by reason, but by principles similar to those of the brutes. His reason is weak at best. It is liable to be impaired or lost, by his own fault, or by other means. In like manner, he may be a free agent, though his freedom of action may have many similar limitations.

The liberty I have described has been represented by some philosophers as inconceivable, and as involving an absurdity.

"Liberty, they say, consists only in a power to act as we will; and it is impossible to conceive in any being a greater liberty than this. Hence it follows, that liberty does not extend to the determinations of the will, but only to the actions consequent to its determination, and depending upon the will. To say that we have power to will such an action, is to say, that we may will it, if we will. This supposes the will to be determined by a prior will; and, for the same reason, that will must be determined by a will prior to it, and so on in an infinite series of wills, which is absurd. To act freely, therefore, can mean nothing more than to act voluntarily; and this is all the liberty that can be conceived in man, or in any being."

This reasoning—first, I think, advanced by Hobbes—has been very generally adopted by the defenders of necessity. It is grounded upon a definition of liberty totally different from that which I have given, and therefore does not apply to moral liberty, as above defined.

But it is said that this is the only liberty that is possible, that is conceivable, that does not involve an absurdity.

It is strange, indeed, if the word *Liberty* has no meaning but this one. I shall mention *three,* all very common. The objection applies to one of them, but to neither of the other two.

Liberty is sometimes opposed to external force or confinement of the body. Sometimes it is opposed to obligation by law, or by lawful authority. Sometimes it is opposed to necessity.

1. It is opposed to confinement of the body by superior force. So we say a prisoner is set at liberty when his fetters are knocked off, and he is discharged from confinement. This is the liberty defined in the objection; and I grant that this liberty extends not to the will, neither does the confinement, because the will cannot be confined by external force.

2. Liberty is opposed to obligation by law, or lawful authority. This liberty is a right to act one way or another, in things which the law has neither commanded nor forbidden; and this liberty is meant when we speak of a man's natural liberty, his civil liberty, his Christian liberty. It is evident that this liberty, as well as the obligation opposed to it, extends to the will: For it is the will to obey that makes obedience; the will to transgress that makes a transgression of the law. Without will there can be neither obedience nor transgression. Law supposes a power to obey or to transgress; it does not take away this power, but proposes the motives of duty and of interest, leaving the power to yield to them, or to take the consequence of transgression.

3. Liberty is opposed to Necessity, and in this sense it extends to the determinations of the will only, and not to what is consequent to the will.

In every voluntary action, the determination of the will is the first part of the action, upon which alone the moral estimation of it depends. It has been made a question among philosophers, *Whether, in every instance, this determination be the necessary consequence of the constitution of the person, and the circumstances in which he is placed; or whether he had not power, in many cases, to determine this way or that?*

This has, by some, been called the *philosophical* notion of liberty and necessity; but it is by no means peculiar to philosophers. The lowest of the vulgar have, in all ages, been prone to have recourse to this necessity, to exculpate themselves or their friends in what they do wrong, though, in the general tenor of their conduct, they act upon the contrary principle.

Whether this notion of moral liberty be *conceivable* or not, every man must judge for himself. To me there appears no difficulty in conceiving it. I consider the determination of the will as an effect. This effect must have a cause which had power to produce it; and the cause must be either the person himself, whose will it is, or some other being. The first is as easily conceived as the last. If the person was the cause of that determination of his own will, he was free in that action, and it is justly imputed to him, whether it be good or bad. But, if another being was the cause of this determination, either by producing it immediately, or by means and instruments under his direction, then the determination is the act and deed of that being, and is solely imputable to him.

But it is said—"That nothing in our power but what depends upon the will, and therefore, the will itself cannot be in our power."

I answer—That this is a fallacy arising from taking a common saying in a sense which it never was intended to convey, and in a sense contrary to what it necessarily implies.

In common life, when men speak of what is, or is not, in a man's power, they attend only to the external and visible effects, which only can be perceived, and which only can affect them. Of these, it is true that nothing is in a man's power but what depends upon his will, and this is all that is meant by this common saying.

But this is so far from excluding his will from being in his power, that it necessarily implies it. For to say that what depends upon the will is in a man's power, but the will is not in his power, is to say that the end is in his power, but the means necessary to that end are not in his power, which is a contradiction.

In many propositions which we express universally, there is an exception necessarily implied, and, therefore, always understood. Thus, when we say that all things depend upon God, God himself is necessarily excepted. In like manner, when we say, that all that is in our power depends upon the will, the will itself is necessarily excepted: for, if the will be not, nothing else can be in our power. Every effect must be in the power of its cause. The determination of the will is an effect, and therefore, must be in the power of its cause, whether that cause be the agent himself, or some other being.

From what has been said in this chapter, I hope the notion of moral liberty will be distinctly understood, and that it appears that this notion is neither inconceivable, nor involves any absurdity or contradiction.

CHAPTER 2 / OF THE WORDS CAUSE *AND* EFFECT, ACTION, *AND* ACTIVE POWER

The writings upon Liberty and Necessity have been much darkened by the ambiguity of the words used in reasoning upon that subject. The words *cause* and *effect, action* and *active power, liberty* and *necessity,* are related to each other: The meaning of one determines the meaning of the rest. When we attempt to define them, we can only do it by synonymous words which need definition as much. There is a strict sense in which those words must be used, if we speak and reason clearly about moral liberty; but to keep to this strict sense is difficult, because, in all languages, they have, by custom, got a great latitude of signification.

As we cannot reason about moral liberty without using those ambiguous words, it is proper to point out, as distinctly as possible, their proper and original meaning in which they ought to be understood in treating of this subject, and to shew from what causes they have become so ambiguous in all languages as to darken and embarrass our reasonings upon it.

Everything that begins to exist, must have a cause of its existence, which had power to give it existence. And everything that undergoes any change, must have some cause of that change.

That neither existence, nor any mode of existence, can begin without an efficient cause, is a principle that appears very early in the mind of man; and it is so universal, and so firmly rooted in human nature, that the most determined scepticism cannot eradicate it.

It is upon this principle that we ground the rational belief of a deity. But that is not the only use to which we apply it. Every man's conduct is governed by it, every day, and almost every hour, of his life. And if it were possible for any man to root out this principle from his mind, he must give up everything that is called common prudence, and be fit only to be confined as insane.

From this principle it follows, *That everything which undergoes any change, must either be the efficient cause of that change in itself, or it must be changed by some other being.*

In the *first* case, it is said to have *active power,* and to *act* in producing that change. In the *second* case, it is merely *passive,* or is *acted upon,* and the active power is in that being only which produces the change.

The name of a *cause* and of an *agent,* is properly given to that being only, which, by its active power, produces some change in itself, or in some other being. The change, whether it be of thought, of will, or of motion, is the *effect.* Active power, therefore, is a quality in the cause, which enables it to produce the effect. And the exertion of that active power in producing the effect, is called *action, agency, efficiency.*

In order to the production of any effect, there must be in the cause, not only power, but the *exertion of that power;* for power that is not exerted produces no effect.

All that is necessary to the production of any effect, is power in an efficient cause to produce the effect, and the exertion of that power; for it is a contradiction to say, that the cause has power to produce the effect, and exerts that power, and yet the effect is not produced. The effect cannot be in his power unless all the means necessary to its production be in his power.

It is no less a contradiction to say, that a cause has power to produce a certain effect, but that he cannot exert that power; for power which cannot be exerted is no power, and is a contradiction in terms.

To prevent mistake, it is proper to observe, that a being may have a power at one time which it has not at another. It may commonly have a power, which, at a particular time, it has not. Thus, a man may commonly have power to walk or to run; but he has not this power when asleep, or when he is confined by superior force. In common language, he may be said to have a power which he cannot then exert. But this popular expression means only that he commonly has this power, and will have it when the cause is removed which at present deprives him of it; for, when we speak strictly and philosophically, it is a contradiction to say that he has this power, at that moment when he is deprived of it.

These, I think, are necessary consequences from the principle first mentioned—That every change which happens in nature must have an efficient cause which had power to produce it.

Another principle, which appears very early in the mind of man, is, *That we are efficient causes in our deliberate and voluntary actions.*

We are conscious of making an exertion, sometimes with difficulty, in order to produce certain effects. And exertion made deliberately and voluntarily, in order to produce an effect, implies a conviction that the effect is in our power. No man can deliberately attempt what he does not believe to be in his power. The language of all mankind, and their ordinary conduct in life, demonstrate that they have a conviction of some active power in themselves to produce certain motions in their own and in other bodies, and to regulate and direct their own thoughts. This conviction we have so early in life, that we have no remembrance when, or in what way, we acquired it.

That such a conviction is at first the necessary result of our constitution, and that it can never be entirely obliterated, is, I think, acknowledged by one of the most zealous defenders of Necessity. "Such are the influences to which all mankind, without distinction, are exposed that they necessarily refer actions (I mean refer them ultimately) first of all to themselves and others; and it is a long time before they begin to consider themselves and others as instruments in the hand of a superior agent. Consequently, the associations which refer actions to themselves get so confirmed that they are never entirely obliterated; and therefore the common language, and the common feelings, of mankind, will be adapted to the first, the limited and imperfect, or rather erroneous, view of things."

It is very probable that the very conception or idea of active power, and of efficient causes, is derived from our voluntary exertions in producing effects; and that, if we were not conscious of such exertion, we should have no conception at all of a cause, or of active power, and consequently no conviction of the necessity of a cause of every change which we observe in nature.

It is certain that we can conceive no kind of active power but what is similar or analogous to that which we attribute to ourselves; that is, a power which is exerted by will and with understanding. Our notion, even of Almighty power, is derived from the notion of human power, by removing from the former those imperfections and limitations to which the latter is subjected.

It may be difficult to explain the origin of our conceptions and belief concerning efficient causes and active power. The common theory, that all our ideas are ideas of Sensation or Reflection, and that all our belief is a perception of the agreement or the disagreement of those ideas, appears to be repugnant, both to the idea of an efficient cause, and to the belief of its necessity.

An attachment to that theory has led some philosophers to deny that we have any conception of an efficient cause, or of active power, because efficiency and active power are not ideas, either of sensation or reflection. They maintain, therefore, that a Cause is only *something prior to the effect, and constantly conjoined with it.* This is Mr Hume's notion of a cause, and seems to be adopted by Dr Priestley, who says, "That a cause cannot be defined to be any thing, but *such previous circumstances as are constantly followed by a certain effect,* the constancy of the result making us conclude that there must be a *sufficient reason,* in the nature of the things, why it should be produced in those circumstances."

But theory ought to stoop to fact, and not fact to theory. Every man who understands the language knows that neither priority, nor constant conjunction, nor both taken together, imply efficiency. . . .

The very dispute, whether we have the conception of an efficient cause, shews that we have. For, though men may dispute about things which have no existence, they cannot dispute about things of which they have no conception.

What has been said in this chapter is intended to shew—That the conception of causes, of action and of active power, in the strict and proper sense of these words, is found in the minds of all men very early, even in the dawn of their rational life. It is therefore probable, that, in all languages, the words by which these conceptions were expressed were at first distinct and unambiguous, yet it is certain that, among the most enlightened nations, these words are applied to so many things of different natures, and used in so vague a manner, that it is very difficult to reason about them distinctly.

This phaenomenon, at first view, seems very unaccountable. But a little reflection may satisfy us, that it is a natural consequence of the slow and gradual progress of human knowledge.

12

A. J. Ayer, "Freedom and Necessity"

Alfred J. Ayer (1910–1989) was a professor at Oxford University and advocated a positivist scientific world view from the 1930s until his death. In this selection he advocates a compatibilist theory of the sort of freedom required for moral responsibility. Ayer maintains that when agents are under constraint *they do not have this sort of freedom. But since agents do act without being constrained, they are morally responsible for some of their actions, despite the truth of causal determinism.*

When I am said to have done something of my own free will it is implied that I could have acted otherwise; and it is only when it is believed that I could have acted otherwise that I am held to be morally responsible for what I have done. For a man is not thought to be morally responsible for an action that it was not in his power to avoid. But if human behaviour is entirely governed by causal laws, it is not clear how any action that is done could ever have been avoided. It may be said of the agent that he would have acted otherwise if the causes of his action had been different, but they being what they were, it seems to follow that he was bound to act as he did. Now it is commonly assumed both that men are capable of acting freely, in the sense that is required to make them morally responsible, and that human behaviour is entirely governed by causal laws: and it is the apparent conflict between these two assumptions that gives rise to the philosophical problem of the freedom of the will.

Confronted with this problem, many people will be inclined to agree with Dr. Johnson: 'Sir, we *know* our will is free, and *there's* an end on't.' But, while this does very well for those who accept Dr. Johnson's premiss, it would hardly convince anyone who denied the freedom of the will. Certainly, if we do know that our wills are free, it follows that they are so. But the logical reply to this might be that since our wills are not free, it follows that no one can know that they are: so that if anyone claims, like Dr. Johnson, to know that they are, he must be mistaken. What is evident, indeed, is that people often believe themselves to be acting freely; and it is

From *Philosophical Essays* by Professor Sir Alfred Ayer (1954, pp. 271–84). Reprinted by permission of Macmillan, London and Basingstoke.

to this 'feeling' of freedom that some philosophers appeal when they wish, in the supposed interests of morality, to prove that not all human action is causally determined. But if these philosophers are right in their assumption that a man cannot be acting freely if his action is causally determined, then the fact that someone feels free to do, or not to do, a certain action does not prove that he really is so. It may prove that the agent does not himself know what it is that makes him act in one way rather than another: but from the fact that a man is unaware of the causes of his action, it does not follow that no such causes exist.

So much may be allowed to the determinist; but his belief that all human actions are subservient to causal laws still remains to be justified. If, indeed, it is necessary that every event should have a cause, then the rule must apply to human behaviour as much as to anything else. But why should it be supposed that every event must have a cause? The contrary is not unthinkable. Nor is the law of universal causation a necessary presupposition of scientific thought. The scientist may try to discover causal laws, and in many cases he succeeds; but sometimes he has to be content with statistical laws, and sometimes he comes upon events which, in the present state of his knowledge, he is not able to subsume under any law at all. In the case of these events he assumes that if he knew more he would be able to discover some law, whether causal or statistical, which would enable him to account for them. And this assumption cannot be disproved. For however far he may have carried his investigation, it is always open to him to carry it further; and it is always conceivable that if he carried it further he would discover the connection which had hitherto escaped him. Nevertheless, it is also conceivable that the events with which he is concerned are not systematically connected with any others: so that the reason why he does not discover the sort of laws that he requires is simply that they do not obtain.

Now in the case of human conduct the search for explanations has not in fact been altogether fruitless. Certain scientific laws have been established; and with the help of these laws we do make a number of successful predictions about the ways in which different people will behave. But these predictions do not always cover every detail. We may be able to predict that in certain circumstances a particular man will be angry, without being able to prescribe the precise form that the expression of his anger will take. We may be reasonably sure that he will shout, but not sure how loud his shout will be, or exactly what words he will use. And it is only a small proportion of human actions that we are able to forecast even so precisely as this. But that, it may be said, is because we have not carried our investigations very far. The science of psychology is still in its infancy and, as it is developed, not only will more human actions be explained, but the explanations will go into greater detail. The ideal of complete explanation may never in fact be attained: but it is theoretically attainable. Well, this may be so: and certainly it is impossible to show *a priori* that it is not so: but equally it cannot be shown that it is. This will not, however, discourage the scientist who, in the field of human behaviour, as elsewhere, will continue to formulate theories and test them by the facts. And in this he is justified. For since he has no reason *a priori* to admit that there is a limit to what he can discover, the fact that he also cannot be sure that there is no limit does not make it unreasonable for him to devise theories, nor, having devised them, to try constantly to improve them.

But now suppose it to be claimed that, so far as men's actions are concerned, there is a limit: and that this limit is set by the fact of human freedom. An obvious objection is that in many cases in which a person feels himself to be free to do, or not to do, a certain action, we are even now able to explain, in causal terms, why it is that he acts as he does. But it might be argued that even if men are sometimes mistaken in believing that they act freely, it does not follow that they are always so mistaken. For it is not always the case that when a man believes that he has acted freely we are in fact able to account for his action in causal terms. A determinist would say that we should be able to account for it if we had more knowledge of the circumstances, and had been able to discover the appropriate natural laws. But until those discoveries have been made, this remains only a pious hope. And may it not be true that, in some cases at least, the reason why we can give no causal explanation is that no causal explanation is available; and that this is because the agent's choice was literally free, as he himself felt it to be?

The answer is that this may indeed be true, inasmuch as it is open to anyone to hold that no explanation is possible until some explanation is actually found. But even so it does not give the moralist what he wants. For he is anxious to show that men are capable of acting freely in order to infer that they can be morally responsible for what they do. But if it is a matter of pure chance that a man should act in one way rather than another, he may be free but can hardly be responsible. And indeed when a man's actions seem to us quite unpredictable, when, as we say, there is no knowing what he will do, we do not look upon him as a moral agent. We look upon him as a lunatic.

To this it may be objected that we are not dealing fairly with the moralist. For when he makes it a condition of my being morally responsible that I should act freely, he does not wish to imply that it is purely a matter of chance that I act as I do. What he wishes to imply is that my actions are the result of my own free choice: and it is because they are the result of my own free choice that I am held to be morally responsible for them.

But now we must ask how it is that I come to make my choice. Either it is an accident that I choose to act as I do or it is not. If it is an accident, then it is merely a matter of chance that I did not choose otherwise; and if it is merely a matter of chance that I did not choose otherwise, it is surely irrational to hold me morally responsible for choosing as I did. But if it is not an accident that I choose to do one thing rather than another, then presumably there is some causal explanation of my choice: and in that case we are led back to determinism.

Again, the objection may be raised that we are not doing justice to the moralist's case. His view is not that it is a matter of chance that I choose to act as I do, but rather that my choice depends upon my character. Nevertheless he holds that I can still be free in the sense that he requires; for it is I who am responsible for my character. But in what way am I responsible for my character? Only, surely, in the sense that there is a causal connection between what I do now and what I have done in the past. It is only this that justifies the statement that I have made myself what I am: and even so this is an over-simplification, since it takes no account of the external influences to which I have been subjected. But, ignoring the external influences, let us assume that it is in fact the case that I have made myself what I am. Then it is still legitimate to ask how it is that I have come to make myself one sort of person rather than another. And if it be answered that it is a matter of my strength of will, we can put the same question in another form by asking how it is that my will has the strength that it has and not some other degree of strength. Once more, either it is an accident or it is not. If it is an accident, then by the same argument as before, I am not morally responsible, and if it is not an accident we are led back to determinism.

Furthermore, to say that my actions proceed from my character or, more colloquially, that I act in character, is to say that my behaviour is consistent and to that extent predictable: and since it is, above all, for the actions that I perform in character that I am held to be morally responsible, it looks as if the admission of moral responsibility, so far from being incompatible with determinism, tends rather to presuppose it. But how can this be so if it is a necessary condition of moral responsibility that the person who is held responsible should have acted freely? It seems that if we are to retain this idea of moral responsibility, we must either show that men can be held responsible for actions which they do not do freely, or else find some way of reconciling determinism with the freedom of the will.

It is no doubt with the object of effecting this reconciliation that some philosophers have defined freedom as the consciousness of necessity. And by so doing they are able to say not only that a man can be acting freely when his action is causally determined, but even that his action must be causally determined for it to be possible for him to be acting freely. Nevertheless this definition has the serious disadvantage that it gives to the word 'freedom' a meaning quite different from any that it ordinarily bears. It is indeed obvious that if we are allowed to give the word 'freedom' any meaning that we please, we can find a meaning that will reconcile it with determinism: but this is no more a solution of our present problem than the fact that the word 'horse' could be arbitrarily used to mean what is ordinarily meant by 'sparrow' is a proof that horses have wings. For suppose that I am compelled by another person to do something 'against my will'. In that case, as the word 'freedom' is ordinarily used, I should not be said to be acting freely: and the fact that I am fully aware of the constraint to which I am subjected makes no difference to the matter. I do not become free by becoming conscious that I am not. It may, indeed, be possible to show that my being aware that my action is causally determined is not incompatible with my acting freely: but it by no means follows that it is in this that my freedom consists. Moreover, I suspect that one of the reasons why people are inclined to define freedom as the consciousness of necessity is that they think that if one is conscious of necessity one may somehow be able to master it. But this is a fallacy. It is like someone's saying that he wishes he could see into the future, because if he did he would know what calamities lay in wait for him and so would be able to avoid them. But if he avoids the calamities then they don't lie in the future and it is not true that he foresees them. And similarly if I am able to master necessity, in the sense of escaping the operation of a necessary law, then the law in question is not necessary. And if the law is not necessary, then neither my freedom nor anything else can consist in my knowing that it is.

Let it be granted, then, when we speak of reconciling freedom with determination we are using the word 'freedom' in an ordinary sense. It still remains for us to make this usage clear: and perhaps the best way to make it clear is to show what it is that freedom, in this sense, is contrasted with. Now we began with the assumption that freedom is contrasted with causality: so that a man cannot be said to be acting freely if his action is causally determined. But this assumption has led us into difficulties and I now wish to suggest that it is mistaken. For it is not, I think, causality that freedom is to be contrasted with, but constraint. And while it is true that being constrained to do an action entails being caused to do it, I shall try to show that the converse does not hold. I shall try to show that from the fact that my action is causally determined it does not necessarily follow that I am constrained to do it: and this is equivalent to saying that it does not necessarily follow that I am not free.

If I am constrained, I do not act freely. But in what circumstances can I legitimately be said to be constrained? An obvious instance is the case in which I am compelled by another person to do what he wants. In a case of this sort the compulsion need not be such as to deprive one of the power of choice. It is not required that the other person should have hypnotized me, or that he should make it physically impossible for me to go against his will. It is enough that he should induce me to do what he wants by making it clear to me that, if I do not, he will bring about some situation that I regard as even more undesirable than the consequences of the action that he wishes me to do. Thus, if the man points a pistol at my head I may still choose to disobey him: but this does not prevent its being true that if I do fall in with his wishes he can legitimately be said to have compelled me. And if the circumstances are such that no reasonable person would be expected to choose the other alternative, then the action that I am made to do is not one for which I am held to be morally responsible.

A similar, but still somewhat different, case is that in which another person has obtained an habitual ascendancy over me. Where this is so, there may be no question of my being induced to act as the other person wishes by being confronted with a still more disagreeable alternative: for if I am sufficiently under his influence this special stimulus will not be necessary. Nevertheless I do not act freely, for the reason that I have been deprived of the power of choice. And this means that I have acquired so strong a habit of obedience that I no longer go through any process of deciding whether or not to do what the other person wants. About other matters I may still deliberate; but as regards the fulfillment of this other person's wishes, my own deliberations have ceased to be a causal factor in my behaviour. And it is in this sense that I may be said to be constrained. It is not, however, necessary that such constraint should take the form of subservience to another person. A kleptomaniac is not a free agent, in respect of his stealing, because he does not go through any process of deciding whether or not to steal. Or rather, if he does go through such a process, it is irrelevant to his behaviour. Whatever he resolved to do, he would steal all the same. And it is this that distinguishes him from the ordinary thief.

But now it may be asked whether there is any essential difference between these cases and those in which the agent is commonly thought to be free. No doubt the ordinary thief does go through a process of deciding whether or not to steal, and no doubt it does affect his behaviour. If he resolved to refrain from stealing, he could carry his resolution out. But if it be allowed that his making or not making this resolution is causally determined, then how can he be any more free than the kleptomaniac? It may be true that unlike the kleptomaniac he could refrain from stealing if he chose: but if there is a cause, or set of causes, which necessitate his choosing as he does, how can he be said to have the power of choice? Again, it may be true that no one now compels me to get up and walk across the room: but if my doing so can be causally explained in terms of my history or my environment, or whatever it may be, then how am I any more free than if some other person had compelled me? I do not have the feeling of constraint that I have when a pistol is manifestly pointed at my head; but the chains of causation by which I am bound are no less effective for being invisible.

The answer to this is that the cases I have mentioned as examples of constraint do differ from the others: and they differ just in the ways that I have tried to bring out. If I suffered from a compulsion neurosis, so that I got up and walked across the room, whether I wanted to or not, or if I did so because somebody else compelled me, then I should not be acting freely. But if I do it now, I shall be acting freely, just because these conditions do not obtain; and the fact that my action may nevertheless have a cause is, from this point of view, irrelevant. For it is not when my action has any cause at all, but only when it has a special sort of cause, that it is reckoned not to be free.

But here it may be objected that, even if this distinction corresponds to ordinary usage, it is still very irrational. For why should we distinguish, with regard to a person's freedom, between the operations of one sort of cause and those of another? Do not all causes equally necessitate? And is it not therefore arbitrary to say that a person is free when he is necessitated in one fashion but not when he is necessitated in another?

That all causes equally necessitate is indeed a tautology, if the word 'necessitate' is taken merely as equivalent to 'cause': but if, as the objection requires, it is taken as equivalent to 'constrain' or 'compel', then I do not think that this proposition is true. For all that is needed for one event to be the cause of another is that, in the given circumstances, the event which is said to be the effect would not have occurred if it had not been for the occurrence of the event which is said to be the cause, or vice versa, according as causes are interpreted as necessary, or sufficient, conditions: and this fact is usually deducible from some causal law which states that whenever an event of the one kind occurs then, given suitable conditions, an event of the other kind will occur in a certain temporal or spatio-temporal relationship to it. In short, there is an invariable concomitance between the two classes of events; but there is no compulsion, in any but a metaphorical sense. Suppose, for example, that a psycho-analyst is able to account for some aspect of my behaviour by referring it to some lesion that I suffered in my childhood. In that case, it may be said that my childhood experience, together with certain other events, necessitates my behaving as I do. But all that this involves is that it is found to be true in general that when people have had certain experiences as children, they subsequently behave in certain specifiable ways; and my case is just another instance of this general law. It is in this way indeed that my behaviour is explained. But from the fact that my behaviour is capable of being explained, in the sense that it can be subsumed under some natural law, it does not follow that I am acting under constraint.

If this is correct, to say that I could have acted otherwise is to say, first, that I should have acted otherwise if I had so chosen; secondly, that my action was voluntary in the sense in which the actions, say, of the kleptomaniac are not; and thirdly, that nobody compelled me to choose as I did: and these three conditions may very well be fulfilled. When they are fulfilled, I may be said to have acted freely. But this is not to say that it was a matter of chance that I acted as I did, or, in other words, that my action could not be explained. And that my actions should be capable of being explained is all that is required by the postulate of determinism.

If more than this seems to be required it is, I think, because the use of the very word 'determinism' is in some degree misleading. For it tends to suggest that one event is somehow in the power of another, whereas the truth is merely that they are factually correlated. And the same applies to the use, in this context, of the word 'necessity' and even of the word 'cause' itself. Moreover, there are various reasons for this. One is the tendency to confuse causal with logical necessitation, and so to infer mistakenly that the effect is contained in the cause. Another is the uncritical use of a concept of force which is derived from primitive experiences of pushing and striking. A third is the survival of an animistic conception of causality, in which all causal relationships are modelled on the example of one person's exercising authority over another. As a result we tend to form an imaginative picture of an unhappy effect trying vainly to escape from the clutches of an overmastering cause. But, I repeat, the fact is simply that when an event of one type occurs, an event of another type occurs also, in a certain temporal or spatio-temporal relation to the first. The rest is only metaphor. And it is because of the metaphor, and not because of the fact, that we come to think that there is an antithesis between causality and freedom.

Nevertheless, it may be said, if the postulate of determinism is valid, then the future can be explained in terms of the past: and this means that if one knew enough about the past one would be able to predict the future. But in that case what will happen in the future is already decided. And how then can I be said to be free? What is going to happen is going to happen and nothing that I do can prevent it. If the determinist is right, I am the helpless prisoner of fate.

But what is meant by saying that the future course of events is already decided? If the implication is that some person has arranged it, then the proposition is false. But if all that is meant is that it is possible, in principle, to deduce it from a set of particular facts about the past, together with the appropriate general laws, then, even if this is true, it does not in the least entail that I am the helpless prisoner of fate. It does not even entail that my actions make no difference to the future: for they are causes as well as effects; so that if they were different their consequences would be different also. What it does entail is that my behaviour can be predicted: but to say that my behaviour can be predicted is not to say that I am acting under constraint. It is indeed true that I cannot escape my destiny if this is taken to mean no more than that I shall do what I shall do. But this is a tautology, just as it is a tautology that what is going to happen is going to happen. And such tautologies as these prove nothing whatsoever about the freedom of the will.

13

P. F. Strawson, "Freedom and Resentment"

Peter F. Strawson (1919–2006) was a professor of philosophy for many years at Oxford University. This article is an influential attempt to detach moral responsibility from metaphysical or scientific doctrines such as universal determinism. For Strawson, it is the participant reactive attitudes—*attitudes such as resentment and gratitude to which we are subject by virtue of participation in ordinary interpersonal relationships—that alone provide the basis for holding people morally responsible. Whether determinism is true is irrelevant to the issue. To secure his case, Strawson argues first for a psychological thesis, that these reactive attitudes cannot be affected by a belief in general determinism, and then for a normative thesis, that they should not be affected by a belief in general determinism.*

I

Some philosophers say they do not know what the thesis of determinism is. Others say, or imply, that they do know what it is. Of these, some—the pessimists perhaps—hold that if the thesis is true, then the concepts of moral obligation and responsibility really have no application, and the practices of punishing and blaming, of expressing moral condemnation and approval, are really unjustified. Others—the optimists perhaps—hold that these concepts and practices in no way lose their *raison d'être* if the thesis of determinism is true. Some hold even that the justification of these concepts and practices requires the truth of the thesis. There is another opinion which is less frequently voiced: the opinion, it might be said, of the genuine moral sceptic. This is that the notions of moral guilt, of blame, of moral responsibility are inherently confused and that we can see this to be so if we consider the consequences either of the truth of determinism or of its falsity. The holders of this opinion agree with the pessimists that these notions lack application if determinism is true, and add simply that they lack it if determinism is false. If I am asked which of these parties I belong to, I must say it is the first of all, the party

 Proceedings of the British Academy 48 (1962), pp. 1–25.

of those who do not know what the thesis of determinism is. But this does not stop me from having some sympathy with the others, and a wish to reconcile them. Should not ignorance, rationally, inhibit such sympathies? Well, of course, though darkling, one has some inkling—some notion of what sort of thing is being talked about. This lecture is intended as a move towards reconciliation; so is likely to seem wrongheaded to everyone.

But can there be any possibility of reconciliation between such clearly opposed opinions as those of pessimists and optimists about determinism? Well, there might be a formal withdrawal on one side in return for a substantial concession on the other. Thus, suppose the optimist's position were put like this: (1) the facts as we know them do not show determinism to be false; (2) the facts as we know them supply an adequate basis for the concepts and practices which the pessimist feels to be imperilled by the possibility of determinism's truth. Now it might be that the optimist is right in this, but is apt to give an inadequate account of the facts as we know them, and of how they constitute an adequate basis for the problematic concepts and practices; that the reasons he gives for the adequacy of the basis are themselves inadequate and leave out something vital. It might be that the pessimist is rightly anxious to get this vital thing back and, in the grip of his anxiety, feels he has to go beyond the facts as we know them; feels that the vital thing can be secure only if, beyond the facts as we know them, there is the further fact that determinism is false. Might *he* not be brought to make a formal withdrawal in return for a vital concession?

II

Let me enlarge very briefly on this, by way of preliminary only. Some optimists about determinism point to the efficacy of the practices of punishment, and of moral condemnation and approval, in regulating behaviour in socially desirable ways.[1] In the fact of their efficacy, they suggest, is an adequate basis for these practices; and this fact certainly does not show determinism to be false. To this the pessimists reply, all in a rush, that *just* punishment and *moral* condemnation imply moral guilt and guilt implies moral responsibility and moral responsibility implies freedom and freedom implies the falsity of determinism. And to this the optimists are wont to reply in turn that it is true that these practices require freedom in a sense, and the existence of freedom in this sense is one of the facts as we know them. But what 'freedom' means here is nothing but the absence of certain conditions the presence of which would

1. Cf. P. H. Nowell-Smith, 'Freewill and the Moral Responsibility', *Mind,* 1948.

make moral condemnation or punishment inappropriate. They have in mind conditions like compulsion by another, or innate incapacity, or insanity, or other less extreme forms of psychological disorder, or the existence of circumstances in which the making of any other choice would be morally inadmissible or would be too much to expect of any man. To this list they are constrained to add other factors which, without exactly being limitations of freedom, may also make moral condemnation or punishment inappropriate or mitigate their force: as some forms of ignorance, mistake, or accident. And the general reason why moral condemnation or punishment is inappropriate when these factors or conditions are present is held to be that the practices in question will be generally efficacious means of regulating behaviour in desirable ways only in cases where these factors are *not* present. Now the pessimist admits that the facts as we know them include the existence of freedom, the occurrence of cases of free action, in the negative sense which the optimist concedes; and admits, or rather insists, that the existence of freedom in this sense is compatible with the truth of determinism. Then what does the pessimist find missing? When he tries to answer this question, his language is apt to alternate between the very familiar and the very unfamiliar.[2] Thus he may say, familiarly enough, that the man who is the subject of justified punishment, blame or moral condemnation must really *deserve* it; and then add, perhaps, that, in the case at least where he is blamed for a positive act rather than an omission, the condition of his really deserving blame is something that goes beyond the negative freedoms that the optimist concedes. It is, say, a genuinely free identification of the will with the act. And this is the condition that is incompatible with the truth of determinism.

The conventional, but conciliatory, optimist need not give up yet. He may say: Well, people often decide to do things, really intend to do what they do, know just what they're doing in doing it: the reasons they think they have for doing what they do, often really are their reasons and not their rationalizations. These facts, too, are included in the facts as we know them. If this is what you mean by freedom—by the identification of the will with the act—then freedom may again be conceded. But again the concession is compatible with the truth of the determinist thesis. For it would not follow from that thesis that nobody decides to do anything; that nobody ever does anything intentionally; that it is false that people sometimes know perfectly well what they are doing. I tried to define freedom

2. As Nowell-Smith pointed out in a later article: 'Determinists and Libertarians', *Mind,* 1954.

negatively. You want to give it a more positive look. But it comes to the same thing. Nobody denies freedom in this sense, or these senses, and nobody claims that the existence of freedom in these senses shows determinism to be false.

But it is here that the lacuna in the optimistic story can be made to show. For the pessimist may be supposed to ask: But *why* does freedom in this sense justify blame, etc.? You turn towards me first the negative, and then the positive, faces of a freedom which nobody challenges. But the only reason you have given for the practices of moral condemnation and punishment in cases where this freedom is present is the efficacy of these practices in regulating behaviour in socially desirable ways. But this is not a sufficient basis, it is not even the right *sort* of basis, for these practices as we understand them.

Now my optimist, being the sort of man he is, is not likely to invoke an intuition of fittingness at this point. So he really has no more to say. And my pessimist, being the sort of man he is, has only one more thing to say; and that is that the admissibility of these practices, as we understand them, demands another kind of freedom, the kind that in turn demands the falsity of the thesis of determinism. But might we not induce the pessimist to give up saying this by giving the optimist something more to say?

III

I have mentioned punishing and moral condemnation and approval; and it is in connection with these practices or attitudes that the issue between optimists and pessimists—or, if one is a pessimist, the issue between determinists and libertarians—is felt to be particularly important. But it is not of these practices and attitudes that I propose, at first, to speak. These practices or attitudes permit, where they do not imply, a certain detachment from the actions or agents which are their objects. I want to speak, at least at first, of something else: of the non-detached attitudes and reactions of people directly involved in transactions with each other; of the attitudes and reactions of offended parties and beneficiaries: of such things as gratitude, resentment, forgiveness, love, and hurt feelings. Perhaps something like the issue between optimists and pessimists arises in this neighbouring field too; and since this field is less crowded with disputants, the issue might here be easier to settle; and if it is settled here, then it might become easier to settle it in the disputant-crowded field.

What I have to say consists largely of commonplaces. So my language, like that of commonplace generally, will be quite unscientific and imprecise. The central commonplace that I want to insist on is the very great importance that we attach to the attitudes and intentions towards us of other human beings, and the great extent to which our personal feelings and reactions depend upon, or involve, our beliefs about these attitudes and intentions. I can give no simple description of the field of phenomena at the centre of which stands this commonplace truth; for the field is too complex. Much imaginative literature is devoted to exploring its complexities; and we have a large vocabulary for the purpose. There are simplifying styles of handling it in a general way. Thus we may, like La Rochfoucauld, put self-love or self-esteem or vanity at the centre of the picture and point out how it may be caressed by the esteem, or wounded by the indifference or contempt, of others. We might speak, in another jargon, of the need for love, and the loss of security which results from its withdrawal; or, in another, of human self-respect and its connection with the recognition of the individual's dignity. These simplifications are of use to me only if they help to emphasize how much we actually mind, how much it matters to us, whether the actions of other people—and particularly of *some* other people—reflect attitudes towards us of goodwill, affection, or esteem on the one hand or contempt, indifference, or malevolence on the other. If someone treads on my hand accidentally, while trying to help me, the pain may be no less acute than if he treads on it in contemptuous disregard of my existence or with a malevolent wish to injure me. But I shall generally feel in the second case a kind and degree of resentment that I shall not feel in the first. If someone's actions help me to some benefit I desire, then I am benefited in any case; but if he intended them so to benefit me because of his general goodwill towards me, I shall reasonably feel a gratitude which I should not feel at all if the benefit was an incidental consequence, unintended or even regretted by him, of some plan of action with a different aim.

These examples are of actions which confer benefits or inflict injuries over and above any conferred or inflicted by the mere manifestation of attitude and intention themselves. We should consider also in how much of our behaviour the benefit or injury resides mainly or entirely in the manifestation of attitude itself. So it is with good manners, and much of what we call kindness, on the one hand; with deliberate rudeness, studied indifference, or insult on the other.

Besides resentment and gratitude, I mentioned just now forgiveness. This is a rather unfashionable subject in moral philosophy at present; but to be forgiven is something we sometimes ask, and forgiving is something we sometimes say we do. To ask to be forgiven is in part to acknowledge that the attitude displayed in our actions was such as might properly be resented and in part to repudiate that attitude for the future (or at least for the immediate future); and to forgive is to accept the repudiation and to forswear the resentment.

We should think of the many different kinds of relationship which we can have with other people—as sharers of a common interest; as members of the same family; as colleagues; as friends; as lovers; as chance parties to an enormous range of transactions and encounters. Then we should think, in each of these connections in turn, and in others, of the kind of importance we attach to the attitudes and intentions towards us of those who stand in these relationships to us, and of the kinds of *reactive* attitudes and feelings to which we ourselves are prone. In general, we demand some degree of goodwill or regard on the part of those who stand in these relationships to us, though the forms we require it to take vary widely in different connections. The range and intensity of our *reactive* attitudes towards goodwill, its absence or its opposite vary no less widely. I have mentioned, specifically, resentment and gratitude; and they are a usefully opposed pair. But, of course, there is a whole continuum of reactive attitude and feeling stretching on both sides of these and—the most comfortable area—in between them.

The object of these commonplaces is to try to keep before our minds something it is easy to forget when we are engaged in philosophy, especially in our cool, contemporary style, viz. what it is actually like to be involved in ordinary inter-personal relationships, ranging from the most intimate to the most casual.

IV

It is one thing to ask about the general causes of these reactive attitudes I have alluded to; it is another to ask about the variations to which they are subject, the particular conditions in which they do or do not seem natural or reasonable or appropriate; and it is a third thing to ask what it would be like, what it *is* like, not to suffer them. I am not much concerned with the first question; but I am with the second; and perhaps even more with the third.

Let us consider, then, occasions for resentment: situations in which one person is offended or injured by the action of another and in which—in the absence of special considerations—the offended person might naturally or normally be expected to feel resentment. Then let us consider what sorts of special considerations might be expected to modify or mollify this feeling or remove it altogether. It needs no saying now how multifarious these considerations are. But, for my purpose, I think they can be roughly divided into two kinds. To the first group belong all those which might give occasion for the employment of such expressions as 'He didn't mean to', 'He hadn't realized', 'He didn't know'; and also all those which might give occasion for the use of the phrase 'He couldn't help it', when this is supported by such phrases as 'He was pushed', 'He had to do it', 'It was the only way', 'They left him no alternative', etc. Obviously these various pleas, and the kinds of situations in which they would be appropriate, differ from each other in striking and important ways. But for my present purpose they have something still more important in common. None of them invites us to suspend towards the agent, either at the time of his action or in general, our ordinary reactive attitudes. They do not invite us to view the *agent* as one in respect of whom these attitudes are in any way inappropriate. They invite us to view the *injury* as one in respect of which a particular one of these attitudes is inappropriate. They do not invite us to see the *agent* as other than a fully responsible agent. They invite us to see the *injury* as one for which he was not fully, or at all, responsible. They do not suggest that the agent is in any way an inappropriate object of that kind of demand for goodwill or regard which is reflected in our ordinary reactive attitudes. They suggest instead that the fact of injury was not in this case incompatible with that demand's being fulfilled, that the fact of injury was quite consistent with the agent's attitude and intentions being just what we demand they should be.[3] The agent was just ignorant of the injury he was causing, or had lost his balance through being pushed or had reluctantly to cause the injury for reasons which acceptably override his reluctance. The offering of such pleas by the agent and their acceptance by the sufferer is something in no way opposed to, or outside the context of, ordinary interpersonal relationships and the manifestation of ordinary reactive attitudes. Since things go wrong and situations are complicated, it is an essential and integral element in the transactions which are the life of these relationships.

The second group of considerations is very different. I shall take them in two subgroups of which the first is far less important than the second.

3. Perhaps not in every case *just* what we demand they should be, but in any case *not* just what we demand they should not be. For my present purpose these differences do not matter.

In connection with the first subgroup we may think of such statements as 'He wasn't himself', 'He has been under very great strain recently', 'He was acting under post-hypnotic suggestion'; in connection with the second, we may think of 'He's only a child', 'He's a hopeless schizophrenic', 'His mind has been systematically perverted', 'That's purely compulsive behaviour on his part'. Such pleas as these do, as pleas of my first general group do not, invite us to suspend our ordinary reactive attitudes toward the agent, either at the time of his action or all the time. They do not invite us to see the agent's action in a way consistent with the full retention of ordinary interpersonal attitudes and merely inconsistent with one particular attitude. They invite us to view the agent himself in a different light from the light in which we should normally view one who has acted as he has acted. I shall not linger over the first subgroup of cases. Though they perhaps raise, in the short term, questions akin to those raised, in the long term, by the second subgroup, we may dismiss them without considering those questions by taking that admirably suggestive phrase, 'He wasn't himself', with the seriousness that—for all its being logically comic—it deserves. We shall not feel resentment against the man he is for the action done by the man he is not; or at least we shall feel less. We normally have to deal with him under normal stresses; so we shall not feel towards him, when he acts as he does under abnormal stresses, as we should have felt towards him had he acted as he did under normal stresses.

The second and more important subgroup of cases allows that the circumstances were normal, but presents the agent as psychologically abnormal—or as morally undeveloped. The agent was himself; but he is warped or deranged, neurotic or just a child. When we see someone in such a light as this, all our reactive attitudes tend to be profoundly modified. I must deal here in crude dichotomies and ignore the ever-interesting and ever-illuminating varieties of case. What I want to contrast is the attitude (or range of attitudes) of involvement or participation in a human relationship, on the one hand, and what might be called the objective attitude (or range of attitudes) to another human being, on the other. Even in the same situation, I must add, they are not altogether *exclusive* of each other; but they are, profoundly, *opposed* to each other. To adopt the objective attitude to another human being is to see him, perhaps, as an object of social policy; as a subject for what, in a wide range of sense, might be called treatment; as something certainly to be taken account, perhaps precautionary account, of; to be managed or handled or cured or trained; perhaps simply to be avoided, though *this* gerundive is not peculiar to cases of objectivity of attitude. The objective attitude may be emotionally toned in many ways, but not in all ways: it may include repulsion or fear, it may include pity or even love, though not all kinds of love. But it cannot include the range of reactive feelings and attitudes which belong to involvement or participation with others in inter-personal human relationships; it cannot include resentment, gratitude, forgiveness, anger, or the sort of love which two adults can sometimes be said to feel reciprocally, for each other. If your attitude towards someone is wholly objective, then though you may fight him, you cannot quarrel with him, and though you may talk to him, even negotiate with him, you cannot reason with him. You can at most pretend to quarrel, or to reason, with him.

Seeing someone, then, as warped or deranged or compulsive in behaviour or peculiarly unfortunate in his formative circumstances—seeing someone so tends, at least to some extent, to set him apart from normal participant reactive attitudes on the part of one who sees him, tends to promote, at least in the civilized, objective attitudes. But there is something curious to add to this. The objective attitude is not only something we naturally tend to fall into in cases like these, where participant attitudes are partially or wholly inhibited by abnormalities or by immaturity. It is also something which is available as a resource in other cases too. We look with an objective eye on the compulsive behaviour of the neurotic or the tiresome behaviour of a very young child, thinking in terms of treatment or training. But we *can* sometimes look with something like the same eye on the behaviour of the normal and the mature. We *have* this resource and can sometimes use it: as a refuge, say, from the strains of involvement; or as an aid to policy; or simply out of intellectual curiosity. Being human, we cannot, in the normal case, do this for long, or altogether. If the strains of involvement, say, continue to be too great, then we have to do something else—like severing a relationship. But what is above all interesting is the tension there is, in us, between the participant attitude and the objective attitude. One is tempted to say: between our humanity and our intelligence. But to say this would be to distort both notions.

What I have called the participant reactive attitudes are essentially natural human reactions to the good or ill will or indifference of others towards us, as displayed in *their* attitudes and actions. The question we have to ask is: What effect would, or should, the acceptance of the truth of a general thesis of determinism have upon these reactive attitudes? More specifically, would, or should, the acceptance of the truth of the thesis lead to the decay or the repudiation of all such attitudes? Would, or should, it mean the end of gratitude, resentment, and forgiveness; of all reciprocated adult loves; of all the essentially *personal* antagonisms?

But how can I answer, or even pose, this question without knowing *exactly* what the thesis of determinism is? Well, there is one thing we do know: that if there is a coherent thesis of determinism, then there must be a sense of 'determined' such that, if that thesis is true, then all behaviour whatever is determined in that sense. Remembering this, we can consider at least what possibilities lie formally open; and then perhaps we shall see that the question can be answered *without* knowing exactly what the thesis of determinism is. We can consider what possibilities lie open because we have already before us an account of the ways in which particular reactive attitudes, or reactive attitudes in general, may be, and, sometimes, we judge, should be, inhibited. Thus I considered earlier a group of considerations which tend to inhibit, and, we judge, should inhibit, resentment, in particular cases of an agent causing an injury, without inhibiting reactive attitudes in general towards that agent. Obviously this group of considerations cannot strictly bear upon our question; for that question concerns reactive attitudes in general. But resentment has a particular interest; so it is worth adding that it has never been claimed as a consequence of the truth of determinism that one or another of *these* considerations was operative in every case of an injury being caused by an agent; that it would follow from the truth of determinism that anyone who caused an injury *either* was quite simply ignorant of causing it *or* had acceptably overriding reasons for acquiescing reluctantly in causing it *or* . . . , etc. The prevalence of this happy state of affairs would not be a consequence of the reign of universal determinism, but of the reign of universal goodwill. We cannot, then, find here the possibility of an affirmative answer to our question, even for the particular case of resentment.

Next, I remarked that the participant attitude, and the personal reactive attitudes in general, tend to give place, and, it is judged by the civilized, should give place, to objective attitudes, just in so far as the agent is seen as excluded from ordinary adult human relationships by deep-rooted psychological abnormality—or simply by being a child. But it cannot be a consequence of any thesis which is not itself self-contradictory that abnormality is the universal condition.

Now this dismissal might seem altogether too facile; and so, in a sense, it is. But whatever is too quickly dismissed in this dismissal is allowed for in the only possible form of affirmative answer that remains. We can sometimes, and in part, I have remarked, look on the normal (those we rate as 'normal') in the objective way in which we have learned to look on certain classified cases of abnormality. And our question reduces to this: could, or should the acceptance of the determinist thesis lead us always to look on everyone exclusively in this way? For this is the only condition worth considering under which the acceptance of determinism could lead to the decay or repudiation of participant reactive attitudes.

It does not seem to be self-contradictory to suppose that this might happen. So I suppose we must say that it is not absolutely inconceivable that it should happen. But I am strongly inclined to think that it is, for us as we are, practically inconceivable. The human commitment to participation in ordinary interpersonal relationships is, I think, too thoroughgoing and deeply rooted for us to take seriously the thought that a general theoretical conviction might so change our world that, in it, there were no longer any such things as inter-personal relationships as we normally understand them; and being involved in inter-personal relationships as we normally understand them precisely is being exposed to the range of reactive attitudes and feelings that is in question.

This, then, is a part of the reply to our question. A sustained objectivity of inter-personal attitude, and the human isolation which that would entail, does not seem to be something of which human beings would be capable, even if some general truth were a theoretical ground for it. But this is not all. There is a further point, implicit in the foregoing, which must be made explicit. Exceptionally, I have said, we can have direct dealings with human beings without any degree of personal involvement, treating them simply as creatures to be handled in our own interests, or our side's, or society's—or even theirs. In the extreme case of the mentally deranged, it is easy to see the connection between the possibility of a wholly objective attitude and the impossibility of what we understand by ordinary inter-personal relationships. Given this latter impossibility, no other civilized attitude is available than that of viewing the deranged person simply as something to be understood and controlled in the most desirable fashion. To view him as outside the reach of personal relationships is already, for the civilized, to view him in this way. For reasons of policy or self-protection we may have occasion, perhaps temporary, to adopt a fundamentally similar attitude to a 'normal' human being; to concentrate, that is, on understanding 'how he works', with a view to determining our policy accordingly or to finding in that very understanding a relief from the strains of involvement. Now it is certainly true that in the case of the abnormal, though not in the case of the normal, our adoption of the objective attitude is a consequence of our viewing the agent as *incapacitated* in some or all respects for ordinary inter-personal relationships. He is thus incapacitated, perhaps, by the fact that his picture of reality is pure fantasy, that he does not, in a sense, live in the real world at all; or by the fact that his behaviour is, in part, an unrealistic acting out of unconscious purposes; or by the fact that he is an idiot, or a moral idiot. But there is something else which, *because* this is true, is equally certainly *not* true. And that is that there is a sense of 'determined' such that (1) if determinism is true, all behaviour is determined in this sense, and (2) determinism might be true, i.e., it is not inconsistent with the facts as we know them to suppose that all behaviour might be determined in this sense, and (3) our adoption of the objective attitude towards the abnormal is the result of prior embracing of the belief that the behaviour, or the relevant stretch of behaviour, of the human being in question *is* determined in this sense. Neither in the case of the normal, then, nor in the case of the abnormal is it true that, when we adopt an objective attitude, we do so *because* we hold such a belief. So my answer has two parts. The first is that we cannot, as we are, seriously envisage ourselves adopting a thoroughgoing objectivity of attitude to others as a result of theoretical conviction of the truth of determinism; and the second is that when we do in fact adopt such an attitude in a particular case, our doing so is not the consequence of a theoretical conviction which might be expressed as 'Determinism in this case', but is a consequence of our abandoning, for different reasons in different cases, the ordinary inter-personal attitudes.

It might be said that all this leaves the real question unanswered, and that we cannot hope to answer it without knowing exactly what the thesis of determinism is. For the real question is not a question about what we actually do, or why we do it. It is not even a question about what we would *in fact* do if a certain theoretical conviction gained general acceptance. It is a question about what it would be *rational* to do if determinism were true, a question about the rational justification of ordinary inter-personal attitudes in general. To this I shall reply, first, that such a question could seem real only to one who had utterly failed to grasp the purport of the preceding answer, the fact of our natural human commitment to ordinary inter-personal attitudes. This commitment is part of the general framework of human life, not something that can come up for review as particular cases can come up for review within this general framework. And I shall reply, second, that if we could imagine what we cannot have, viz. a choice in this matter, then we could choose rationally only in the light of an assessment of the gains and losses to human life, its enrichment or impoverishment; and the truth or falsity of a general thesis of determinism would not bear on the rationality of *this* choice.[4]

4. The question, then, of the connection between rationality and the adoption of

V

The point of this discussion of the reactive attitudes in their relation—or lack of it—to the thesis of determinism was to bring us, if possible, nearer to a position of compromise in a more usual area of debate. We are not now to discuss reactive attitudes which are essentially those of offended parties or beneficiaries. We are to discuss reactive attitudes which are essentially not those, or only incidentally are those, of offended parties or beneficiaries, but are nevertheless, I shall claim, kindred attitudes to those I have discussed. I put resentment in the centre of the previous discussion. I shall put moral indignation—or, more weakly, moral disapprobation—in the centre of this one.

The reactive attitudes I have so far discussed are essentially reactions to the quality of others' wills towards us, as manifested in their behaviour: to their good or ill will or indifference or lack of concern. Thus resentment, or what I have called resentment, is a reaction to injury or indifference. The reactive attitudes I have now to discuss might be described as the sympathetic or vicarious or impersonal or disinterested or generalized analogues of the reactive attitudes I have already discussed. They are reactions to the qualities of others' wills, not towards ourselves, but towards others. Because of this impersonal or vicarious character, we give them different names. Thus one who experiences the vicarious analogue of resentment is said to be indignant or disapproving, or morally indignant or disapproving. What we have here is, as it were, resentment on behalf of another, where one's own interest and dignity are not involved; and it is this impersonal or vicarious character of the attitude, added to its others, which entitle it to the qualification 'moral'. Both my description of, and my name for, these attitudes are, in one important respect, a little misleading. It is not that these attitudes are essentially vicarious—one can feel indignation on one's own account—but that they are essentially capable of being vicarious. But I shall retain the name for the sake of is suggestive-

---

the objective attitude to others is misposed when it is made to seem dependent on the issue of determinism. But there is another question which should be raised, if only to distinguish it from the misposed question. Quite apart from the issue of determinism might it not be said that we should be nearer to being purely rational creatures in proportion as our relation to others was in fact dominated by the objective attitude? I think this might be said; only it would have to be added, once more, that if such a choice were possible, it would not necessarily be rational to choose to be more purely rational than we are.

ness; and I hope that what is misleading about it will be corrected in what follows.

The personal reactive attitudes rest on, and reflect, an expectation of, and demand for, the manifestation of a certain degree of goodwill or regard on the part of other human beings towards ourselves; or at least on the expectation of, and demand for, an absence of the manifestation of active ill will or indifferent disregard. (What will, in particular cases, *count* as manifestations of good or ill will or disregard will vary in accordance with the particular relationship in which we stand to another human being.) The generalized or vicarious analogues of the personal reactive attitudes rest on, and reflect, exactly the same expectation or demand in a generalized form; they rest on, or reflect, that is, the demand for the manifestation of a reasonable degree of goodwill or regard, on the part of others, not simply towards oneself, but towards all those on whose behalf moral indignation may be felt, i.e., as we now think, towards all men. The generalized and nongeneralized forms of demand, and the vicarious and personal reactive attitudes which rest upon, and reflect, them are connected not merely logically. They are connected humanly; and not merely with each other. They are connected also with yet another set of attitudes which I must mention now in order to complete the picture. I have considered from two points of view the demands we make on others and our reactions to their possibly injurious actions. These were the points of view of one whose interest was directly involved (who suffers, say, the injury) and of others whose interest was not directly involved (who do not themselves suffer the injury). Thus I have spoken of personal reactive attitudes in the first connection and of their vicarious analogues in the second. But the picture is not complete unless we consider also the correlates of these attitudes on the part of those on whom the demands are made, on the part of the agents. Just as there are personal and vicarious reactive attitudes associated with demands on others for oneself and demands on others for others, so there are self-reactive attitudes associated with demands on oneself for others. And here we have to mention such phenomena as feeling bound or obliged (the 'sense of obligation'); feeling compunction; feeling guilty or remorseful or at least responsible; and the more complicated phenomenon of shame.

All these three types of attitude are humanly connected. One who manifested the personal reactive attitudes in a high degree but showed no inclination at all to their vicarious analogues would appear as an abnormal case of moral egocentricity, as a kind of moral solipsist. Let him be supposed fully to acknowledge the claims to regard that others had on him, to be susceptible of the whole range of self-reactive attitudes. He would then see himself as unique both as one (*the* one) who had a general claim on human regard and as one (*the* one) on whom human beings in general had such a claim. This would be a kind of moral solipsism. But it is barely more than a conceptual possibility; if it is that. In general, though within varying limits, we demand of others for others, as well as of ourselves for others, something of the regard which we demand of others for ourselves. Can we imagine, besides that of the moral solipsist, any other case of one or two of these three types of attitude being fully developed, but quite unaccompanied by any trace, however slight, of the remaining two or one? If we can, then we imagine something far below or far above the level of our common humanity—a moral idiot or a saint. For all these types of attitude alike have common roots in our human nature and our membership of human communities.

Now, as of the personal reactive attitudes, so of their vicarious analogues, we must ask in what ways, and by what considerations, they tend to be inhibited. Both types of attitude involve, or express, a certain sort of demand for inter-personal regard. The fact of injury constitutes a prima-facie appearance of this demand's being flouted or unfulfilled. We saw, in the case of resentment, how one class of considerations may show this appearance to be mere appearance, and hence inhibit resentment, *without* inhibiting, or displacing, the sort of demand of which resentment can be an expression, without in any way tending to make us suspend our ordinary inter-personal attitudes to the agent. Considerations of this class operate in just the same way, for just the same reasons, in connection with moral disapprobation or indignation; they inhibit indignation without in any way inhibiting the sort of demand on the agent of which indignation can be an expression, the range of attitudes towards him to which it belongs. But in this connection we may express the facts with a new emphasis. We may say, stressing the moral, the generalized aspect of the demand, considerations of this group have no tendency to make us see the agent as other than a morally responsible agent; they simply make us see the injury as one for which he was not morally responsible. The offering and acceptance of such exculpatory pleas as are here in question in no way detract in our eyes from the agent's status as a term of moral relationships. On the contrary, since things go wrong and situations are complicated, it is an essential part of the life of such relationships.

But suppose we see the agent in a different light: as one whose picture of the world is an insane delusion; or as one whose behaviour, or a part of whose behaviour, is unintelligible to us, perhaps even to him, in terms of conscious purposes, and intelligible only in terms of unconscious purposes; or even, perhaps, as one wholly impervious to the self-reactive attitudes I spoke of, wholly lacking, as we say, in moral sense. Seeing an agent in such a light as this tends, I said, to inhibit resentment in a wholly different way. It tends to inhibit resentment because it tends to inhibit ordinary inter-personal attitudes in general, and the kind of demand and expectation which those attitudes involve; and tends to promote instead the purely objective view of the agent as one posing problems simply of intellectual understanding, management, treatment, and control. Again the parallel holds for those generalized or moral attitudes towards the agent which we are now concerned with. The same abnormal light which shows the agent to us as one in respect of whom the personal attitudes, the personal demand, are to be suspended, shows him to us also as one in respect of whom the impersonal attitudes, the generalized demand, are to be suspended. Only, abstracting now from direct personal interest, we may express the facts with a new emphasis. We may say: to the extent to which the agent is seen in this light, he is not seen as one on whom demands and expectations lie in that particular way in which we think of them as lying when we speak of moral obligation; he is not, to that extent, seen as a morally responsible agent, as a term of moral relationships, as a member of the moral community.

I remarked also that the suspension of ordinary inter-personal attitudes and the cultivation of a purely objective view is sometimes possible even when we have no such reasons for it as I have just mentioned. Is this possible also in the case of the moral reactive attitudes? I think so; and perhaps it is easier. But the motives for a total suspension of moral reactive attitudes are fewer, and perhaps weaker; fewer, because only where there is antecedent personal involvement can there be the motive of seeking refuge from the strains of such involvement; perhaps weaker, because the tension between objectivity of view and the moral reactive attitudes is perhaps less than the tension between objectivity of view and the personal reactive attitudes, so that we can in the case of the moral reactive attitudes more easily secure the speculative or political gains of objectivity of view by a kind of setting on one side, rather than a total suspension, of those attitudes.

These last remarks are uncertain; but also, for the present purpose, unimportant. What concerns us now is to inquire, as previously in connection with the personal reactive attitudes, what relevance any general thesis of determinism might have to their vicarious analogues. The answers once more are parallel; though I shall take them in a slightly different order. First, we must note, as before, that when the suspension of such an attitude or such attitudes occurs in a particular case, it is *never* the consequence of the belief that the piece of behaviour in question was determined in a sense such that all behaviour *might be,* and, if determinism is true, all behaviour *is,* determined in that sense. For it is not a consequence of any general thesis of determinism which might be true that nobody knows what he's doing or that everybody's behaviour is unintelligible in terms of conscious purposes or that everybody lives in a world of delusion or that nobody has a moral sense, i.e. is susceptible of self-reactive attitudes, etc. In fact no such sense of 'determined' as would be required for a general thesis of determinism is ever relevant to our actual suspensions of moral reactive attitudes. Second, suppose it granted, as I have already argued, that we cannot take seriously the thought that theoretical conviction of such a general thesis would lead to the total decay of the personal reactive attitudes. Can we then take seriously the thought that such a conviction—a conviction, after all, that many have held or said they held—would nevertheless lead to the total decay or repudiation of the vicarious analogues of these attitudes? I think that the change in our social world which would leave us exposed to the personal reactive attitudes but not to all their vicarious analogues, the generalization of abnormal egocentricity which this would entail, is perhaps even harder for us to envisage as a real possibility than the decay of both kinds of attitude together. Though there are some necessary and some contingent differences between the ways and cases in which these two kinds of attitudes operate or are inhibited in their operation, yet, as general human capacities or pronenesses, they stand or lapse together. Finally, to the further question whether it would not be *rational,* given a general theoretical conviction of the truth of determinism, so to change our world that in it all these attitudes were wholly suspended. I must answer, as before, that one who presses this question has wholly failed to grasp the import of the preceding answer, the nature of the human commitment that is here involved: it is *useless* to ask whether it would not be rational for us to do what it is not in our nature to (be able to) do. To this I must add, as before, that if there were, say, for a moment open to us the possibility of such a godlike choice, the rationality of making or refusing it would be determined by quite other considerations than the truth or falsity of the general theoretical doctrine in question. The latter would be simply irrelevant; and this becomes ironically clear when we remember that for those convinced that the truth of determinism nevertheless really would make the one choice rational, there has always been the insuperable difficulty of explaining in intelligible terms how its falsity would make the opposite choice rational.

I am aware that in presenting the arguments as I have done, neglecting the ever-interesting varieties of case, I have presented nothing more than a schema, using sometimes a crude opposition of phrase where we have a great intricacy of phenomena. In particular the simple opposition of objective attitudes on the one hand and the various contrasted attitudes which I have opposed to them must seem as grossly crude as it is central. Let me pause to mitigate this crudity a little, and also to strengthen one of my central contentions, by mentioning some things which straddle these contrasted kinds of attitude. Thus parents and others concerned with the care and upbringing of young children cannot have to their charges either kind of attitude in a pure or unqualified form. They are dealing with creatures who are potentially and increasingly capable both of holding, and being objects of, the full range of human and moral attitudes, but are not yet truly capable of either. The treatment of such creatures must therefore represent a kind of compromise, constantly shifting in one direction, between objectivity of attitude and developed human attitudes. Rehearsals insensibly modulate towards true performances. The punishment of a child is both like and unlike the punishment of an adult. Suppose we try to relate this progressive emergence of the child as a responsible being, as an object of non-objective attitudes, to that sense of 'determined' in which, if determinism is a possibly true thesis, all behaviour *may* be determined, and in which, if it is a true thesis, all behaviour *is* determined. What bearing *could* such a sense of 'determined' have upon the progressive modification of attitudes towards the child? Would it not be grotesque to think of the development of the child as a progressive or patchy emergence from an area in which its behaviour is in this sense determined into an area in which it isn't? Whatever sense of 'determined' is required for stating the thesis of determinism, it can scarcely be such as to allow of compromise, borderline-style answers to the question. 'Is this bit of behaviour determined or isn't it?' But in this matter of young children, it is essentially a borderline, penumbral area that we move in. Again, consider—a very different matter—the strain in the attitude of a psychoanalyst to his patient. *His* objectivity of attitude, *his* suspension of ordinary moral reactive attitudes, is profoundly modified by the fact that the aim of the enterprise is to make such suspension unnecessary or less necessary. Here we may and do naturally speak of restoring the agent's freedom. But here the restoring of freedom means bringing it about that the agent's behaviour shall be intelligible in terms of conscious purposes rather than in terms only of unconscious purposes. *This* is the object of the enterprise; and it is in so far as *this* object is attained that the suspension, or half-suspension, of ordinary moral attitudes is deemed no longer necessary or appropriate. And in this we see once again the *irrelevance* of that concept of 'being determined' which must be the central concept of determinism. For we cannot both agree that this object is attainable and that its attainment has this consequence and yet hold (1) that neurotic behaviour is determined in a sense in which, it may be, all behaviour is determined, and (2) that it is because neurotic behaviour is determined in this sense that objective attitudes are deemed appropriate to neurotic behaviour. Not, at least, without accusing ourselves of incoherence in our attitude to psychoanalytic treatment.

VI

And now we can try to fill in the lacuna which the pessimist finds in the optimist's account of the concept of moral responsibility, and of the bases of moral condemnation and punishment; and to fill it in from the facts as we know them. For, as I have already remarked, when the pessimist himself seeks to fill it in, he rushes beyond the facts as we know them and proclaims that it cannot be filled in at all unless determinism is false.

Yet a partial sense of the facts as we know them is certainly present to the pessimist's mind. When his opponent, the optimist, undertakes to show that the truth of determinism would not shake the foundations of the concept of moral responsibility and of the practices of moral condemnation and punishment, he typically refers, in a more or less elaborated way, to the efficacy of these practices in regulating behaviour in socially desirable ways. These practices are represented solely as instruments of policy, as methods of individual treatment and social control. The pessimist recoils from this picture; and in his recoil there is, typically, an element of emotional shock. He is apt to say, among much else, that the humanity of the offender himself is offended by *this* picture of his condemnation and punishment.

The reasons for this recoil—the explanation of the sense of an emotional, as well as a conceptual, shock—we have already before us. The picture painted by the optimists is painted in a style appropriate to a situation envisaged as wholly dominated by objectivity of attitude. The only operative notions invoked in this picture are such as those of policy, treatment, control. But a thoroughgoing objectivity of attitude, excluding as it does the moral reactive attitudes, excludes at the same time essential elements in the concepts of *moral* condemnation and *moral* responsibility. This is the reason for the conceptual shock. The deeper emotional shock is a reaction, not simply to an inadequate conceptual analysis, but to the suggestion of a change in our world. I have remarked that it is possible to cultivate an exclusive objectivity of attitude in some cases, and for some reasons, where the object of the attitude is not set aside from developed inter-personal and moral attitudes by immaturity or abnormality. And the suggestion which seems to be contained in the optimist's account is that such an attitude should be universally adopted to all offenders. This is shocking enough in the pessimist's eyes. But, sharpened by shock, his eyes see further. It would be hard to make *this* division in our natures. If to all offenders, then to all mankind. Moreover, to whom could this recommendation be, in any real sense, addressed? Only to the powerful, the authorities. So abysses seem to open.[5]

But we will confine our attention to the case of the offenders. The concepts we are concerned with are those of responsibility and guilt, qualified as 'moral', on the one hand—together with that of membership of a moral community; of demand, indignation, disapprobation and condemnation, qualified as 'moral', on the other hand—together with that of punishment. Indignation, disapprobation, like resentment, tend to inhibit or at least to limit our goodwill towards the object of these attitudes, tend to promote an at least partial and temporary withdrawal of goodwill; they do so in proportion as they are strong; and their strength is in general proportioned to what is felt to be the magnitude of the injury and to the degree to which the agent's will is identified with, or indifferent to, it. (These, of course, are not contingent connections.) But these attitudes of disapprobation and indignation are precisely the correlates of the moral demand in the case where the demand is felt to be disregarded. The making of the demand *is* the proneness to such attitudes. The holding of them does not, as the holding of objective attitudes does, involve as a part of itself viewing their object other than as a member of the moral community. The partial withdrawal of goodwill which *these* attitudes entail, the modification *they* entail of the general demand that another should, if possible, be spared suffering, is, rather, the consequence of *continuing* to view him as a member of the moral community; only as one who has offended against its demands. So the preparedness to acquiesce in that

5. See J.D. Mabbott's 'Freewill and Punishment', in *Contemporary British Philosophy,* 3rd ser. (London: Allen & Unwin, 1956).

infliction of suffering on the offender which is an essential part of punishment is all of a piece with this whole range of attitudes of which I have been speaking. It is not only moral reactive attitudes towards the offender which are in question here. We must mention also the self-reactive attitudes of offenders themselves. Just as the other-reactive attitudes are associated with a readiness to acquiesce in the infliction of suffering on an offender, within the 'institution' of punishment, so the self-reactive attitudes are associated with a readiness on the part of the offender to acquiesce in such infliction *without* developing the reactions (e.g. of resentment) which he would normally develop to the infliction of injury upon him; i.e. with a readiness, as we say, to accept punishment[6] as 'his due' or as 'just'.

I am not in the least suggesting that these readinesses to acquiesce, either on the part of the offender himself or on the part of others, are always or commonly accompanied or preceded by indignant boilings or remorseful pangs; only that we have here a continuum of attitudes and feelings to which these readinesses to acquiesce themselves belong. Nor am I in the least suggesting that it belongs to this continuum of attitudes that we should be ready to acquiesce in the infliction of injury on offenders in a fashion which we saw to be quite indiscriminate or in accordance with procedures which we know to be wholly useless. On the contrary, savage or civilized, we have some belief in the utility of practices of condemnation and punishment. But the social utility of these practices, on which the optimist lays such exclusive stress, is not what is now in question. What is in question is the pessimist's justified sense that to speak in terms of social utility alone is to leave out something vital in our conception of these practices. The vital thing can be restored by attending to that complicated web of attitudes and feelings which form an essential part of the moral life as we know it, and which are quite opposed to objectivity of attitude. Only by attending to this range of attitudes can we recover from the facts as we know them a sense of what we mean, i.e., of *all* we mean, when, speaking the language of morals, we speak of desert, responsibility, guilt, condemnation, and justice. But we *do* recover it from the facts as we know them. We do not have to go beyond them. Because the optimist neglects or misconstrues these attitudes, the pessimist rightly claims to find a lacuna in his account. We can fill the lacuna for him. But in return we must demand of the pessimist a surrender of his metaphysics.

Optimist and pessimist misconstrue the facts in very different styles.

6. Of course not *any* punishment for *anything* deemed an offence.

But in a profound sense there is something in common to their misunderstandings. Both seek, in different ways, to overintellectualize the facts. Inside the general structure or web of human attitudes and feelings of which I have been speaking, there is endless room for modification, redirection, criticism, and justification. But questions of justification are internal to the structure or relate to modifications internal to it. The existence of the general framework of attitudes itself is something we are given with the fact of human society. As a whole, it neither calls for, nor permits, an external 'rational' justification. Pessimist and optimist alike show themselves, in different ways, unable to accept this.[7] The optimist's style of overintellectualizing the facts is that of a characteristically incomplete empiricism, a one-eyed utilitarianism. He seeks to find an adequate basis for certain social practices in calculated consequences, and loses sight (perhaps wishes to lose sight) of the human attitudes of which these practices are, in part, the expression. The pessimist does not lose sight of these attitudes, but is unable to accept the fact that it is just these attitudes themselves which fill the gap in the optimist's account. Because of this, he thinks the gap can be filled only if some general metaphysical proposition is repeatedly verified, verified in all cases where it is appropriate to attribute moral responsibility. This proposition he finds it as difficult to state coherently and with intelligible relevance as its determinist contradictory. Even when a formula has been found ('contracausal freedom' or something of the kind) there still seems to remain a gap between its applicability in particular cases and its supposed moral consequences. Sometimes he plugs this gap with an intuition of fittingness—a pitiful intellectualist trinket for a philosopher to wear as a charm against the recognition of his own humanity.

Even the moral sceptic is not immune from his own form of the wish to overintellectualize such notions as those of moral responsibility, guilt, and blame. He sees that the optimist's account is inadequate and the pessimist's libertarian alternative inane; and finds no resource except to declare that the notions in question are inherently confused, that 'blame is metaphysical'. But the metaphysics was in the eye of the metaphysician. It is a

7. Compare the question of the justification of induction. The human commitment to inductive belief-formation is original, natural, non-rational (not *ir*rational), in no way something we choose or could give up. Yet rational criticism and reflection can refine standards and their application, supply 'rules for judging of cause and effect'. Ever since the facts were made clear by Hume, people have been resisting acceptance of them.

pity that talk of the moral sentiments has fallen out of favour. The phrase would be quite a good name for that network of human attitudes in acknowledging the character and place of which we find, I suggest, the only possibility of reconciling these disputants to each other and the facts.

There are, at present, factors which add, in a slightly paradoxical way, to the difficulty of making this acknowledgment. These human attitudes themselves, in their development and in the variety of their manifestations, have to an increasing extent become objects of study in the social and psychological sciences; and this growth of human selfconsciousness, which we might expect to reduce the difficulty of acceptance, in fact increases it in several ways. One factor of comparatively minor importance is an increased historical and anthropological awareness of the great variety of forms which these human attitudes may take at different times and in different cultures. This makes one rightly chary of claiming as essential features of the concept of morality in general, forms of these attitudes which may have a local and temporary prominence. No doubt to some extent my own descriptions of human attitudes have reflected local and temporary features of our own culture. But an awareness of variety of forms should not prevent us from acknowledging also that in the absence of *any* forms of these attitudes it is doubtful whether we should have anything that *we* could find intelligible as a system of human relationships, as human society. A quite different factor of greater importance is that psychological studies have made us rightly mistrustful of many particular manifestations of the attitudes I have spoken of. They are a prime realm of self-deception, of the ambiguous and the shady, of guilt-transference, unconscious sadism and the rest. But it is an exaggerated horror, itself suspect, which would make us unable to acknowledge the facts because of the seamy side of the facts. Finally, perhaps the most important factor of all is the prestige of these theoretical studies themselves. That prestige is great, and is apt to make us forget that in philosophy, though it also is a theoretical study, we have to take account of the facts in *all* their bearings; we are not to suppose that we are required, or permitted, as philosophers, to regard ourselves, as human beings, as detached from the attitudes which, as scientists, we study with detachment. This is in no way to deny the possibility and desirability of redirection and modification of our human attitudes in the light of these studies. But we may reasonably think it unlikely that our progressively greater understanding of certain aspects of ourselves will lead to the total disappearance of those aspects. Perhaps it is not inconceivable that it should; and perhaps, then, the dreams of some philosophers will be realized.

If we sufficiently, that is *radically*, modify the view of the optimist, his view is the right one. It is far from wrong to emphasize the efficacy of all those practices which express or manifest our moral attitudes, in regulating behaviour in ways considered desirable; or to add that when certain of our beliefs about the efficacy of some of these practices turns out to be false, then we may have good reason for dropping or modifying those practices. What *is* wrong is to forget that these practices, and their reception, the reactions to them, really *are* expressions of our moral attitudes and not merely devices we calculatingly employ for regulative purposes. Our practices do not merely exploit our natures, they express them. Indeed the very understanding of the kind of efficacy these expressions of our attitudes have turns on our remembering this. When we do remember this, and modify the optimist's position accordingly, we simultaneously correct its conceptual deficiencies and ward off the dangers it seems to entail, without recourse to the obscure and panicky metaphysics of libertarianism.

14

Roderick Chisholm, "Human Freedom and the Self"

Roderick Chisholm (1916–1999) was a philosophy professor at Brown University for many years. In this lecture, Chisholm develops a libertarian agent-causal theory of action, according to which freedom of the sort required for moral responsibility is accounted for by the existence of agents who possess a causal power to make choices without being determined to do so. In this view, it is crucial that the kind of causation involved in an agent's making a free choice is not reducible to causation between events but is rather irreducibly an instance of a substance causing a choice. When such an agent acts freely, she can be inclined but not causally determined to act by factors such as reasons, desires, and beliefs.

> 'A staff moves a stone, and is moved by a hand, which is moved by a man.' Aristotle, *Physics*, 256a.

1. The metaphysical problem of human freedom might be summarized in the following way: Human beings are responsible agents; but this fact appears to conflict with a deterministic view of human action (the view that every event that is involved in an act is caused by some other event); and it *also* appears to conflict with an indeterministic view of human action (the view that the act, or some event that is essential to the act, is not caused at all.) To solve the problem, I believe, we must make somewhat far-reaching assumptions about the self or the agent—about the man who performs the act.

Perhaps it is needless to remark that, in all likelihood, it is impossible to say anything significant about this ancient problem that has not been said before.[1]

2. Let us consider some deed, or misdeed, that may be attributed to a responsible agent: one man, say, shot another. If the man *was* responsible for what he did, then, I would urge, what was to happen at the time of the shooting was something that was entirely up to the man himself. There was a moment at which it was true, both that he could have fired the shot and also that he could have refrained from firing it. And if this is so, then, even though he did fire it, he could have done something else instead. (He didn't find himself firing the shot 'against his will', as we say.) I think we can say, more generally, then, that if a man is responsible for a certain event or a certain state of affairs (in our example, the shooting of another man), then that event or state of affairs was brought about by some act of his, and the act was something that was in his power either to perform or not to perform.

But now if the act which he *did* perform was an act that was also in his power *not* to perform, then it could not have been caused or determined by any event that was not itself within his power either to bring about or not to bring about. For example, if what we say he did was really something that was brought about by a second man, one who forced his hand upon the trigger, say, or who, by means of hypnosis, compelled him to perform the act, then since the act was caused by the *second* man it was nothing that was within the power of the *first* man to prevent. And precisely the same thing is true, I think, if instead of referring to a second man who compelled the first one, we speak instead of the *desires* and *beliefs* which the first man happens to have had. For if what we say he did was really something that was brought about by his own beliefs and desires, if these beliefs and desires in the particular situation in which he happened to have found himself caused him to do just what it was that we say he did do, then, since *they* caused it, *he* was unable to do anything other than just what it was that he did do. It makes no difference whether the cause of the deed was internal or external; if the cause was some state or event for

1. The general position to be presented here is suggested in the following writings, among others: Aristotle, *Eudemian Ethics,* bk. ii ch. 6; *Nicomachean Ethics,* bk. iii, ch. 1–5; Thomas Reid, *Essays on the Active Powers of Man;* C. A. Campbell, 'Is "Free Will" a Pseudo-Problem?' *Mind,* 1951, 441–65; Roderick M. Chisholm, 'Responsibility and Avoidability', and Richard Taylor, 'Determination and the Theory of Agency," in *Determination and Freedom in the Age of Modern Science,* ed. Sidney Hook (New York, 1958).

which the man himself was not responsible, then he was not responsible for what we have been mistakenly calling his act. If a flood caused the poorly constructed dam to break, then, given the flood and the constitution of the dam, the break, we may say, had to occur and nothing could have happened in its place. And if the flood of desire caused the weak-willed man to give in, then he, too, had to do just what it was that he did do and he was no more responsible than was the dam for the results that followed. (It is true, of course, that if the man is responsible for the beliefs and desires that he happens to have, then he may also be responsible for the things they lead him to do. But the question now becomes: *is* he responsible for the beliefs and desires he happens to have? If he is, then there was a time when they were within his power either to acquire or not to acquire, and we are left, therefore, with our general point.)

One may object: But surely if there were such a thing as a man who is really *good,* then he would be responsible for things that he would do; yet, he would be unable to do anything other than just what it is that he does do, since, being good, he will always choose to do what is best. The answer, I think, is suggested by a comment that Thomas Reid makes upon an ancient author. The author had said of Cato, 'He was good because he could not be otherwise', and Reid observes: 'This saying, if understood literally and strictly, is not the praise of Cato, but of his constitution, which was no more the work of Cato than his existence'.[2] If Cato was himself responsible for the good things that he did, then Cato, as Reid suggests, was such that, although he had the power to do what was not good, he exercised his power only for that which was good.

All of this, if it is true, may give a certain amount of comfort to those who are tender-minded. But we should remind them that it also conflicts with a familiar view about the nature of God—with the view that St. Thomas Aquinas expresses by saying that 'every movement both of the will and of nature proceeds from God as the Prime Mover'.[3] If the act of the sinner *did* proceed from God as the Prime Mover, then God was in the position of the second agent we just discussed—the man who forced the trigger finger, or the hypnotist—and the sinner, so-called, was *not* responsible for what he did. (This may be a bold assertion, in view of the history of western theology, but I must say that I have never encountered a single good reason for denying it.)

2. Thomas Reid, *Essays on the Active Powers of Man,* essay iv, ch. 4 (*Works,* 600).

3. *Summa Theologica,* First Part of the Second Part, qu vi ('On the Voluntary and Involuntary').

There is one standard objection to all of this and we should consider it briefly.

3. The objection takes the form of a stratagem—one designed to show that determinism (and divine providence) is consistent with human responsibility. The stratagem is one that was used by Jonathan Edwards and by many philosophers in the present century, most notably, G. E. Moore.[4]

One proceeds as follows: The expression

(a) He could have done otherwise,

it is argued, means no more nor less than

(b) If he had chosen to do otherwise, then he would have done otherwise.

(In place of 'chosen', one might say 'tried', 'set out', 'decided', 'undertaken', or 'willed'.) The truth of statement (b), it is then pointed out, is consistent with determinism (and with divine providence); for even if all of the man's actions were causally determined, the man could still be such that, *if* he had chosen otherwise, then he would have done otherwise. What the murderers saw, let us suppose, along with his beliefs and desires, *caused* him to fire the shot; yet he was such that *if,* just then, he had chosen or decided *not* to fire the shot, then he would not have fired it. All of this is certainly possible. Similarly, we could say, of the dam, that the flood caused it to break and also that the dam was such that, *if* there had been no flood or any similar pressure, then the dam would have remained intact. And therefore, the argument proceeds, if (b) is consistent with determinism, and if (a) and (b) say the same thing, then (a) is also consistent with determinism; hence we can say that the agent *could* have done otherwise even though he was caused to do what he did do; and therefore determinism and moral responsibility are compatible.

Is the argument sound? The conclusion follows from the premises, but the catch, I think, lies in the first premiss—the one saying that statement (a) tells us no more nor less than what statement (b) tells us. For (b), it would seem, could be true while (a) is false. That is to say, our man might be such that, if he had chosen to do otherwise, then he would have done otherwise, and yet *also* such that he could not have done otherwise. Suppose, after all, that our murderer could not have *chosen,* or could not have *decided,* to do otherwise. Then the fact that he happens also to be a man

4. Jonathan Edwards, *Freedom of the Will* (New Haven, 1957); G. E. Moore, *Ethics* (Home University Library, 1912), ch. 6.

such that, if he had chosen not to shoot he would not have shot, would make no difference. For if he could *not* have chosen *not* to shoot, then he could not have done anything other than just what it was that he did do. In a word: from our statement (b) above ('If he had chosen to do otherwise, then he would have done otherwise'), we cannot make an inference to (a) above ('He could have done otherwise') unless we can *also* assert:

(c) He could have chosen to do otherwise.

And therefore, if we must reject this third statement (c), then, even though we may be justified in asserting (b), we are not justified in asserting (a). If the man could not have chosen to do otherwise, then he would not have done otherwise—*even if* he was such that, if he *had* chosen to do otherwise, then he would have done otherwise.

The stratagem in question, then, seems to me not to work, and I would say, therefore, that the ascription of responsibility conflicts with a deterministic view of action.

4. Perhaps there is less need to argue that the ascription of responsibility also conflicts with an indeterministic view of action—with the view that the act, or some event that is essential to the act, is not caused at all. If the act—the firing of the shot—was not caused at all, if it was fortuitous or capricious, happening so to speak out of the blue, then, presumably, no one—and nothing—was responsible for the act. Our conception of action, therefore, should be neither deterministic nor indeterministic. Is there any other possibility?

5. We must not say that every event involved in the act is caused by some other event; and we must not say that the act is something that is not caused at all. The possibility that remains, therefore, is this: We should say that at least one of the events that are involved in the act is caused, not by any other events, but by something else instead. And this something else can only be the agent—the man. If there is an event that is caused, not by other events, but by the man, then there are some events involved in the act that are not caused by other events. But if the event in question is caused by the man then it *is* caused and we are not committed to saying that there is something involved in the act that is not caused at all.

But this, of course, is a large consequence, implying something of considerable importance about the nature of the agent or the man.

6. If we consider only inanimate natural objects, we may say that causation, if it occurs, is a relation between *events* or *states of affairs*. The dam's breaking was an event that was caused by a set of other events—the dam

being weak, the flood being strong, and so on. But if a man is responsible for a particular deed, then, if what I have said is true, there is some event, or set of events, that is caused, *not* by other events or states of affairs, but by the agent, whatever he may be.

I shall borrow a pair of medieval terms, using them, perhaps, in a way that is slightly different from that for which they were originally intended. I shall say that when one event or state of affairs (or set of events or states of affairs) causes some other event or state of affairs, then we have an instance of *transeunt* causation. And I shall say that when an *agent,* as distinguished from an event, causes an event or state of affairs, then we have an instance of *immanent* causation.

The nature of what is intended by the expression 'immanent causation' may be illustrated by this sentence from Aristotle's *Physics:* 'thus, a staff moves a stone, and is moved by a hand, which is moved by a man.' (VII, 5, 256a, 6–8) If the man was responsible, then we have in this illustration a number of instances of causation—most of them transeunt but at least one of them immanent. What the staff did to the stone was an instance of transeunt causation, and thus we may describe it as a relation between events: 'the motion of the staff caused the motion of the stone.' And similarly for what the hand did to the staff: 'the motion of the hand caused the motion of the staff'. And, as we know from physiology, there are still other events which caused the motion of the hand. Hence we need not introduce the agent at this particular point, as Aristotle does—we *need* not, though we *may.* We *may* say that the hand was moved by the man, but we may *also* say that the motion of the hand was caused by the motion of certain muscles; and we may say that the motion of the muscles was caused by certain events that took place within the brain. But some event, and presumably one of those that took place within the brain, was caused by the agent and not by any other events.

There are, of course, objections to this way of putting the matter; I shall consider the two that seem to me to be most important.

7. One may object, firstly: 'If the *man* does anything, then, as Aristotle's remark suggests, what he does is to move the *hand.* But he certainly does not *do* anything to his brain—he may not even know that he *has* a brain. And if he doesn't do anything to the brain, and if the motion of the hand was caused by something that happened within the brain, then there is no point in appealing to "immanent causation" as being something incompatible with "transeunt causation"—for the whole thing, after all, is a matter of causal relations among events or states of affairs.'

The answer to this objection, I think, is this: It is true that the agent does not *do* anything with his brain, or to his brain, in the sense in which he *does* something with his hand and does something to the staff. But from this it does not follow that the agent was not the immanent cause of something that happened within his brain.

We should note a useful distinction that has been proposed by Professor A. I. Melden—namely, the distinction between 'making something A happen' and 'doing A'.[5] If I reach for the staff and pick it up, then one of the things that I *do* is just that—reach for the staff and pick it up. And if it is something that I do, then there is a very clear sense in which it may be said to be something that I know that I do. If you ask me, 'Are you doing something, or trying to do something, with the staff?' I will have no difficulty in finding an answer. But in doing something with the staff, I also make various things happen which are not in this same sense things that I do: I will make various air-particles move; I will free a number of blades of grass from the pressure that had been upon them; and I may cause a shadow to move from one place to another. If these are merely things that I make happen, as distinguished from things that I do, then I may know nothing whatever about them; I may not have the slightest idea that, in moving the staff, I am bringing about any such thing as the motion of air-particles, shadows, and blades of grass.

We may say, in answer to the first objection, therefore, that it is true that our agent does nothing to his brain or with his brain; but from this it does not follow that the agent is not the immanent cause of some event within his brain; for the brain event may be something which, like the motion of the air-particles, he made happen in picking up the staff. The only difference between the two cases is this: in each case, he made something happen when he picked up the staff; but in the one case—the motion of the air-particles or of the shadows—it was the motion of the staff that caused the event to happen; and in the other case—the event that took place in the brain—it was this event that caused the motion of the staff.

The point is, in a word, that whenever a man does something A, then (by 'immanent causation') he makes a certain cerebral event happen, and this cerebral event (by 'transeunt causation') makes A happen.

8. The second objection is more difficult and concerns the very concept of 'immanent causation', or causation by an agent, as this concept is to be interpreted here. The concept is subject to a difficulty which has long been associated with that of the prime mover unmoved. We have said that

5. A. I. Melden, *Free Action* (London, 1961), especially ch. 3. Mr. Melden's own views, however, are quite the contrary of those that are proposed here.

there must be some event A, presumably some cerebral event, which is caused not by any other event, but by the agent. Since A was not caused by any other event, then the agent himself cannot be said to have undergone any change or produced any other event (such as 'an act of will' or the like) which brought A about. But if, when the agent made A happen, there was no event involved other than A itself, no event which could be described as *making* A happen, what did the agent's causation consist of? What, for example, is the difference between A's just happening, and the agents' *causing* A to happen? We cannot attribute the difference to any event that took place within the agent. And so far as the event A itself is concerned, there would seem to be no discernible difference. Thus Aristotle said that the activity of the prime mover is nothing in addition to the motion that it produces, and Suarez said that 'the action is in reality nothing but the effect as it flows from the agent'.[6] Must we conclude, then, that there is no more to the man's action in causing event A than there is to the event A's happening by itself? Here we would seem to have a distinction without a difference—in which case we have failed to find a *via media* between a deterministic and an indeterministic view of action.

The only answer, I think, can be this: that the difference between the man's causing A, on the one hand, and the event A just happening, on the other, lies in the fact that, in the first case but not the second, the event A *was* caused and was caused by the man. There was a brain event A; the agent did, in fact, cause the brain event; but there was nothing that he did to cause it.

This answer may not entirely satisfy and it will be likely to provoke the following question: 'But what are you really *adding* to the assertion that A happened when you utter the words "The agent *caused* A to happen"?' As soon as we have put the question this way, we see, I think, that whatever difficulty we may have encountered is one that may be traced to the concept of causation generally—whether 'immanent' or 'transeunt'. The problem, in other words, is not a problem that is peculiar to our conception of human action. It is a problem that must be faced by anyone who makes use of the concept of causation at all; and therefore, I would say, it is a problem for everyone but the complete indeterminist.

For the problem, as we put it, referring just to 'immanent causation', or causation by an agent, was this; 'What is the difference between saying, of an event A, that A just happened and saying that someone caused A to

6. Aristotle, *Physics*, bk. iii, ch. 3; Suarez, *Disputations Metaphysicae*, Disputation 18, s. 10.

happen?' The analogous problem, which holds for 'transeunt causation', or causation by an event, is this: 'What is the difference between saying, of two events A and B, that B happened and then A happened, and saying that B's happening was the *cause* of A's happening?' And the only answer that one can give is this—that in the one case the agent was the cause of A's happening and in the other case event B was the cause of A's happening. The nature of transeunt causation is no more clear than is that of immanent causation.

9. But we may plausibly say—and there is a respectable philosophical tradition to which we may appeal—that the notion of immanent causation, or causation by an agent, is in fact more clear than that of transeunt causation, or causation by an event, and that it is only by understanding our own causal efficacy, as agents, that we can grasp the concept of *cause* at all. Hume may be said to have shown that we do not derive the concept of *cause* from what we perceive of external things. How, then, do we derive it? The most plausible suggestion, it seems to me, is that of Reid, once again: namely that 'the conception of an efficient cause may very probably be derived from the experience we have had . . . of our own power to produce certain effects'.[7] If we did not understand the concept of immanent causation, we would not understand that of transeunt causation.

10. It may have been noted that I have avoided the term 'free will' in all of this. For even if there is such a faculty as 'the will', which somehow sets our acts agoing, the question of freedom, as John Locke said, is not the question '*whether the will be free*'; it is the question '*whether a man be free*'.[8] For if there is a 'will', as a moving faculty, the question is whether the man is free to will to do these things that he does will to do—and also whether he is free *not* to will any of those things that he does will to do, and, again, whether he is free to will any of those things that he does not will to do. Jonathan Edwards tried to restrict himself to the question—'Is the man free to do what it is that he wills?'—but the answer to this question will not tell us whether the man is responsible for what it is that he *does* will to do. Using still another pair of medieval terms, we may say that the metaphysical problem of freedom does not concern the *actus imperatus;* it does not concern the question whether we are free to accomplish whatever it is that we will or set out to do; it concerns the *actus elicitus*, the question whether we are free to will or to set out to do those things that we do will or set out to do.

7. Reid, *Works*, 524.

8. *Essay Concerning Human Understanding*, bk. ii. ch. 21.

11. If we are responsible, and if what I have been trying to say is true, then we have a prerogative which some would attribute only to God: each of us, when we act, is a prime mover unmoved. In doing what we do, we cause certain events to happen, and nothing—or no one—causes us to cause those events to happen.

12. If we are thus prime movers unmoved and if our actions, or those for which we are responsible, are not causally determined, then they are not causally determined by our *desires.* And this means that the relation between what we want or what we desire, on the one hand, and what it is that we do, on the other, is not as simple as most philosophers would have it.

We may distinguish between what we might call the 'Hobbist approach' and what we might call the 'Kantian approach' to this question. The Hobbist approach is the one that is generally accepted at the present time, but the Kantian approach, I believe, is the one that is true. According to Hobbism, if we *know,* of some man, what his beliefs and desires happen to be and how strong they are, if we know what he feels certain of, what he desires more than anything else, and if we know the state of his body and what stimuli he is being subjected to, then we may *deduce,* logically, just what it is that he will do—or, more accurately, just what it is that he will try, set out, or undertake to do. Thus Professor Melden has said that 'the connection between wanting and doing is logical'.[9] But according to the Kantian approach to our problem, and this is the one that I would take, there is no such logical connection between wanting and doing, nor need there even be a causal connection. No set of statements about a man's desires, beliefs, and stimulus situation at any time implies any statement telling us what the man will try, set out, or undertake to do at that time. As Reid put it, though we may 'reason from men's motives to their actions and, in many cases, with great probability', we can never do so 'with absolute certainty'.[10]

This means that, in one very strict sense of the terms, there can be no science of man. If we think of science as a matter of finding out what laws happen to hold, and if the statement of a law tells us what kinds of events are caused by what other kinds of events, then there will be human actions which we cannot explain by subsuming them under any laws. We cannot say, 'It is causally necessary that, given such and such desires and beliefs, and being subject to such and such stimuli, the agent will do so and so'.

9. Melden, 166.

10. Reid, *Works,* 608, 612.

For at times the agent, if he chooses, may rise above his desires and do something else instead.

But all of this is consistent with saying that, perhaps more often than not, our desires do exist under conditions such that those conditions necessitate us to act. And we may also say, with Leibniz, that at other times our desires may 'incline without necessitating'.

13. Leibniz's phrase presents us with our final philosophical problem. What does it mean to say that a desire, or a motive, might 'incline without necessitating'? There is a temptation, certainly, to say that 'to incline' means to cause and that 'not to necessitate' means not to cause, but obviously we cannot have it both ways.

Nor will Leibniz's own solution do. In his letter to Coste, he puts the problem as follows: 'When a choice is proposed, for example to go out or not to go out, it is a question whether, with all the circumstances, internal and external, motives, perceptions, dispositions, impressions, passions, inclinations taken together, I am still in a contingent state, or whether I am necessitated to make the choice, for example, to go out; that is to say, whether this proposition true and determined in fact, *In all these circumstances taken together I shall choose to go out,* is contingent or necessary.'[11] Leibniz's answer might be put as follows: in one sense of the terms 'necessary' and 'contingent', the proposition 'In all these circumstances taken together I shall choose to go out', may be said to be contingent and not necessary, and in another sense of these terms, it may be said to be necessary and not contingent. But the sense in which the proposition may be said to be contingent, according to Leibniz, is only this: there is no logical contradiction involved in denying the proposition. And the sense in which it may be said to be necessary is this: since 'nothing ever occurs without cause or determining reason', the proposition is causally necessary. 'Whenever all the circumstances taken together are such that the balance of deliberation is heavier on one side than on the other, it is certain and infallible that that is the side that is going to win out'. But if what we have been saying is true, the proposition 'In all these circumstances taken together I shall choose to go out', may be causally as well as logically contingent. Hence we must find another interpretation for Leibniz's statement that our motives and desires may incline us, or influence us, to choose without thereby necessitating us to choose.

Let us consider a public official who has some moral scruples but who

11. 'Lettre à Mr. Coste de la Nécessité et de la Contingence' (1707) in *Opera Philosophica,* ed. Erdmann, 447 9.

also, as one says, could be had. Because of the scruples that he does have, he would never take any positive steps to receive a bribe—he would not actively solicit one. But his morality has its limits and he is also such that, if we were to confront him with a *fait accompli* or to let him see what is about to happen ($10,000 in cash is being deposited behind the garage), then he would succumb and be unable to resist. The general situation is a familiar one and this is one reason that people pray to be delivered from temptation. (It also justifies Kant's remark: 'And how many there are who may have led a long blameless life, who are only *fortunate* in having escaped so many temptations'.[12] Our relation to the misdeed that we contemplate may not be a matter simply of being able to bring it about or not to bring it about. As St. Anselm noted, there are at least four possibilities. We may illustrate them by reference to our public official and the event which is his receiving the bribe, in the following way: (i) he may be able to bring the event about himself (*facere esse*), in which case he would actively cause himself to receive the bribe; (ii) he may be able to refrain from bringing it about himself (*non facere esse*), in which case he would not himself do anything to insure that he receive the bribe; (iii) he may be able to do something to prevent the event from occurring (*facere non esse*), in which case he would make sure that the $10,000 was *not* left behind the garage; or (iv) he may be unable to do anything to prevent the event from occurring (*non facere non esse*), in which case, though he may not solicit the bribe, he would allow himself to keep it.[13] We have envisaged our official as a man who can resist the temptation to (i) but cannot resist the temptation to (iv): he can refrain from bringing the event about himself, but he cannot bring himself to do anything to prevent it.

Let us think of 'inclination without necessitation', then, in such terms as these. First we may contrast the two propositions:

(1) He can resist the temptation to do something in order to make A happen;

(2) He can resist the temptation to allow A to happen (i.e. to do nothing to prevent A from happening).

12. In the Preface to the *Metaphysical Element of Ethics*, in Kant's *Critique of Practical Reason and Other Works on the Theory of Ethics*, ed. T. K. Abbott (London, 1959), 303.

13. Cf. D. P. Henry, 'Saint Anselm's *De "Grammatico"*', *Philosophical Quarterly*, x (1960), 115–26. St. Anselm noted that (i) and (iii), respectively, may be thought of as forming the upper left and the upper right corners of a square of opposition, and (ii) and (iv) the lower left and the lower right.

We may suppose that the man has some desire to have A happen and thus has a motive for making A happen. His motive for making A happen, I suggest, is one that *necessitates* provided that, because of the motive, (1) is false; he cannot resist the temptation to do something in order to make A happen. His motive for making A happen is one that *inclines* provided that, because of the motive, (2) is false; like our public official, he cannot bring himself to do anything to prevent A from happening. And therefore we can say that this motive for making A happen is one that *inclines but does not necessitate* provided that, because of the motive, (1) is true and (2) is false; he can resist the temptation to make it happen but he cannot resist the temptation to allow it to happen.

15

Harry Frankfurt, "Alternate Possibilities and Moral Responsibility"

Harry Frankfurt was a philosophy professor at Yale University for many years and is now a professor emeritus at Princeton University. In this selection Frankfurt argues that despite a common assumption, one can be morally responsible for one's actions even if one could not have done otherwise. He develops a series of examples to support his view. Because this article challenges so fundamental an intuition about moral responsibility, it has provoked a very substantial response, and it can thus be considered a milestone in the debate about free will and moral responsibility.

A dominant role in nearly all recent inquiries into the free-will problem has been played by a principle which I shall call "the principle of alternate possibilities." This principle states that a person is morally responsible for what he has done only if he could have done otherwise. Its exact meaning is a subject of controversy, particularly concerning whether someone who accepts it is thereby committed to believing that moral responsibility and determinism are incompatible. Practically no one, however, seems inclined to deny or even to question that the principle of alternate possibilities (construed in some way or other) is true. It has generally seemed so overwhelmingly plausible that some philosophers have even characterized it as an *a priori* truth. People whose accounts of free will or of moral responsibility are radically at odds evidently find in it a firm and convenient common ground upon which they can profitably take their opposing stands.

But the principle of alternate possibilities is false. A person may well be morally responsible for what he has done even though he could not have done otherwise. The principle's plausibility is an illusion, which can be made to vanish by bringing the relevant moral phenomena into sharper focus.

"Alternate Possibilities and Moral Responsibility" first appeared in the *Journal of Philosophy*, 66 (December 1969), 828–39, copyright © 1969 by the *Journal of Philosophy*, and is reprinted here by permission of Harry Frankfurt and the *Journal of Philosophy*.

I

In seeking illustrations of the principle of alternate possibilities, it is most natural to think of situations in which the same circumstances both bring it about that a person does something and make it impossible for him to avoid doing it. These include, for example, situations in which a person is coerced into doing something, or in which he is impelled to act by a hypnotic suggestion, or in which some inner compulsion drives him to do what he does. In situations of these kinds there are circumstances that make it impossible for the person to do otherwise, and these very circumstances also serve to bring it about that he does whatever it is that he does.

However, there may be circumstances that constitute sufficient conditions for a certain action to be performed by someone and that therefore make it impossible for the person to do otherwise, but that do not actually impel the person to act or in any way produce his action. A person may do something in circumstances that leave him no alternative to doing it, without these circumstances actually moving him or leading him to do it—without them playing any role, indeed, in bringing it about that he does what he does.

An examination of situations characterized by circumstances of this sort casts doubt, I believe, on the relevance to questions of moral responsibility of the fact that a person who has done something could not have done otherwise. I propose to develop some examples of this kind in the context of a discussion of coercion and to suggest that our moral intuitions concerning these examples tend to disconfirm the principle of alternate possibilities. Then I will discuss the principle in more general terms, explain what I think is wrong with it, and describe briefly and without argument how it might appropriately be revised.

II

It is generally agreed that a person who has been coerced to do something did not do it freely and is not morally responsible for having done it. Now the doctrine that coercion and moral responsibility are mutually exclusive may appear to be no more than a somewhat particularized version of the principle of alternate possibilities. It is natural enough to say of a person who has been coerced to do something that he could not have done otherwise. And it may easily seem that being coerced deprives a person of freedom and of moral responsibility simply because it is a special case of being unable to do otherwise. The principle of alternate possibilities may in this way derive some credibility from its association with the very plausible proposition that moral responsibility is excluded by coercion.

It is not right, however, that it should do so. The fact that a person was coerced to act as he did may entail both that he could not have done otherwise and that he bears no moral responsibility for his action. But his lack of moral responsibility is not entailed by his having been unable to do otherwise. The doctrine that coercion excludes moral responsibility is not correctly understood, in other words, as a particularized version of the principle of alternate possibilities.

Let us suppose that someone is threatened convincingly with a penalty he finds unacceptable and that he then does what is required of him by the issuer of the threat. We can imagine details that would make it reasonable for us to think that the person was coerced to perform the action in question, that he could not have done otherwise, and that he bears no moral responsibility for having done what he did. But just what is it about situations of this kind that warrants the judgment that the threatened person is not morally responsible for his act?

This question may be approached by considering situations of the following kind. Jones decides for reasons of his own to do something, then someone threatens him with a very harsh penalty (so harsh that any reasonable person would submit to the threat) unless he does precisely that, and Jones does it. Will we hold Jones morally responsible for what he has done? I think this will depend on the roles we think were played, in leading him to act, by his original decision and by the threat.

One possibility is that $Jones_1$ is not a reasonable man: he is, rather, a man who does what he has once decided to do no matter what happens next and no matter what the cost. In that case, the threat actually exerted no effective force upon him. He acted without any regard to it, very much as if he were not aware that it had been made. If this is indeed the way it was, the situation did not involve coercion at all. The threat did not lead $Jones_1$ to do what he did. Nor was it in fact sufficient to have prevented him from doing otherwise: if his earlier decision had been to do something else, the threat would not have deterred him in the slightest. It seems evident that in these circumstances the fact that $Jones_1$ was threatened in no way reduces the moral responsibility he would otherwise bear for his act. This example, however, is not a counterexample either to the doctrine that coercion excuses or to the principle of alternate possibilities. For we have supposed that $Jones_1$ is a man upon whom the threat had no coercive effect and, hence, that it did not actually deprive him of alternatives to doing what he did.

Another possibility is that $Jones_2$ was stampeded by the threat. Given that threat, he would have performed that action regardless of what decision he had already made. The threat upset him so profoundly, moreover, that he completely forgot his own earlier decision and did what was demanded of him entirely because he was terrified of the penalty with which he was threatened. In this case, it is not relevant to his having performed the action that he had already decided on his own to perform it. When the chips were down he thought of nothing but the threat, and fear alone led him to act. The fact that at an earlier time $Jones_2$ had decided for his own reasons to act in just that way may be relevant to an evaluation of his character; he may bear full moral responsibility for having made *that* decision. But he can hardly be said to be morally responsible for his action. For he performed the action simply as a result of the coercion to which he was subjected. His earlier decision played no role in bringing it about that he did what he did, and it would therefore be gratuitous to assign it a role in the moral evaluation of his action.

Now consider a third possibility. $Jones_3$ was neither stampeded by the threat nor indifferent to it. The threat impressed him, as it would impress any reasonable man, and he would have submitted to it wholeheartedly if he had not already made a decision that coincided with the one demanded of him. In fact, however, he performed the action in question on the basis of the decision he had made before the threat was issued. When he acted, he was not actually motivated by the threat but solely by the considerations that had originally commended the action to him. It was not the threat that led him to act, though it would have done so if he had not already provided himself with a sufficient motive for performing the action in question.

No doubt it will be very difficult for anyone to know, in a case like this one, exactly what happened. Did $Jones_3$ perform the action because of the threat, or were his reasons for acting simply those which had already persuaded him to do so? Or did he act on the basis of two motives, each of which was sufficient for his action? It is not impossible, however, that the situation should be clearer than situations of this kind usually are. And suppose it is apparent to us that $Jones_3$ acted on the basis of his own decision and not because of the threat. Then I think we would be justified in regarding his moral responsibility for what he did as unaffected by the threat even though, since he would in any case have submitted to the threat, he could not have avoided doing what he did. It would be entirely reasonable for us to make the same judgment concerning his moral responsibility that we would have made if we had not known of the threat.

For the threat did not in fact influence his performance of the action. He did what he did just as if the threat had not been made at all.

III

The case of $Jones_3$ may appear at first glance to combine coercion and moral responsibility, and thus to provide a counterexample to the doctrine that coercion excuses. It is not really so certain that it does so, however, because it is unclear whether the example constitutes a genuine instance of coercion. Can we say of $Jones_3$ that he was coerced to do something, when he had already decided on his own to do it and when he did it entirely on the basis of that decision? Or would it be more correct to say that $Jones_3$ was not coerced to do what he did, even though he himself recognized that there was an irresistible force at work in virtue of which he had to do it? My own linguistic intuitions lead me toward the second alternative, but they are somewhat equivocal. Perhaps we can say either of these things, or perhaps we must add a qualifying explanation to whichever of them we say.

This murkiness, however, does not interfere with our drawing an important moral from an examination of the example. Suppose we decide to say that $Jones_3$ was *not* coerced. Our basis for saying this will clearly be that it is incorrect to regard a man as being coerced to do something unless he does it *because* of the coercive force exerted against him. The fact that an irresistible threat is made will not, then, entail that the person who receives it is coerced to do what he does. It will also be necessary that the threat is what actually accounts for doing it. On the other hand, suppose we decide to say that $Jones_3$ *was* coerced. Then we will be bound to admit that being coerced does not exclude being morally responsible. And we will also surely be led to the view that coercion affects the judgment of a person's moral responsibility only when the person acts as he does because he is coerced to do so—i.e., when the fact that he is coerced is what accounts for his action.

Whichever we decide to say, then, we will recognize that the doctrine that coercion excludes moral responsibility is not a particularized version of the principle of alternate possibilities. Situations in which a person who does something cannot do otherwise because he is subject to coercive power are either not instances of coercion at all, or they are situations in which the person may still be morally responsible for what he does if it is not because of the coercion that he does it. When we excuse a person who has been coerced, we do not excuse him because he was unable to do otherwise. Even though a person is subject to a coercive force that precludes his performing any action but one, he may nonetheless bear full moral responsibility for performing that action.

IV

To the extent that the principle of alternate possibilities derives its plausibility from association with the doctrine that coercion excludes moral responsibility, a clear understanding of the latter diminishes the appeal of the former. Indeed the case of $Jones_3$ may appear to do more than illuminate the relationship between the two doctrines. It may well seem to provide a decisive counterexample to the principle of alternate possibilities and thus to show that this principle is false. For the irresistibility of the threat to which $Jones_3$ is subjected might well be taken to mean that he cannot but perform the action he performs. And yet the threat, since $Jones_3$ performs the action without regard to it, does not reduce his moral responsibility for what he does.

The following objection will doubtless be raised against the suggestion that the case of $Jones_3$ is a counterexample to the principle of alternate possibilities. There is perhaps a sense in which $Jones_3$ cannot do otherwise than perform the action he performs, since he is a reasonable man and the threat he encounters is sufficient to move any reasonable man. But it is not this sense that is germane to the principle of alternate possibilities. His knowledge that he stands to suffer an intolerably harsh penalty does not mean that $Jones_3$, strictly speaking, *cannot* perform any action but the one he does perform. After all it is still open to him, and this is crucial, to defy the threat if he wishes to do so and to accept the penalty his action would bring down upon him. In the sense in which the principle of alternate possibilities employs the concept of "could have done otherwise," $Jones_3$'s inability to resist the threat does not mean that he cannot do otherwise than perform the action he performs. Hence the case of $Jones_3$ does not constitute an instance contrary to the principle.

I do not propose to consider in what sense the concept of "could have done otherwise" figures in the principle of alternate possibilities, nor will I attempt to measure the force of the objection I have just described.[1] For I believe that whatever force this objection may be thought to have can be

1. The two main concepts employed in the principle of alternate possibilities are "morally responsible" and "could have done otherwise." To discuss the principle without analyzing either of these concepts may well seem like an attempt at piracy. The reader should take notice that my Jolly Roger is now unfurled.

deflected by altering the example in the following way.[2] Suppose someone—Black, let us say—wants $Jones_4$ to perform a certain action. Black is prepared to go to considerable lengths to get his way, but he prefers to avoid showing his hand unnecessarily. So he waits until $Jones_4$ is about to make up his mind what to do, and he does nothing unless it is clear to him (Black is an excellent judge of such things) that $Jones_4$ is going to decide to do something *other* than what he wants him to do. If it does become clear that $Jones_4$ is going to decide to do something else, Black takes effective steps to ensure that $Jones_4$ decides to do, and that he does do, what he wants him to do.[3] Whatever $Jones_4$'s initial preferences and inclinations, then, Black will have his way.

What steps will Black take, if he believes he must take steps, in order to ensure that $Jones_4$ decides and acts as he wishes? Anyone with a theory concerning what "could have done otherwise" means may answer this question for himself by describing whatever measures he would regard as sufficient to guarantee that, in the relevant sense, $Jones_4$ cannot do otherwise. Let Black pronounce a terrible threat, and in this way both force $Jones_4$ to perform the desired action and prevent him from performing a forbidden one. Let Black give $Jones_4$ a potion, or put him under hypnosis, and in some such way as these generate in $Jones_4$ an irresistible inner compulsion to perform the act Black wants performed and to avoid others. Or let Black manipulate the minute processes of $Jones_4$'s brain and nervous system in some more direct way, so that causal forces running in and out of his synapses and along the poor man's nerves determine that he

2. After thinking up the example that I am about to develop I learned that Robert Nozick, in lectures given several years ago, had formulated an example of the same general type and had proposed it as a counterexample to the principle of alternate possibilities.

3. The assumption that Black can predict what $Jones_4$ will decide to do does not beg the question of determinism. We can imagine that $Jones_4$, has often confronted the alternatives—*A* and *B*—that he now confronts, and that his face has invariably twitched when he was about to decide to do *A* and never when he was about to decide to do *B*. Knowing this, and observing the twitch, Black would have a basis for prediction. This does, to be sure, suppose that there is some sort of causal relation between $Jones_4$'s state at the time of the twitch and his subsequent states. But any plausible view of decision or of action will allow that reaching a decision and performing an action both involve earlier and later phases, with causal relations between them, and such that the earlier phases are not themselves part of the decision or of the action. The example does not require that these earlier phases be deterministically related to still earlier events.

chooses to act and that he does act in the one way and not in any other. Given any conditions under which it will be maintained that $Jones_4$ cannot do otherwise, in other words, let Black bring it about that those conditions prevail. The structure of the example is flexible enough, I think, to find a way around any charge of irrelevance by accommodating the doctrine on which the charge is based.[4]

Now suppose that Black never has to show his hand because $Jones_4$, for reasons of his own, decides to perform and does perform the very action Black wants him to perform. In that case, it seems clear, $Jones_4$ will bear precisely the same moral responsibility for what he does as he would have borne if Black had not been ready to take steps to ensure that he do it. It would be quite unreasonable to excuse $Jones_4$ for his action, or to withhold the praise to which it would normally entitle him, on the basis of the fact that he could not have done otherwise. This fact played no role at all in leading him to act as he did. He would have acted the same even if it had not been a fact. Indeed, everything happened just as it would have happened without Black's presence in the situation and without his readiness to intrude into it.

In this example there are sufficient conditions for $Jones_4$'s performing the action in question. What action he performs is not up to him. Of course it is in a way up to him whether he acts on his own or as a result of Black's intervention. That depends upon what action he himself is inclined to perform. But whether he finally acts on his own or as a result of Black's intervention, he performs the same action. He has no alternative but to do what Black wants him to do. If he does it on his own, however, his moral responsibility for doing it is not affected by the fact that Black was lurking in the background with sinister intent, since this intent never comes into play.

V

The fact that a person could not have avoided doing something is a sufficient condition of his having done it. But, as some of my examples show, this fact may play no role whatever in the explanation of why he did

4. The example is also flexible enough to allow for the elimination of Black altogether. Anyone who thinks that the effectiveness of the example is undermined by its reliance on a human manipulator, who imposes his will on $Jones_4$, can substitute for Black a machine programmed to do what Black does. If this is still not good enough, forget both Black and the machine and suppose that their role is played by natural forces involving no will or design at all.

it. It may not figure at all among the circumstances that actually brought it about that he did what he did, so that his action is to be accounted for on another basis entirely. Even though the person was unable to do otherwise, that is to say, it may not be the case that he acted as he did *because* he could not have done otherwise. Now if someone had no alternative to performing a certain action but did not perform it because he was unable to do otherwise, then he would have performed exactly the same action even if he *could* have done otherwise. The circumstances that made it impossible for him to do otherwise could have been subtracted from the situation without affecting what happened or why it happened in any way. Whatever it was that actually led the person to do what he did, or that made him do it, would have led him to do it or made him do it even if it had been possible for him to do something else instead.

Thus it would have made no difference, so far as concerns his action or how he came to perform it, if the circumstances that made it impossible for him to avoid performing it had not prevailed. The fact that he could not have done otherwise clearly provides no basis for supposing that he *might* have done otherwise if he had been able to do so. When a fact is in this way irrelevant to the problem of accounting for a person's action it seems quite gratuitous to assign it any weight in the assessment of his moral responsibility. Why should the fact be considered in reaching a moral judgment concerning the person when it does not help in any way to understand either what made him act as he did or what, in other circumstances, he might have done?

This, then, is why the principle of alternate possibilities is mistaken. It asserts that a person bears no moral responsibility—that is, he is to be excused—for having performed an action if there were circumstances that made it impossible for him to avoid performing it. But there may be circumstances that make it impossible for a person to avoid performing some action without those circumstances in any way bringing it about that he performs that action. It would surely be no good for the person to refer to circumstances of this sort in an effort to absolve himself of moral responsibility for performing the action in question. For those circumstances, by hypothesis, actually had nothing to do with his having done what he did. He would have done precisely the same thing, and he would have been led or made in precisely the same way to do it, even if they had not prevailed.

We often do, to be sure, excuse people for what they have done when they tell us (and we believe them) that they could not have done otherwise. But this is because we assume that what they tell us serves to explain why they did what they did. We take it for granted that they are not being disingenuous, as a person would be who cited as an excuse the fact that he could not have avoided doing what he did but who knew full well that it was not at all because of this that he did it.

What I have said may suggest that the principle of alternate possibilities should be revised so as to assert that a person is not morally responsible for what he has done if he did it because he could not have done otherwise. It may be noted that this revision of the principle does not seriously affect the arguments of those who have relied on the original principle in their efforts to maintain that moral responsibility and determinism are incompatible. For if it was causally determined that a person perform a certain action, then it will be true that the person performed it because of those causal determinants. And if the fact that it was causally determined that a person perform a certain action means that the person could not have done otherwise, as philosophers who argue for the incompatibility thesis characteristically suppose, then the fact that it was causally determined that a person perform a certain action will mean that the person performed it because he could not have done otherwise. The revised principle of alternate possibilities will entail, on this assumption concerning the meaning of 'could have done otherwise', that a person is not morally responsible for what he has done if it was causally determined that he do it. I do not believe, however, that this revision of the principle is acceptable.

Suppose a person tells us that he did what he did because he was unable to do otherwise; or suppose he makes the similar statement that he did what he did because he had to do it. We do often accept statements like these (if we believe them) as valid excuses, and such statements may well seem at first glance to invoke the revised principle of alternate possibilities. But I think that when we accept such statements as valid excuses it is because we assume that we are being told more than the statements strictly and literally convey. We understand the person who offers the excuse to mean that he did what he did *only because* he was unable to do otherwise, or *only because* he had to do it. And we understand him to mean, more particularly, that when he did what he did it was not because that was what he really wanted to do. The principle of alternate possibilities should thus be replaced, in my opinion, by the following principle: a person is not morally responsible for what he has done if he did it only because he could not have done otherwise. This principle does not appear to conflict with the view that moral responsibility is compatible with determinism.

The following may all be true: there were circumstances that made it impossible for a person to avoid doing something; these circumstances actually played a role in bringing it about that he did it, so that it is correct to say that he did it because he could not have done otherwise; the person really wanted to do what he did; he did it because it was what he really wanted to do, so that it is not correct to say that he did what he did only because he could not have done otherwise. Under these conditions, the person may well be morally responsible for what he has done. On the other hand, he will not be morally responsible for what he has done if he did it only because he could not have done otherwise, even if what he did was something he really wanted to do.

16

Harry Frankfurt, "Freedom of the Will and the Concept of a Person"

In this article Frankfurt develops an account of personhood and of freedom of the will. He also advocates a compatibilist account of the freedom required for moral responsibility (which, in his view, is distinct from freedom of the will). To have the sort of freedom required for moral responsibility the agent must, first of all, will *to perform the action. For Frankfurt this means that the agent must have a desire to perform the action, and that this desire actually be effective in producing the action. But furthermore, she must also possess* a desire to will *to perform the action. Finally, her will must be her will because she has this second-order desire.*

What philosophers have lately come to accept as analysis of the concept of a person is not actually analysis of *that* concept at all. Strawson, whose usage represents the current standard, identifies the concept of a person as "the concept of a type of entity such that *both* predicates ascribing states of consciousness *and* predicates ascribing corporeal characteristics . . . are equally applicable to a single individual of that single type."[1] But there are many entities besides persons that have both mental and physical properties. As it happens—though it seems extraordinary that this should be so—there is no common English word for the type of entity Strawson has

"Freedom of the Will and the Concept of a Person," first appeared in the *Journal of Philosophy*, 68 (January 1971), 5–20, copyright © 1971 by the *Journal of Philosophy*, and is reprinted here by permission of Harry Frankfurt and the *Journal of Philosophy*.

1. P. F. Strawson, *Individuals* (London: Methuen, 1959), pp. 101–102. Ayer's usage of 'person' is similar: "it is characteristic of persons in this sense that besides having various physical properties . . . they are also credited with various forms of consciousness" [A. J. Ayer, *The Concept of a Person* (New York: St. Martin's, 1963), p. 82]. What concerns Strawson and Ayer is the problem of understanding the relation between mind and body, rather than the quite different problem of understanding what it is to be a creature that not only has a mind and a body but is also a person.

in mind, a type that includes not only human beings but animals of various lesser species as well. Still, this hardly justifies the misappropriation of a valuable philosophical term.

Whether the members of some animal species are persons is surely not to be settled merely by determining whether it is correct to apply to them, in addition to predicates ascribing corporeal characteristics, predicates that ascribe states of consciousness. It does violence to our language to endorse the application of the term 'person' to those numerous creatures which do have both psychological and material properties but which are manifestly not persons in any normal sense of the word. This misuse of language is doubtless innocent of any theoretical error. But although the offense is "merely verbal," it does significant harm. For it gratuitously diminishes our philosophical vocabulary, and it increases the likelihood that we will overlook the important area of inquiry with which the term 'person' is most naturally associated. It might have been expected that no problem would be of more central and persistent concern to philosophers than that of understanding what we ourselves essentially are. Yet this problem is so generally neglected that it has been possible to make off with its very name almost without being noticed and, evidently, without evoking any widespread feeling of loss.

There is a sense in which the word 'person' is merely the singular form of 'people' and in which both terms connote no more than membership in a certain biological species. In those senses of the word which are of greater philosophical interest, however, the criteria for being a person do not serve primarily to distinguish the members of our own species from the members of other species. Rather, they are designed to capture those attributes which are the subject of our most humane concern with ourselves and the source of what we regard as most important and most problematical in our lives. Now these attributes would be of equal significance to us even if they were not in fact peculiar and common to the members of our own species. What interests us most in the human condition would not interest us less if it were also a feature of the condition of other creatures as well.

Our concept of ourselves as persons is not to be understood, therefore, as a concept of attributes that are necessarily species-specific. It is conceptually possible that members of novel or even of familiar nonhuman species should be persons; and it is also conceptually possible that some members of the human species are not persons. We do in fact assume, on the other hand, that no member of another species is a person. Accordingly, there is a presumption that what is essential to persons is a set of characteristics that we generally suppose—whether rightly or wrongly—to be uniquely human.

It is my view that one essential difference between persons and other creatures is to be found in the structure of a person's will. Human beings are not alone in having desires and motives, or in making choices. They share these things with the members of certain other species, some of whom even appear to engage in deliberation and to make decisions based upon prior thought. It seems to be peculiarly characteristic of humans, however, that they are able to form what I shall call "second-order desires" or "desires of the second order."

Besides wanting and choosing and being moved *to do* this or that, men may also want to have (or not to have) certain desires and motives. They are capable of wanting to be different, in their preferences and purposes, from what they are. Many animals appear to have the capacity for what I shall call "first-order desires" or "desires of the first order," which are simply desires to do or not to do one thing or another. No animal other than man, however, appears to have the capacity for reflective self-evaluation that is manifested in the formation of second-order desires.[2]

I

The concept designated by the verb 'to want' is extraordinarily elusive. A statement of the form "*A* wants to *X*"—taken by itself, apart from a context that serves to amplify or to specify its meaning—conveys remarkably little information. Such a statement may be consistent, for example, with each of the following statements: (a) the prospect of doing *X* elicits no sensation or introspectible emotional response in *A;* (b) *A* is unaware that he wants to *X;* (c) *A* believes that he does not want to *X;* (d) *A* wants to refrain from *X*-ing; (e) *A* wants to *Y* and believes that it is impossible for him both to *Y* and to *X;* (f) *A* does not "really" want to *X;* (g) *A* would rather die than *X;* and so on. It is therefore hardly sufficient to formulate

2. For the sake of simplicity, I shall deal only with what someone wants or desires, neglecting related phenomena such as choices and decisions. I propose to use the verbs 'to want' and 'to desire' interchangeably, although they are by no means perfect synonyms. My motive in forsaking the established nuances of these words arises from the fact that the verb 'to want', which suits my purposes better so far as its meaning is concerned, does not lend itself so readily to the formation of nouns as does the verb 'to desire'. It is perhaps acceptable, albeit graceless, to speak in the plural of someone's "wants." But to speak in the singular of someone's "want" would be an abomination.

the distinction between first-order and second-order desires, as I have done, by suggesting merely that someone has a first-order desire when he wants to do or not to do such-and-such, and that he has a second-order desire when he wants to have or not to have a certain desire of the first order.

As I shall understand them, statements of the form "*A* wants to *X*" cover a rather broad range of possibilities.[3] They may be true even when statements like (a) through (g) are true: when *A* is unaware of any feelings concerning *X*-ing, when he is unaware that he wants to *X*, when he deceives himself about what he wants and believes falsely that he does not want to *X*, when he also has other desires that conflict with his desire to *X*, or when he is ambivalent. The desires in question may be conscious or unconscious, they need not be univocal, and *A* may be mistaken about them. There is a further source of uncertainty with regard to statements that identify someone's desires, however, and here it is important for my purposes to be less permissive.

Consider first those statements of the form "*A* wants to *X*" which identify first-order desires—that is, statements in which the term 'to *X*' refers to an action. A statement of this kind does not, by itself, indicate the relative strength of *A*'s desire to *X*. It does not make it clear whether this desire is at all likely to play a decisive role in what *A* actually does or tries to do. For it may correctly be said that *A* wants to *X* even when his desire to *X* is only one among his desires and when it is far from being paramount among them. Thus, it may be true that *A* wants to *X* when he strongly prefers to do something else instead; and it may be true that he wants to *X* despite the fact that, when he acts, it is not the desire to *X* that motivates him to do what he does. On the other hand, someone who states that *A* wants to *X* may mean to convey that it is this desire that is motivating or moving *A* to do what he is actually doing or that *A* will in fact be moved by this desire (unless he changes his mind) when he acts.

It is only when it is used in the second of these ways that, given the special usage of 'will' that I propose to adopt, the statement identifies *A*'s will. To identify an agent's will is either to identify the desire (or desires) by which he is motivated in some action he performs or to identify the

3. What I say in this paragraph applies not only to cases in which 'to *X*' refers to a possible action or inaction. It also applies to cases in which 'to *X*' refers to a first-order desire and in which the statement that '*A* wants to *X*' is therefore a shortened version of a statement—"*A* wants to want to *X*"—that identifies a desire of the second order.

desire (or desires) by which he will or would be motivated when or if he acts. An agent's will, then, is identical with one or more of his first-order desires. But the notion of the will, as I am employing it, is not coextensive with the notion of first-order desires. It is not the notion of something that merely inclines an agent in some degree to act in a certain way. Rather, it is the notion of an *effective* desire—one that moves (or will or would move) a person all the way to action. Thus the notion of the will is not coextensive with the notion of what an agent intends to do. For even though someone may have a settled intention to do *X*, he may nonetheless do something else instead of doing *X* because, despite his intention, his desire to do *X* proves to be weaker or less effective than some conflicting desire.

Now consider those statements of the form "*A* wants to *X*" which identify second-order desires—that is, statements in which the term 'to *X*' refers to a desire of the first order. There are also two kinds of situation in which it may be true that *A* wants to want to *X*. In the first place, it might be true of *A* that he wants to have a desire to *X* despite the fact that he has a univocal desire, altogether free of conflict and ambivalence, to refrain from *X*-ing. Someone might want to have a certain desire, in other words, but univocally want that desire to be unsatisfied.

Suppose that a physician engaged in psychotherapy with narcotics addicts believes that his ability to help his patients would be enhanced if he understood better what it is like for them to desire the drug to which they are addicted. Suppose that he is led in this way to want to have a desire for the drug. If it is a genuine desire that he wants, then what he wants is not merely to feel the sensations that addicts characteristically feel when they are gripped by their desires for the drug. What the physician wants, insofar as he wants to have a desire, is to be inclined or moved to some extent to take the drug.

It is entirely possible, however, that, although he wants to be moved by a desire to take the drug, he does not want this desire to be effective. He may not want it to move him all the way to action. He need not be interested in finding out what it is like to take the drug. And insofar as he now wants only to *want* to take it, and not to *take* it, there is nothing in what he now wants that would be satisfied by the drug itself. He may now have, in fact, an altogether univocal desire *not* to take the drug; and he may prudently arrange to make it impossible for him to satisfy the desire he would have if his desire to want the drug should in time be satisfied.

It would thus be incorrect to infer, from the fact that the physician now wants to desire to take the drug, that he already does desire to take it. His second-order desire to be moved to take the drug does not entail that he has a first-order desire to take it. If the drug were now to be administered to him, this might satisfy no desire that is implicit in his desire to want to take it. While he wants to want to take the drug, he may have *no* desire to take it; it may be that *all* he wants is to taste the desire for it. That is, his desire to have a certain desire that he does not have may not be a desire that his will should be at all different than it is.

Someone who wants only in this truncated way to want to *X* stands at the margin of preciosity, and the fact that he wants to want to *X* is not pertinent to the identification of his will. There is, however, a second kind of situation that may be described by '*A* wants to want to *X*'; and when the statement is used to describe a situation of this second kind, then it does pertain to what *A* wants his will to be. In such cases the statement means that *A* wants the desire to *X* to be the desire that moves him effectively to act. It is not merely that he wants the desire to *X* to be among the desires by which, to one degree or another, he is moved or inclined to act. He wants this desire to be effective—that is, to provide the motive in what he actually does. Now when the statement that *A* wants to want to *X* is used in this way, it does entail that *A* already has a desire to *X*. It could not be true both that *A* wants the desire to *X* to move him into action and that he does not want to *X*. It is only if he does want to *X* that he can coherently want the desire to *X* not merely to be one of his desires but, more decisively, to be his will.[4]

Suppose a man wants to be motivated in what he does by the desire to concentrate on his work. It is necessarily true, if this supposition is correct, that he already wants to concentrate on his work. This desire is now among his desires. But the question of whether or not his second-order desire is fulfilled does not turn merely on whether the desire he wants is one of his desires. It turns on whether this desire is, as he wants it to be, his effective desire or will. If, when the chips are down, it is his desire to

4. It is not so clear that the entailment relation described here holds in certain kinds of cases, which I think may fairly be regarded as nonstandard, where the essential difference between the standard and the nonstandard cases lies in the kind of description by which the first-order desire in question is identified. Thus, suppose that *A* admires *B* so fulsomely that, even though he does not know what *B* wants to do, he wants to be effectively moved by whatever desire effectively moves *B*, without knowing what *B*'s will is, in other words, *A* wants his own will to be the same. It certainly does not follow that *A* already has, among his desires, a desire like the one that constitutes *B*'s will. I shall not pursue here the questions of whether there are genuine counterexamples to the claim made in the text or of how, if there are, that claim should be altered.

concentrate on his work that moves him to do what he does, then what he wants at that time is indeed (in the relevant sense) what he wants to want. If it is some other desire that actually moves him when he acts, on the other hand, then what he wants at that time is not (in the relevant sense) what he wants to want. This will be so despite the fact that the desire to concentrate on his work continues to be among his desires.

II

Someone has a desire of the second order either when he wants simply to have a certain desire or when he wants a certain desire to be his will. In situations of the latter kind, I shall call his second-order desires "second-order volitions" or "volitions of the second order." Now it is having second-order volitions, and not having second-order desires generally, that I regard as essential to being a person. It is logically possible, however unlikely, that there should be an agent with second-order desires but with no volitions of the second order. Such a creature, in my view, would not be a person. I shall use the term 'wanton' to refer to agents who have first-order desires but who are not persons because, whether or not they have desires of the second order, they have no second-order volitions.[5]

The essential characteristic of a wanton is that he does not care about his will. His desires move him to certain things, without its being true of him either that he wants to be moved by those desires or that he prefers to be moved by other desires. The class of wantons includes all nonhuman animals that have desires and all very young children. Perhaps it also includes some adult human beings as well. In any case, adult humans may be more or less wanton; they may act wantonly, in response to first-order desires concerning which they have no volitions of the second order, more or less frequently.

The fact that a wanton has no second-order volitions does not mean that each of his first-order desires is translated heedlessly and at once into action. He may have no opportunity to act in accordance with some of his

5. Creatures with second-order desires but no second-order volitions differ significantly from brute animals, and, for some purposes, it would be desirable to regard them as persons. My usage, which withholds the designation 'person' from them, is thus somewhat arbitrary. I adopt it largely because it facilitates the formulation of some of the points I wish to make. Hereafter, whenever I consider statements of the form "*A* wants to want to *X*," I shall have in mind statements identifying second-order volitions and not statements identifying second-order desires that are not second-order volitions.

desires. Moreover, the translation of his desires into action may be delayed or precluded either by conflicting desires of the first order or by the intervention of deliberation. For a wanton may possess and employ rational faculties of a high order. Nothing in the concept of a wanton implies that he cannot reason or that he cannot deliberate concerning how to do what he wants to do. What distinguishes the rational wanton from other rational agents is that he is not concerned with the desirability of his desires themselves. He ignores the question of what his will is to be. Not only does he pursue whatever course of action he is most strongly inclined to pursue, but he does not care which of his inclinations is the strongest.

Thus a rational creature, who reflects upon the suitability to his desires of one course of action or another, may nonetheless be a wanton. In maintaining that the essence of being a person lies not in reason but in will, I am far from suggesting that a creature without reason may be a person. For it is only in virtue of his rational capacities that a person is capable of becoming critically aware of his own will and of forming volitions of the second order. The structure of a person's will presupposes, accordingly, that he is a rational being.

The distinction between a person and a wanton may be illustrated by the difference between two narcotics addicts. Let us suppose that the physiological condition accounting for the addiction is the same in both men, and that both succumb inevitably to their periodic desires for the drug to which they are addicted. One of the addicts hates his addiction and always struggles desperately, although to no avail, against its thrust. He tries everything that he thinks might enable him to overcome his desires for the drug. But these desires are too powerful for him to withstand, and invariably, in the end, they conquer him. He is an unwilling addict, helplessly violated by his own desires.

The unwilling addict has conflicting first-order desires: he wants to take the drug, and he also wants to refrain from taking it. In addition to these first-order desires, however, he has a volition of the second order. He is not a neutral with regard to the conflict between his desire to take the drug and his desire to refrain from taking it. It is the latter desire, and not the former, that he wants to constitute his will: it is the latter desire, rather than the former, that he wants to be effective and to provide the purpose that he will seek to realize in what he actually does.

The other addict is a wanton. His actions reflect the economy of his first-order desires, without his being concerned whether the desires that move him to act are desires by which he wants to be moved to act. If he encounters problems in obtaining the drug or in administering it to himself, his responses to his urges to take it may involve deliberation. But it never occurs to him to consider whether he wants the relations among his desires to result in his having the will he has. The wanton addict may be an animal, and thus incapable of being concerned about his will. In any event he is, in respect of his wanton lack of concern, no different from an animal.

The second of these addicts may suffer a first-order conflict similar to the first-order conflict suffered by the first. Whether he is human or not, the wanton may (perhaps due to conditioning) both want to take the drug and want to refrain from taking it. Unlike the unwilling addict, however, he does not prefer that one of his conflicting desires should be paramount over the other; he does not prefer that one first-order desire rather than the other should constitute his will. It would be misleading to say that he is neutral as to the conflict between his desires, since this would suggest that he regards them as equally acceptable. Since he has no identity apart from his first-order desires, it is true neither that he prefers one to the other nor that he prefers not to take sides.

It makes a difference to the unwilling addict, who is a person, which of his conflicting first-order desires wins out. Both desires are his, to be sure; and whether he finally takes the drug or finally succeeds in refraining from taking it, he acts to satisfy what is in a literal sense his own desire. In either case he does something he himself wants to do, and he does it not because of some external influence whose aim happens to coincide with his own but because of his desire to do it. The unwilling addict identifies himself, however, through the formation of a second-order volition, with one rather than with the other of his conflicting first-order desires. He makes one of them more truly his own and, in so doing, he withdraws himself from the other. It is in virtue of this identification and withdrawal, accomplished through the formation of a second-order volition, that the unwilling addict may meaningfully make the analytically puzzling statements that the force moving him to take the drug is a force other than his own, and that it is not of his own free will but rather against his will that this force moves him to take it.

The wanton addict cannot or does not care which of his conflicting first-order desires wins out. His lack of concern is not due to his inability to find a convincing basis for preference. It is due either to his lack of the capacity for reflection or to his mindless indifference to the enterprise of evaluating his own desires and motives.[6] There is only one issue in the

6. In speaking of the evaluation of his own desires and motives as being characteristic of a person, I do not mean to suggest that a person's second-order volitions

struggle to which his first-order conflict may lead: whether the one or the other of his conflicting desires is the stronger. Since he is moved by both desires, he will not be altogether satisfied by what he does no matter which of them is effective. But it makes no difference *to him* whether his craving or his aversion gets the upper hand. He has no stake in the conflict between them and so, unlike the unwilling addict, he can neither win nor lose the struggle in which he is engaged. When a *person* acts, the desire by which he is moved is either the will he wants or a will he wants to be without. When a *wanton* acts, it is neither.

III

There is a very close relationship between the capacity for forming second-order volitions and another capacity that is essential to persons—one that has often been considered a distinguishing mark of the human condition. It is only because a person has volitions of the second order that he is capable both of enjoying and of lacking freedom of the will. The concept of a person is not only, then, the concept of a type of entity that has both first-order desires and volitions of the second order. It can also be construed as the concept of a type of entity for whom the freedom of its will may be a problem. This concept excludes all wantons, both infrahuman and human, since they fail to satisfy an essential condition for the enjoyment of freedom of the will. And it excludes those suprahuman beings, if any, whose wills are necessarily free.

Just what kind of freedom is the freedom of the will? This question calls for an identification of the special area of human experience to which the concept of freedom of the will, as distinct from the concepts of other sorts of freedom, is particularly germane. In dealing with it, my aim will be primarily to locate the problem with which a person is most immediately concerned when he is concerned with the freedom of his will.

According to one familiar philosophical tradition, being free is fundamentally a matter of doing what one wants to do. Now the notion of an

---

necessarily manifest a *moral* stance on his part toward his first-order desires. It may not be from the point of view of morality that the person evaluates his first-order desires. Moreover, a person may be capricious and irresponsible in forming his second-order volitions and give no serious consideration to what is at stake. Second-order volitions express evaluations only in the sense that they are preferences. There is no essential restriction on the kind of basis, if any, upon which they are formed.

agent who does what he wants to do is by no means an altogether clear one: both the doing and the wanting, and the appropriate relation between them as well, require elucidation. But although its focus needs to be sharpened and its formulation refined, I believe that this notion does capture at least part of what is implicit in the idea of an agent who *acts* freely. It misses entirely, however, the peculiar content of the quite different idea of an agent whose *will* is free.

We do not suppose that animals enjoy freedom of the will, although we recognize that an animal may be free to run in whatever direction it wants. Thus, having the freedom to do what one wants to do is not a sufficient condition of having a free will. It is not a necessary condition either. For to deprive someone of his freedom of action is not necessarily to undermine the freedom of his will. When an agent is aware that there are certain things he is not free to do, this doubtless affects his desires and limits the range of choices he can make. But suppose that someone, without being aware of it, has in fact lost or been deprived of his freedom of action. Even though he is no longer free to do what he wants to do, his will may remain as free as it was before. Despite the fact that he is not free to translate his desires into actions or to act according to the determinations of his will, he may still form those desires and make those determinations as freely as if his freedom of action had not been impaired.

When we ask whether a person's will is free we are not asking whether he is in a position to translate his first-order desires into actions. That is the question of whether he is free to do as he pleases. The question of the freedom of his will does not concern the relation between what he does and what he wants to do. Rather, it concerns his desires themselves. But what question about them is it?

It seems to me both natural and useful to construe the question of whether a person's will is free in close analogy to the question of whether an agent enjoys freedom of action. Now freedom of action is (roughly, at least) the freedom to do what one wants to do. Analogously, then, the statement that a person enjoys freedom of the will means (also roughly) that he is free to want what he wants to want. More precisely, it means that he is free to will what he wants to will, or to have the will he wants. Just as the question about the freedom of an agent's action has to do with whether it is the action he wants to perform, so the question about the freedom of his will has to do with whether it is the will he wants to have.

It is in securing the conformity of his will to his second-order volitions, then, that a person exercises freedom of the will. And it is in the discrepancy between his will and his second-order volitions, or in his awareness that their coincidence is not his own doing but only a happy chance, that a person who does not have this freedom feels its lack. The unwilling addict's will is not free. This is shown by the fact that it is not the will he wants. It is also true, though in a different way, that the will of the wanton addict is not free. The wanton addict neither has the will he wants nor has a will that differs from the will he wants. Since he has no volitions of the second order, the freedom of his will cannot be a problem for him. He lacks it, so to speak, by default.

People are generally far more complicated than my sketchy account of the structure of a person's will may suggest. There is as much opportunity for ambivalence, conflict, and self-deception with regard to desires of the second order, for example, as there is with regard to first-order desires. If there is an unresolved conflict among someone's second-order desires, then he is in danger of having no second-order volition; for unless this conflict is resolved, he has no preference concerning which of his first-order desires is to be his will. This condition, if it is so severe that it prevents him from identifying himself in a sufficiently decisive way with *any* of his conflicting first-order desires, destroys him as a person. For it either tends to paralyze his will and to keep him from acting at all, or it tends to remove him from his will so that his will operates without his participation. In both cases he becomes, like the unwilling addict though in a different way, a helpless bystander to the forces that move him.

Another complexity is that a person may have, especially if his second-order desires are in conflict, desires and volitions of a higher order than the second. There is no theoretical limit to the length of the series of desires of higher and higher orders; nothing except common sense and, perhaps, a saving fatigue prevents an individual from obsessively refusing to identify himself with any of his desires until he forms a desire of the next higher order. The tendency to generate such a series of acts of forming desires, which would be a case of humanization run wild, also leads toward the destruction of a person.

It is possible, however, to terminate such a series of acts without cutting it off arbitrarily. When a person identifies himself *decisively* with one of his first-order desires, this commitment "resounds" throughout the potentially endless array of higher orders. Consider a person who, without reservation or conflict, wants to be motivated by the desire to concentrate on his work. The fact that his second-order volition to be moved by this desire is a decisive one means that there is no room for questions concerning the pertinence of desires or volitions of higher orders. Suppose the person is asked whether he wants to want to want to concentrate on his work. He can properly insist that this question concerning a third-order desire does not arise. It would be a mistake to claim that, because he has not considered whether he wants the second-order volition he has formed, he is indifferent to the question of whether it is with this volition or with some other that he wants his will to accord. The decisiveness of the commitment he has made means that he has decided that no further question about his second-order volition, at any higher order, remains to be asked. It is relatively unimportant whether we explain this by saying that this commitment implicitly generates an endless series of confirming desires of higher orders, or by saying that the commitment is tantamount to a dissolution of the pointedness of all questions concerning higher orders of desire.

Examples such as the one concerning the unwilling addict may suggest that volitions of the second order, or of higher orders, must be formed deliberately and that a person characteristically struggles to ensure that they are satisfied. But the conformity of a person's will to his higher-order volitions may be far more thoughtless and spontaneous than this. Some people are naturally moved by kindness when they want to be kind, and by nastiness when they want to be nasty, without any explicit forethought and without any need for energetic self-control. Others are moved by nastiness when they want to be kind and by kindness when they intend to be nasty, equally without forethought and without active resistance to these violations of their higher-order desires. The enjoyment of freedom comes easily to some. Others must struggle to achieve it.

IV

My theory concerning the freedom of the will accounts easily for our disinclination to allow that this freedom is enjoyed by the members of any species inferior to our own. It also satisfies another condition that must be met by any such theory, by making it apparent why the freedom of the will should be regarded as desirable. The enjoyment of a free will means the satisfaction of certain desires—desires of the second or of higher orders—whereas its absence means their frustration. The satisfactions at stake are those which accrue to a person of whom it may be said that his will is his own. The corresponding frustrations are those suffered by a person of whom it may be said that he is estranged from himself, or that he finds himself a helpless or a passive bystander to the forces that move him.

A person who is free to do what he wants to do may yet not be in a position to have the will he wants. Suppose, however, that he enjoys both freedom of action and freedom of the will. Then he is not only free to do what he wants to do; he is also free to want what he wants to want. It seems to me that he has, in that case, all the freedom it is possible to desire or to conceive. There are other good things in life, and he may not possess some of them. But there is nothing in the way of freedom that he lacks.

It is far from clear that certain other theories of the freedom of the will meet these elementary but essential conditions: that it be understandable why we desire this freedom and why we refuse to ascribe it to animals. Consider, for example, Roderick Chisholm's quaint version of the doctrine that human freedom entails an absence of causal determination.[7] Whenever a person performs a free action, according to Chisholm, it's a miracle. The motion of a person's hand, when the person moves it, is the outcome of a series of physical causes; but some event in this series, "and presumably one of those that took place within the brain, was caused by the agent and not by any other events." A free agent has, therefore, "a prerogative which some would attribute only to God: each of us, when we act, is a prime mover unmoved."

This account fails to provide any basis for doubting that animals of subhuman species enjoy the freedom it defines. Chisholm says nothing that makes it seem less likely that a rabbit performs a miracle when it moves its leg than that a man does so when he moves his hand. But why, in any case, should anyone *care* whether he can interrupt the natural order of causes in the way Chisholm describes? Chisholm offers no reason for believing that there is a discernible difference between the experience of a man who miraculously initiates a series of causes when he moves his hand and a man who moves his hand without any such breach of the normal causal sequence. There appears to be no concrete basis for preferring to be involved in the one state of affairs rather than in the other.[8]

It is generally supposed that, in addition to satisfying the two conditions I have mentioned, a satisfactory theory of the freedom of the will necessarily provides an analysis of one of the conditions of moral responsibility. The most common recent approach to the problem of understanding the

7. "Freedom and Action," in K. Lehrer, ed., *Freedom and Determinism* (New York: Random House, 1966), pp. 11–14.

8. I am not suggesting that the alleged difference between these two states of affairs is unverifiable. On the contrary, physiologists might well be able to show that Chisholm's conditions for a free action are not satisfied, by establishing that there is no relevant brain event for which a sufficient physical cause cannot be found.

freedom of the will has been, indeed, to inquire what is entailed by the assumption that someone is morally responsible for what he has done. In my view, however, the relation between moral responsibility and the freedom of the will has been very widely misunderstood. It is not true that a person is morally responsible for what he has done only if his will was free when he did it. He may be morally responsible for having done it even though his will was not free at all.

A person's will is free only if he is free to have the will he wants. This means that, with regard to any of his first-order desires, he is free either to make that desire his will or to make some other first-order desire his will instead. Whatever his will, then, the will of the person whose will is free could have been otherwise; he could have done otherwise than to constitute his will as he did. It is a vexed question just how 'he could have done otherwise' is to be understood in contexts such as this one. But although this question is important to the theory of freedom, it has no bearing on the theory of moral responsibility. For the assumption that a person is morally responsible for what he has done does not entail that the person was in a position to have whatever will he wanted.

This assumption *does* entail that the person did what he did freely, or that he did it of his own free will. It is a mistake, however, to believe that someone acts freely only when he is free to do whatever he wants or that he acts of his own free will only if his will is free. Suppose that a person has done what he wanted to do, that he did it because he wanted to do it, and that the will by which he was moved when he did it was his will because it was the will he wanted. Then he did it freely and of his own free will. Even supposing that he could have done otherwise, he would not have done otherwise; and even supposing that he could have had a different will, he would not have wanted his will to differ from what it was. Moreover, since the will that moved him when he acted was his will because he wanted it to be, he cannot claim that his will was forced upon him or that he was a passive bystander to its constitution. Under these conditions, it is quite irrelevant to the evaluation of his moral responsibility to inquire whether the alternatives that he opted against were actually available to him.[9]

In illustration, consider a third kind of addict. Suppose that his addiction has the same physiological basis and the same irresistible thrust as the addictions of the unwilling and wanton addicts, but that he is altogether

9. For another discussion of the considerations that cast doubt on the principle that a person is morally responsible for what he has done only if he could have done otherwise, see Chapter 6, pp. 143–152. [Reference to original work.]

delighted with his condition. He is a willing addict, who would not have things any other way. If the grip of his addiction should somehow weaken, he would do whatever he could to reinstate it; if his desire for the drug should begin to fade, he would take steps to renew its intensity.

The willing addict's will is not free, for his desire to take the drug will be effective regardless of whether or not he wants this desire to constitute his will. But when he takes the drug, he takes it freely and of his own free will. I am inclined to understand his situation as involving the overdetermination of his first-order desire to take the drug. This desire is his effective desire because he is physiologically addicted. But it is his effective desire also because he wants it to be. His will is outside his control, but, by his second-order desire that his desire for the drug should be effective, he has made this will his own. Given that it is therefore not only because of his addiction that his desire for the drug is effective, he may be morally responsible for taking the drug.

My conception of the freedom of the will appears to be neutral with regard to the problem of determinism. It seems conceivable that it should be causally determined that a person is free to want what he wants to want. If this is conceivable, then it might be causally determined that a person enjoys a free will. There is no more than an innocuous appearance of paradox in the proposition that it is determined, ineluctably and by forces beyond their control, that certain people have free wills and that others do not. There is no incoherence in the proposition that some agency other than a person's own is responsible (even *morally* responsible) for the fact that he enjoys or fails to enjoy freedom of the will. It is possible that a person should be morally responsible for what he does of his own free will and that some other person should also be morally responsible for his having done it.[10]

10. There is a difference between being *fully* responsible and being *solely* responsible. Suppose that the willing addict has been made an addict by the deliberate and calculated work of another. Then it may be that both the addict and this other person are fully responsible for the addict's taking the drug, while neither of them is solely responsible for it. That there is a distinction between full moral responsibility and sole moral responsibility is apparent in the following example. A certain light can be turned on or off by flicking either of two switches, and each of these switches is simultaneously flicked to the "on" position by a different person, neither of whom is aware of the other. Neither person is solely responsible for the light's going on, nor do they share the responsibility in the sense that each is partially responsible; rather, each of them is fully responsible.

On the other hand, it seems conceivable that it should come about by chance that a person is free to have the will he wants. If this is conceivable, then it might be a matter of chance that certain people enjoy freedom of the will and that certain others do not. Perhaps it is also conceivable, as a number of philosophers believe, for states of affairs to come about in a way other than by chance or as the outcome of a sequence of natural causes. If it is indeed conceivable for the relevant states of affairs to come about in some third way, then it is also possible that a person should in that third way come to enjoy the freedom of the will.

17

Peter van Inwagen, "The Incompatibility of Free Will and Determinism"

Peter van Inwagen is a professor of philosophy at the University of Notre Dame and an advocate of incompatibilism. In this article he develops the consequence argument *for the claim that if causal determinism is true, no agent could have chosen otherwise than she in fact did and that as a result free will and determinism are not compatible.*

In this paper I shall define a thesis I shall call 'determinism', and argue that it is incompatible with the thesis that we are able to act otherwise than we do (i.e. is incompatible with 'free will'). Other theses, some of them very different from what *I* shall call 'determinism', have at least an equal right to this name, and, therefore, I do not claim to show that *every* thesis that could be called 'determinism' without historical impropriety is incompatible with free will. I shall, however, assume without argument that what I call 'determinism' is legitimately so called.

In Part I, I shall explain what I mean by 'determinism'. In Part II, I shall make some remarks about 'can'. In Part III, I shall argue that free will and determinism are incompatible. In Part IV, I shall examine some possible objections to the argument of Part III. I shall not attempt to establish the truth or falsity of determinism, or the existence or non-existence of free will.

I

In defining 'determinism', I shall take for granted the notion of a proposition (that is, of a non-linguistic bearer of truth-value), together with certain allied notions such as denial, conjunction, and entailment.

"The Incompatibility of Free Will and Determinism" first appeared in *Philosophical Studies* 27 (1975), pp. 185–99, copyright © 1975 by D. Reidel Publishing Company, Dordrecht, Holland. Reprinted with kind permission from Springer Science and Business Media.

Nothing in this paper will depend on the special features of any particular account of propositions. The reader may think of them as functions from possible worlds to truth-values or in any other way he likes, provided they have their usual features (e.g. they are either true or false; the conjunction of a true and a false proposition is a false proposition; they obey the law of contraposition with respect to entailment).

Our definition of 'determinism' will also involve the notion of 'the state of the entire physical world' (hereinafter, 'the state of the world') at an instant. I shall leave this notion largely unexplained, since the argument of this paper is very nearly independent of its content. Provided the following two conditions are met, the reader may flesh out 'the state of the world' in any way he likes:

(i) Our concept of 'state' must be such that, given that the world is in a certain state at a certain time, nothing follows *logically* about its states at other times. For example, we must not choose a concept of 'state' that would allow as part of a description of the momentary state of the world, the clause, '. . . and, at *t*, the world is such that Jones's left hand will be raised 10 seconds later than *t*.'

(ii) If there is some observable change in the way things are (e.g. if a white cloth becomes blue, a warm liquid cold, or if a man raises his hand), this change must entail some change in the state of the world. That is, our concept of 'state' must not be so theoretical, so divorced from what is observably true, that it be possible for the world to be in the *same* state at t_1 and t_2, although (for example) Jones's hand is raised at t_1 and not at t_2.

We may now define 'determinism'. We shall apply this term to the conjunction of these two theses:

(a) For every instant of time, there is a proposition that expresses the state of the world at that instant.

(b) If *A* and *B* are any propositions that express the state of the world at some instants, then the conjunction of *A* with the laws of physics entails *B*.

By a proposition that expresses the state of the world at time *t*, I mean a true proposition that asserts of some state that, at *t*, the world is in that state. The reason for our first restriction on the content of 'state' should now be evident: if it were not for this restriction, 'the state of the world' could be defined in such a way that determinism was trivially true. We could, without this restriction, build sufficient information about the past and future into each proposition that expresses the state of the world at an instant, that, for every pair of such propositions, each *by itself* entails the other. And in that case, determinism would be a mere tautology, a thesis applicable to every conceivable state of affairs.

This amounts to saying that the 'laws of physics' clause on our definition does some work: whether determinism is true depends on the character of the laws of physics. For example, if all physical laws were vague propositions like 'In every nuclear reaction, momentum is *pretty nearly* conserved', or 'Force is *approximately* equal to mass times acceleration', then determinism would be false.

This raises the question, What is a law of physics? First, a terminological point. I do not mean the application of this term to be restricted to those laws that belong to physics in the narrowest sense of the word. I am using 'law of physics' in the way some philosophers use 'law of nature'. Thus, a law about chemical valences is a law of physics in my sense, even if chemistry is not ultimately 'reducible' to physics. I will not use the term 'law of nature', because, conceivably, *psychological* laws, including laws (if such there be) about the voluntary behaviour of rational agents, might be included under this term.[1] Rational agents are, after all, in some sense part of 'Nature'. Since I do not think that everything I shall say about laws of physics is true of such 'voluntaristic laws', I should not want to use, instead of 'laws of physics', some term like 'laws of nature' that might legitimately be applied to voluntaristic laws. Thus, for all that is said in this paper, it may be that some version of determinism based on voluntaristic laws is compatible with free will.[2] Let us, then, understand by 'law of physics' a law of nature that is not about the voluntary behaviour of rational agents.

1. For example, 'If a human being is not made to feel ashamed of lying before his twelfth birthday, then he will lie whenever he believes it to be to his advantage.'

2. In 'The Compatibility of Free Will and Determinism', *Philosophical Review*, 1962, J. V. Canfield argues convincingly for a position that we might represent in this terminology as the thesis that a determinism based on voluntaristic laws could be compatible with free will.

But this does not tell us what 'laws of nature' are. There would probably be fairly general agreement that a proposition cannot be a law of nature unless it is true and contingent, and that no proposition is a law of nature if it entails the existence of some concrete individual, such as Caesar or the earth. But the proposition that there is no solid gold sphere 20 feet in diameter (probably) satisfies these conditions, though it is certainly not a law of nature.

It is also claimed sometimes that a law of nature must 'support its counterfactuals'. There is no doubt something to this. Consider, however, the proposition, 'Dogs die if exposed to virus V'. The claim that this proposition supports its counter-factuals is, I think, equivalent to the claim that 'Every dog is such that if it were exposed to virus V, it would die' is *true.* Let us suppose that this latter proposition *is* true, the quantification being understood as being over all dogs, past, present, and future. Its truth, it seems to me, is quite consistent with its being the case that dog-breeders *could* (but will not) institute a programme of selective breeding that *would* produce a sort of dog that is immune to virus V. But if dog-breeders *could* do this, then clearly 'Dogs die if exposed to virus V' is not a law of nature, since in that case the truth of the corresponding universally quantified counterfactual depends upon an accidental circumstance: if dog-breeders were to institute a certain programme of selective breeding they are quite capable of instituting, then 'Every dog is such that if it were exposed to virus V, it would die' would be false. Thus a proposition may 'support its counterfactuals' and yet not be a law of nature.

I do not think that any philosopher has succeeded in giving a (non-trivial) set of individually necessary and jointly sufficient conditions for a proposition's being a law of nature or of physics. *I* certainly do not know of any such set. Fortunately, for the purposes of this paper we need not know how to analyse the concept 'law of physics'. I shall, in Part III, argue that certain statements containing 'law of physics' are analytic. But this can be done in the absence of a satisfactory analysis of 'law of physics'. In fact, it would hardly be possible for one to *provide* an analysis of some concept if one had no pre-analytic convictions about what statements involving that concept are analytic.

For example, we do not have to have a satisfactory analysis of memory to know that 'No one can remember future events' is analytic. And if someone devised an analysis of memory according to which it was possible to remember future events, then, however attractive the analysis was in other respects, it would have to be rejected. The analyticity of 'No one can remember future events' is one of the *data* that anyone who investigates the concept of memory must take account of. Similarly, the claims I shall make on behalf of the concept of physical law seem to me to be basic and evident enough to be data that an analysis of this concept must take account of: any analysis on which these claims did not 'come out true' would be for that very reason defective.

II

It seems to be generally agreed that the concept of free will should be understood in terms of the *power* or *ability* of agents to act otherwise than they in fact do. To deny that men have free will is to assert that what a man does do and what he *can* do coincide. And almost all philosophers[3] agree that a necessary condition for holding an agent responsible for an act is believing that that agent *could have* refrained from performing that act.[4]

There is, however, considerably less agreement as to how 'can' (in the relevant sense) should be analysed. This is one of the most difficult questions in philosophy. It is certainly a question to which I do not know any nontrivial answer. But, as I said I should do in the case of 'law of physics', I shall make certain conceptual claims about 'can' (in the 'power' or 'ability' sense) in the absence of any analysis. Any suggested analysis of 'can' that does not support these claims will either be neutral with respect to them, in which case it will be incomplete, since it will not settle *all* conceptual questions about 'can', or it will be inconsistent with them, in which case the arguments I shall present in support of these claims will, in effect, be arguments that the analysis fails. In Part IV, I shall expand on this point as it applies to one particular analysis of 'can', the well-known 'conditional' analysis.

I shall say no more than this about the meaning of 'can'. I shall, however, introduce an idiom that will be useful in talking about ability and inability in complicated cases. Without this idiom, the statement of our

3. See, however, Harry Frankfurt, 'Alternate Possibilities and Moral Responsibility', *Journal of Philosophy,* 1969. [Selection 15 in this volume.]

4. Actually, the matter is rather more complicated than this, since we may hold a man responsible for an act we believe he could not have refrained from, provided we are prepared to hold him responsible for his being unable to refrain.

argument would be rather unwieldy. We shall sometimes make claims about an agent's abilities by using sentences of the form:

S can render [could have rendered] . . . false.

where ' . . . ' may be replaced by names of propositions.[5] Our ordinary claims about ability can easily be translated into this idiom. For example, we translate:

He could have reached Chicago by midnight.

as

He could have rendered the proposition that he did not reach Chicago by midnight false.

and, of course, the translation from the special idiom to the ordinary idiom is easy enough in such simple cases. If we were interested only in everyday ascriptions of ability, the new idiom would be useless. Using it, however, we may make ascriptions of ability that it would be very difficult to make in the ordinary idiom. Consider, for example, the last true proposition asserted by Plato. (Let us assume that this description is, as logicians say, 'proper'.) One claim that we might make about Aristotle is that he could have rendered this proposition false. Now, presumably, we have no way of discovering *what* proposition the last true proposition asserted by Plato was. Still, the claim about Aristotle would seem to be either true or false. To discover its truth-value, we should have to discover under what conditions the last true proposition asserted by Plato (i.e. that proposition having as one of its accidental properties, the property of being the last true proposition asserted by Plato) would be false, and then discover whether it was within Aristotle's power to produce these conditions. For example, suppose that if Aristotle had lived in Athens from the time of Plato's death till the time of his own death, then the last true proposition asserted by Plato (whatever it was) would be false. Then, if Aristotle could

5. In all the cases we shall consider, ' . . . ' will be replaced by names of *true* propositions. For the sake of logical completeness, we may stipulate that any sentence formed by replacing ' . . . ' with the name of a *false* proposition is trivially true. Thus, 'Kant could have rendered the proposition that 7 + 5 = 13 false' is trivially true.

have lived (i.e. if he had it within his power to live) in Athens throughout this period, he could have rendered the last true proposition asserted by Plato false. On the other hand, if the last true proposition asserted by Plato is the proposition that the planets do not move in perfect circles, then Aristotle could not have rendered the last true proposition asserted by Plato false, since it was not within his power to produce any set of conditions sufficient for the falsity of this proposition.[6]

It is obvious that the proposition expressed by 'Aristotle could have rendered the last true proposition asserted by Plato false', is a proposition that we should be hard put to express without using the idiom of rendering propositions false, or, at least, without using some very similar idiom. We shall find this new idiom very useful in discussing the relation between free will (a thesis about abilities) and determinism (a thesis about certain propositions).

III

I shall now imagine a case in which a certain man, after due deliberation, refrained from performing a certain contemplated act. I shall then argue that, if determinism is true, then that man *could not have* performed that act. Because this argument will not depend on any features peculiar to our imagined case, the incompatibility of free will and determinism *in general* will be established, since, as will be evident, a parallel argument could easily be constructed for the case of any agent and any unperformed act.

Here is the case. Let us suppose there was once a judge who had only to raise his right hand at a certain time, *T*, to prevent the execution of a sentence of death upon a certain criminal, such a hand-raising being the sign, according to the conventions of the judge's country, of a granting of special clemency. Let us further suppose that the judge—call him '*J*'—refrained from raising his hand at that time, and that this inaction resulted

6. Richard Taylor has argued (most explicitly in 'Time, Truth and Ability' by 'Diodorus Cronus', *Analysis*, 1965) that every true proposition is such that, necessarily, no one is able to render it false. On my view, this thesis is mistaken, and Taylor's arguments for it can be shown to be unsound. I shall not, however, argue for this here. I shall argue in Part III that we are unable to render *certain sorts of* true proposition false, but my arguments will depend on special features of these sorts of proposition. I shall, for example, argue that no one can render false a law of physics; but I shall not argue that this is the case because laws of physics are *true*, but because of other features that they possess.

in the criminal's being put to death. We may also suppose that the judge was unbound, uninjured, and free from paralysis; that he decided not to raise his hand at *T* only after a period of calm, rational, and relevant deliberation; that he had not been subjected to any 'pressure' to decide one way or the other about the criminal's death; that he was not under the influence of drugs, hypnosis, or anything of that sort; and finally, that there was no element in his deliberations that would have been of any special interest to a student of abnormal psychology.

Now the argument. In this argument, which I shall refer to as the 'main argument', I shall use 'T_0' to denote some instant of time earlier than *J*'s birth, 'P_0' to denote the proposition that expresses the state of the world at T_Q, '*P*' to denote the proposition that expresses the state of the world at *T*, and '*L*' to denote the conjunction into a single proposition of all laws of physics. (I shall regard *L* itself as a law of physics, on the reasonable assumption that if *A* and *B* are laws of physics, then the conjunction of *A* and *B* is a law of physics.) The argument consists of seven statements, the seventh of which follows from the first six:

(1) If determinism is true, then the conjunction of P_0 and *L* entails *P*.

(2) If *J* had raised his hand at *T*, then *P* would be false.

(3) If (2) is true, then if *J* could have raised his hand at *T*, *J* could have rendered *P* false.[7]

(4) If *J* could have rendered *P* false, and if the conjunction of P_0 and *L* entails *P*, then *J* could have rendered the conjunction of P_0 and *L* false.

(5) If *J* could have rendered the conjunction of P_0 and *L* false, then *J* could have rendered *L* false.

(6) *J* could not have rendered *L* false.

(7) If determinism is true, *J* could not have raised his hand at *T*.

That (7) follows from (1) through (6) can easily be established by truth-functional logic. Note that all conditionals in the argument except for (2)

7. '*J* could have raised his hand at *T*' is ambiguous. It might mean either (roughly) '*J* possessed, at *T*, the ability to raise his hand', or '*J* possessed the ability to bring it about that his hand rose at *T*'. If *J* was unparalysed at *T* but paralysed at all earlier instants, then the latter of these would be false, though the former might be true. I mean '*J* could have raised his hand at *T*' in the latter sense.

are truth-functional. For purposes of establishing the *validity* of this argument, (2) may be regarded as a simple sentence. Let us examine the premises individually.

(1) This premiss follows from the definition of determinism.

(2) If *J* had raised his hand at T, then the world would have been in a different state at *T* from the state it was in fact in. (See our second condition on the content of 'the state of the world'.) And, therefore, if *J* had raised his hand at *T*, some contrary of *P* would express the state of the world at *T*. It should be emphasized that '*P*' does not *mean* 'the proposition that expresses the state of the world at *T*'. Rather, '*P*' *denotes* the proposition that expresses the state of the world at *T*. In Kripke's terminology, '*P*' is being used as a *rigid designator*, while 'the proposition that expresses the state of the world at *T*' is perforce non-rigid.[8]

(3) Since *J*'s hand being raised at *T* would have been sufficient for the falsity of *P*, there is, if *J* could have raised his hand, at least one condition sufficient for the falsity of *P* that *J* could have produced.

(4) This premiss may be defended as an instance of the following general principle:

> If *S* can render *R* false, and if *Q* entails *R*, then *S* can render *Q* false.

This principle seems to be analytic. For if *Q* entails *R*, then the denial of *R* entails the denial of *Q*. Thus, any condition sufficient for the falsity of *R* is also sufficient for the falsity of *Q*. Therefore, if there is some condition that *S* can produce that is sufficient for the falsity of *R*, there is some condition (that same condition) that *S* can produce that is sufficient for the falsity of *Q*.

(5) This premiss may be defended as an instance of the following general principle, which I take to be analytic:

> If *Q* is a true proposition that concerns only states of affairs that obtained before *S*'s birth, and if *S* can render the conjunction of *Q* and *R* false, then *S* can render *R* false.

Consider, for example, the propositions expressed by

> The Spanish Armada was defeated in 1588.

and

8. See Saul Kripke, 'Identity and Necessity', in *Identity and Individuation,* ed. Milton K. Munitz (New York, 1971).

Peter van Inwagen never visits Alaska.

The conjunction of these two propositions is quite possibly true. At any rate, let us assume it is true. Given that it is true, it seems quite clear that I can render it false if and only if I can visit Alsaka. If, for some reason, it is not within my power ever to visit Alaska, then I *cannot* render it false. This is a quite trivial assertion, and the general principle (above) of which it is an instance is hardly less trivial. And it seems incontestable that premiss (5) is also an instance of this principle.

(6) I shall argue that if anyone *can* (i.e. has it within his power to) render some proposition false, then that proposition is not a law of physics. This I regard as a conceptual truth, one of the data that must be taken account of by anyone who wishes to give an analysis of 'can' or 'law'. It is this connection between these two concepts, I think, that is at the root of the incompatibility of free will and determinism.

In order to see this connection, let us suppose that both of the following are true:

(A) Nothing ever travels faster than light.

(B) Jones, a physicist, can construct a particle accelerator that would cause protons to travel at twice the speed of light.

It follows from (A) that Jones will never exercise the power that (B) ascribes to him. But whatever the reason for Jones's failure to act on his ability to render (A) false, it is clear that (A) and (B) are consistent, and that (B) entails that (A) is not a law of physics. For given that (B) is true, then Jones is able to conduct an experiment that would falsify (A); and surely it is a feature of any proposition that is a physical law that no one *can* conduct an experiment that would show it to be false.

Of course, most propositions that look initially as if they might be physical laws, but which are later decided to be non-laws, are rejected because of experiments that are actually performed. But this is not essential. In order to see this, let us elaborate the example we have been considering. Let us suppose that Jones's ability to render (A) false derives from the fact that he has discovered a mathematically rigorous proof that under certain conditions *C*, realizable in the laboratory, protons would travel faster than light. And let us suppose that this proof proceeds from premisses so obviously true that all competent physicists accept his conclusion without reservation. But suppose that conditions *C* never obtain in nature, and that actually to produce them in the laboratory would require such an expenditure of resources that Jones and his colleagues decide not to carry out the experiment. And suppose that, as a result, conditions *C* are never realized and nothing ever travels faster than light. It is evident that if all this were true, we should have to say that (A), while *true,* is not a law of physics. (Though, of course, 'Nothing ever travels faster than light except under conditions *C*' might be a law.)

The laboratories and resources that figure in this example are not essential to its point. If Jones *could* render some proposition false by performing *any* act he does not in fact perform, even such a simple act as raising his hand at a certain time, this would be sufficient to show that that proposition is not a law of physics.

This completes my defence of the premisses of the main argument. In the final part of this paper, I shall examine objections to this argument suggested by the attempts of various philosophers to establish the compatibility of free will and determinism.

IV

The most useful thing a philosopher who thinks that the main argument does not prove its point could do would be to try to show that some premiss of the argument is false or incoherent, or that the argument begs some important question, or contains a term that is used equivocally, or something of that sort. In short, he should get down to cases. Some philosophers, however, might continue to hold that free will and determinism, in the sense of Part I, are compatible, but decline to try to point out a mistake in the argument. For (such a philosopher might argue) we have, in everyday life, *criteria* for determining whether an agent could have acted otherwise than he did, and these criteria determine the *meaning* of 'could have acted otherwise'; to know the meaning of this phrase is simply to know how to apply these criteria. And since these criteria make no mention of determinism, anyone who thinks that free will and determinism are incompatible is simply confused.[9]

As regards the argument of Part III (this philosopher might continue), this argument is very complex, and this complexity must simply serve to hide some error, since its conclusion is absurd. We must treat this argument like the infamous 'proof' that zero equals one: It may be amusing and even instructive to find the hidden error (if one has nothing better to

9. Cf. Antony Flew, 'Divine Omniscience and Human Freedom', *New Essays in Philosophical Theology,* ed. Antony Flew and Alasdair MacIntyre (London: SCM Press, 1955), 149–51 in particular.

do), but it would be a waste of time to take seriously any suggestion that it is sound.

Now I suppose we do have 'criteria', in some sense of this over-used word, for the application of 'could have done otherwise', and I will grant that knowing the criteria for the application of a term can plausibly be identified with knowing its meaning. Whether the criteria for applying 'could have done otherwise' can (as at least one philosopher has supposed[10]) be taught by simple ostension is another question. However this may be, the 'criteria' argument is simply invalid. To see this, let us examine a simpler argument that makes the same mistake.

Consider the doctrine of 'predestinarianism'. Predestinarians hold (i) that if an act is foreseen it is not free, and (ii) that all acts are foreseen by God. (I do not claim that anyone has ever held this doctrine in precisely this form.) Now suppose we were to argue that predestinarianism must be compatible with free will, since our criteria for applying 'could have done otherwise' make no reference to predestinarianism. Obviously this argument would be invalid, since predestinarianism is incompatible with free will. And the only difference I can see between this argument and the 'criteria' argument for the compatibility of free will and determinism is that predestinarianism, unlike determinism, is *obviously* incompatible with free will. But, of course, theses may be incompatible with one another even if this incompatibility is not obvious. Even if determinism cannot, like predestinarianism, be seen to be incompatible with free will on the basis of a simple formal inference, there is, nonetheless, a conceptual connection between the two theses (as we showed in our defence of premiss (6)). The argument of Part III is intended to draw out the implications of this connection. There may well be a mistake in the argument, but I do not see why anyone should think that the very idea of such an argument is misconceived.

It has also been argued that free will *entails* determinism, and, being itself a consistent thesis, is *a fortiori* compatible with determinism. The argument, put briefly, is this. To say of some person on some particular occasion that he acted freely is obviously to say at least that *he* acted on that occasion. Suppose, however, that we see someone's arm rise and it later turns out that there was *no cause whatsoever* for his arm's rising. Surely we should have to say that *he* did not really raise his arm at all. Rather, his arm's rising was a mere chance happening, that, like a muscular twitch, had nothing to do with *him,* beyond the fact that it happened to involve a

10. Ibid.

part of his body. A necessary condition for this person's really having raised his hand is that *he* caused his hand to rise. And surely '*he* caused' means '*his* character, desires, and beliefs caused'.[11]

I think that there is a great deal of confusion in this argument, but to expose this confusion would require a lengthy discussion of many fine points in the theory of agency. I shall only point out that if this argument is supposed to refute the conclusion of Part III, it is an *ignoratio elenchi.* For I did not conclude that free will is incompatible with the thesis that every event has a cause, but rather with determinism as defined in Part I. And the denial of this thesis does not entail that there are uncaused events.

Of course, one might try to construct a similar but relevant argument for the falsity of the conclusion of Part III. But, so far as I can see, the plausibility of such an argument would depend on the plausibility of supposing that if the present movements of one's body are not completely determined by physical law and the state of the world before one's birth, then these present movements are not one's own doing, but, rather, mere random happenings. And I do not see the least shred of plausibility in this supposition.

I shall finally consider the popular 'conditional analysis' argument for the compatibility of free will and determinism. According to the advocates of this argument—let us call them 'conditionalists'—what statements of the form:

(8) S could have done X

mean is:

(9) If S had chosen to do X, S would have done X.[12]

11. Cf. R. E. Hobart, 'Free Will as Involving Determination and Inconceivable Without It', *Mind,* 1934; A. J. Ayer, 'Freedom and Necessity', in his collected *Philosophical Essays* (New York, 1954) [Selection 12 in this collection]; P. H. Nowell-Smith, 'Freewill and Moral Responsibility,' *Mind,* 1948; J. J. C. Smart, 'Free Will, Praise, and Blame', *Mind,* 1961.

12. Many other verbs besides 'choose' figure in various philosophers' conditional analyses of ability: e.g. 'wish', 'want', 'will', 'try', 'set oneself'. Much of the important contemporary work on this analysis, by G. E. Moore, P. H. Nowell-Smith, J. L. Austin, Keith Lehrer, Roderick Chisholm, and others, is collected in *The Nature of Human Action,* ed. Myles Brand (Glenview, Ill., 1970). See also 'Fatalism and Determinism', by Wilfrid Sellars, in *Freedom and Determinism,* ed. Keith Lehrer (New York, 1966), 141–74.

For example, 'Smith could have saved the drowning child' means, 'If Smith had chosen to save the drowning child, Smith would have saved the drowning child.' Thus, even if determinism is true (the conditionalists argue), it is possible that Smith did not save but *could have* saved the drowning child, since the conjunction of determinism with 'Smith did not save the child' does not entail the falsity of 'If Smith had chosen to save the child, Smith would have saved the child'.

Most of the controversy about this argument centres around the question whether (9) is a correct analysis of (8). I shall not enter into the debate about whether this analysis is correct. I shall instead question the relevance of this debate to the argument of Part III. For it is not clear that the main argument would be unsound if the conditional analysis *were* correct. Clearly the argument is *valid* whether or not (8) and (9) mean the same. But suppose the premisses of the main argument were rewritten so that every clause they contain that is of form (8) is replaced by the corresponding clause of form (9)—should we then see that any of these premisses is false? Let us try this with premiss (6), which seems, prima facie, to be the crucial premiss of the argument. We have:

> (6a) It is not the case that if *J* had chosen to render *L* false, *J* would have rendered *L* false.

Now (6a) certainly seems true: If someone chooses to render false some proposition *R*, and if *R* is a law of physics, then surely he will fail. This little argument for (6a) *seems* obviously sound. But we cannot overlook the possibility that someone might discover a mistake in it and, perhaps, even construct a convincing argument that (6a) is false. Let us, therefore, assume for the sake of argument that (6a) is demonstrably false. What would this show? I submit that it would show that (6a) does not mean the same as (6), since (6) is, as I have argued, *true.*

The same dilemma confronts the conditionalist if he attempts to show, on the basis of the conditional analysis, that any of the other premisses of the argument is false. Consider the argument got by replacing every clause of form (8) in the main argument with the corresponding clause of form (9). If all the premisses of this new argument are true, the main argument is, according to the conditionalist's own theory, sound. If, on the other hand, any of the premisses of the new argument is false, then (*I* would maintain) this premiss is a counter-example to the conditional analysis. I should not be begging the question against the conditionalist in maintaining this, since I have given arguments for the truth of each of the premisses of the main argument, and nowhere in these arguments do I assume that the conditional analysis is wrong.

Of course, any or all of my arguments in defence of the premisses of the main argument may contain some mistake. But unless the conditionalist could point to some such mistake, he would not accomplish much by showing that some statement he *claimed* was equivalent to one of its premisses was false.[13]

13. For an argument in some respects similar to what I have called the 'main argument', see Carl Ginet's admirable article, 'Might We Have No choice?' in Lehrer, 87–104. Another argument similar to the main argument, which is (formally) much simpler than the main argument, but which is stated in language very different from that of traditional statements of the free-will problem, can be found in my 'A Formal Approach to the Problem of Free Will and Determinism', *Theoria*, 1974.

18

Susan Wolf, "Asymmetrical Freedom"

Susan Wolf is a professor of philosophy at the University of North Carolina, Chapel Hill. In this article she argues for incompatibilism about blameworthiness but compatibilism about praiseworthiness. Whereas deserved blame cannot be justified if psychological determinism is true, deserved praise does not collapse along with it. In her view, being psychologically determined to perform good actions is compatible with deserving praise for them.

In order for a person to be morally responsible, two conditions must be satisfied. First, he must be a free agent—an agent, that is, whose actions are under his own control. For if the actions he performs are not up to him to decide, he deserves no credit or discredit for doing what he does. Second, he must be a moral agent—an agent, that is, to whom moral claims apply. For if the actions he performs can be neither right nor wrong, then there is nothing to credit or discredit him with. I shall call the first condition, *the condition of freedom,* and the second, *the condition of value.* Those who fear that the first condition can never be met worry about the problem of free will. Those who fear that the second condition can never be met worry about the problem of moral skepticism. Many people believe that the condition of value is dependent on the condition of freedom—that moral prescriptions make sense only if the concept of free will is coherent. In what follows, I shall argue that the converse is true—that the condition of freedom depends on the condition of value. Our doubts about the existence of true moral values, however, will have to be left aside.

I shall say that an agent's action is *psychologically determined* if his action is determined by his interests—that is, his values or desires—and his interests are determined by his heredity or environment. If all our actions are so determined, then the thesis of psychological determinism is true. This description is admittedly crude and simplistic. A more plausible description of psychological determination will include among possible

"Asymetrical Freedom" first appeared in the *Journal of Philosophy,* 77 (March 1980), 151–66, copyright © 1980 by the *Journal of Philosophy,* and is reprinted here by permission of Susan Wolf and the *Journal of Philosophy.*

determining factors a wider range of psychological states. There are, for example, some beliefs and emotions which cannot be analyzed as values or desires and which clearly play a role in the psychological explanations of why we act as we do. For my purposes, however, it will be easier to leave the description of psychological determinism uncluttered. The context should be sufficient to make the intended application understood.

Many people believe that if psychological determinism is true, the condition of freedom can never be satisfied. For if an agent's interests are determined by heredity and environment, they claim, it is not up to the agent to have the interests he has. And if his actions are determined by his interests as well, then he cannot but perform the actions he performs. In order for an agent to satisfy the condition of freedom, then, his actions must not be psychologically determined. Either his actions must not be determined by his interests, or his interests must not be determined by anything external to himself. They therefore conclude that the condition of freedom requires the absence of psychological determinism. And they think this is what we mean to express when we state the condition of freedom in terms of the requirement that the agent "could have done otherwise."

Let us imagine, however, what an agent who satisfied this condition would have to be like. Consider first what it would mean for the agent's actions not to be determined by his interests—for the agent, in other words, to have the ability to act despite his interests. This would mean, I think, that the agent has the ability to act against everything he believes in and everything he cares about. It would mean, for example, that if the agent's son were inside a burning building, the agent could just stand there and watch the house go up in flames. Or that the agent, though he thinks his neighbor a fine and agreeable fellow, could just get up one day, ring the doorbell, and punch him in the nose. One might think such pieces of behavior should not be classified as actions at all—that they are rather more like spasms that the agent cannot control. If they are actions, at least, they are very bizarre, and an agent who performed them would have to be insane. Indeed, one might think he would have to be insane if he had even the ability to perform them. For the rationality of an agent who could perform such irrational actions as these must hang by a dangerously thin thread.

So let us assume instead that his actions are determined by his interests, but that his interests are not determined by anything external to himself. Then of any of the interests he happens to have, it must be the case that he does not have to have them. Though perhaps he loves his wife, it must be possible for him not to love her. Though perhaps he cares about people in general, it must be possible for him not to care. This agent, moreover, could not have reasons for his interests—at least no reasons of the sort we normally have. He cannot love his wife, for example, because of the way his wife is—for the way his wife is is not up to him to decide. Such an agent, presumably, could not be much committed to anything; his interests must be something like a matter of whim. Such an agent must be able not to care about the lives of others, and, I suppose, he must be able not to care about his own life as well. An agent who didn't care about these things, one might think, would have to be crazy. And again, one might think he would have to be crazy if he had even the ability not to care.

In any case, it seems, if we require an agent to be psychologically undetermined, we cannot expect him to be a moral agent. For if we require that his actions not be determined by his interests, then *a fortiori* they cannot be determined by his moral interests. And if we require that his interests not be determined by anything else, then *a fortiori* they cannot be determined by his moral reasons.

When we imagine an agent who performs right actions, it seems, we imagine an agent who is rightly determined: whose actions, that is, are determined by the right sorts of interests, and whose interests are determined by the right sorts of reasons. But an agent who is not psychologically determined cannot perform actions that are right in this way. And if his actions can never be appropriately right, then in not performing right actions, he can never be wrong. The problem seems to be that the undetermined agent is so free as to be free *from moral reasons.* So the satisfaction of the condition of freedom seems to rule out the satisfaction of the condition of value.

This suggests that the condition of freedom was previously stated too strongly. When we require that a responsible agent "could have done otherwise" we cannot mean that it was not determined that he did what he did. It has been proposed that 'he could have done otherwise' should be analyzed as a conditional instead. For example, we might say that 'he could have done otherwise' means that he would have done otherwise, if he had tried. Thus the bank robber is responsible for robbing the bank, since he would have restrained himself if he had tried. But the man he locked up is not responsible for letting him escape, since he couldn't have stopped him even if he had tried.

Incompatibilists, however, will quickly point out that such an analysis is insufficient. For an agent who would have done otherwise if he had tried cannot be blamed for his action if he could not have tried. The compatibilist might try to answer this objection with a new conditional analysis of 'he could have tried.' He might say, for example, that 'he could have tried to do otherwise' be interpreted to mean he would have tried to do otherwise, if he had chosen. But the incompatibilist now has a new objection to make: namely, what if the agent could not have chosen?

It should be obvious that this debate might be carried on indefinitely with a proliferation of conditionals and a proliferation of objections. But if an agent is determined, no conditions one suggests will be conditions that an agent could have satisfied.

Thus, any conditional analysis of 'he could have done otherwise' seems too weak to satisfy the condition of freedom. Yet if 'he could have done otherwise' is not a conditional, it seems too strong to allow the satisfaction of the condition of value. We seem to think of ourselves one way when we are thinking about freedom, and to think of ourselves another way when we are thinking about morality. When we are thinking about the condition of freedom, our intuitions suggest that the incompatibilists are right. For they claim that an agent can be moral only insofar as his actions are psychologically determined. If our intuitions require that both these claims are right, then the concept of moral responsibility must be incoherent. For then a free agent can never be moral, and a moral agent can never be free.

In fact, however, I believe that philosophers have generally got our intuitions wrong. There is an asymmetry in our intuitions about freedom which has generally been overlooked. As a result, it has seemed that the answer to the problem of free will can lie in only one of two alternatives: Either the fact that an agent's action was determined is always compatible with his being responsible for it, or the fact that the agent's action was determined will always rule his responsibility out. I shall suggest that the solution lies elsewhere—that both compatibilists and incompatibilists are wrong. What we need in order to be responsible beings, I shall argue, is a suitable combination of determination and indetermination.

When we try to call up our intuitions about freedom, a few stock cases come readily to mind. We think of the heroin addict and the kleptomaniac, of the victim of hypnosis, and the victim of a deprived childhood. These cases, I think, provide forceful support for our incompatibilist intuitions. For of the kleptomaniac it may well be true that he would have done otherwise if he had tried. The kleptomaniac is not responsible because he could not have tried. Of the victim of hypnosis it may well be true that he would have done otherwise if he had chosen. The victim of hypnosis is not responsible because he could not have chosen.

The victim of the deprived childhood who, say, embezzles some money, provides the most poignant example of all. For this agent is not coerced nor overcome by an irresistible impulse. He is in complete possession of normal adult faculties of reason and observation. He seems, indeed, to have as much control over his behavior as we have of ours. He acts on the basis of his choice, and he chooses on the basis of his reasons. If there is any explanation of why this agent is not responsible, it would seem that it must consist simply in the fact that his reasons are determined.

These examples are all peculiar, however, in that they are examples of people doing bad things. If the agents in these cases were responsible for their actions, this would justify the claim that they deserve to be blamed. We seldom look, on the other hand, at examples of agents whose actions are morally good. We rarely ask whether an agent is truly responsible if his being responsible would make him worthy of praise.

There are a few reasons why this might be so which go some way in accounting for the philosophers' neglect. First, acts of moral blame are more connected with punishment than acts of moral praise are connected with reward. So acts of moral blame are likely to be more public, and examples will be readier to hand. Second, and more important, I think, we have stronger reasons for wanting acts of blame to be justified. If we blame someone or punish him, we are likely to be causing him some pain. But if we praise someone or reward him, we will probably only add to his pleasures. To blame someone undeservedly is, in any case, to do him an injustice. Whereas to praise someone undeservedly is apt to be just a harmless mistake. For this reason, I think, our intuitions about praise are weaker and less developed than our intuitions about blame. Still, we do have some intuitions about cases of praise, and it would be a mistake to ignore them entirely.

When we ask whether an agent's action is deserving of praise, it seems we do not require that he could have done otherwise. If an agent does the right thing for just the right reasons, it seems absurd to ask whether he could have done the wrong. "I cannot tell a lie," "He couldn't hurt a fly" are not exemptions from praiseworthiness but testimonies to it. If a friend presents you with a gift and says "I couldn't resist," this suggests the strength of his friendship and not the weakness of his will. If one feels one "has no choice" but to speak out against injustice, one ought not to be upset about the depth of one's commitment. And it seems I should be grateful for the fact that if I were in trouble, my family "could not help" but come to my aid.

Of course, these phrases must be given an appropriate interpretation if they are to indicate that the agent is deserving of praise. "He couldn't hurt a fly" must allude to someone's gentleness—it would be perverse to say this of someone who was in an iron lung. It is not admirable in George Washington that he cannot tell a lie, if it is because he has a tendency to stutter that inhibits his attempts. 'He could not have done otherwise' as it is used in the context of praise, then, must be taken to imply something like 'because he was too good'. An action is praiseworthy only if it is done for the right reasons. So it must be only in light of and because of these reasons that the praiseworthy agent "could not help" but do the right thing.

But when an agent does the right thing for the right reasons, the fact that, having the right reasons, he *must* do the right should surely not lessen the credit he deserves. For presumably the reason he cannot do otherwise is that his virtue is so sure or his moral commitment so strong.

One might fear that if the agent really couldn't have acted differently, his virtue must be *too* sure or his commitment *too* strong. One might think, for example, that if someone literally couldn't resist buying a gift for a friend, his generosity would not be a virtue—it would be an obsession. For one can imagine situations in which it would be better if the agent did resist—if, for example, the money that was spent on the gift was desperately needed for some other purpose. Presumably, in the original case, though, the money was not desperately needed—we praise the agent for buying a gift for his friend rather than, say, a gift for himself. But from the fact that the man could not resist in this situation it doesn't follow that he couldn't resist in another. For part of the explanation of why he couldn't resist in this situation is that in this situation he has no reason to try to resist. This man, we assume, has a generous nature—a disposition, that is, to perform generous acts. But, then, if he is in a situation that presents a golden opportunity, and has no conflicting motive, how could he act otherwise?

One might still be concerned that if his motives are determined, the man cannot be truly deserving of praise. If he cannot help but have a generous character, then the fact that he is generous is not up to him. If a man's motives are determined, one might think, then *he* cannot control them, so it cannot be to his credit if his motives turn out to be good. But whether a man is in control of his motives cannot be decided so simply. We must know not only whether his motives are determined, but how they are determined as well.

We can imagine, for example, a man with a generous mother who becomes generous as a means of securing her love. He would not have been generous had his mother been different. Had she not admired generosity, he would not have developed this trait. We can imagine further that once this man's character had been developed, he would never subject it to question or change. His character would remain unthinkingly rigid, carried over from a childhood over which he had no control. As he developed a tendency to be generous, let us say, he developed other tendencies—a tendency to brush his teeth twice a day, a tendency to avoid the company of Jews. The explanation for why he developed any one of these traits is more or less the same as the explanation for why he has developed any other. And the explanation for why he has retained any one of these tendencies is more or less the same as the explanation for why he has retained any other. These tendencies are all, for him, merely habits which he has never thought about breaking. Indeed, they are habits which, by hypothesis, it was determined he would never think about breaking. Such a man, perhaps, would not deserve credit for his generosity, for his generosity might be thought to be senseless and blind. But we can imagine a different picture in which no such claim is true, in which a generous character might be determined and yet under the agent's control.

We might start again with a man with a generous mother who starts to develop his generosity out of a desire for her love. But his reasons for developing a generous nature need not be his reasons for retaining it when he grows more mature. He may notice, for example, that his generous acts provide an independent pleasure, connected to the pleasure he gives the person on whom his generosity is bestowed. He may find that being generous promotes a positive fellow feeling and makes it easier for him to make friends than it would otherwise be. Moreover, he appreciates being the object of the generous acts of others, and he is hurt when others go to ungenerous extremes. All in all, his generosity seems to cohere with his other values. It fits in well with his ideals of how one ought to live.

Such a picture, I think, might be as determined as the former one. But it is compatible with the exercise of good sense and an open frame of mind. It is determined, because the agent does not create his new reasons for generosity any more than he created his old ones. He does not *decide* to feel an independent pleasure in performing acts of generosity, or decide that such acts will make it easier for him to make friends. He discovers that these are consequences of a generous nature—and if he is observant and perceptive, he cannot help but discover this. He does not choose to be the object of the generous acts of others, or to be the victim of less generous acts of less virtuous persons. Nor does he choose to be grateful to the one and hurt by the other. He cannot help but have these experiences—they are beyond his control. So it seems that what reasons he *has* for being generous depends on what reasons there *are.*

If the man's character is determined in this way, however, it seems absurd to say that it is not under his control. His character is determined on the basis of his reasons, and his reasons are determined by what reasons there are. What is not under his control, then, is that generosity be a virtue, and it is only because he realizes this that he remains a generous man. But one cannot say for *this* reason that his generosity is not praiseworthy. This is the best reason for being generous that a person could have.

So it seems that an agent can be morally praiseworthy even though he is determined to perform the action he performs. But we have already seen that an agent cannot be morally blameworthy if he is determined to perform the action he performs. Determination, then, is compatible with an agent's responsibility for a good action, but incompatible with an agent's responsibility for a bad action. The metaphysical conditions required for an agent's responsibility will vary according to the value of the action he performs.

The condition of freedom, as it is expressed by the requirement that an agent could have done otherwise, thus appears to demand a conditional analysis after all. But the condition must be one that separates the good actions from the bad—the condition, that is, must be essentially value-laden. An analysis of the condition of freedom that might do the trick is:

> He could have done otherwise if there had been good and sufficient reason.

where the 'could have done otherwise' in the analysans is not a conditional at all. For presumably an action is morally praiseworthy only if there are no good and sufficient reasons to do something else. And an action is morally blameworthy only if there are good and sufficient reasons to do something else. Thus, when an agent performs a good action, the condition of freedom is a counterfactual: though it is required that the agent would have been able to do otherwise *had there been* good and sufficient reason to do so, the situation in which the good-acting agent actually found himself is a situation in which there was no such reason. Thus, it is compatible with the satisfaction of the condition of freedom that the agent in this case could not actually have done other than what he actually did. When an agent performs a bad action, however, the condition of freedom is not a counterfactual. The bad-acting agent does what he does in the face of good and sufficient reasons to do otherwise. Thus the condition of freedom requires that the agent in this case could have done otherwise in just the situation in which he was actually placed. An agent, then, can be determined to perform a good action and still be morally praiseworthy. But if an agent is to be blameworthy, he must unconditionally have been able to do something else.

It may be easier to see how this analysis works, and how it differs from conditional analyses that were suggested before, if we turn back to the case in which these previous analyses failed—namely, the case of the victim of a deprived childhood.

We imagined a case, in particular, of a man who embezzled some money, fully aware of what he was doing. He was neither coerced nor overcome by an irresistible impulse, and he was in complete possession of normal adult faculties of reason and observation. Yet it seems he ought not to be blamed for committing his crime, for, from his point of view, one cannot reasonably expect him to see anything wrong with his action. We may suppose that in his childhood he was given no love—he was beaten by his father, neglected by his mother. And that the people to whom he was exposed when he was growing up gave him examples only of evil and selfishness. From his point of view, it is natural to conclude that respecting other people's property would be foolish. For presumably no one had ever respected his. And it is natural for him to feel that he should treat other people as adversaries.

In light of this, it seems that this man shouldn't be blamed for an action we know to be wrong. For if we had had his childhood, we wouldn't have known it either. Yet this agent seems to have as much control over his life as we are apt to have over ours: he would have done otherwise, if he had tried. He would have tried to do otherwise, if he had chosen. And he would have chosen to do otherwise, if he had had reason. It is because he couldn't have had reason that this agent should not be blamed.

Though this agent's childhood was different from ours, it would seem to be neither more nor less binding. The good fortune of our childhood is no more to our credit than the misfortune of his is to his blame. So if he is not free because of the childhood he had, then it would appear that we are not free either. Thus it seems no conditional analysis of freedom will do—for there is nothing internal to the agent which distinguishes him from us.

My analysis, however, proposes a condition that is not internal to the agent. And it allows us to state the relevant difference: namely that, whereas our childhoods fell within a range of normal decency, his was severely deprived. The consequence this has is that he, unlike us, could not have had reasons even though there were reasons around. The problem is not that his reason was functioning improperly, but that his data were unfortuitously selective. Since the world for him was not suitably cooperating, his reason cannot attain its appropriate goal.

The goal, to put it bluntly, is the True and the Good. The freedom we want is the freedom to find it. But such a freedom requires not only that we, as agents, have the right sorts of abilities—the abilities, that is, to direct and govern our actions by our most fundamental selves. It requires as well that the world cooperate in such a way that our most fundamental selves have the opportunity to develop into the selves they ought to be.

If the freedom necessary for moral responsibility is the freedom to be determined by the True and the Good, then obviously we cannot know whether we have such a freedom unless we know, on the one hand, that there *is* a True and a Good and, on the other, that there *are* capacities for finding them. As a consequence of this, the condition of freedom cannot be stated in purely metaphysical terms. For we cannot know which capacities and circumstances are necessary for freedom unless we know which capacities and circumstances will enable us to form the *right* values and perform the *right* actions. Strictly speaking, I take it, the capacity to reason is not enough—we need a kind of sensibility and perception as well. But these are capacities, I assume, that most of us have. So when the world cooperates, we are morally responsible.

I have already said that the condition of freedom cannot be stated in purely metaphysical terms. More specifically, the condition of freedom cannot be stated in terms that are value-free. Thus, the problem of free will has been misrepresented insofar as it has been thought to be a purely metaphysical problem. And, perhaps, this is why the problem of free will has seemed for so long to be hopeless.

That the problem should have seemed to be a purely metaphysical problem is not, however, unnatural or surprising. For being determined by the True and the Good is very different from being determined by one's garden variety of causes, and I think it not unnatural to feel as if one rules out the other. For to be determined by the Good is not to be determined by the Past. And to do something because it is the right thing to do is not to do it because one has been taught to do it. One might think, then, that one can be determined only by one thing or the other. For if one is going to do whatever it is right to do, then it seems one will do it whether or not one has been taught. And if one is going to do whatever one has been taught to do, then it seems one will do it whether or not it is right.

In fact, however, such reasoning rests on a category mistake. These two explanations do not necessarily compete, for they are explanations of different kinds. Consider, for example, the following situation: you ask me to name the capital of Nevada, and I reply "Carson City." We can explain why I give the answer I do give in either of the following ways: First, we can point out that when I was in the fifth grade I had to memorize the capitals of the fifty states. I was taught to believe that Carson City was the capital of Nevada, and was subsequently positively reinforced for doing so. Second, we can point out that Carson City *is* the capital of Nevada, and that this was, after all, what you wanted to know. So on the one hand, I gave my answer because I was taught. And on the other, I gave my answer because it was right.

Presumably, these explanations are not unrelated. For if Carson City were not the capital of Nevada, I would not have been taught that it was. And if I hadn't been taught that Carson City was the capital of Nevada, I wouldn't have known that it was. Indeed, one might think that if the answer I gave weren't right, I *couldn't* have given it because I was taught. For no school board would have hired a teacher who got such facts wrong. And if I hadn't been taught that Carson City was the capital of Nevada, perhaps I couldn't have given this answer because it was right. For that Carson City is the capital of Nevada is not something that can be known a priori.

Similarly, we can explain why a person acts justly in either of the following ways: First, we can point out that he was taught to act justly, and was subsequently positively reinforced for doing so. Second, we can point out that it is right to act justly, and go on to say why he knows this is so. Again, these explanations are likely to be related. For if it weren't right to act justly, the person may well not have been taught that it was. And if the person hadn't been taught that he ought to act justly, the person may not have discovered this on his own. Of course, the explanations of both kinds in this case will be more complex than the explanations in the previous case. But what is relevant here is that these explanations are compatible: that one can be determined by the Good and determined by the Past.

In order for an agent to be morally free, then, he must be capable of being determined by the Good. Determination by the Good is, as it were, the goal we need freedom to pursue. We need the freedom *to* have our actions determined by the Good, and the freedom to be or to become the sorts of persons whose actions will continue to be so determined. In light of this, it should be clear that no standard incompatibilist views about the conditions of moral responsibility can be right, for, according to these views, an agent is free only if he is the sort of agent whose actions are not causally determined at all. Thus, an agent's freedom would be incompatible with the realization of the goal for which freedom is required. The agent would be, in the words, though not in the spirit, of Sartre, "condemned to be free"—he could not both be free and realize a moral ideal.

Thus, views that offer conditional analyses of the ability to do otherwise, views that, like mine, take freedom to consist in the ability *to be determined* in a particular way, are generally compatibilist views. For insofar as an agent *is* determined in the right way, the agent can be said to be acting freely. Like the compatibilists, then, I am claiming that whether an agent is morally responsible depends not on whether but on how that agent is determined. My view differs from theirs only in what I take the satisfactory kind of determination to be.

However, since on my view the satisfactory kind of determination is determination by reasons that an agent ought to have, it will follow that an agent can be both determined and responsible only insofar as he performs actions that he ought to perform. If an agent performs a morally bad action, on the other hand, then his actions can't be determined in the appropriate way. So if an agent is ever to be responsible for a bad action, it must be the case that his action is not psychologically determined at all. According to my view, then, in order for both moral praise and moral blame to be justified, the thesis of psychological determinism must be false.

Is it plausible that this thesis is false? I think so. For though it appears that some of our actions are psychologically determined, it appears that others are not. It appears that some of our actions are not determined by our interests, and some of our interests are not determined at all. That is, it seems that some of our actions are such that no set of psychological facts are sufficient to explain them. There are occasions on which a person takes one action, but there seems to be no reason why he didn't take another.

For example, we sometimes make arbitrary choices—to wear the green shirt rather than the blue, to have coffee rather than tea. We make such choices on the basis of no reason—and it seems that we might, in these cases, have made a different choice instead.

Some less trivial and more considered choices may also be arbitrary. For one may have reasons on both sides which are equally strong. Thus, one may have good reasons to go to graduate school and good reasons not to;

good reasons to get married, and good reasons to stay single. Though we might want, in these cases, to choose on the basis of reasons, our reasons simply do not settle the matter for us. Other psychological events may be similarly undetermined, such as the chance occurrence of thoughts and ideas. One is just struck by an idea, but for no particular reason—one might as easily have had another idea or no idea at all. Or one simply forgets an appointment one has made, even though one was not particularly distracted by other things at the time.

On retrospect, some of the appearance of indetermination may turn out to be deceptive. We decide that unconscious motives dictated a choice that seemed at the time to be arbitrary. Or a number of ideas that seemed to occur to us at random reveal a pattern too unusual to be the coincidence we thought. But if some of the appearances of indetermination are deceptive, I see no reason to believe that all of them should be.

Let us turn, then, to instances of immoral behavior, and see what the right kind of indetermination would be. For indetermination, in this context, is indetermination among some number of fairly particular alternatives—and if one's alternatives are not of the appropriate kind, indetermination will not be sufficient to justify moral blame. It is not enough, for example, to know that a criminal who happened to rob a bank might as easily have chosen to hold up a liquor store instead. What we need to know, in particular, is that when an agent performs a wrong action, he could have performed the right action for the right reasons instead. That is, first, the agent could have had the interests that the agent ought to have had, and second, the agent could have acted on the interests on which he ought to have acted.

Corresponding to these two possibilities, we can imagine two sorts of moral failure: the first corresponds to a form of negligence, the second to a form of weakness. Moral negligence consists in a failure to recognize the existence of moral reasons that one ought to have recognized. For example, a person hears that his friend is in the hospital, but fails to attend to this when planning his evening. He doesn't stop to think about how lonely and bored his friend is likely to be—he simply reaches for the *TV Guide* or for his novel instead. If the person could have recognized his friend's sorry predicament, he is guilty of moral negligence. Moral weakness, on the other hand, consists in the failure to act on the reasons that one knows one ought, for moral reasons, to be acting on. For example, a person might go so far as to conclude that he really ought to pay his sick friend a visit, but the thought of the drive across town is enough to convince him to stay at home with his book after all. If the person could have made the visit, he is guilty of moral weakness.

There is, admittedly, some difficulty in establishing that an agent who performs a morally bad action satisfies the condition of freedom. It is hard to know whether an agent who did one thing could have done another instead. But presumably we decide such questions now on the basis of statistical evidence—and, if, in fact, these actions are not determined, this is the best method there can be. We decide, in other words, that an agent could have done otherwise if others in his situation have done otherwise, and these others are like him in all apparently relevant ways. Or we decide that an agent could have done otherwise if he himself has done otherwise in situations that are like this one in all apparently relevant ways.

It should be emphasized that the indetermination with which we are here concerned is indetermination only at the level of psychological explanation. Such indetermination is compatible with determination at other levels of explanation. In particular, a sub-psychological, or physiological, explanation of our behavior may yet be deterministic. Some feel that if this is the case, the nature of psychological explanations of our behavior cannot be relevant to the problem of free will. Though I am inclined to disagree with this view, I have neither the space nor the competence to argue this here.

Restricting the type of explanation in question appropriately, however, it is a consequence of the condition of freedom I have suggested that the explanation for why a responsible agent performs a morally bad action must be, at some level, incomplete. There must be nothing that made the agent perform the action he did, nothing that prevented him from performing a morally better one. It should be noted that there may be praiseworthy actions for which the explanations are similarly incomplete. For the idea that an agent who could have performed a morally bad action actually performs a morally good one is no less plausible than the idea that an agent who could have performed a morally good action actually performs a morally bad one. Presumably, an agent who does the right thing for the right reasons deserves praise for his action whether it was determined or not. But whereas indetermination is compatible with the claim that an agent is deserving of praise, it is essential to the justification of the claim that an agent is deserving of blame.

Seen from a certain perspective, this dealing out of praise and blame may seem unfair. In particular, we might think that if it is truly undetermined whether a given agent in a given situation will perform a good action or a bad one, then it must be a matter of chance that the agent ends up doing what he does. If the action is truly undetermined, then it is not determined by the agent himself. One might think that in this case the agent has no more control over the moral quality of his action than does anything else.

However, the fact that it is not determined whether the agent will perform a good action or a bad one does not imply that which action he performs can properly be regarded as a matter of chance. Of course, in some situations an agent might choose to make it a matter of chance. For example, an agent struggling with the decision between fulfilling a moral obligation and doing something immoral that he very much wants to do might ultimately decide to let the toss of a coin settle the matter for him. But, in normal cases, the way in which the agent makes a decision involves no statistical process or randomizing event. It appears that the claim that there is no complete explanation of why the agent who could have performed a better action performed a worse one or why the agent who could have performed a worse action performed a better one rules out even the explanation that it was a matter of chance.

In order to have control over the moral quality of his actions, an agent must have certain requisite abilities—in particular, the abilities necessary to see and understand the reasons and interests he ought to see and understand and the abilities necessary to direct his actions in accordance with these reasons and interests. And if, furthermore, there is nothing that interferes with the agent's use of these abilities—that is, no determining cause that prevents him from using them and no statistical process that, as it were, takes out of his hands the control over whether or not he uses them—then it seems that these are all the abilities that the agent needs to have. But it is compatible with the agent's having these abilities and with there being no interferences to their use that it is not determined whether the agent will perform a good action or a bad one. The responsible agent who performs a bad action fails to exercise these abilities sufficiently, though there is no complete explanation of why he fails. The responsible agent who performs a good action does exercise these abilities—it may or may not be the case that it is determined that he exercise them.

The freedom required for moral responsibility, then, is the freedom to be good. Only this kind of freedom will be neither too much nor too little. For then the agent is not so free as to be free from moral reasons, nor so unfree as to make these reasons ineffective.

John Martin Fischer, "My Compatibilism"

John Martin Fischer is a professor of philosophy at the University of California, Riverside and an advocate of an influential compatibilist point of view. With Frankfurt he rejects the claim that free will requires the ability to do otherwise, and he contends that instead it requires an ability to guide our actions by reasons, an ability not threatened by determinism.

I. Introduction

Thinking about it in one way, compatibilism seems very plausible. For now, take "compatibilism" to be the doctrine that both some central notion of freedom and also genuine, robust moral responsibility are compatible with the doctrine of causal determinism (which, among other things, entails that every bit of human behavior is causally necessitated by events in the past together with the natural laws). Of course, compatibilism, as thus understood, does not in itself take any stand on whether causal determinism is true.

Compatibilism can seem plausible because it appears so obvious to us that we (most of us) are at least sometimes free and morally responsible, and yet we also realize that causal determinism could turn out to be true. That is, for all we know, it is true that all events (including human behavior) are the results of chains of necessitating causes that can be traced indefinitely into the past. Put slightly differently, I could certainly imagine waking up some morning to the newspaper headline, "Causal Determinism Is True!" (Most likely this would not be in the *National Inquirer* or even *People*—but perhaps the *New York Times*. . . .) I could imagine reading the article and subsequently (presumably over some time) becoming convinced that causal determinism is true—that the generalizations that describe the relationships between complexes of past events and laws of nature, on the one hand, and subsequent events, on the other, are

Reprinted with permission from Blackwell Publishers and the author. This is an abridged version, with revisions, of a longer essay that appeared in Manuel Vargas, ed., *Four Views on Free Will: A Debate* (Malden, MA: Blackwell, 2007).

universal generalizations with 100 percent probabilities associated with them. And I feel confident that this would not, nor should it, change my view of myself and others as (sometimes) free and robustly morally responsible agents—deeply different from other animals. The mere fact that these generalizations or conditionals have 100 percent probabilities associated with them, rather than 99.9 percent (say), would not and should not have any effect on my views about the existence of freedom and moral responsibility. My basic views of myself and others as free and responsible are and should be resilient with respect to such a discovery about the arcane and "close" facts pertaining to the generalizations of physics. (This of course is not to say that these basic views are resilient to *any* empirical discovery—just to this sort of discovery.)

So, when I deliberate I often take it that I am free in the sense that I have more than one option that is genuinely open to me. Since causal determinism (in the sense sketched above) might, for all we know, be true, compatibilism seems extremely attractive. Similarly, it is very natural to distinguish those agents who are compelled to behave as they do from those who act freely; we make this distinction, and mark the two classes of individuals, in common sense and also the law. But since causal determinism might, for all we know, be true, compatibilism is extremely attractive. If causal determinism turned out to be true, and incompatibilism were also true, then it would seem that all behavior would be put into one class—the distinctions we naturally and intuitively draw in common sense and law would be in jeopardy of disappearing.

And yet there are deep problems with compatibilism. Perhaps these are what have led some philosophers to condemn it in such vigorous terms: "wretched subterfuge" (Kant), "quagmire of evasion" (James), and "the most flabbergasting instance of the fallacy of changing the subject to be encountered anywhere in the complete history of sophistry . . . [a ploy that] was intended to take in the vulgar, but which has beguiled the learned in our time" (Wallace Matson).

In this short essay I will start by highlighting the attractions of compatibilism and sketching and motivating an appealing version of traditional compatibilism. I shall then present a basic challenge to such a compatibilism. Given this challenge, I suggest an alternative version of compatibilism, which I call "semicompatibilism," and I develop some of the advantages of such an approach. My goal will be to present the beginning of a defense of semicompatibilism (highlighting the main attractions), rather than a detailed elaboration or full defense of the doctrine.

II. The Lure of Compatibilism

As I pointed out above, often it seems to me that I have more than one path open to me. The paths into the future branch out from the present, and they represent different ways I could proceed into the future. When I deliberate now about whether to go to the lecture or to the movies tonight, I now think I genuinely can go to the lecture, and I genuinely can go to the movies (but perhaps I cannot do both). And I often have this view about the future—the view of the future as a "garden of forking paths" (in Borges' wonderful phrase). But I also can be brought to recognize that, for all I know, causal determinism is true; its truth would not necessarily manifest itself to me phenomenologically. Thus, compatibilism is extremely attractive: it allows me to keep both the view that I (sometimes at least) have more than one path genuinely open to me and also that causal determinism may be true. (I can keep both of these views in the same mental compartment, so to speak; they need not be compartmentalized into different mental slots or thought to apply to different realms or perspectives.)

It is incredibly natural—almost inevitable phenomenologically—to think that I could either go to the movies or to the lecture tonight, that I could either continue working on this essay or take a coffee break, and so forth. It would be jarring to discover that, despite the appearance of the availability of these options, only one path into the future is genuinely available to me. A compatibilist need not come to the one-path conclusion, in the event that theoretical physicists conclusively establish that the conditionals discussed above have associated with them 100 percent probabilities, rather than (say) 99.9 percent probabilities. A compatibilist can embrace the resiliency of this fundamental view of ourselves as agents who (help to) *select* the path the world takes into the future, among various paths it genuinely *could* take. A compatibilist can capture the intuitive idea that a tiny difference (between 100 percent and 99.9 percent) should not make such a huge difference (between our having more than one genuinely available pathway into the future and this pervasive phenomenological fact being just a big delusion). How could such a small change—of the sort envisaged in the probabilities associated with the arcane conditionals of theoretical physics—make such a big difference?

Similarly, it is natural and extraordinarily "basic" for human beings to think of ourselves as (sometimes at least) morally accountable for our choices and behavior. Typically, we think of ourselves as morally responsible precisely in virtue of exercising a distinctive kind of freedom or control;

this freedom is traditionally thought to involve exactly the sort of "selection" from among genuinely available alternative possibilities alluded to above. When an agent is morally responsible for his behavior, we typically suppose that he could have (at least at some relevant time) done otherwise.

The assumption that we human beings—most of us, at least—are morally responsible agents (at least sometimes) is extremely important and pervasive. In fact, it is hard to imagine human life without it. (At the very least, such life would be very different from the way we currently understand our lives—less richly textured and, arguably, not better or more attractive.) A compatibilist need not give up this assumption, even if he were to wake up to the headline, "Causal Determinism Is True!" (and he were convinced of its truth). Nor need the compatibilist give up any of his basic metaphysical views—apparently a priori metaphysical truths that support his views about free will—simply because the theoretical physicists have established that the relevant probabilities are 100 percent rather than 99 percent. Wouldn't it be bizarre to give up a principle such as that the past is fixed and out of our control or that logical truths are fixed and out of our control, simply because one has been convinced that the probabilities in question are 100 percent rather than 99 percent? A compatibilist need not "flip-flop" in this weird and unappealing way.

In ordinary life, and in our moral principles and legal system, we distinguish individuals who behave freely from those who do not. Sam is a "normal" adult human being, who grew up in favorable circumstances (roughly those described in the American TV series, *Leave It to Beaver*). He has no unusual neurophysiological or psychological anomalies or disorders, and he is not in a context in which he is manipulated, brainwashed, coerced, or otherwise "compelled" to do what he does. More specifically, no factors that uncontroversially function to undermine, distort, or thwart the normal human faculty of practical reasoning or execution of the outputs of such reasoning are present. He deliberates in the "normal way" about whether to deliberately withhold pertinent information on his income tax forms, and, although he knows it is morally wrong, he decides to withhold the information and cheat on his taxes anyway.

According to our common sense way of looking at the world and even our more theoretical moral and legal perspectives, Sam freely chooses to cheat on his income taxes and freely cheats. It is plausible that, given the assumptions I have sketched, he was free just prior to his decision and action *not* to so decide and behave. Insofar as Sam selected his own path, he acted freely and can be held both morally and legally accountable for cheating on his taxes.

On the other hand, we tend to exempt certain agents from *any* moral responsibility in virtue of their lacking even the *capacity* to control their choices and actions; we take it that such individuals are so impaired in their cognitive and/or executive capacities that they cannot *freely* select their path into the future (even if various paths present themselves as genuinely available). Such agents may have significant brain damage or neurological or psychological disorders in virtue of which they are not even capable of exercising the distinctive human capacity of control in any morally significant context. Other agents may have the basic features that underwrite this capacity, but they nevertheless are locally rather than globally exempt from moral responsibility.

On the common sense view, even as structured and refined by moral and legal analysis, agents who are brainwashed (without their consent), involuntarily subjected to hypnosis or subliminal advertising or other forms of behavioral conditioning, or even direct stimulation of the brain, are not morally responsible for the relevant behavior. But they may be morally responsible for choices and actions that are not the result of these "stock" examples of freedom-undermining and thus responsibility-undermining factors.

Of course, there are difficult cases of significant coercion, or pressure that falls short of genuine compulsion, or subliminal suggestion that is influential but not determinative, about which reasonable persons may disagree. Further, there is considerable controversy over the role and significance of early childhood experiences, deprivations, poverty, physical and psychological abuse, and so forth. But even though there are "hard cases," common sense—and moral and legal theory—has it that there are clear cases of freedom and responsibility, on the one hand, and clear cases of the lack of it, on the other.

A compatibilist can maintain this distinction, even if it turns out that the physicists convince us that the probabilities associated with the relevant conditionals—the conditionals linking the past and laws with the present in physics—are 100 percent, rather than 99.9 percent. And this is a significant and attractive feature of compatibilism. Incompatibilism would seem to lead to a collapse of the important distinction between agents such as Sam and thoroughly manipulated or brainwashed or coerced agents. A compatibilist need not deny what seems so obvious, even if the conditionals have attached to them probabilities of 100 percent: there is an important difference between agents such as Sam, who act freely and can be held morally responsible, and individuals who are completely or partially exempt from moral responsibility in virtue of *special* hindrances and disabilities that impair their functioning. Again, a compatibilist's view of human beings as (sometimes) both free and morally responsible agents is *resilient* to the particular empirical discovery that causal determinism is true. Wouldn't it be bizarre if our basic view of ourselves as free and morally responsible, and our distinction between responsible agents and those who are insane or literally unable to control their behavior, would hang on whether the probabilities of the conditionals are 99.9 percent or 100 percent? Again, how can such a tiny change make such a monumental difference?

III. A Compatibilist Account of Freedom

One might distinguish between the forward-looking aspects of agency, including practical reasoning, planning, and deliberation, and the backward-looking aspects of agency, including accountability and moral (and legal) responsibility. I have noted that it is extremely natural and plausible—almost inevitable—to think of ourselves as (sometimes at least) having more than one path branching into the future. This same assumption appears to frame both our deliberation and (retrospectively) our attributions of responsibility. I shall here take it that the possibilities in question are the *same* in both forward-looking and backward-looking aspects of agency: when we deliberate, we naturally presuppose that we have different paths into the future, and when we assign responsibility, we suppose (typically) that the relevant agent had available to him a different path.

In both forward-looking and backward-looking contexts, it is appealing to suppose that the relevant sort of possibility or freedom is analyzed as a certain sort of choice-dependence. That is, when I'm deliberating, it is plausible to suppose that I genuinely can do whatever it is that I would do, if I were so to act: I can go to the movies later insofar as I would go to the movies, if I were to choose to go to the movies, and I can go to the lecture insofar as I would go to the lecture, if I were to choose to go to the lecture, and so forth. On this view, I can do, in the relevant sense of "can," whatever is a (suitable) function of my "will" or choices: the scope of my deliberation about the future is the set of paths along which my behavior is a function of my choices. I do not deliberate about whether to jump to the moon, because (in part at least) I would not successfully jump to the moon, even if I were to choose to jump to the moon.

Similarly, given the assumption of the unity of forward-looking and backward-looking features of agency, the alternative possibilities pertinent to the attribution of responsibility are understood in terms of choice-dependence. That is, on this approach an agent is morally responsible for a certain action only if he could have done otherwise, and he could have done otherwise just in case he would have done otherwise, if he had chosen to do otherwise.

This compatibilist analysis of freedom (or the distinctive sort of possibility relevant to deliberation and responsibility) is called the "conditional analysis" because it suggests that our freedom can be understood in terms of certain conditional statements ("if-then" statements). More specifically, the conditional analysis commends to us the view that an agent *S*'s freedom to do *X* can be understood in terms of the truth of a statement such as, "If S were to choose (will, decide, and so forth) to do *X*, *S* would do *X*." The subjunctive conditional specifies the relevant notion of "dependence." The analysis seems to capture important elements of our intuitive picture of what is within the legitimate scope of our deliberation and planning for the future. It also helps to sort out at least some cases in which agents are not morally responsible for their behavior—and to distinguish these from cases in which agents are responsible. If someone is kidnapped and chained, he is presumably not morally responsible for not helping someone in distress insofar as he would still be in chains (and thus would not succeed in helping) even if he were to choose (decide, will) to help.

But despite its considerable attractions, the conditional analysis, as presented thus far, has fatal problems—problems that should be seen to be fatal even by the compatibilist. First, note that it may be that some upshot is choice-dependent in the way specified by the conditional analysis, and yet there may be some factor that (uncontroversially) impairs or hinders the relevant agent's capacity for choice (in the circumstances in question). This factor could render the agent powerless (in the sense presumably relevant to moral responsibility), even though the upshot is choice-dependent.

So consider the following example due to Keith Lehrer.[1] As a boy, Thomas had a terrible and traumatic experience with a snake. He thus has a pathological aversion to snakes that renders him psychologically incapable of bringing himself to choose to touch a snake (much less pick one up),

1. Lehrer discusses such cases in various places, including Keith Lehrer, "'Can' in Theory and Practice: A Possible-Worlds Analysis," in Myles Brand and Kendall Walton, eds., *Action Theory* (Dordrecht: Reidel Publishing Co., 1976), pp. 241–70.

even as an adult. A snake is in a basket right in front of Thomas. Whereas it is true that *if* Thomas were to choose to pick up the snake, he would do so, it is nevertheless true that Thomas cannot choose to pick up the snake. Intuitively, Thomas cannot pick up the snake—and yet the conditional analysis would have it that he can (in the relevant sense). This is a problem that even a compatibilist should see as significant; the problem clearly does not come from causal determination per se. The general form of the problem is that the relevant subjunctive conditional can be true consistently with the actual operation of some factor that intuitively (and apart from any contentious views about the compatibility of causal determinism and freedom) makes it the case that the agent is psychologically incapable of choosing (the act in question) and thus unable to perform the act. Factors that would seem to render an agent psychologically incapable of choice (and which could be seen to do so even by a compatibilist) might include past trauma, subliminal advertising, aversive conditioning, hypnosis, and even direct electric stimulation of the brain.

To make the point starkly, an individual could have his brain directly manipulated (without his consent) so as to choose *Y*. This would presumably render it true that he cannot do *X*, even though it might well be the case that *if* he had chosen to do *X*, he would have done *X*. (Of course, if the individual were to choose *X*, then he would not have been subject to the actual manipulation to which he has been subjected—manipulation that issues in his choosing *Y*.) Think of a demonic (or even well-intentioned) neuroscientist (or even a team including very nice neurophilosophers and neuroscientists!) who can manipulate parts of the brain by using (say) a laser; metaphorically, the laser beam can be thought of as a line that comes from some external source—some source physically external to the individual who is being manipulated and out of his control—at the "end" of which is the individual's choice to do *Y*. The neuroscientist knows the systematic workings of the brain so that she knows what sort of laser-induced manipulation is bound to produce a choice to do *Y*. Under such circumstances, it would seem ludicrous to suppose that the individual is free to do *X*; and yet it may well be true that *if* he were to choose *X*, the neuroscientist would not have intervened and the individual would successfully do *X*. The upshot is choice-dependent, but the individual is clearly powerless (in the relevant sense).

Some compatibilists about freedom and causal determinism have given up on the conditional analysis in light of such difficulties. Others have sought to give a more refined conditional analysis. So we might distinguish between the generally discredited "simple" conditional analysis, and what might be called the "refined" conditional analysis. Different philosophers have suggested different ways of refining the simple analysis, but the basic idea is somehow to rule out the factors that uncontroversially (that is, without making any assumptions that are contentious within the context of an evaluation of the compatibility of causal determinism and freedom) render an agent unable to choose (and thus unable to act). Along these lines, one might try something like this: an agent *S* can do *X* just in case (i) if *S* were to choose to do *X*, *S* would do *X*, and (ii) the agent is not subject to clandestine hypnosis, subliminal advertising, psychological compulsion resulting from past traumatic experiences, direct stimulation of the brain, neurological damage due to a fall or accident, and so forth. . . .

An obvious problem with the refined analysis is the "and so forth. . . ." It would seem that an indefinitely large number of other conditions (apparently heterogeneous in nature) could in principle be thought to issue in the relevant sort of incapacity. Additionally, there should be a certain discomfort in countenancing as part of the analysis a list of disparate items with no explanation of what ties them together as a class; from a philosophical point of view, condition (ii) posits an unseemly miscellany. How could one evaluate a proposed addition to the list in a principled way?

Perhaps the compatibilist could simply admit these problems and revise condition (ii) in the following way: (ii) the agent is not subject to *any* factor that would uncontroversially (that is, without making any assumptions that are contentious within the context of an evaluation of the compatibility of causal determinism and freedom) render an agent unable to choose the act in question (and thus unable to act). Despite the obvious problems of incompleteness in this analysis, it might capture something useful; it might capture much of what a compatibilist means by the relevant notion of freedom.

Unfortunately, the proposed revision renders the analysis completely useless in seeking to resolve the controversial issue of whether causal determinism is compatible with freedom (in the relevant sense). This is because all actual choices will be the result of a causally deterministic sequence, if causal determinism is true. Since causal determination obviously is *not* a factor that uncontroversially renders an agent unable to choose (and thus unable to act), the revised analysis will have results congenial to compatibilism. But it would be dialectically unfair to the incompatibilist to suppose that the revised analysis can be seen uncontroversially to be acceptable; that is, it would clearly beg the question against the incompatibilist to contend that the refined conditional analysis can be seen to be a plausible analysis of the sort of freedom that is under consideration.

To see this more clearly, recall again the metaphor of the line from the neuroscientist to the individual's choice. When the neuroscientist uses clandestine and unconsented-to manipulation by a laser beam, it is plausible that the individual could not have chosen otherwise. Note that, under the circumstances, the only way the individual would have chosen otherwise (would have chosen *X* instead of *Y*) would have been if the neuroscientist had not employed the laser beam as she actually did; that is, it was a necessary condition of the individual's choosing otherwise that the line not have been present, as it were. But the incompatibilist will ask how, exactly, causal determination of the choice to do *Y* is any different from the neuroscientist's employment of her laser beam to manipulatively induce a choice to do *Y*. The laser beam is not experienced as coercive—it is by hypothesis not experienced at all. The laser is a "subtle" and phenomenologically inaccessible influence that starts entirely "outside" the agent (physically external to the agent and not within his control) and issues (via a process over which the agent has no control) in a choice to do *Y*. But if causal determinism is true, then there is *some* causally deterministic sequence that starts entirely "outside" the agent (physically external to the agent and not within his control) and issues (via a deterministic process) in a choice to do *Y*. The incompatibilist will legitimately ask what exactly the difference between the laser beam and the causally deterministic sequence is. Metaphorically, they are both lines that start outside the agent and end with the same choice, and both lines must be "erased" to get a different choice.

Now a compatibilist might grant this, but insist on a crucial point—that not all causal sequences are "created equal." More specifically, the compatibilist wishes to insist that not all causally deterministic sequences undermine freedom; a straightforward and "upfront" commitment of the compatibilist is to the idea that we can distinguish among causally deterministic sequences and, more specifically, that we can distinguish those that involve "compulsion" (or some freedom- and responsibility-undermining factor) from those that do not. Returning to the pictorial metaphor: it may well be that an individual cannot choose or do otherwise when being manipulated by the neuroscientist's laser beam—in this case the individual cannot erase the line from the neuroscientist to his choice. On the other hand, according to the compatibilist, there is no reason to suppose that I am not free either to go to the lecture or to go to the movies later. Even if I do in fact go to the movies, there is no reason—no reason stemming merely from the truth of causal determinism—to suppose that my behavior is causally determined in a *special way*—a way uncontroversially recognized to rule out freedom and responsibility. Thus, even if I do in fact go to the movies later, the compatibilist might say that there is no reason (stemming merely from the truth of causal determinism) to think that I will not be free (at the relevant time) to go to the lecture instead—and thus no reason to suppose that I will not be free (at the relevant time) to erase the line that does in fact connect the past to my choice to go to the movies.

IV. The Consequence Argument

Yes, it is a basic commitment of the compatibilist—to which I promise we will return below—that not all causally deterministic sequences undermine freedom equally. But there is nevertheless an argument that presents a significant challenge to this commitment and also to the common-sense idea that we can be confident in distinguishing cases of freedom and responsibility from cases where some freedom- and responsibility-undermining factor operates. This argument is a "skeptical argument," rather like the skeptical argument from the possibility of illusion to the conclusion that we don't know what we ordinarily take ourselves to know about the external world. The skeptical argument in epistemology employs basic ingredients of common sense to challenge other parts of common sense; that is, it employs ordinary ideas about the possibility of illusion and the concept of knowledge (putatively) to generate the intuitively jarring result that we don't know what we take ourselves to know about the external world. Similarly, the skeptical argument about our freedom employs ordinary ideas about the fixity of the past and the fixity of the natural laws (putatively) to generate the intuitively jarring result that we are not ever free, if causal determinism turns out to be true (something we can't rule out a priori). If this skeptical argument is sound, it calls into question *any* compatibilist analysis of freedom (that is, freedom of the sort under consideration—involving the capacity for selection among open alternatives). If the argument is sound, then not only both the simple and refined conditional analysis, but *any* compatibilist analysis (of the relevant sort of freedom) must be rejected. It is thus an extremely powerful and disturbing argument. I think that any honest and serious discussion of compatibilism must address this argument, to which I turn now.

The skeptical argument has been around in one form or another for a very long time. Actually, a structurally similar argument was originally presented thousands of years ago; then, the worry was fatalism (more specifically, the idea that the truth values of statements about the future must be fixed and thus we lack freedom). Then in the Middle Ages the worry stemmed from the doctrine of God's essential omniscience. In the Modern era, our attention has focused primarily (although by no means exclusively) on the threat posed by science—more specifically, the possibility that causal determinism is true. At this point, we simply do not know whether causal determinism is true or not. If it turns out to be true, then all our behavior could in principle be deduced from a complete description of the past and laws of nature. Alternatively, if causal determinism is true, then true propositions about the past and propositions that express the laws of nature entail all our current and future choices and actions.

Here's the argument (very informally). Suppose that causal determinism is indeed true. Given the definition of causal determinism, it follows that my current choice to continue typing (and not take an admittedly much-needed coffee break) is entailed by true propositions about the past and laws of nature. Thus, if I were free (just prior to my actual choice) to choose (and subsequently do) otherwise, then I must have been free so to behave that the past would have been different or the natural laws would have been different. But intuitively the past is "fixed" and out of my control and so are the natural laws. I cannot now do anything that is such that, if I were to do it, the past would have been different (say, John F. Kennedy never would have been assassinated) or the natural laws would be different (say, some things would travel faster than the speed of light [if I've got the natural law in question correct!]). It appears to follow that, despite the natural and almost ineluctable sense I have that I am (sometimes, at least) free to choose and do otherwise, I am never free to choose and do otherwise, if causal determinism obtains.

Although the compatibilist wishes to say that not all causally deterministic sequences equally threaten freedom, the Consequence Argument—so-called by Peter van Inwagen because under causal determinism all our behavior is the consequence of the past plus the laws of nature—appears to imply that causal determinism per se rules out the relevant sort of freedom.[2] If the Consequence Argument is sound—and it relies on intuitively plausible ingredients, such as the fixity of the past and natural laws—then the common-sense distinction between cases of "compulsion" and ordinary cases in which moral responsibility is present would vanish,

2. Peter van Inwagen, *An Essay on Free Will* (Oxford: Clarendon Press, 1983).

if causal determinism were true; and since we do not know that causal determinism is false, our basic views about ourselves (as free and morally responsible agents) would be called into question.

Recall that it would be uncontroversial that I would not be morally responsible if I were subjected to clandestine (and unconsented to) manipulation by a neuroscientist's laser beam. As I said above, in such a context, in order for a different choice to have occurred, the laser beam must not have connected the neurosurgeon with my actual choice. Similarly, if causal determinism were true, then the Consequence Argument brings out the fact that—even in the most "ordinary" circumstances (that is, in the absence of anything that would uncontroversially constitute compulsion)—in order for a different choice to have occurred, the past or the natural laws would have had to have been different: the "line" connecting the past to my choice (via the laws) would have had to have been broken (or erased). The line posited by causal determination appears to be equivalent to the laser beam.

Another way to look at the ingredients that go into the Consequence Argument is to consider the intuitive idea that (as Carl Ginet puts the point) my freedom now is the freedom to add to the given past, holding fixed the laws of nature.[3] In terms of our metaphor, my freedom (on this view) is the freedom to draw a line that *extends* the line that connects the actual past with the present (holding fixed the natural laws). The future may well be a garden of forking paths (in Borges' lovely phrase), but the forking paths all branch off a single line (presumably). The Consequence Argument throws into relief an intuitively jarring implication of compatibilism: the compatibilist cannot embrace the almost undeniable picture of our freedom as the freedom to add to the past, given the laws. If the past is a set of dots, then for our freedom truly to be understandable, we must be able to connect the dots—in more ways than one. Some have said that responsibility involves "making a connection" with values of a certain sort, or "tracking values" in a certain way; but there is even a more fundamental way in which our freedom involves making a connection: we must be able to connect our current actions with our past (holding the natural laws fixed).

In my opinion, the Consequence Argument is a powerful and highly plausible argument. On the other hand, it certainly falls short of being indisputably sound. Some compatibilists—Multiple-Pasts Compatibilists—

3. Carl Ginet, *On Action* (Cambridge: Cambridge University Press, 1990), pp. 102–3.

are willing to say that we can sometimes so act that the past would have been different from what it actually was; alternatively, these compatibilists say that our freedom need not be construed as the freedom to extend the given past, holding the natural laws fixed. On such a view, I might have access to a possibility with a different past associated with it (a possible world with a different past from the actual past) insofar as there are no special "obstacles" in the actual course of events (or the actual world) that "block" such access. Other compatibilists—Local-Miracle Compatibilists—are willing to say that we can sometimes so act that a natural law that actually obtains would not have obtained; some such compatibilists are also willing to countenance small changes in the past as well as the laws. On this sort of view, I might have access to a possibility (or possible world) with slightly different natural laws from those that obtain actually, as long as these alternative scenarios do not involve widespread and big changes in the laws. This view is defended in a classic paper by David Lewis.[4]

So there is room for compatibilism about causal determinism and the sort of freedom that involves genuine access to alternative possibilities, even in light of the Consequence Argument; excellent philosophers have opted for some response to the Consequence Argument (such as Local-Miracle or Multiple-Pasts Compatibilism). As I said above, the Consequence Argument is not indisputably sound, and thus there is no knockdown argument available that the responses are inadequate.

I do in fact find the Consequence Argument highly plausible, and I am inclined to accept its soundness. I thus think it is important to argue that there is an attractive kind of compatibilism that is indeed consistent with accepting the Consequence Argument as sound. The doctrine of semicompatibilism is the claim that causal determinism is compatible with moral responsibility quite apart from whether causal determinism rules out the sort of freedom that involves access to alternative possibilities. Note that semicompatibilism in itself does not take a stand on whether the Consequence Argument is sound; it is consistent with acceptance or rejection of the Consequence Argument. My main goal is to defend semicompatibilism, although I am also inclined to accept the soundness of the Consequence Argument. The total package of views I am inclined to accept includes more than semicompatibilism, but semicompatibilism is the principle doctrine I seek to defend here.

4. David Lewis, "Are We Free to Breathe the Laws?" *Theoria* (1981), pp. 113–21.

V. Semicompatiblism and the Frankfurt-examples

Let's say you are driving your car and it is functioning normally. You want to go to the coffee house, so you guide the car to the right (into the parking lot for the coffee house). Your choice to go to the coffee house is based on your own reasons in the normal way, and the car's steering apparatus functions normally. Here you have a certain distinctive kind of control of the car's movements—you have "guidance control" of the car's going to the right. This is more than mere causation or even causal determination; you might have causally determined the car's going to the right by sneezing (and thus jerking the steering wheel to the right) or having an epileptic seizure (and thus slumping over the wheel and causing it to turn to the right) without having exercised this specific and distinctive sort of *control.* Supposing that there are no "special" factors at work—that is, no special psychological impairments, brain lesions, neurological disorders, causal determination, and so forth—and imagining (as above) that the car's steering apparatus is not broken, you had it in your power (just prior to your actual decision to turn to the right) to continue going straight ahead, or to turn the car to the left, and so forth. That is, although you exercise guidance control in turning the car to the right, you presumably (and apart from special assumptions) possessed freedom to choose and do otherwise: you had "regulative control" over the car's movements. In the normal case, we assume that agents have both guidance and regulative control—a signature sort of control of the car's movements, as well as a characteristic kind of control *over* the car's movements.

Whereas these two sorts of control are typically presumed to go together, they can be prized apart. Suppose that everything is as above, but that the steering apparatus of your car is broken in such a way that, if you had tried to guide the car in any direction other than the one in which you actually guide it, it would have gone to the right anyway—in just the trajectory it actually traveled. The defect in the steering apparatus plays no role in the actual sequence of events, but it would have played a role in the alternative scenario (or range of such scenarios). Given this sort of preemptive overdetermination, although you exhibit guidance control of the car's going to the right, you do *not* have regulative control over the car's movements: it would have gone in precisely the same way, no matter what you were to choose or try.

Of course, in this context you *do* possess *some* regulative control: you could have chosen otherwise, and you could have tried to guide the car in some other direction. This is reminiscent of John Locke's famous example in his *Essay Concerning Human Understanding.* Here a man is transported into a room while he is asleep. When the man awakens, he considers leaving, but he decides to stay in the room for his own reasons. Locke says he voluntarily chooses to stay in the room and voluntarily stays in the room. Unbeknownst to the man, the door to the room is locked, and thus he could not have left the room. According to Locke, the man voluntarily stays in the room, although he does not have the power to leave the room. He exhibits a certain sort of control of his staying in the room (what I would call guidance control), even though he cannot do otherwise than stay in the room (and thus he lacks regulative control over staying in the room). But note that, as in the second car example above, the man could have chosen to leave the room, and he could have tried to do so.

Can structurally similar examples be given in which there is guidance control but *no* regulative control? This is where the "Frankfurt-examples" come in. The contemporary philosopher, Harry Frankfurt, has sought to provide just such an example.[5] One could say that he seeks to put the locked door inside the mind (in terms of Locke's example). In Locke's example, some factor (the locked door) plays no role in the individual's deliberations or choice, and yet its presence renders it true that the individual could not have done otherwise (could not have left the room). Frankfurt posits some factor that plays an analogous role in the context of the agent's mind: it plays no role in the agent's actual deliberations or choice, and yet its presence (allegedly) renders it true that the individual could not have chosen otherwise (or done otherwise). If Frankfurt's examples work, then one could in principle entirely prize apart guidance control from regulative control.

Here is my favorite version of a Frankfurt-type case. Jones has left his political decision until the last moment, just as some diners leave their decision about what to order at a restaurant to the moment when the waiter turns to them. In any case, Jones goes into the voting booth, deliberates in the "normal" way, and chooses to vote for the Democrat. On the basis of this choice, Jones votes for the Democrat. Unbeknownst to Jones, he has a chip in his brain that allows a very nice and highly progressive neurosurgeon (Black) to monitor his brain. The neurosurgeon wants Jones to vote for the Democrat, and if she sees that Jones is about to do so, she does not intervene in any way—she merely monitors the brain. If, on the other hand, the neurosurgeon sees that Jones is about to choose to vote

5. See Selection 15 in this volume.

for the Republican, she swings into action with her nifty electronic probe and stimulates Jones's brain in such a way as to ensure that he chooses to vote for the Democrat (and goes ahead and votes for the Democrat). Given the set-up, it seems that Jones freely chooses to vote for the Democrat and freely votes for the democrat, although he could not have chosen or done otherwise: it seems that Jones exhibits guidance control of his vote, but he lacks regulative control over his choice and also his vote. The neurosurgeon's chip and electronic device has brought Locke's locked door into the mind. Just as the locked door plays no role in Locke's man's choice or behavior but nevertheless renders it true that he could not have done otherwise, the Black set-up plays no role in Jones's actual choice or behavior, but it apparently renders it true that he could not have chosen or done otherwise.

How exactly does the neurosurgeon's device reliably know how Jones is about to vote? Frankfurt himself is vague about this point, but let us imagine that Jones's brain registers a certain neurological pattern if Jones is about to choose to vote for the Democrat, and a different pattern if Jones is about to choose to vote Republican. The chip can subtly convey this information to the neurosurgeon, which she can then use to good effect. Of course, the mere possibility of exhibiting a certain neurological pattern is not sufficiently robust to ground ascriptions of moral responsibility, on the picture that requires access to alternative possibilities. That is, if moral responsibility requires the sort of control that involves selection from among various paths that are genuinely open to an agent, the mere possibility of involuntarily exhibiting a certain neurological pattern would not seem to count as the relevant sort of "selection." Put slightly differently, just as it is not enough to secure moral responsibility that a different choice could have *randomly* occurred, it does not seem to be enough to secure moral responsibility that a different neurological pattern could have been exhibited *involuntarily*. Such an exiguous possibility is a mere "flicker of freedom" and not sufficiently robust to ground moral responsibility, given the picture that requires regulative control for moral responsibility. How could something as important as moral responsibility come from something so thin—and something entirely involuntary?

It is tempting then to suppose that one could have a genuine kind of control—guidance control—that can be entirely prized apart from regulative control and that is all the freedom required for moral responsibility. So even if the Consequence Argument were valid and thus all causally deterministic sequences were equally potent in ruling out the sort of control that requires access to alternative possibilities (regulative control), it would *not* follow that all causally deterministic sequences equally threaten guidance control and moral responsibility. That is, if moral responsibility does not require the sort of control that involves access to alternative possibilities, then this opens the possibility of defending a kind of compatibilism, even granting the soundness of the Consequence Argument.

But various philosophers have resisted the temptation to suppose that one can expunge all vestiges of regulative control while at the same time preserving guidance control. They have pointed out that the appearance that Frankfurt-type cases can help to separate guidance from (all) regulative control may be misleading. Perhaps the most illuminating way to put their argument is in terms of a dilemma. The first horn assumes that indeterminism is true in the Frankfurt-examples; in particular, it assumes that the relationship between the "prior sign" (read by the progressive neurosurgeon Black) is causally indeterministic. It follows that right up until the time Jones begins to choose, he can begin to choose otherwise; after all, the prior sign (together with other factors) fall short of causally determining the actual choice. Thus, there emerges a robust alternative possibility—the possibility of beginning to choose otherwise. This is no mere flicker of freedom; although it may be blocked or thwarted before it is completed or comes to fruition, it is nevertheless a voluntary episode—the initiation of choice.

The second horn of the dilemma assumes that causal determinism is true in the examples. Given the assumption of causal determination, it would appear to be straightforwardly question-begging to say that Jones is obviously morally responsible for his choice and behavior (despite lacking genuine access to alternative possibilities). After all, this (the compatibility of causal determination and moral responsibility) is precisely what is at issue!

The dilemma is powerful, but I am not convinced that it presents an insuperable objection to the employment of the Frankfurt-examples as part of a general strategy of defending compatibilism; as a matter of fact, I reject it. First, there have been various attempts at providing explicitly indeterministic versions of the Frankfurt-cases , and I think some of them are promising. I don't think it is obvious that one could not construct a Frankfurt-example (under the explicit assumption of causal indeterminism) in which there are *no* robust alternative possibilities. Recall that it is not enough for the proponent of the regulative control requirement to identify just any sort of alternative possibility; rather, he needs to find an alternative possibility that is sufficiently *robust* to ground attributions of moral responsibility, given the regulative control picture. If the ground of moral responsibility is a certain sort of *selection* from genuinely available paths into the future, then paths with mere accidental or arbitrary events would seem to be irrelevant. This is the idea of the irrelevance of exiguous alternatives. In my view, to seek to get responsibility out of mere flickers of freedom is akin to alchemy. Here I am in agreement with the libertarian Robert Kane, who insists on the "dual-voluntariness" constraint on moral responsibility.[6]

On the second horn of the dilemma, causal determinism is assumed. I agree that it would be dialectically rash to conclude precipitously from mere inspection of the example presented above that Jones is morally responsible for his choice and voting behavior. Rather, my approach would be rather more circumspect. First, I would note that the distinctive contribution of the Frankfurt-examples is to suggest that if Jones is not morally responsible for his choice and behavior, this is *not* because he lacks genuine access to (robust) alternative possibilities. After all, in the example, Black's set-up is sufficient for Jones's choosing and acting as he actually does, but intuitively it is *irrelevant* to Jones's moral responsibility. That is, we can identify a factor—Black's elaborate set-up—that is (perhaps in conjunction with other features of the example) sufficient for Jones's actual kind of choice and behavior, but it plays no actual role in Jones's deliberations or actions; Black's set-up could have been subtracted from the situation and the actual sequence would have flowed in exactly the way it actually did. When something is in this way irrelevant to what happens in the actual sequence issuing in an agent's choice and behavior, it would seem to be irrelevant to his moral responsibility.

So the distinctive element added by the Frankfurt-examples, under the assumption of causal determinisim, is this: if the relevant agent is not morally responsible, it is not because of his lack of regulative control. Alternatively, we could say that they show that it is not the lack of genuine access to alternative possibilities (regulative control) in itself (and apart from pointing to other factors) that rules out moral responsibility. Now we can ask whether there is some other factor—some factor that plays a role in the actual sequence—that rules out moral responsibility, if causal determinism obtains. We will turn to a more thorough and careful consideration

6. Robert Kane, *The Significance of Free Will* (New York: Oxford University Press, 1996), pp. 109–15.

of such "actual-sequence factors" below. For now, I simply wish to note that there is nothing question-begging or dialectically inappropriate about how I have invoked the Frankfurt-examples thus far (on the second horn), and their distinctive role is to call into question the relevance or importance of regulative control in grounding moral responsibility (in the way described above).

Taking stock, in Section IV I presented the Consequence Argument. I did not officially endorse its conclusion, although I am inclined to believe that the argument is valid and further that its premises are based on extremely plausible ingredients. I suggested that it would be prudent to seek a defense of compatibilism that does not presuppose that the Consequence Argument is unsound. Here I have presented the rudimentary first steps toward the elaboration of just such a compatibilism. I have invoked the Frankfurt-examples (the prototypes of which are in John Locke) to support the contention that moral responsibility does not require regulative control (or the sort of freedom that involves genuine access to alternative possibilities), but only guidance control. (In the following section, I shall give a sketch of an account of guidance control.) Further, I have suggested that (thus far at least) there is no reason to suppose that causal determinism is inconsistent with guidance control. Better: I have contended that even if causal determinism threatens regulative control, it does not thereby threaten guidance control. In a more comprehensive defense of the sort of compatibilism I find attractive, one would explore whether there are other reasons (apart from regulative control) in virtue of which causal determinism is incompatible with moral responsibility (and offer reasons why it isn't).

VI. An Account of Guidance Control

An insight from the Frankfurt-cases helps to shape the account of guidance control: moral responsibility is a matter of the history of an action (or behavior)—of how the actual sequence unfolds—rather than the genuine metaphysical availability of alternative possibilities. On this view, alternative scenarios or non-actual possible worlds might be relevant to moral responsibility in virtue of helping to specify or analyze modal properties of the actual sequence, but not in virtue of indicating or providing an analysis of genuine access to alternative possibilities.

Note that, in a Frankfurt-type case, the actual sequence proceeds "in the normal way" or via the "normal" process of practical reasoning.

In contrast, in the alternative scenario (which never actually gets triggered and thus never becomes part of the actual sequence of events in our world), there is (say) direct electronic stimulation of the brain—intuitively, a different way or a different kind of mechanism. (By "mechanism" I simply mean, roughly speaking, "way"—I do not mean to reify anything.) I assume that we have intuitions at least about clear cases of "same mechanism," and "different mechanism." The actually operating mechanism (in a Frankfurt-type cases)—ordinary human practical reasoning, unimpaired by direct stimulation by neurosurgeons, and so forth—is in a salient sense responsive to reasons. That is, holding fixed that mechanism, the agent would presumably choose and act differently in a range of scenarios in which he is presented with good reasons to do so.

The above discussion suggests the rudiments of an account of guidance control of action. On this account, we hold fixed the kind of mechanism that actually issues in the choice and action, and we see whether the agent responds suitably to reasons (some of which are moral reasons). My account presupposes that the agent can recognize reasons, and, in particular, recognize certain reasons as moral reasons. The account distinguishes between reasons-recognition (the ability to recognize the reasons that exist) and reasons-reactivity (choice in accordance with reasons that are recognized as good and sufficient), and it makes different demands on reasons-recognition and reasons-reactivity. The sort of reasons-responsiveness linked to moral responsibility, on my view, is "moderate reasons-responsiveness."

A bit more carefully, we can build up to the conditions for moderate reasons-responsiveness by starting with "weak reasons-responsiveness":

> An agent is *weakly reasons-responsive* when a certain kind K of mechanism, which involves the agent's rational consideration of reasons relevant to the situation, issues in action, and in *at least some alternative circumstances* in which there are sufficient reasons for her to do otherwise than she actually does, she would be receptive to these reasons and would have chosen and done otherwise by the efficacy of the same mechanism that actually results in the action.[7]

Now moderate reasons-responsiveness is the same as weak reasons-responsiveness, except for the following changes:

7. John Martin Fischer, *The Metaphysics of Free Will* (Oxford: Blackwell Publishing Co., 1994), p. 164.

a) In the alternative situation in which there is sufficient reason to do otherwise and the agent does otherwise, the agent performs the action for that (sufficient) reason.
b) The agent must show regularity in recognizing reasons—the agent must be receptive to a pattern of reasons. (This condition rules out situations in which an agent is weakly reason-responsive but recognizes only random elements in a pattern of reasons.)
c) The agent must be receptive to a range of reasons that includes moral reasons.[8]

But one could exhibit the right sort of reasons-responsiveness as a result (say) of clandestine, unconsented-to electronic stimulation of the brain (or hypnosis, brainwashing, and so forth). So moderate reasons-responsiveness of the actual-sequence mechanism is necessary but not sufficient for moral responsibility. I contend that there are two elements of guidance control: reasons-sensitivity of the appropriate sort and mechanism ownership. That is, the mechanism that issues in the behavior must (in an appropriate sense) be the *agent's own* mechanism. (When one is secretly manipulated through clandestine mind control as in *The Manchurian Candidate,* one's practical reasoning is not *one's own.*)

I argue for a subjective approach to mechanism ownership. On this approach, one's mechanism becomes one's own in virtue of one's having certain beliefs about one's own agency and its effects in the world, that is, in virtue of *seeing oneself in a certain way.* (Of course, it is *not* simply a matter of saying certain things—one actually has to have the relevant constellation of beliefs.) On my view, an individual becomes morally responsible in part at least by taking responsibility; he makes his mechanism his own by taking responsibility for acting from that kind of mechanism. In a sense, then, one acquires control by *taking control.*

More carefully, the conditions for taking responsibility for the mechanism on which one acts are as follows:

a) The individual must see himself as an agent; he must see that his choices and actions are efficacious in the world. This condition

8. John Martin Fischer and Mark Ravizza, *Responsibility and Control: A Theory of Moral Responsibility* (New York: Oxford University Press, 1998), pp. 69–82. In presenting the view in a clear and condensed way, I am very grateful to Derk Pereboom, *Living without Free Will* (New York: Cambridge University Press, 2001), pp. 108–9.

includes the claim that the individual sees that if he were to choose and act differently, different upshots would occur in the world.

b) The individual must accept that he is a fair target of the reactive attitudes as a result of how he exercises this agency in certain contexts.

c) The individual's view of himself specified in the first two conditions must be based, in an appropriate way, on the evidence.[9]

I ended my 1982 paper, "Responsibility and Control," by saying that we must "decode the information in the actual sequence" leading to behavior for which the agent can legitimately be held morally responsible and ascertain whether it is compatible with causal determination. The account of guidance control—with the two chief ingredients, moderate reasons-responsiveness and mechanism-ownership—are the secrets revealed by close scrutiny of the actual sequence, and I have argued that they are entirely compatible with causal determination. (Note that they are also entirely compatible with causal indeterminism; thus, on my approach, moral responsibility does *not* hang on a thread.)

Further, I have shown how we can build a *comprehensive* account of guidance control from an account of guidance control of *actions.*[10] That is, we can develop an account of guidance control of omissions, consequence-particulars, consequence-universals, and perhaps even emotions and character traits by invoking certain basic ingredients contained in the account of guidance control of actions. I argue that it is a point in favor of my account of moral responsibility that it can give a comprehensive account that builds on simple, basic ingredients. Additionally, I contend that this comprehensive account systematizes our intuitive judgments about a wide range of examples involving moral responsibility. It thus helps us to achieve a philosophical homeostasis, or, in John Rawls's famous term, a reflective equilibrium.

VII. Conclusion: The Lure of Semicompatibilism

John Perry has told me that I need a new name for the position, and I agree that "semicompatibilism" is not very exciting. (My only consolation is that the other names for positions in the Free Will debates are equally

9. Fischer and Ravizza, 1998, pp. 210–14.

10. Fischer and Ravizza, 1998.

uninspiring; could you imagine going to the barricades for "hard incompatibilism"?) What is important, however, is not what's in the name, but what's in the doctrine. In this essay I have focused mainly on trying to explain the appeal of this form of compatibilism. That is, I have attempted to provide a *general* motivation for compatibilism, and also an explanation of the appeal of *this specific form* of compatibilism (as opposed to traditional compatibilism). The idea here has not been to develop detailed elaborations of the ideas or sustained defenses of the positions; rather, I have simply presented in sketchy form the attractions of the overall view (and some of the difficulties faced by its competitors).

One of the main virtues of compatibilism is that our deepest and most basic views about our agency—our freedom and moral responsibility—are not held hostage to views in physics. A semicompatibilist would not have to revise these beliefs in light of a future discovery of the truth of causal determinism. Nor need he be prepared to revise his basic metaphysical views—such as that the past is fixed or the laws of nature are fixed or that powerlessness can be transmitted via the Principle of Transfer of Powerlessness—in light of such a discovery. A libertarian, it seems, must claim that he knows from his armchair (or philosophical Barcalounger) that causal determinism is false; but how could we know in advance the truth or falsity of such an empirical thesis? These are significant virtues of semicompatibilism: a proponent of this doctrine need not purport to know a priori some (presumably) empirical thesis in physics, or be prepared to give up his basic views about our agency, or engage in unattractive "metaphysical flip-flopping" (giving up some or one's basic metaphysical principles in light of some empirical truth in physics).

Semicompatibilism combines the best features of compatibilism and incompatibilism. It can accommodate the most compelling insights of the incompatibilist (as crystallized in the Consequence Argument) and also the basic appeal of compatibilism—that not all causally deterministic sequences equally rule out the sort of control that grounds moral responsibility. Thus, semicompatibilism allows us to track common sense (suitably conceptualized in moral and legal theory) in making distinctions between those factors that operate in such a way as to undermine responsibility and those that do not. And a semicompatibilist need not give up the idea that sometimes individuals robustly deserve punishment for their behavior, whereas on other occasions they robustly deserve moral commendation and reward. That is, a semicompatibilist need not etiolate or reconfigure the widespread and natural idea that individuals *morally deserve* to be treated harshly in certain circumstances and kindly in others. We need not in any way damp down our revulsion at heinous deeds or our admiration for human goodness and even heroism. Thus, even if the name is unexciting, the idea is beautiful.[11]

John Martin Fischer

11. This essay is (in part) based on my contribution to John Martin Fischer, Robert Kane, Derk Pereboom, and Manuel Vargas, *Four Views on Free Will* (Oxford: Blackwell Publishing Co., 2007), pp. 44–84. I have attempted to present, defend, and elaborate semicompatibilism in: Fischer, 1994; Fischer and Ravizza, 1998; and John Martin Fischer, *My Way: Essays on Moral Responsibility* (New York: Oxford University Press, 2006). For further reflections on various features of my account of guidance control (and thus the freedom-relevant component of moral responsibility), see John Martin Fischer, "The Free Will Revolution," part of a book symposium on John Martin Fischer and Mark Ravizza, *Responsibility and Control: A Theory of Moral Responsibility, Philosophical Explorations* 8 (2005), pp. 145–56; "*The Free Will Revolution (Continued),*" (part of a special issue on the work [pertaining to moral responsibility] of John Martin Fischer), *Journal of Ethics* 10 (2006), pp. 315–45; "*My Way* and Life's Highway," *Journal of Ethics* 12 (2008), pp. 167–89.

There are certain features of my account of guidance control that a disconcerting cohort of (otherwise!) thoughtful philosophers have found rather less than irresistible, especially the subjective element and the contention that "reactivity is all of a piece." In the trio of articles referred to in the paragraph above, I argue (among other things) that (if need be) I could adjust my account so as to do without these contentious features while still maintaining all of my major claims: that moral responsibility does not require regulative control, that causal determination is compatible with moral responsibility, that moral responsibility is an essentially historical notion, and so forth.

I am grateful to Derk Pereboom for helpful comments on a previous version of this paper.

20

Robert Kane, "Free Will: New Foundations for an Ancient Problem"

Robert Kane is a professor emeritus at the University of Texas at Austin. He has defended a sophisticated version of event-causal libertarianism, the essentials of which he describes in this article.

1. Introduction

For several decades I have been developing a distinctive view of free will that has come to be called in the philosophical literature a *causal indeterminist* or *event-causal libertarian* view of free will. When I first started thinking about free will more than forty years ago, no such view of free will existed in any developed form.

The landscape of free will debate was simpler back then. The unstated assumption was that if you had scientific leanings, you should be a *compatibilist* about free will (believing it to be compatible with determinism). That is, you should be a compatibilist, *if* you did not deny we had free will altogether (as did skeptics and hard determinists). And if you were a *libertarian* about free will—believing in a free will that is *incompatible* with determinism—you must (in order to make sense of such a free will) inevitably appeal to uncaused causes, immaterial minds, noumenal selves, non-event agent causes, prime movers unmoved, or other examples of what P. F. Strawson called the "panicky metaphysics" of libertarianism (in his influential 1962 essay "Freedom and Resentment").[1]

The challenge I set for myself back then was to see if one could give a traditional incompatibilist or libertarian account of free will (one that required indeterminism) that could be reconciled with modern science without having to appeal to any of the mysterious forms of agency or causation to which past libertarians had invariably appealed and which

1. *Proceedings of the British Academy* 48 (1962), pp. 1–25.

Strawson had dubbed "panicky metaphysics." I found that to solve this problem one had to rethink the long history of debates about free will from the ground up.

The first step required rethinking the whole question of why we should believe that free will is incompatible with determinism in the first place, as many philosophers and ordinary persons have believed down through history. Call this the Compatibility Question. The second step would be to show how a free will requiring indeterminism could be made intelligible without reducing free choices to mere chance events, and how such an indeterminist free will could be reconciled with modern images of human beings in the physical, biological, psychological, social, and neuro-sciences. Call this the Intelligibility Question. I found that meeting the challenge I had set for myself required departing from the conventional wisdom on both these questions.

2. The Compatibility Question: Alternative Possibilities (AP)

Consider the Compatibility Question first. The first thing to note is that if the Compatibility Question is formulated as in many familiar discussions of free will—"Is freedom compatible or incompatible with determinism?"—the question is too simple and misleading. The reason is there are many meanings of "freedom" (as one would expect of such a protean and much-used term); and many of them are compatible with determinism. Even in a determined world, we would want to distinguish persons who are free from such things as physical restraint, addiction, coercion, compulsion, covert control, or political oppression from persons who are not free from these things; and having these freedoms would be preferable to not having them even in a determined world.

Those who believe free will is incompatible with determinism—that is, those who are incompatibilists and libertarians about free will—should simply grant this point to their compatibilist opponents, namely that many kinds of freedom worth wanting are compatible with determinism. What incompatibilists should rather insist upon is that there is *at least one* kind of freedom worth wanting that is not compatible with determinism. This additional important freedom, as I see it, is "free *will*," which I define as "the power to be the ultimate creator and sustainer of some of one's own ends or purposes." To acknowledge the importance of this further freedom is not to deny the importance of other everyday compatibilist freedoms from coercion, compulsion, political oppression, and so on; it is only to say that human concerns about freedom and responsibility go beyond these everyday freedoms.

This is one departure from conventional wisdom on the Compatibility Question that I came to emphasize. But there is another of more importance. Most philosophical debate about the Compatibility Question in the past century has focused on the question of whether determinism is compatible with "the condition of alternative possibilities" (which I call AP)—the requirement that the free agent must have had alternative possibilities and hence had the "power" or "ability" to have "done otherwise." Most arguments for the incompatibility of free will and determinism (of which the so-called Consequence Argument of Peter van Inwagen and others is the most well known) appeal to this AP condition in one way or another.[2] These arguments claim that if determinism were true, agents could not have done otherwise, since only one alternative future would have been possible, given the past and laws of nature; and agents do not now have the power or ability to change either the past or the laws of nature. Compatibilist critics of such arguments have either denied that the power or ability to do otherwise (the AP condition) conflicts with determinism or have denied that being able to do otherwise is required for moral responsibility or free will in the first place.

As I view these persisting debates about alternative possibilities and incompatibilism, they inevitably tend to stalemate over conflicting interpretations of "can," "power," "ability," and "could have done otherwise." And I think there are good reasons for these stalemates having to do with the different meanings of freedom just mentioned. In response, I argue that to answer the Compatibility Question, we have to think about it in new ways. The alternative possibilities condition, or AP, is not sufficient to rest the case for the incompatibility of free will and determinism upon it alone: the Compatibility debate cannot be resolved by focusing on alternative possibilities alone.

3. Ultimate Responsibility (UR)

Fortunately, if one looks into the long history of debates about free will, one can find another criterion fueling incompatibilist intuitions that, to my mind, is even more important than AP, though it has often been neglected. I call it the condition of ultimate responsibility, or UR. The

2. See van Inwagen, *An Essay on Free Will* (Oxford: Oxford University Press, 1983).

basic idea is this: *To be ultimately responsible for an action, an agent must be responsible for anything that is a sufficient reason (condition, cause, or motive) for the action's occurring.*[3] If, for example, a choice should issue from, and can be sufficiently explained by appealing to, an agent's character and motives (together with other conditions), then to be *ultimately* responsible for the choice, the agent must have been at least in part responsible by virtue of choices or actions voluntarily performed in the past for having the character and motives he or she now has. Compare Aristotle's claim that if a man is responsible for wicked acts that flow from his character, he must at some time in the past have been responsible for forming the wicked character from which these acts flow.

This UR condition accounts for the "ultimate" in the earlier definition of free will: "The power of agents to be the *ultimate* creators and sustainers of some of their own ends or purposes." Now UR does not require that we could have done otherwise (AP) for *every* act done of our own free wills. It thus vindicates the claims of those philosophers, such as Harry Frankfurt, John Martin Fischer, and Daniel Dennett, who insist that we can be held morally responsible for many acts even when we could not have done otherwise. But the vindication is only partial. For the UR condition *does* require that we could have done otherwise with respect to *some* acts in our past life histories by which we formed our present characters. I call these *self-forming actions,* or SFAs.

Consider Dennett's example of Martin Luther.[4] When Luther finally broke with the Church at Rome, he famously said, "Here I stand, I can do no other." Dennett asks us to suppose that Luther was literally speaking the truth at that moment. Given his character and motives, he could not then and there have done otherwise. Does this mean, Dennett asks, that Luther was not morally responsible, not subject to praise or blame, for his act, or that he was not acting of his own free will? "Not at all," says Dennett. In saying "I can do no other," Luther was not disowning responsibility for his action, but taking full responsibility for acting of his own free will. So "could have done otherwise," or AP, says Dennett, is not required for moral responsibility or free will.

My response to this argument is to grant that Luther could have been responsible for this act, even *ultimately* responsible in the sense of UR, though he could not have done otherwise then and there and even if his act

3. For a formal statement and defense of this condition, see my book *The Significance of Free Will* (New York: Oxford University Press, 1996), Ch. 3.

4. From *Elbow Room* (Cambridge, MA: MIT Press, 1984), p. 133.

was determined. But this would be the case to the extent that Luther was responsible for his present motives and character by virtue of many earlier struggles and self-forming choices (SFAs) that brought him to this point where he could not have done otherwise. We often act from a will already formed. But it is "our own free will" by virtue of the fact that we formed it by other self-forming choices or actions in the past (SFAs) for which we could have done otherwise. If this were not so, there is *nothing we could have ever done differently in our entire lifetimes to make ourselves different than we are*—a consequence that I believe is incompatible with our being (at least to some degree) ultimately responsible for what we are. So, while SFAs are not the only acts in life for which we are ultimately responsible and which are done "of our own free will," if none of our acts were self-forming in this way, we would not be *ultimately* responsible for anything we did.

If the case for the incompatibility of free will and determinism cannot be made by appealing to AP alone, it can be made if UR is added. If agents must be responsible to some degree for anything that is a sufficient cause or motive for their actions, an impossible infinite regress of past actions would be required unless some actions in the life histories of the agent (namely, SFAs) did not have either sufficient causes or motives. Lacking sufficient causes would mean that the occurrence of such actions was not inevitable, given the past and the laws of nature, and hence that the actions were not determined.

Focusing on UR also tells us something else of paramount importance about free will. It tells us why the free will issue is about the freedom of the *will* and not merely about freedom of action. There has been a tendency in the modern era of philosophy, beginning with Hobbes and Locke in the seventeenth century and coming to fruition in the twentieth century, to reduce the problem of free will to a problem of freedom of action. I have been arguing for some time that such a reduction oversimplifies the problem. Free will is not just about free action. It is about "self-formation," about the formation of our "wills," or how we got to be the kinds of persons we are, with the characters, motives, and purposes we now have. Were we ultimately responsible to some degree for having the wills we do have, or can the sources of our wills be completely traced backwards to something over which we had no control—to Fate or to God's decrees, physical causes and laws of nature, heredity and environment, social conditioning or hidden controllers? Therein, I believe, lies the core of the traditional "problem of free will."

4. Plurality Conditions

But if one can arrive at the incompatibility of free will and determinism from UR alone, is AP needed at all for free will? One may be tempted to think at this point that one could dispense with AP altogether. Indeed, some recent incompatibilists, who are impressed by arguments of the above kinds, have done just that. These "narrow" or "uncompromising" *source incompatibilists,* as they are often called, insist that, while free will is incompatible with determinism (by virtue of a source or ultimacy condition, such as UR), alternative possibilities or AP are not needed at all for free will or moral responsibility.[5] I think this is a mistake. Although I am usually regarded as one of the original "source incompatibilists," because of my emphasis on UR, I have never been a "narrow" or "uncompromising" source incompatibilist of this kind. *Both* conditions, I believe—UR and AP—are needed for free will. But the reasons why both are needed and the relations between them are more subtle than has generally been realized.

This brings me to my third departure from conventional wisdom regarding the Compatibility Question. It is normally assumed that all incompatibilists need for free will are alternative possibilities or the ability to do otherwise (AP) *plus* indeterminism. But it turns out interestingly that these two conditions—AP and indeterminism—are not jointly sufficient for free will, even if each should be necessary. One can see why by considering a significant class of actions for which the agents could have done otherwise (had AP) *and* the actions are undetermined—and yet the agents lack free *will.*

I call these "Austin-style examples," after J. L. Austin, one of the first to emphasize examples of these kinds, though Austin and others used them for a different purpose and did not notice the use to which I put them.[6] Consider three examples of this kind, starting with Austin's own

5. Uncompromising source incompatibilists often appeal to so-called "Frankfurt-style examples" to show that alternative possibilities are not needed for moral responsibility and free will. See Derk Pereboom, *Living without Free Will* (Cambridge: Cambridge University Press, 2001) for a discussion of source incompatibilism in relation to Frankfurt-style examples. I do not believe that Frankfurt-style examples show that alternative possibilities are not needed for free will and ultimate moral responsibility, but the issue is too complex to be taken up in this essay.

6. Austin, "Ifs and Cans," in *Philosophical Papers* (Oxford: Oxford University Press, 1961), pp. 153–60.

example. He imagined that he must hole a three-foot putt to win a golf match, but owing to a nervous twitch in his arm, he misses. Here are two other examples I have used on other occasions. An assassin is trying to kill the prime minister with a high-powered rifle when, owing to a nervous twitch, he misses and kills the minister's aide instead. I am standing in front of a coffee machine intending to press the button for coffee without cream when, owing to a brain cross, I accidentally press the button for coffee with cream. As Austin suggests, in each of these cases, we can suppose that some genuine indeterminacy is involved in the outgoing neural pathways of his arm or the arm of the assassin or the impulses in my brain making the outcomes undetermined. We can thus imagine, for instance, that Austin's holing the putt is a genuinely undetermined event. He might miss it by chance and, in the example, does miss it by chance.

Now Austin asked an interesting question about his example: Can we say in such circumstances that "he could have done otherwise" than miss the putt? And his answer was that we can indeed say this. For he had made many similar putts of this short length in the past (he had the *capacity* and the *opportunity*). In addition, since the outcome of this putt was undetermined, he might well have succeeded in holing it, as he was trying to do. But this means that his missing the putt is an action that is (i) *undetermined* and (ii) such that the agent *could have done otherwise* (it satisfies AP). But missing the putt is not something that we regard as *freely* done in any normal sense of the term because it is not under the agent's voluntary control. He doesn't do it voluntarily. The same is true of the assassin's missing his intended target and my accidentally pressing the wrong button on the coffee machine.

Now one might think these occurrences are not *actions* at all because they are undetermined and happen by accident. But Austin rightly warns against such a conclusion. Missing the putt, he argues, was clearly something he *did,* even though it was admittedly *not* what he wanted or intended to do. Similarly, killing the aide was something the assassin did, though unintentionally; and pressing the wrong button was something I did, even if only by accident or inadvertently. The point here, and it is an important one, is that many of the things we do *by accident* or *mistake, unintentionally* or *inadvertently,* are things we *do.* We may sometimes be absolved of responsibility for doing them (though we are not always absolved, as in the case of the assassin). But it is for *doing* them that we are absolved of responsibility; and this can be true even if the accidents or mistakes are genuinely undetermined.

To grasp what this implies about free will, consider the following scenario. Suppose God created a world in which there was much more genuine indeterminism or chance in human affairs and action. In this world, people set out to do things—to assassinate prime ministers, hole putts, press buttons, punch computer keys, jump fences—often succeeding, but sometimes failing by mistake or accident in the manner of Austin-style examples. Further imagine that all actions in this world, whether the agents succeed in their purposes or not, are such that their reasons, motives, and purposes for trying to act as they do are always predetermined or pre-settled by God. Though many events in this world are undetermined, the motives and purposes for which agents act are all determined by conditions over which the agents have no control. Whether the assassin misses the prime minister, his *intention* to kill is predetermined in this world. Whether Austin misses his putt, his *wanting* and *trying* to make it are predetermined in this world. Whether I press the button for coffee without cream, my wanting to do so is predetermined by my preferences; and so it is for all persons and all actions in this imagined world.

I would argue that persons in such a world lack free *will,* even though it is often the case that they have *alternative possibilities* and their actions are *undetermined.* For while they can do otherwise, they can do so only in the Austinian manner—by mistake or accidentally, unwillingly or inadvertently—and this is a limited kind of freedom at best. What they cannot do in any instance is *will* otherwise; for all of their motives and purposes have been pre-set by God. We may say their wills in every situation have already been "set one way" before and when they act, so that if they do otherwise, it will not be "in accordance with their wills."

What we learn from this example and others like it is that when we wonder about whether the *wills* of agents are free, it is not merely whether they could have done otherwise that concerns us, *even if the doing otherwise is undetermined.* What interests us is whether they could have done otherwise *voluntarily* (or *willingly*), intentionally, and *rationally.* Or, putting the matter more generally, we are interested in whether they could have acted voluntarily, intentionally, and rationally in *more than one way,* rather than that they could have acted voluntarily, intentionally, and rationally in only one way, and in other ways only by accident or mistake, unintentionally, inadvertently, or irrationally. ("Voluntarily" and "willingly" here mean acting "in accordance with one's will [motives and purposes]"; "intentionally" means "knowingly" [as opposed to "inadvertently"] and "on purpose" [as opposed to "accidentally"]; and "rationally" means "having reasons for so acting and acting for those reasons.")

I call these conditions of *more-than-one-way* voluntariness, intentionality, and rationality, "plurality conditions" for free will.[7] They seem to be deeply embedded in our intuitions about freedom of choice and action. Consider that most of us naturally assume that our freedom and responsibility would be deficient if it were always the case that we could *only* do otherwise by accident or mistake, unintentionally, involuntarily, or irrationally. But then it follows that if these plurality conditions must hold for some free acts, if we are to have freedom of *will,* then alternative possibilities or AP must hold for some free acts as well, if we are to have free will. For, if agents are able to *do* and to *do otherwise voluntarily, intentionally, and rationally,* then it follows that they are able to *do* and to *do otherwise.* That is, they have alternative possibilities and satisfy AP.

5. The Dual Regress of Free Will

So AP is required for free will after all. But how then are we to make sense of the fact that one can argue for incompatibilism of free will and determinism from UR alone without appealing to AP? The answer lies in UR. *Both* AP and indeterminism follow from UR, but *by different argumentative routes.* I have called this in the past "the dual regress of free will."[8] For it turns out that there are two separate regresses associated with UR. The first begins with the requirement that agents be responsible by virtue of past voluntary actions for anything that is a sufficient ground or reason for their actions in the sense of a *sufficient cause.* Reflecting on this regress leads to the conclusion that *some* actions in the life histories of agents, if the agents are to be ultimately responsible, must be undetermined (must lack sufficient causes). The second regress begins with the requirement that agents be responsible for anything that is a sufficient ground or reason for their actions in the sense of a *sufficient motive;* and it leads (by way of will-setting and plurality conditions) to the conclusion that some actions in the life histories of agents must be such that the agents could have done otherwise (AP).

The first of these regresses results from the requirement that we be ultimate sources of some of our *actions,* the second from the requirement that we be ultimate sources of our *wills* (to perform those actions). If this

7. *The Significance of Free Will,* pp. 107–11.

8. Kane, "The Dual Regress of Free Will and the Role of Alternative Possibilities," *Philosophical Perspectives* 14 (Oxford: Blackwell Publishers, 2000), pp. 57–80.

second requirement were not added, one might have a world in which all the will-setting was done by God, or someone, or something, other than the agents themselves. Agents in such a world might be unhindered in the pursuit of some of their purposes, and their actions might sometimes be undetermined. But it would never be "up to them" what *purposes* they pursued. They would have some freedom of action, but not freedom of will.

In this manner, both the requirements of *indeterminism* and *alternative possibilities* have a common origin in the idea that we must be the ultimate sources or grounds of our willed actions. But the two requirements are arrived at by different routes, corresponding to two senses of sufficient "grounds"—i.e., *causes* and *reasons* (or motives). In Aristotle's terms, these grounds are respectively the *archai* (sources, causes) and *aitiai* (reasons, explanations) of our willed actions. The actions that stop *both* regresses are the "self-forming actions" or SFAs required at some point in our lives, if UR is to be satisfied.[9] Such "self-forming" actions must be undetermined and satisfy the plurality conditions.

6. The Intelligibility Question

But this new approach to the Compatibility Question through UR raises a host of further difficult questions about the very possibility of a free will so conceived. Indeed, the requirement of UR that we be responsible for anything that is a sufficient cause or motive for our actions seems to involve us in an infinite regress. If we must have formed our present wills (our characters and motives) by earlier voluntary choices or actions, then UR would require that if any of these earlier choices or actions *also* had sufficient causes or motives when we performed *them,* then we must have also been responsible for those earlier sufficient causes or motives by virtue of forming them by *still earlier* voluntary choices or actions, and so on backwards indefinitely into our past. Eventually we would come to infancy or to a time before our birth when we could not have formed our own wills.

The only way to stop this regress is to suppose that *some* acts in our life histories must lack *sufficient* causes and motives altogether, and hence must be *undetermined.* These would be the *self-forming* actions or SFAs required at some point in our lives, if we are to be ultimately responsible for our wills. But how can undetermined actions lacking both sufficient

9. The argument for this is spelled out in the essay cited in note 8.

causes and motives themselves be free and responsible actions in the agent's control? Indeterminism means: same past, different possible futures. How is it possible, one might ask, that different actions could arise voluntarily and intentionally from exactly the same past, the same psychological history of the agent, without occurring merely by luck or chance?

This question has had a hypnotic effect on those who think about free will. One imagines that if free choices are undetermined, then which one occurs must be like spinning a wheel in one's mind or one must just pop out by chance. If a choice occurred as a result of a quantum jump or other undetermined event in one's brain, would that amount to a free and responsible choice? I'll not trouble you with all the arguments, like these and others, by which philosophers have argued that undetermined choices or actions would occur as a matter of chance and hence would be "arbitrary," or "capricious," or "random," "irrational," "inexplicable, "mere matters of luck" and not under the "control" of the agents, hence not free and responsible actions at all.

No wonder those who have believed in a traditional notion of free will requiring ultimate responsibility have felt the need to appeal to various mysterious forms of agency to explain their view. Immanuel Kant, for example, said that while we need such a notion of free will for morality, we cannot explain it in scientific terms, but must appeal to the agency of a "noumenal self" outside space and time. Others appealed to an immaterial self or soul that intervenes in the natural order. Still others have appealed to unusual forms of agent causation that cannot be accounted for in terms of the ordinary kinds of scientific causation, and so on. It seems that we have a trilemma here: either an infinite regress *or* mere chance *or* some extra mysterious factor to fill the gaps left in nature by mere chance—that is, an infinite regress or chance or mystery.

7. Indeterminism and Responsibility

Is there another way to go to escape this trilemma? I think there is. But it requires rethinking issues about indeterminism and responsibility—and hence rethinking the Intelligibility Question—from the ground up, just as we did with the Compatibility Question. The first step is to recall that all acts that are done "of our own free wills" for which we are ultimately responsible, do not have to be undetermined by our prior characters and motives, but only those acts by which we formed our present characters and motives and made ourselves into the kinds of persons we are, namely, the "self-forming actions" or SFAs mentioned earlier.

Now I believe these undetermined self-forming actions or SFAs occur at those difficult times of life when we are torn between competing visions of what we should do or become. We may for example be torn between doing the moral thing or acting from ambition, or between powerful present desires and long-term projects, or we may be faced with difficult tasks for which we have aversions. In all such cases, we are faced with competing motivations and have to make an effort to overcome temptation to do something else we may also strongly want. There is tension and uncertainty in our minds about what to do at such times, I suggest, that is reflected in appropriate regions of our brains by movement away from thermodynamic equilibrium. In short, there is a kind of "stirring up of chaos" in the brain that makes it sensitive to micro-indeterminacies at the neuronal level. The uncertainty and inner tension we feel at such soul-searching moments of self-formation would thus be reflected in the indeterminacy of our neural processes themselves, so that what is experienced internally as uncertainty would correspond physically to the opening of a window of opportunity that temporarily screens off complete determination by influences of the past.

When deciding under such conditions of uncertainty, the outcome would not be determined because of the preceding indeterminacy—and yet the outcome could be willed (and hence rational and voluntary) either way owing to the fact that in such self-formation, the agents' prior wills are divided by conflicting motives. Consider an example: A businesswoman is on her way to an important meeting when she sees an assault taking place in an alley. An inner struggle ensues between her conscience, which tells her to stop and call for help, and her career ambitions, which tell her she cannot miss this important meeting for her career. She has to make an effort of will to overcome the temptation to go on. If she does overcome this temptation, it will be the result of her effort, but if she fails, it will be because she did not *allow* her effort to succeed. And this is because, while she willed to overcome temptation, she also willed to fail, for quite different and incommensurable reasons. When we, like the woman, decide in such circumstances, and the indeterminate efforts we are making become determinate choices, we *make* one set of competing reasons or motives prevail over the others then and there *by deciding.*

Now let us add an additional piece to the puzzle. Just as indeterminism need not undermine rationality and voluntariness, so indeterminism in and of itself need not undermine control and responsibility. Suppose you are trying to think through a difficult problem, say, a mathematical problem, and there is some indeterminacy in your neural processes complicating the task—a kind of chaotic background. It would be like trying to concentrate and solve a problem with background noise or distraction. Whether you are going to succeed is uncertain and undetermined because of the distracting neural noise. Yet, if you do concentrate and solve the problem nonetheless, there is reason to say you did it and are responsible for it though it was undetermined whether you would succeed. The indeterministic noise would have been an obstacle that you overcame by your effort.

There are many examples supporting this point, where indeterminism functions as an obstacle to success without precluding responsibility (including some of the Austin-style examples mentioned earlier). Consider the assassin who is trying to shoot the prime minister, but may miss because of some undetermined events in his nervous system that may lead to a wavering of his arm. If he does succeed in hitting his target, despite the indeterminism, can he be held responsible? The answer is clearly yes, because he voluntarily and intentionally succeeded in doing what he was *trying* to do—kill the prime minister. Yet his action, killing the prime minister, was undetermined. Here is another example: A husband is arguing with his wife when, in a fit of rage, he swings his arm down on her favorite glass table top intending to break it. Again, let us suppose that some indeterminism in his outgoing neural pathways makes the momentum of his arm indeterminate so that it is not determined whether the table will break right up to the very moment when it is struck. Whether the husband breaks the table or not is undetermined. Yet he is clearly responsible if he does break it. (It would hardly be an effective excuse for him to say to his wife: "Chance did it, not me." Though there was a chance he wouldn't break it, chance didn't do it, he did.)

Now these examples—of the mathematical problem, the assassin, and the husband—are only part of the story. They do not give us all we want, since they do not amount to genuine exercises of free will in SFAs, like the businesswoman's, where the will is divided between conflicting motives. The assassin's will is not divided like the businesswoman's. He wants to kill the prime minister. But he does not also want to fail. (If he fails, therefore, it will be *merely* by chance.) Yet these examples of the assassin, the husband, and the like, do provide some clues. To go further, we have to add some additional thoughts.

Let us imagine that in cases of inner conflict characteristic of self-forming actions or SFAs, like the businesswoman's, the indeterministic noise that is creating an obstacle to her overcoming temptation is not coming from an external source but is coming from her own will, since she also deeply wants to do the opposite. Imagine that two crossing recurrent neural networks are involved, each influencing the other, and representing her conflicting motives. (Recurrent neural networks are complex networks of interconnected neurons in the brain circulating impulses in feedback loops that are generally involved in higher-level cognitive processing.)[10] The input of one of these neural networks consists in the woman's motives for acting morally and stopping to help the victim; the input of the other network consists in her ambitious motives for going on to her meeting. The two networks are connected, so that the indeterministic noise that is an obstacle to her making one of the choices is generated by her desire to make the other, and vice versa. The indeterminism thus arises from a tension-creating conflict in the will, as suggested earlier. In such circumstances, when either of the pathways reaches an activation threshold (which amounts to choice), it would be like your solving the mathematical problem by overcoming the background noise produced by the other pathway. And just as when you solved the mathematical problem by overcoming the distracting noise, one can say you did it and are responsible for it, so one can say this as well, I argue, in the present case, *whichever one is chosen.* The pathway through which the woman succeeds in reaching a choice will have overcome the obstacle in the form of indeterministic noise generated by the other.

Not that, under such conditions, the choices either way would not be "inadvertent," "accidental," "capricious," or "merely random" (as critics of indeterminism say), because they would be *willed* by the agents either way when they are made, and done for *reasons* either way—reasons that the agents then and there *endorse.* But these are the conditions that are usually required to say something is done "on purpose," rather than accidentally, capriciously, or merely by chance. Moreover, as I have argued elsewhere, these conditions rule out each of the reasons one might have for saying that agents act but do not have *control* over their actions (conditions such as compulsion, coercion, constraint, inadvertence, accident, control by others, and so on).[11]

10. Readable and accessible introductions to the role of neural networks (including recurrent networks) in cognitive processing include P. M. Churchland, *The Engine of Reason, the Seat of the Soul* (1996), and Manfred Spitzer, *The Mind within the Net* (1999), both from MIT Press in Cambridge, MA.

11. Further assumptions about the case must be made to rule out some of these conditions, e.g., that no one is holding a gun to the woman's head forcing her to go back, that she is not paralyzed, etc. But the point is that none of these conditions is inconsistent with the case of the woman as we have imagined it.

Indeed, the agents have what I have called "plural voluntary control" over the options in the following sense: "They are able to bring about *whichever* of the options they will, *when* they will to do so, *for* the *reasons* they will to do so, *on purpose* rather than accidentally or by mistake, without being coerced or compelled in doing so or in willing to do so, or otherwise controlled in doing or willing to do so by any other agents or mechanisms." In my 1996 book, I show that each of these conditions can be satisfied for SFAs as conceived above.[12] Taken together, they amount to satisfying the *plurality conditions* of section 4. These conditions can be summed up by saying that the agents can choose either way, *at will*.

This account of self-forming choices, it should be noted, amounts to a kind of "doubling" of the mathematical problem. It is as if an agent faced with such a choice is *trying* or making an effort to solve *two* cognitive problems at once, or to complete two competing deliberative tasks at once. In our example, that would be to make a moral choice and to make a conflicting self-interested choice (the two efforts corresponding to the two competing neural networks involved). Each task is being thwarted by the indeterminism generated by the other, so it might fail. But if it succeeds, then the agents can be held responsible because, as in the case of solving the mathematical problem, they will have succeeded in doing what they were knowingly and voluntarily trying to do.

Return to the assassin and the husband. Owing to indeterminacies in their nervous systems, the assassin might miss his target or the husband fail to break the table. But if they *succeed,* they are responsible, despite the possibility of failure, because they will have succeeded in doing what they were trying to do. And so it is, I suggest, with self-forming choices or SFAs, except that in the case of self-forming choices, *whichever way the agents* choose they will have succeeded in doing what they were trying to do because they were simultaneously trying to make both choices, and one of the choices is going to succeed. Their failure to do one thing will therefore not be a *mere* failure, but a voluntary succeeding in doing the other.

Does it make sense to talk about the agent's trying to do two competing things at once in this way, or to solve two cognitive problems at once? Well, there is now considerable evidence that the brain is a parallel processor; it can simultaneously process different kinds of information pertinent to tasks such as perception or recognition through different neural pathways. I believe such a capacity is essential to the exercise of free will. Agents

12. *The Significance of Free Will,* Chapter 8.

engaged in self-formation (SFAs) are simultaneously trying to resolve plural and competing cognitive tasks. They are, as we often say, "of two minds," without being two separate persons. They are not dissociated from either task. The businesswoman who wants to stop to help the assault victim is the same ambitious woman who wants to go to her meeting. She is torn inside by different images of who she is and what she wants to be, as we all are from time to time. But this, I am suggesting, is the kind of complexity that is needed for genuine self-formation and hence for free will. And when the woman succeeds in doing one of the things she is trying to do, she will endorse that as *her* resolution of the conflict in her will, voluntarily and intentionally and not by accident or mistake.

8. Responsibility, Luck, and Chance

Despite these remarks, I am aware how difficult it is to shake the intuitions that if choices are undetermined, they *must* happen merely by chance—and so must be "random," "capricious," "uncontrolled," "irrational," and all other things claimed. Such intuitions are deeply embedded. But if we are to understand free will, I think we have to break familiar habits of thought that support such intuitions. The first step in doing this is to question the intuitive connection in most people's minds between "indeterminism's being involved in something" and "its happening merely as a matter of chance or luck." "Chance" and "luck" are terms of ordinary language that carry the connotation of "its being out of my control." So using them already begs certain questions. "Indeterminism" by contrast is a technical term that merely precludes *deterministic* causation, though not causation altogether. Indeterminism is consistent with probabilistic causation, where outcomes are not inevitable. It is one of the most common mistakes in debates about free will to assume that "undetermined" means "uncaused," so that if choices are undetermined they must be uncaused.

Consider another related source of misunderstanding. Because the choice that results from the businesswoman's effort is undetermined up to the last minute, we may imagine her first making an effort to overcome the temptation to go on to her meeting and then at the last instant "chance takes over" and decides the issue for her. That, however, is misleading, since one cannot separate the indeterminism and the effort, so that *first* the effort occurs *followed* by chance or luck. Rather the effort *is* indeterminate and the indeterminism is a property of the effort, not something separate that occurs after or before it. The fact that the effort has the property of being indeterminate does not make it any less the woman's *effort.* The complex recurrent neural network that realizes the effort in the brain is circulating impulses in feedback loops and there is some indeterminacy in these circulating impulses. But the whole process is the woman's effort of will, and it persists right up to the moment when the choice is made. There is no point at which the effort stops and chance "takes over." She chooses as a result of the effort, even though she might have failed. In the same way, the husband breaks the table as a result of his effort, even though he might have failed because of the indeterminacy. (That is why his excuse, "chance broke the table, not me," is so lame.)

Similarly, expressions like "she got lucky" can mislead in such contexts, just as expressions like "she chose *by* chance" can mislead. One might say of the assassin and husband, for example, that "they got lucky" in killing the prime minister and breaking the table because their actions were undetermined. Yet they were responsible for what they did. So ask yourself this question: Why is it false to say "he got lucky, *so he was not responsible*" in the cases of the husband and the assassin? The first part of an answer has to do with the point made earlier that "luck," like "chance," has question-begging implications in ordinary language that are not necessarily implications of "indeterminism" (which implies only the absence of deterministic causation). The meaning of "he got lucky" in the assassin and husband cases, which *is* implied by indeterminism, I suggest, is that "he succeeded *despite the probability or chance of failure*"; and this core meaning does not imply lack of responsibility, *if he succeeds.*

The second reason why it is false to say "he got lucky, so he was not responsible" in the cases of the assassin and the husband is that *what* they succeeded in doing was what they were *trying* and wanting to do all along (kill the minister and break the table). And the third reason is that *when* they succeeded, their reaction was not "oh dear, that was a mistake or accident—something that *happened* to me, not something I *did.*" Rather they *endorsed* the outcomes as something they were trying and wanting to do all along, not something that happened by mistake or accident.

But now note that these conditions are satisfied in the businesswoman's case as well, *either way* she chooses. Whether she succeeds in choosing to return to help the victim (or to go on to her meeting) (i) she will have "succeeded *despite the probability or chance of failure,*" (ii) she will have succeeded in doing what she was *trying* and *wanting* to do all along (for she wanted both outcomes very much, though for different reasons, and was trying to make those reasons prevail in both cases), and (iii) when she succeeded (in choosing to return to help) her reaction was not "that was a mistake, an accident—something that happened to me, not something I did." Rather she *endorsed* the outcome as something she was trying and wanting to do all along and recognized it as her resolution of the conflict in her will.

But wouldn't the presence of indeterminism at least *diminish* the control persons have over their choices and other actions? Is it not the case that the assassin's control over whether the prime minister is killed is lessened by the undetermined impulses in his arm—and so also for the husband and his purposes of breaking the table? This limitation seems to be connected with another objection often made against libertarian freedom, namely, that indeterminism, wherever it occurs, seems to be a *hindrance* or *obstacle* to our realizing our purposes and hence an obstacle to our freedom rather than an enhancement of our freedom.

There is some truth to these claims. But I think what is true in them reveals something else of importance about free will. We should concede that indeterminism, wherever it occurs, *does* diminish control over what we are trying to do and *is* a hindrance or obstacle to the realization of our purposes. But we must recall that in the case of the businesswoman (and of SFAs generally), the indeterminism that is diminishing her control over one thing she is trying to do (the moral act of helping the victim) *is coming from her own will*—from her desire and effort to do the opposite (go to her business meeting), and vice versa. So, in each case, the indeterminism *is* functioning as a hindrance or obstacle to her realizing one of her purposes—a hindrance or obstacle in the form of resistance within her will that has to be overcome by effort.

If there were no such hindrance—if there were no resistance in her will—she would in a sense have "complete control" over one of her options. For there would be no competing motives standing in the way of her choosing it. But in that case also she would not be free to rationally and voluntarily choose the opposing purpose because she would have no good competing reasons to do so. Thus, by *being* a hindrance to realizing some of our purposes, indeterminism paradoxically opens up the genuine possibility of pursuing other purposes—of choosing or doing *otherwise* in accordance with, rather than against, our wills. To be genuinely self-forming agents—to have free will—there must at times in life be obstacles and hindrances in our wills of this sort that we must overcome. Self-formation is not a gift, but a struggle.

Another objection that has been made to the preceding view is that we are not introspectively or consciously aware of making dual efforts and performing multiple cognitive tasks in self-forming choice or SFA situations. Some philosophers who make this objection are inclined to dismiss the view on these grounds alone. But such a dismissal is too hasty. For I am not claiming that agents are introspectively aware of making dual efforts. What persons are introspectively aware of in SFA situations is that they are trying to decide about which of two options to choose, and that either choice is a difficult one because there are resistant motives pulling them in different directions that will have to be overcome, whichever choice is made. In such introspective conditions, I am theorizing that what is actually going on underneath is a kind of distributed processing in the brain that involves separate efforts or endeavorings to resolve competing cognitive tasks.

This point is related to a more important point on which I have frequently insisted, that introspective evidence cannot give us the whole story about free will. Stay on the surface and free will is likely to appear obscure or mysterious. What is needed is a *theory* about what might be going on behind the scenes when we exercise free will, not merely a description of what we immediately experience; and in this regard new scientific ideas can be a help rather than a hindrance to making sense of free will. It is now widely believed, for example, that parallel processing takes place in the brain in such cognitive phenomena as visual perception. The theory is that the brain separately processes different features of the visual scene, such as object and background, through distributed and parallel, though interacting, neural pathways or streams.[13]

Suppose someone objected that we are not introspectively aware of such distributed processing in ordinary cases of perception. That would hardly be a decisive objection to this new theory of vision. For the claim is that this is what we are doing in visual perception, not necessarily that we are introspectively aware of doing it. And I am making a similar claim about free will. *If parallel distributed processing takes place on the input side of the cognitive ledger (in perception), then why not consider that it also takes place on the output side (in practical reasoning, choice, and action)?* That is what we should suppose, I am suggesting, if we are to make sense of libertarian free will.

13. For an overview of recent research supporting such views, see "Decomposing and Localizing Vision: An Exemplar for Cognitive Neuroscience" by William Bechtel, in *Philosophy and the Neurosciences: A Reader,* ed. by W. Bechtel, Pete Mandik, Jennifer Mundale, and Robert Stufflebaum (Oxford: Blackwell, 2001), pp. 225–49.

It has also been commonly objected that it is irrational to make efforts to do incompatible things. I concede that in most ordinary situations it is. But I contend that there are special circumstances in which it is not irrational to make competing efforts: these include circumstances in which (i) we are deliberating between competing options; (ii) we intend to choose one or the other, but cannot choose both; (iii) we have powerful motives for wanting to choose each of the options for different and incommensurable reasons; (iv) there is a consequent resistance in our will to either choice, so that (v) if either choice is to have a chance of being made, effort will have to be made to overcome the temptation to make the other choice; and most importantly, (vi) we want to give each choice a fighting chance of being made because the motives for each choice are important to us. The motives for each choice define in part what sort of person we are; and we would be taking them lightly if we did not make an effort in their behalf. These conditions, one should note, are the conditions for SFAs.

Let me conclude with a final objection. Even if one granted that persons, such as the businesswoman, could make genuine self-forming choices that were undetermined, wouldn't it be true that such choices would be *arbitrary?* Arbitrariness seems to remain in all SFA choices since the agents cannot in principle have sufficient or overriding *prior* reasons for making one option and one set of reasons prevail over the other. This is again true, but it is also one of those truths that tells us something important about free will. It tells us that every undetermined self-forming free choice is the initiation of what I have elsewhere called a "value experiment" whose justification lies in the future and is not fully explained by the past. In making such a choice we say, in effect, "Let's try this. It is not required by my past, but it is consistent with my past and is one branching pathway my life can now meaningfully take. Whether it is the right choice, only time will tell. Meanwhile, I am willing to take responsibility for it one way or the other."[14]

I have often made the point in my writings that the term "arbitrary" comes from the Latin term *arbitrium,* which means "judgment"—as in *liberum arbitrium voluntatis,* "free judgment of the will," which was the medieval philosophers' designation for free will. Consider the author of a novel whose heroine faces a crisis and the writer has not yet developed her character in sufficient detail to say exactly how she will react. The author must makes a "judgment" about this that is not determined by the

14. *The Significance of Free Will,* pp. 145–6.

heroine's already formed past, which does not give unique direction. The judgment (*arbitrium*) of how the heroine will react is in this sense "arbitrary," but not entirely so. It had input from the heroine's fictional past and in turn gave input to her projected future.

In an analogous way, moral agents who exercise free will are both authors of and characters in their own stories all at once. By virtue of "self-forming" judgments of the will (*arbitria voluntatis*) (or what I call SFAs), they are "arbiters" of their own lives, "making themselves" out of a past that, if they are truly free, does not limit their future pathways to one. If it were objected that these agent did not have *sufficient* or *conclusive* prior reasons for choosing as they did, they may respond as follows: "True enough. But I did have *good* reasons for choosing as I did, which I'm willing to stand by *and take responsibility for.* If they were not sufficient or conclusive reasons, that's because, like the heroine of the novel, I was not a fully formed person before I chose (and still am not, for that matter). Like the author of the novel, I am in the process of writing an unfinished story and forming an unfinished character who, in my case, is myself."

21

Galen Strawson, "The Impossibility of Ultimate Moral Responsibility"

Galen Strawson is a professor of philosophy at the University of Reading. In this selection, he crafts an argument for the claim that we lack true or ultimate moral responsibility whether or not determinism is true. Given either determinism or indeterminism, we cannot have the sort of control over choice and action that this sort of responsibility demands.

1

There is an argument, which I will call the Basic Argument, which appears to prove that we cannot be truly or ultimately morally responsible for our actions. According to the Basic Argument, it makes no difference whether determinism is true or false. We cannot be truly or ultimately morally responsible for our actions in either case.

The Basic Argument has various expressions in the literature of free will, and its central idea can be quickly conveyed. (1) Nothing can be *causa sui*—nothing can be the cause of itself. (2) In order to be truly morally responsible for one's actions one would have to be *causa sui*, at least in certain crucial mental respects. (3) Therefore nothing can be truly morally responsible.

In this paper I want to reconsider the Basic Argument, in the hope that anyone who thinks that we can be truly or ultimately morally responsible for our actions will be prepared to say exactly what is wrong with it. I think that the point that it has to make is obvious, and that it has been underrated in recent discussion of free will—perhaps because it admits of no answer. I suspect that it is obvious in such a way that insisting on it too much is likely to make it seem less obvious than it is, given the innate contra-suggestibility of human beings in general and philosophers in particular. But I am not worried about making it seem less obvious than it is so long as it gets adequate attention. As far as its validity is concerned, it can look after itself.

A more cumbersome statement of the Basic Argument goes as follows.[1]

(1) Interested in free action, we are particularly interested in actions that are performed for a reason (as opposed to "reflex" actions or mindlessly habitual actions).

(2) When one acts for a reason, what one does is a function of how one is, mentally speaking. (It is also a function of one's height, one's strength, one's place and time, and so on. But the mental factors are crucial when moral responsibility is in question.)

(3) So if one is to be truly responsible for how one acts, one must be truly responsible for how one is, mentally speaking—at least in certain respects.

(4) But to be truly responsible for how one is, mentally speaking, in certain respects, one must have brought it about that one is the way one is, mentally speaking, in certain respects. And it is not merely that one must have caused oneself to be the way one is, mentally speaking. One must have consciously and explicitly chosen to be the way one is, mentally speaking, in certain respects, and one must have succeeded in bringing it about that one is that way.

(5) But one cannot really be said to choose, in a conscious, reasoned fashion, to be the way one is mentally speaking, in any respect at all, unless one already exists, mentally speaking, already equipped with some principles of choice, "P1"—preferences, values, pro-attitudes, ideals—in the light of which one chooses how to be.

(6) But then to be truly responsible, on account of having chosen to be the way one is, mentally speaking, in certain respects, one must be truly responsible for one's having the principles of choice P1 in the light of which one chose how to be.

(7) But for this to be so one must have chosen P1, in a reasoned, conscious, intentional fashion.

(8) But for this, that is, (7), to be so one must already have had some principles of choice P2, in the light of which one chose P1.

(9) And so on. Here we are setting out on a regress that we cannot stop. True self-determination is impossible because it requires the actual completion of an infinite series of choices of principles of choice.[2]

1. Adapted from G. Strawson, 1986: 28–30.
2. That is, the infinite series must have a beginning and an end, which is impossible.

(10) So true moral responsibility is impossible, because it requires true self-determination, as noted in (3).

This may seem contrived, but essentially the same argument can be given in a more natural form. (1) It is undeniable that one is the way one is, initially, as a result of heredity and early experience, and it is undeniable that these are things for which one cannot be held to be in any way responsible (morally or otherwise). (2) One cannot at any later stage of life hope to accede to true moral responsibility for the way one is by trying to change the way one already is as a result of heredity and previous experience. For (3) both the particular way in which one is moved to try to change oneself, and the degree of one's success in one's attempt at change, will be determined by how one already is as a result of heredity and previous experience. And (4) any further changes that one can bring about only after one has brought about certain initial changes will in turn be determined, via the initial changes, by heredity and previous experience. (5) This may not be the whole story, for it may be that some changes in the way one is are traceable not to heredity and experience but to the influence of indeterministic or random factors. But it is absurd to suppose that indeterministic or random factors, for which one is *ex hypothesi* in no way responsible, can in themselves contribute in any way to one's being truly morally responsible for how one is.

The claim, then, is not that people cannot change the way they are. They can, in certain respects (which tend to be exaggerated by North Americans and underestimated, perhaps, by Europeans). The claim is only that people cannot be supposed to change themselves in such a way as to be or become truly or ultimately morally responsible for the way they are, and hence for their actions.

2

I have encountered two main reactions to the Basic Argument. On the one hand it convinces almost all the students with whom I have discussed the topic of free will and moral responsibility.[3] On the other hand it often tends to be dismissed, in contemporary discussion of free will and moral responsibility, as wrong, or irrelevant, or fatuous, or too rapid, or an

3. Two have rejected it in fifteen years. Both had religious commitments, and argued, on general and radical sceptical grounds, that we can know almost nothing, and cannot therefore know that true moral responsibility is not possible in some way that we do not understand.

expression of metaphysical megalomania. I think that the Basic Argument is certainly valid in showing that we cannot be morally responsible in the way that many suppose. And I think that it is the natural light, not fear, that has convinced the students I have taught that this is so. That is why it seems worthwhile to restate the argument in a slightly different—simpler and looser—version, and to ask again what is wrong with it.

Some may say that there is nothing wrong with it, but that it is not very interesting, and not very central to the free will debate. I doubt whether any non-philosopher or beginner in philosophy would agree with this view. If one wants to think about free will and moral responsibility, consideration of some version of the Basic Argument is an overwhelmingly natural place to start. It certainly has to be considered at some point in a full discussion of free will and moral responsibility, even if the point it has to make is obvious. Belief in the kind of absolute moral responsibility that it shows to be impossible has for a long time been central to the Western religious, moral, and cultural tradition, even if it is now slightly on the wane (a disputable view). It is a matter of historical fact that concern about moral responsibility has been the main motor—indeed the *ratio essendi*—of discussion of the issue of free will. The only way in which one might hope to show (1) that the Basic Argument is not central to the free will debate would be to show (2) that the issue of moral responsibility is not central to the free will debate. There are, obviously, ways of taking the word "free" in which (2) can be maintained. But (2) is clearly false nonetheless.[4]

In saying that the notion of moral responsibility criticized by the Basic Argument is central to the Western tradition, I am not suggesting that it is some artificial and local Judeo-Christian–Kantian construct that is found nowhere else in the history of the peoples of the world, although even if it were that would hardly diminish its interest and importance for us. It is natural to suppose that Aristotle also subscribed to it,[5] and it is significant that anthropologists have suggested that most human societies can be classified either as "guilt cultures" or as "shame cultures." It is true that neither of these two fundamental moral emotions necessarily presupposes a conception of oneself as truly morally responsible for what one has done. But the fact that both are widespread, does at least suggest that a

4. It is notable that both Robert Kane (1989) and Alfred Mele (1995), in two of the best recent incompatibilist discussions of free will and autonomy, have relatively little to say about moral responsibility.

5. Cf. *Nicomachean Ethics* III.5.

conception of moral responsibility similar to our own is a natural part of the human moral-conceptual repertoire.

In fact the notion of moral responsibility connects more tightly with the notion of guilt than with the notion of shame. In many cultures shame can attach to one because of what some member of one's family—or government—has done, and not because of anything one has done oneself; and in such cases the feeling of shame need not (although it may) involve some obscure, irrational feeling that one is somehow responsible for the behaviour of one's family or government. The case of guilt is less clear. There is no doubt that people can feel guilty (or can believe that they feel guilty) about things for which they are not responsible, let alone morally responsible. But it is much less obvious that they can do this without any sense or belief that they are in fact responsible.

3

Such complications are typical of moral psychology, and they show that it is important to try to be precise about what sort of responsibility is under discussion. What sort of "true" moral responsibility is being said to be both impossible and widely believed in?

An old story is very helpful in clarifying this question. This is the story of heaven and hell. As I understand it, true moral responsibility is responsibility of such a kind that, if we have it, then it *makes sense,* at least, to suppose that it could be just to punish some of us with (eternal) torment in hell and reward others with (eternal) bliss in heaven. The stress on the words "makes sense" is important, for one certainly does not have to believe in any version of the story of heaven and hell in order to understand the notion of true moral responsibility that it is being used to illustrate. Nor does one have to believe in any version of the story of heaven and hell in order to believe in the existence of true moral responsibility. On the contrary: many atheists have believed in the existence of true moral responsibility. The story of heaven and hell is useful simply because it illustrates, in a peculiarly vivid way, the *kind* of absolute or ultimate accountability or responsibility that many have supposed themselves to have, and that many do still suppose themselves to have. It very clearly expresses its scope and force.

But one does not have to refer to religious faith in order to describe the sorts of everyday situation that are perhaps primarily influential in giving rise to our belief in true responsibility. Suppose you set off for a shop on the evening of a national holiday, intending to buy a cake with your last ten-pound note. On the steps of the shop someone is shaking an Oxfam tin. You stop, and it seems completely clear to you that it is entirely up to you what you do next. That is, it seems to you that you are truly, radically free to choose, in such a way that you will be ultimately morally responsible for whatever you do choose. Even if you believe that determinism is true, and that you will in five minutes time be able to look back and say that what you did was determined, this does not seem to undermine your sense of the absoluteness and inescapability of your freedom, and of your moral responsibility for your choice. The same seems to be true even if you accept the validity of the Basic Argument stated in §1, which concludes that one cannot be in any way ultimately responsible for the way one is and decides. In both cases, it remains true that as one stands there, one's freedom and true moral responsibility seem obvious and absolute to one.

Large and small, morally significant or morally neutral, such situations of choice occur regularly in human life. I think they lie at the heart of the experience of freedom and moral responsibility. They are the fundamental source of our inability to give up belief in true or ultimate moral responsibility. There are further questions to be asked about why human beings experience these situations of choice as they do. It is an interesting question whether any cognitively sophisticated, rational, self-conscious agent must experience situations of choice in this way.[6] But they are the experiential rock on which the belief in true moral responsibility is founded.

4

I will restate the Basic Argument. First, though, I will give some examples of people who have accepted that some sort of true or ultimate responsibility for the way one is is a necessary condition of true or ultimate moral responsibility for the way one acts, and who, certain that they are ultimately morally responsible for the way they act, have believed the condition to be fulfilled.[7]

6. Cf. MacKay (1960), and the discussion of the "Genuine Incompatibilist Determinist" in Strawson 1986: 281–6.

7. I suspect that they have started out from their subjective certainty that they have ultimate moral responsibility. They have then been led by reflection to the realization that they cannot really have such moral responsibility if they are not in some crucial way responsible for being the way they are. They have accordingly concluded that they are indeed responsible for being the way they are.

E. H. Carr held that "normal adult human beings are morally responsible for their own personality." Jean-Paul Sartre talked of "the choice that each man makes of his personality," and held that "man is responsible for what he is." In a later interview he judged that his earlier assertions about freedom were incautious; but he still held that "in the end one is always responsible for what is made of one" in some absolute sense. Kant described the position very clearly when he claimed that "man *himself* must make or have made himself into whatever, in a moral sense, whether good or evil, he is to become. Either condition must be an effect of his free choice; for otherwise he could not be held responsible for it and could therefore be *morally* neither good nor evil." Since he was committed to belief in radical moral responsibility, Kant held that such self-creation does indeed take place, and wrote accordingly of "man's character, which he himself creates," and of "knowledge of oneself as a person who . . . is his own originator." John Patten, a former British Minister for Education and a Catholic apparently preoccupied by the idea of sin, claimed that "it is . . . self-evident that as we grow up each individual chooses whether to be good or bad." It seems clear enough that he saw such choice as sufficient to give us true moral responsibility of the heaven-and-hell variety.[8]

The rest of us are not usually so reflective, but it seems that we do tend, in some vague and unexamined fashion, to think of ourselves as responsible for—answerable for—how we are. The point is quite a delicate one, for we do not ordinarily suppose that we have gone through some sort of active process of self-determination at some particular past time. Nevertheless it seems accurate to say that we do unreflectively experience ourselves, in many respects, rather as we might experience ourselves if we did believe that we had engaged in some such activity of self-determination.

8. Carr in *What Is History?*, p. 89; Sartre in *Being and Nothingness*, *Existentialism and Humanism*, p. 29, and in the *New Left Review* 1969 (quoted in Wiggins 1975); Kant in *Religion within the Limits of Reason Alone*, p. 40, *The Critique of Practical Reason*, p. 101 (Ak. V. 98), and in *Opus Postumum*, p. 213; Patten in *The Spectator*, January 1992.

These quotations raise many questions which I will not consider. It is often hard, for example, to be sure what Sartre is saying. But the occurrence of the quoted phrases is significant on any plausible interpretation of his views. As for Kant, it may be thought to be odd that he says what he does, insofar as he grounds the possibility of our freedom in our possession of an unknowable, non-temporal noumenal nature. It is, however, plausible to suppose that he thinks that radical or ultimate self-determination must take place even in the noumenal realm, in some unintelligibly non-temporal manner, if there is to be true moral responsibility.

Sometimes a part of one's character—a desire or tendency—may strike one as foreign or alien. But it can do this only against a background of character traits that are not experienced as foreign, but are rather "identified" with (it is a necessary truth that it is only relative to such a background that a character trait can stand out as alien). Some feel tormented by impulses that they experience as alien, but in many a sense of general identification with their character predominates, and this identification seems to carry within itself an implicit sense that one is, generally, somehow in control of and answerable for how one is (even, perhaps, for aspects of one's character that one does not like). Here, then, I suggest that we find, semi-dormant in common thought, an implicit recognition of the idea that true or ultimate moral responsibility for what one does somehow involves responsibility for how one is. Ordinary thought is ready to move this way under pressure.

There is, however, another powerful tendency in ordinary thought to think that one can be ultimately morally responsible even if one's character is ultimately wholly non-self-determined—simply because one is fully self-consciously aware of oneself as an agent facing choices. I will return to this point later on.

5

Let me now restate the Basic Argument in very loose—as it were conversational—terms. New forms of words allow for new forms of objection, but they may be helpful nonetheless.

(1) You do what you do, in any situation in which you find yourself, because of the way you are. So

(2) To be truly morally responsible for what you do you must be truly responsible for the way you are—at least in certain crucial mental respects.

Or:
(1) What you intentionally do, given the circumstances in which you (believe you) find yourself, flows necessarily from how you are.

Hence

(2) You have to get to have some responsibility for how you are in order to get to have some responsibility for what you intentionally do, given the circumstances in which you (believe you) find yourself.

Comment: once again the qualification about "certain mental respects" is one I will take for granted. Obviously one is not responsible for one's sex, one's basic body pattern, one's height, and so on. But if one were not responsible for anything about oneself, how could one be responsible for what one did, given the truth of (1)? This is the fundamental question, and it seems clear that if one is going to be responsible for any aspect of oneself, it had better be some aspect of one's mental nature.

I take it that (1) is incontrovertible, and that it is (2) that must be resisted. For if (1) and (2) are conceded, the case seems lost, because the full argument runs as follows.

(1) You do what you do because of the way you are.

So

(2) To be truly morally responsible for what you do you must be truly responsible for the way you are—at least in certain crucial mental respects.

But

(3) You cannot be truly responsible for the way you are, so you cannot be truly responsible for what you do.

Why can't you be truly responsible for the way you are? Because

(4) To be truly responsible for the way you are, you must have intentionally brought it about that you are the way you are, and this is impossible.

Why is it impossible? Well, suppose it is not. Suppose that

(5) You have somehow intentionally brought it about that you are the way you now are, and that you have brought this about in such a way that you can now be said to be truly responsible for being the way you are now.

For this to be true

(6) You must already have had a certain nature N in the light of which you intentionally brought it about that you are as you now are.

But then

(7) For it to be true you and you alone are truly responsible for how you now are, you must be truly responsible for having had the nature N in

the light of which you intentionally brought it about that you are the way you now are.

So

(8) You must have intentionally brought it about that you had that nature N, in which case you must have existed already with a prior nature in the light of which you intentionally brought it about that you had the nature N in the light of which you intentionally brought it about that you are the way you now are . . .

Here one is setting off on the regress. Nothing can be *causa sui* in the required way. Even if such causal "aseity" is allowed to belong unintelligibly to God, it cannot plausibly be supposed to be possessed by ordinary finite human beings. "The *causa sui* is the best self-contradiction that has been conceived so far," as Nietzsche remarked in 1886:

> it is a sort of rape and perversion of logic. But the extravagant pride of man has managed to entangle itself profoundly and frightfully with just this nonsense. The desire for "freedom of the will" in the superlative metaphysical sense, which still holds sway, unfortunately, in the minds of the half-educated; the desire to bear the entire and ultimate responsibility for one's actions oneself, and to absolve God, the world, ancestors, chance, and society involves nothing less than to be precisely this *causa sui* and, with more than Baron Munchhausen's audacity, to pull oneself up into existence by the hair, out of the swamps of nothingness. (*Beyond Good and Evil,* §21)

The rephrased argument is essentially exactly the same as before, although the first two steps are now more simply stated. It may seem pointless to repeat it, but the questions remain. Can the Basic Argument simply be dismissed? Is it really of no importance in the discussion of free will and moral responsibility? (No and No.) Shouldn't any serious defence of free will and moral responsibility thoroughly acknowledge the respect in which the Basic Argument is valid before going on to try to give its own positive account of the nature of free will and moral responsibility? Doesn't the argument go to the heart of things if the heart of the free will debate is a concern about whether we can be truly or ultimately morally responsible in the absolute way that we ordinarily suppose? (Yes and Yes.)

We are what we are, and we cannot be thought to have made ourselves *in such a way* that we can be held to be free in our actions *in such a way* that we can be held to be morally responsible for our actions *in such a way* that any punishment or reward for our actions is ultimately just or fair. Punishments and rewards may seem deeply appropriate or intrinsically "fitting" to us in spite of this argument, and many of the various institutions of punishment and reward in human society appear to be practically indispensable in both their legal and non-legal forms. But if one takes the notion of justice that is central to our intellectual and cultural tradition seriously, then the evident consequence of the Basic Argument is that there is a fundamental sense in which no punishment or reward is ever ultimately just. It is exactly as just to punish or reward people for their actions as it is to punish or reward them for the (natural) colour of their hair or the (natural) shape of their faces. The point seems obvious, and yet it contradicts a fundamental part of our natural self-conception, and there are elements in human thought that move very deeply against it. When it comes to questions of responsibility, we tend to feel that we are somehow responsible for the way we are. Even more importantly, perhaps, we tend to feel that our explicit self-conscious awareness of ourselves as agents who are able to deliberate about what to do, in situations of choice, suffices to constitute us as morally responsible free agents in the strongest sense, whatever the conclusion of the Basic Argument.

6

I have suggested that it is step (2) of the restated Basic Argument that must be rejected, and of course it can be rejected, because the phrases "truly responsible" and "truly morally responsible" can be defined in many ways. I will briefly consider three sorts of response to the Basic Argument, and I will concentrate on their more simple expressions, in the belief that truth in philosophy, especially in areas of philosophy like the present one, is almost never very complicated.

(i) The first response is *compatibilist*. Compatibilists believe that one can be a free and morally responsible agent even if determinism is true. Roughly, they claim, with many variations of detail, that one may correctly be said to be truly responsible for what one does, when one acts, just so long as one is not caused to act by any of a certain set of constraints (kleptomaniac impulses, obsessional neuroses, desires that are experienced as alien, post-hypnotic commands, threats, instances of *force majeure,* and so on). Clearly, this sort of compatibilist responsibility does not require that one should be truly responsible for how one is in any way at all, and so step (2) of the Basic Argument comes out as false. One can have compatibilist responsibility even if the way one is is totally determined by factors entirely outside one's control.

It is for this reason, however, that compatibilist responsibility famously fails to amount to any sort of true *moral* responsibility, given the natural, strong understanding of the notion of true moral responsibility (characterized above by reference to the story of heaven and hell). One does what one does entirely because of the way one is, and one is in no way ultimately responsible for the way one is. So how can one be justly punished for anything one does? Compatibilists have given increasingly refined accounts of the circumstances in which punishment may be said to be appropriate or intrinsically fitting. But they can do nothing against this basic objection.

Many compatibilists have never supposed otherwise. They are happy to admit the point. They observe that the notions of true moral responsibility and justice that are employed in the objection cannot possibly have application to anything real, and suggest that the objection is therefore not worth considering. In response, proponents of the Basic Argument agree that the notions of true moral responsibility and justice in question cannot have application to anything real; but they make no apologies for considering them. They consider them because they are central to ordinary thought about moral responsibility and justice. So far as most people are concerned, they are the subject, if the subject is moral responsibility and justice.

(ii) The second response is *libertarian.* Incompatibilists believe that freedom and moral responsibility are incompatible with determinism, and some of them are libertarians, who believe that that we are free and morally responsible agents, and that determinism is therefore false. In an ingenious statement of the incompatibilist libertarian case, Robert Kane argues that agents in an undetermined world can have free will, for they can "have the power to make choices for which they have ultimate responsibility." That is, they can "have the power to make choices which can only and finally be explained in terms of their own wills (i.e., character, motives, and efforts of will)."[9] Roughly, Kane sees this power as grounded in the possible occurrence, in agents, of efforts of will that have two main features: first, they are partly indeterministic in their nature, and hence indeterminate in their outcome; second, they occur in cases in which agents are trying to make a difficult choice between the options that their

9. Kane 1989: 254. I have omitted some italics.

characters dispose them to consider. (The paradigm cases will be cases in which they face a conflict between moral duty and non-moral desire.)

But the old objection to libertarianism recurs. How can this indeterminism help with moral responsibility? Granted that the truth of determinism rules out true moral responsibility, how can the falsity of determinism help? How can the occurrence of partly random or indeterministic events contribute in any way to one's being truly morally responsible either for one's actions or for one's character? If my efforts of will shape my character in an admirable way, and in so doing are partly indeterministic in nature, while also being shaped (as Kane grants) by my already existing character, why am I not merely lucky?

The general objection applies equally whether determinism is true or false, and can be restated as follows. We are born with a great many genetically determined predispositions for which we are not responsible. We are subject to many early influences for which we are not responsible. These decisively shape our characters, our motives, the general bent and strength of our capacity to make efforts of will. We may later engage in conscious and intentional shaping procedures—call them S-procedures—designed to affect and change our characters, motivational structure, and wills. Suppose we do. The question is then why we engage in the particular S-procedures that we do engage in, and why we engage in them in the particular way that we do. The general answer is that we engage in the particular S-procedures that we do engage in, given the circumstances in which we find ourselves, because of certain features of the way we already are. (Indeterministic factors may also play a part in what happens, but these will not help to make us responsible for what we do.) And these features of the way we already are—call them character features, or C-features—are either wholly the products of genetic or environmental influences, deterministic or random, for which we are not responsible, or are at least partly the result of earlier S-procedures, which are in turn either wholly the product of C-features for which we are not responsible, or are at least partly the product of still earlier S-procedures, which are in turn either the products of C-features for which we are not responsible, or the product of such C-features together with still earlier S-procedures—and so on. In the end, we reach the first S-procedure, and this will have been engaged in, and engaged in the particular way in which it was engaged in, as a result of genetic or environmental factors, deterministic or random, for which we were not responsible.

Moving away from the possible role of indeterministic factors in character or personality formation, we can consider their possible role in particular instances of deliberation and decision. Here too it seems clear that indeterministic factors cannot, in influencing what happens, contribute to true moral responsibility in any way. In the end, whatever we do, we do it either as a result of random influences for which we are not responsible, or as a result of non-random influences for which we are not responsible, or as a result of influences for which we are proximally responsible but not ultimately responsible. The point seems obvious. Nothing can be ultimately *causa sui* in any respect at all. Even if God can be, we can't be.

Kane says little about moral responsibility in his paper, but his position seems to be that true moral responsibility is possible if indeterminism is true. It is possible because in cases of "moral, prudential and practical struggle we . . . are truly 'making ourselves' in such a way that we are ultimately responsible for the outcome." This "making of ourselves" means that "we can be ultimately responsible for our present motives and character by virtue of past choices which helped to form them and for which we were ultimately responsible" (op. cit: 252). It is for this reason that we can be ultimately responsible and morally responsible not only in cases of struggle in which we are "making ourselves," but also for choices and actions which do not involve struggle, flowing unopposed from our character and motives.

In claiming that we can be ultimately responsible for our present motives and character, Kane appears to *accept* step (2) of the Basic Argument. He appears to accept that we have to "make ourselves," and so be ultimately responsible for ourselves, in order to be morally responsible for what we do.[10] The problem with this suggestion is the old one. In Kane's view, a person's "ultimate responsibility" for the outcome of an effort of will depends essentially on the partly indeterministic nature of the outcome. This is because it is only the element of indeterminism that prevents prior character and motives from fully explaining the outcome of the effort of will (op. cit.: 236). But how can this indeterminism help with moral responsibility? How can the fact that my effort of will is indeterministic in such a way that its outcome is indeterminate make me truly responsible for it, or even help to make me truly responsible for it? How can it help in any way at all with moral responsibility? How can it make punishment—or reward—ultimately just?

10. He cites van Inwagen 1989 in support of this view.

There is a further, familiar problem with the view that moral responsibility depends on indeterminism. If one accepts the view, one will have to grant that it is impossible to know whether any human being is ever morally responsible. For moral responsibility now depends on the falsity of determinism, and determinism is unfalsifiable. There is no more reason to think that determinism is false than that it is true, in spite of the impression sometimes given by scientists and popularizers of science.

(iii) The third response begins by accepting that one cannot be held to be ultimately responsible for one's character or personality or motivational structure. It accepts that this is so whether determinism is true or false. It then directly challenges step (2) of the Basic Argument. It appeals to a certain picture of the self in order to argue that one can be truly free and morally responsible in spite of the fact that one cannot be held to be ultimately responsible for one's character or personality or motivational structure. This picture has some support in the "phenomenology" of human choice—we sometimes experience our choices and decisions as if the picture were an accurate one. But it is easy to show that it cannot be accurate in such a way that we can be said to be truly or ultimately morally responsible for our choices or actions.

It can be set out as follows. One is free and truly morally responsible because one's self is, in a crucial sense, independent of one's character or personality or motivational structure—one's CPM, for short. Suppose one is in a situation which one experiences as a difficult choice between A, doing one's duty, and B, following one's non-moral desires. Given one's CPM, one responds in a certain way. One's desires and beliefs develop and interact and constitute reasons for both A and B. One's CPM makes one tend towards A or B. So far the problem is the same as ever: whatever one does, one will do what one does because of the way one's CPM is, and since one neither is nor can be ultimately responsible for the way one's CPM is, one cannot be ultimately responsible for what one does.

Enter one's self, S. S is imagined to be in some way independent of one's CPM. S (i.e., one) considers the deliverances of one's CPM and decides in the light of them, but it—S—incorporates a power of decision that is independent of one's CPM in such a way that one can after all count as truly and ultimately morally responsible in one's decisions and actions, even though one is not ultimately responsible for one's CPM. Step (2) of the Basic Argument is false because of the existence of S.[11]

11. Cf. C. A. Campbell 1957.

The trouble with the picture is obvious. S (i.e., one) decides on the basis of the deliverances of one's CPM. But whatever S decides, it decides as it does because of the way it is (or else because partly or wholly because of the occurrence in the decision process of indeterministic factors for which it—i.e., one—cannot be responsible, and which cannot plausibly be thought to contribute to one's true moral responsibility). And this returns us to where we started. To be a source of true or ultimate responsibility, S must be responsible for being the way it is. But this is impossible, for the reasons given in the Basic Argument.

The story of S and CPM adds another layer to the description of the human decision process, but it cannot change the fact that human beings cannot be ultimately self-determining in such a way as to be ultimately morally responsible for how they are, and thus for how they decide and act. The story is crudely presented, but it should suffice to make clear that no move of this sort can solve the problem.

"Character is destiny," as Novalis is often reported as saying.[12] The remark is inaccurate, because external circumstances are part of destiny, but the point is well taken when it comes to the question of moral responsibility. Nothing can be *causa sui,* and in order to be truly morally responsible for one's actions one would have to be *causa sui,* at least in certain crucial mental respects. One cannot institute oneself in such a way that one can take over true or assume moral responsibility for how one is in such a way that one can indeed be truly morally responsible for what one does. This fact is not changed by the fact that we may be unable not to think of ourselves as truly morally responsible in ordinary circumstances. Nor is it changed by the fact that it may be a very good thing that we have this inability—so that we might wish to take steps to preserve it, if it looked to be in danger of fading. As already remarked, many human beings are unable to resist the idea that it is their capacity for fully explicit self-conscious deliberation, in a situation of choice, that suffices to constitute them as truly morally responsible agents in the strongest possible sense. The Basic Argument shows that this is a mistake. However self-consciously aware we are, as we deliberate and reason, every act and operation of our mind happens as it does as a result of features for which we are ultimately in no way responsible. But the conviction that self-conscious awareness of

12. E.g., by George Eliot in *The Mill on the Floss,* bk. 6, ch. 6. Novalis wrote, "Oft fühl ich jetzt . . . [und] je tiefer einsehe, dass Schicksal und Gemüt Namen eines Begriffes sind"—"I often feel, and ever more deeply realize, that fate and character are the same concept." He was echoing Heraclitus, Fragment 119 DK.

one's situation can be a sufficient foundation of strong free will is very powerful. It runs deeper than rational argument, and it survives untouched, in the everyday conduct of life, even after the validity of the Basic Argument has been admitted.

7

There is nothing new in the somewhat incantatory argument of this paper. It restates certain points that may be in need of restatement. "Everything has been said before," said Andre Gide, echoing La Bruyere, "but since nobody listens we have to keep going back and beginning all over again." This is an exaggeration, but it may not be a gross exaggeration, so far as general observations about the human condition are concerned.

The present claim, in any case, is simply this: time would be saved, and a great deal of readily available clarity would be introduced into the discussion of the nature of moral responsibility, if the simple point that is established by the Basic Argument were more generally acknowledged and clearly stated. Nietzsche thought that thoroughgoing acknowledgement of the point was long overdue, and his belief that there might be moral advantages in such an acknowledgement may deserve further consideration.[13]

References

Aristotle. c. 330 BCE/1953. *Nichomachean Ethics.* Trans. J. A. K. Thomson. London: Allen and Unwin.

Campbell, C. A. 1957. "Has the Self 'Free Will'?" In C. A. Campbell, *On Selfhood and Godhood.* London: Allen and Unwin.

Carr, E. H. 1961. *What Is History?* London: Macmillan.

Eliot, G. 1860/1960. *The Mill on the Floss.* Harmondsworth, U.K.: Penguin.

Kane, R. 1989. "Two Kinds of Incompatibilism." *Philosophy and Phenomenological Research* 50: 219–54.

Kant, I. 1785/1956. *Critique of Practical Reason.* Trans. L. W. Beck. Indianapolis: Bobbs-Merrill.

Kant, I. 1793/1960. *Religion within the Limits of Reason Alone.* Trans. T. M. Greene and H. H. Hudson. New York: Harper and Row.

13. Cf. R. Schacht 1983: 304–9. The idea that there might be moral advantages in the clear-headed admission that true or ultimate moral responsibility is impossible has been developed in another way by Saul Smilansky (1994).

Kant, I. 1993. *Opus Postumum.* Trans. E. Förster and M. Rosen. Cambridge: Cambridge University Press.

MacKay, D. M. 1960. "On the Logical Indeterminacy of Free Choice." *Mind* 69: 31–40.

Mele, A. 1995. *Autonomous Agents: From Self-Control to Autonomy.* New York: Oxford University Press.

Nietzsche, F. 1886/1966. *Beyond Good and Evil.* Trans. Walter Kaufmann. New York: Random House.

Novalis. 1802. *Heinrich von Ofterdingen.* Edited by Friedrich Schlegel. Berlin.

Sartre, J.-P. 1943/1969. *Being and Nothingness.* Trans. Hazel E. Barnes. London: Methuen.

Sartre, J.-P. 1946/1989. *Existentialism and Humanism.* Trans. Philip Mairet. London: Methuen.

Schacht, R. 1983. *Nietzsche.* London: Routledge and Kegan Paul.

Smilansky, S. 1994. "The Ethical Advantages of Hard Determinism." *Philosophy and Phenomenological Research* 55 (1994): 355–63.

Strawson, G. 1986. *Freedom and Belief.* Oxford: Clarendon Press.

Van Inwagen, P. 1989. "When Is the Will Free?" *Philosophical Perspectives* 3: 399–422.

Wiggins, D. 1975. "Towards a Reasonable Libertarianism." In T. Honderich, ed., *Essays on Freedom of Action.* London: Routledge.

Derk Pereboom, "Determinism *al Dente*"

Derk Pereboom is a professor of philosophy at Cornell University. In this article, he defends the claim that we lack the sort of free will required for moral responsibility and proposes that the consequences of denying that we could ever be praiseworthy or blameworthy are not as harmful as one might initially suspect. Even if we believe that we are never morally responsible for our actions, it will make sense to pursue projects that give our lives meaning, we will have adequate reason to do what is right, and good interpersonal relationships will not be undermined.

> *Al dente* means "firm to the bite," and that is how Italians eat pasta. Soft pasta is no more fit to eat than a limp and soggy slice of bread. As soon as pasta begins to lose its stiffness and becomes just tender enough so that you can bite through without snapping it, it is done. Once you have learned to cook and eat pasta *al dente,* you'll accept it no other way. (Marcella Hazan, *The Classic Italian Cookbook,* pp. 90–1)

The demographic profile of the free will debate reveals a majority of soft determinists, who claim that we possess the freedom required for moral responsibility, that determinism is true, and that these views are compatible. Libertarians, incompatibilist champions of the freedom required for moral responsibility, constitute a minority. Not only is this the distribution in the contemporary philosophical population, but in Western philosophy it has always been the pattern. Seldom has hard determinism—the incompatibilist endorsement of determinism and rejection of the freedom required for moral responsibility—been defended.[1] One

"Determinism *al Dente*" first appeared in *Noûs* 29 (1995), pp. 21–45. Reprinted by permission of *Noûs.*

1. The terms 'soft determinism' and 'hard determinism' originate in William James' essay "The Dilemma of Determinism," in *The Will to Believe and Other Essays* (New York: Longman, 1909). The most prominent attempts to develop a hard determinist theory are in Baruch de Spinoza, *Ethics* (especially Part II, Proposition 48, and Part III, Scholium to Proposition 2), in Baron d'Holbach,

would expect hard determinism to have few proponents, given its apparent renunciation of morality. I believe, however, that the argument for hard determinism is powerful, and furthermore, that the reasons against it are not as compelling as they might at first seem.

The categorization of the determinist position by 'hard' and 'soft' masks some important distinctions, and thus one might devise a more fine-grained scheme. Actually, within the conceptual space of both hard and soft determinism there is a range of alternative views. The softest version of soft determinism maintains that we possess the freedom required for moral responsibility, that having this sort of freedom is compatible with determinism, that this freedom includes the ability to do otherwise than what one actually will do, and that even though determinism is true, one is yet deserving of blame upon having performed a wrongful act. The hardest version of hard determinism claims that since determinism is true, we lack the freedom required for moral responsibility, and hence, not only do we never deserve blame, but, moreover, no moral principles or values apply to us. But both hard and soft determinism encompass a number of less extreme positions. The view I wish to defend is somewhat softer than the hardest of the hard determinisms, and in this respect it is similar to some aspects of the position recently developed by Ted Honderich.[2] In the view we will explore, since determinism is true,

---

System of Nature (1770), and in John Hospers, "Meaning and Free Will," *Philosophy and Phenomenological Research* X (1950), pp. 313–330, and *Human Conduct* (New York: Harcourt, Brace, and World, 1961), pp. 493–524. For Charles Stevenson, morality accords with determinism only because the backward-looking elements that many have thought to be essential to morality are not genuinely so; see "Ethical Judgments and Avoidability," *Mind* 47, (1938), and *Facts and Values* (New Haven and London: Yale University Press, 1963) pp. 138–152. The view I develop is similar to Stevenson's in that I argue that there is a conception of ethics, different from the common sense version, which is compatible with determinism, but I contend, while Stevenson does not, that any conception which is compatible with determinism must relinquish moral responsibility. Elizabeth Beardsley argues that the hard deterministic perspective must be taken seriously, but only as one among several perspectives, each of which has its proper role in the moral life, "Determinism and Moral Perspectives," *Philosophy and Phenomenological Research* XXI (1960), pp. 1–20.

2. My attention was drawn to Honderich's position in *A Theory of Determinism* (Oxford: Oxford University Press, 1988) by a referee for *Noûs*. I do not endorse Honderich's strategies for arguing against soft determinism and libertarianism, and my approach for undermining these views differs from his. Neither do I sympathize with his contention that determinism is true despite the evidence of

we lack the freedom required for moral responsibility. But although we therefore never deserve blame for having performed a wrongful act, most moral principles and values are not thereby undermined.

I

Let us, for the sake of counterargument, devise a soft-determinist position that incorporates the essential features of three widespread compatibilist notions of freedom. First, perhaps the most prominent compatibilist conception is found in the Humean tradition—a notion of freedom of action. In this view, an action is free in the sense required for moral responsibility when it is one the agent really wanted to perform. More precisely, an action is free in the right sense just in case desires that genuinely belong to the agent make up the immediate causal history of the action. An action is unfree, by contrast, when, for example, it is performed as a result of brainwashing or some types of mental illness. In such cases, desires that genuinely belong to the agent do not play the causal role necessary for the action to be genuinely free.[3]

Second, in Harry Frankfurt's view, to be morally responsible, one's effective desires to perform actions must conform to one's second-order desires.[4] Frankfurt has us suppose "that a person has done what he wanted

---

quantum mechanics. But despite Honderich's claim to reject both compatibilism and incompatibilism, I agree with several important aspects of his conception of *affirmation* (pp. 488–540), as will become evident as this discussion progresses. Honderich believes that he can reject both compatibilism and incompatibilism because, contrary to tradition, he does not construe these notions as jointly exhaustive of the determinist positions on freedom and morality. Compatibilism, in his schema, is the claim that determinism is compatible with all of our practices of moral evaluation, that it "leaves moral approval and disapproval untouched," whereas incompatibilism is the claim that determinism is compatible with none of these practices, that it "destroys [moral approval and disapproval]" (p. 539, cf. pp. 451–487). In my conception, compatibilism is the view that determinism is compatible with whatever sort of freedom is sufficient for moral responsibility, while incompatibilism is the view that determinism is not compatible with this type of freedom.

3. David Hume, *A Treatise of Human Nature,* L. A. Selby-Bigge, ed. (Oxford: Oxford University Press, 1962), pp. 399–412; *An Enquiry Concerning Human Understanding,* Eric Steinberg, ed. (Indianapolis: Hackett Publishing Co., 1981), §8; A. J. Ayer, "Freedom and Necessity," in *Free Will,* Gary Watson, ed. (Oxford: Oxford University Press, 1982), pp. 15–23 [Selections 7, 8, and 12 in this volume].

4. Harry Frankfurt, "Freedom of the Will and the Concept of a Person," in Gary Watson, ed., *Free Will* (Oxford: Oxford University Press, 1982), pp. 81–95 [Selection 16 in this volume].

to do, that he did it because he wanted to do it, and that the will by which he was moved when he did it was his will because it was the will he wanted."[5] Such a person, in his view, acted freely in the sense required for moral responsibility.

Third, Bernard Gert and Timothy Duggan have argued that the type of freedom required for moral responsibility is *the ability to will,* or, in John Fischer's development of this view, *responsiveness to reasons.*[6] For an action to be free in the right sense, it must result from the agent's rational consideration of reasons relevant to the situation, such that, in at least some alternative circumstances in which there are sufficient reasons for her to do otherwise than she actually does, she would be receptive to these reasons and would have done otherwise by the efficacy of the same deliberative mechanism that actually results in the action. Hence, I am free in the right sense when I decide to harvest the wheat next week rather than this week, if, in circumstances in which I knew it would rain next week, I would, by the deliberative mechanism that actually results in my deciding to harvest next week, appreciate the different reasons and harvest this week instead. If my practical reasoning would not differ in varying circumstances, I am neither free nor morally responsible.[7]

Let us consider a situation involving an action that is free in all of the three senses we have just discussed. Mr. Green kills Ms. Peacock for the sake of some personal advantage. His act of murder is caused by desires that are genuinely his, and his desire to kill Ms. Peacock conforms to his second-order desires. Mr. Green's desires are modified, and some of them

5. Frankfurt, p. 94.

6. Bernard Gert and Timothy J. Duggan, "Free Will as the Ability to Will," *Noûs XIII* (May 1979), pp. 197–217, reprinted in *Moral Responsibility,* John Martin Fischer, ed. (Ithaca: Cornell University Press, 1986), pp. 205–224; John Martin Fischer, "Responsiveness and Moral Responsibility," in *Responsibility, Character, and the Emotions,* Ferdinand Schoeman, ed. (Cambridge: Cambridge University Press, 1987), pp. 81–106, at pp. 88–9.

7. In Honderich's view, compatibilists ignore a widespread attitude about our actions, that moral responsibility presupposes *origination,* or agent causation. He claims, accordingly, that compatibilists are *intransigent* in maintaining their notions of moral responsibility in the face of determinism, and that this counts against them (pp. 482–7). While I agree that moral responsibility presupposes origination, I also believe that pointing out that compatibilists ignore this conception has little force against their position. What is needed is an argument against the view that the types of freedom that soft determinisms have advocated are sufficient for moral responsibility, and I develop such an argument here.

arise, by his rational consideration of the relevant reasons, and his process of deliberation is reasons-responsive. For instance, if he knew that the bad consequences for him resulting from his crime would be much more severe than they are actually likely to be, he would not have murdered Ms. Peacock. Given that determinism is true, is it plausible that Mr. Green is responsible for his action?

In the deterministic view, the first- and second-order desires and the reasons-responsive process that result in Mr. Green's crime are inevitable given their causes, and those causes are inevitable given their causes. In assessing moral responsibility for his act of murder, we wind our way back along the deterministic chain of causes that results in his reasoning and desires, and we eventually reach causal factors that are beyond his control—causal factors that he could not have produced, altered, or prevented. The incompatibilist intuition is that if an action results from a deterministic causal process that traces back to factors beyond the control of the agent, he is not morally responsible for the action.

A compatibilist rejoinder to this intuition is that moral responsibility does not leave Mr. Green behind as the deterministic causal process traces backwards in time. Even though the chain of sufficient causes for his crime reaches far beyond him, to a time before he ever existed, he retains moral responsibility. Mr. Green is morally responsible for the act of murder because *his* first-order desires caused the action, and these first-order desires conform to *his* second-order desires, and all of these desires are generated in a context of *his* rational evaluation of reasons. Since the causal history of his action has the right pattern, he is free and morally responsible.

Let us consider a series of different ways in which the above type of situation might come about, in order to undermine soft determinism and to support the contrary claim that moral responsibility precludes being determined in virtue of a causal process that traces back to factors beyond the agent's control.[8]

Case 1: Mr. Green is like an ordinary human being, except that he was created by neuroscientists, who can manipulate him directly through the use of radio-like technology. Suppose these neuroscientists directly manipulate Mr. Green to undertake the process of reasoning by which his desires are modified and produced, and his effective first-order desire to kill Ms. Peacock conforms to his second-order desires. The

8. Richard Taylor discusses cases of these sorts in *Metaphysics* (Englewood Cliffs, NJ: Prentice Hall, 1983), pp. 43–4.

> neuroscientists manipulate him by, among other things, pushing a series of buttons just before he begins to reason about his situation, thereby causing his reasoning process to be rationally egoistic. His reasoning process is reasons-responsive, because it would have resulted in different choices in some situations in which the egoistic reasons were otherwise. Mr. Green does not think and act contrary to character, since the neuroscientists typically manipulate him to be rationally egoistic.

Mr. Green's action would seem to meet the criteria of the various compatibilist theories of freedom we have examined. But intuitively, he is not morally responsible because he is determined by the neuroscientists' actions, which are beyond his control.

The intuitions generated by this case challenge the suppositions of many soft determinists. Fischer argues that in "case of direct manipulation of the brain, it is likely that the process issuing in the action is not reasons-responsive, whereas the fact that a process is causally deterministic does not in itself bear on whether it is reasons-responsive."[9] He claims that although Frankfurt's sort of freedom can be induced neurophysiologically, a process that is reasons-responsive cannot.[10] But Fischer's claim is mistaken. As long as a process requires only abilities that are physically realized, it can be induced by sufficiently equipped scientists.

One might argue that although in Case 1 the process resulting in the action is reasons-responsive, it is induced by direct manipulation near the time of the action, and this makes the case very much like one of brainwashing. Or one might contend that Mr. Green's reasons-responsiveness is too superficial, because the neuroscientists could make him lack reasons-responsiveness just by controlling him differently. It is not clear how deeply these objections cut, but in reply, let us consider a further case:

> Case 2: Mr. Green is like an ordinary human being, except that he was created by neuroscientists, who, although they cannot control him directly, have programmed him to be a rational egoist, so that, in any circumstances like those in which he now finds himself, he is causally determined to undertake the reasons-responsive process and to possess the set of first and second-order desires that results in his killing Ms. Peacock.

9. Fischer, p. 102.
10. Fischer, pp. 104–5.

Case 2 is more similar than Case 1 to the ordinary human situation, since the agent is not directly manipulated near the time of the action. But again, although the agent is free in each of our compatibilist senses, intuitively he is not morally responsible because he is determined in virtue of the neuroscientists' actions, which are beyond his control. Furthermore, it would seem unprincipled to claim that whether Mr. Green is morally responsible depends on the length of the temporal interval between the programming and the action. Whether the programming takes place two seconds or thirty years before the action is irrelevant.

> Case 3: Mr. Green is an ordinary human being, except that he was determined by the rigorous training practices of his home and community to be a rational egoist. His training took place at too early an age for him to have had the ability to prevent or alter the practices that determined his character. Mr. Green is thereby caused to undertake the reasons-responsive process and to possess the organization of first and second-order desires that result in his killing Ms. Peacock.

If the compatibilist wishes to argue that Mr. Green is morally responsible under these circumstances, he must point out a morally relevant feature present in Case 3 but not in the first two cases, and such a difference is difficult to detect. In each of these cases Mr. Green is free in all of the compatibilist senses. Causal determination by agents whose determining activity is beyond Mr. Green's control most plausibly explains his lack of moral responsibility in the first two cases, and accordingly, we would seem forced to concede that he is not morally responsible in the third case as well.

> Case 4: Physicalist determinism is true. Mr. Green is a rationally egoistic but (otherwise) ordinary human being, raised in normal circumstances. Mr. Green's killing of Ms. Peacock comes about as a result of his undertaking the reasons-responsive process of deliberation, and he has the specified organization of first and second-order desires.

Just as in Cases 1–3, Mr. Green's action in Case 4 results from a deterministic causal process that traces back to factors beyond his control. Given that we are constrained to deny moral responsibility to Mr. Green in the first three cases, what principled reason do we have for holding him morally responsible in this more ordinary case? One distinguishing feature of Case 4 is that the causal determination of Mr. Green's crime is not, in the last analysis, brought about by other agents.[11] But if we were to revise the first three cases so that the determination is brought about by a spontaneously generated, mindless machine, the intuition that Mr. Green is not morally responsible would persist. Hence, the best explanation for this intuition in these first three cases is just that Mr. Green's action results from a deterministic causal process that traces back to factors beyond his control. Consequently, because Mr. Green is also causally determined in this way in Case 4, we must, despite our initial predilections, conclude that here too Mr. Green is not morally responsible. And more generally, if every action results from a deterministic causal process that traces back to factors beyond the agent's control, then no agents are ever morally responsible for their actions.

The soft determinist might point out that according to ordinary intuitions, in Case 4 Mr. Green is morally responsible, and that these intuitions should be given more weight than we have given them. But in the incompatibilist view, one consequence of determinism is that ordinary intuitions about moral responsibility in specific cases are based on a mistake. In making moral judgments in everyday life, we do not assume that agents' choices and actions result from deterministic causal processes that trace back to factors beyond their control. Our ordinary intuitions do not presuppose that determinism is true, and they may even presuppose that it is false. Indeed, in Case 4 it is specified that determinism is true, but ordinary intuitions are likely to persist regardless of this stipulation, especially if the implications of determinism are not thoroughly internalized. If we did assume determinism and internalize its implications, our intuitions might well be different. Consequently, a reply to incompatibilism requires something more powerful than an analysis of freedom and moral responsibility designed to capture ordinary intuitions about moral responsibility in specific cases. What is needed is an argument against the fundamental incompatibilist claim, that if one's action results from a deterministic causal process that traces back to factors beyond one's control, to factors that one could not have produced, altered, or prevented, then one is not free in the sense required for moral responsibility.[12]

11. For example, in the course of developing his soft determinist view, William G. Lycan argues that in the kinds of cases Richard Taylor discusses (in *Metaphysics*, pp. 43–4) the agent lacks responsibility just because he "is a puppet of another person" and not simply because he is causally determined (*Consciousness*, Cambridge, MA: MIT Press, 1987, pp. 117–8).

12. Some compatibilists might argue that one should construe the slide to slope

II

It has often been assumed that there is an alternative and equivalent statement of the fundamental incompatibilist claim. According to this variant formulation, moral responsibility requires that, given all of the factors that precede one's choice, one could have done otherwise than what one actually did.[13] Furthermore, some have argued that because this variant formulation can be defeated, the incompatibilist view is mistaken. But the variant formulation is not equivalent to the original, and since the original is more forceful, it would be best to reject the view that a successful challenge to the "responsibility only if she could have done otherwise" intuition also undermines the "responsibility only if her action does not result from a deterministic causal process that traces back to factors beyond her control" intuition.

As Peter van Inwagen points out, if physicalist determinism is true, there is a clear sense in which no agent could have done otherwise than what he in fact did.[14] By van Inwagen's characterization, physicalist determinism is true just in case a proposition that expresses the entire state of the universe at some instant in time, in conjunction with the physical laws, entails any proposition that expresses the state of the universe at any other instant.[15] So if physicalist determinism is true, given the entire state of the universe at some instant in time, every subsequent state of the universe is thereby rendered inevitable. Suppose Ms. White murdered Mr. Green last Tuesday. Given physicalist determinism, Ms. White's crime is inevitable given the state of the universe 100 years before she was born and the natural laws. So if Ms. White was able to do otherwise last Tuesday, then

---

the other way. One should begin with one's strong intuition that in Case 4 Mr. Green is morally responsible, and since there are no good reasons to believe that there is a morally relevant distinction between Mr. Green in Case 4 and his counterpart in Cases 1–3, one should conclude that Mr. Green in the first three cases is also morally responsible. My own intuition that Mr. Green in Cases 1 and 2 is not morally responsible is much stronger than my intuition that Mr. Green in Case 4 is, but some compatibilists may differ. What follows may provide these compatibilists with a clearer picture of an alternative view.

13. Honderich, for example, seems to suppose that these intuitions, on some interpretation of 'could have done otherwise,' are equivalent, e.g., pp. 400–9.

14. Peter van Inwagen, "The Incompatibility of Free Will and Determinism," in *Free Will*, Gary Watson, ed. (Oxford, 1982), pp. 96–110 [Selection 17 in this volume]; *An Essay on Free Will* (Oxford: Oxford University Press, 1983), pp. 55–78.

15. "The Incompatibility of Free Will and Determinism," p. 47.

she must at that time have been able to alter the state of the universe 100 years before she was born, or to change the natural laws. Since she was able to do neither, last Tuesday she could not have done otherwise than to murder Mr. Green.

But soft determinists have argued that one can be morally responsible for one's actions even if one could not have done otherwise. Frankfurt has devised a case similar to this one:

> Ms. Scarlet is seriously considering whether to kill Colonel Mustard. Meanwhile Professor Plum, a neuroscientist, very much wants the Colonel dead, and is worried that Ms. Scarlet will not choose to kill him. So Professor Plum has implanted a device in Ms. Scarlet's brain, which, just in case Ms. Scarlet were to be swayed by a reason not to kill Colonel Mustard, would cause her to choose to kill him. But Ms. Scarlet chooses to kill, and carries out the deed, without even beginning to be swayed by a reason for making the alternative choice.[16]

Our intuition is that Ms. Scarlet is responsible for killing Colonel Mustard, although she could not have done otherwise, and thus, the conclusion of Frankfurt's argument is that the variant intuition is mistaken. This argument is powerful and resilient. For example, it succeeds not only against the intuition that moral responsibility requires the ability to *do* otherwise, but also against the intuition that it requires the ability to *choose* otherwise. For Ms. Scarlet could not even have chosen otherwise, because the device would have arrested the deliberative process before it resulted in any alternative choice.

Frankfurt's argument strongly suggests that the incompatibilist (and everyone else) must relinquish the "responsibility only if she could have done otherwise" intuition. As Fischer has shown, however, this type of argument does not establish that the incompatibilist must also abandon the claim that moral responsibility requires that one's action not be causally determined, or, in my formulation, that moral responsibility requires that one's action not result from a deterministic causal process that traces back to factors beyond one's control.[17] (One might note that Frank-

16. Harry Frankfurt, "Alternate Possibilities and Moral Responsibility," *Journal of Philosophy* 1969, pp. 828–39 [Selection 15 in this volume]. For a precursor to certain elements of my variation on Frankfurt's case see John Martin Fischer, "Responsibility and Control," *Moral Responsibility*, Fischer, ed., pp. 174–90.

17. Fischer, "Responsibility and Control," pp. 182–5.

furt does not state that his argument has this result). In the Frankfurt-style example it is not specified that Ms. Scarlet is causally determined to choose or act as she did. Our intuition that she is responsible might well depend on the assumption that although the device prevents her from being able to choose to do otherwise, her choice does not result from a deterministic causal process that traces back to factors beyond her control. And indeed, if it were specified that her choice is caused in this way, incompatibilists, among others, would no longer agree that Ms. Scarlet is morally responsible.

That one's choice and action result from a deterministic causal process that traces back to factors beyond one's control entails that one cannot choose to do otherwise (in at least one sense), but not vice versa. For as Fischer points out, it is possible that one's choice not come about as a result of a deterministic process at all, and yet there be mechanisms that prevent one's choosing to do otherwise.[18] Ms. Scarlet might have been the undetermined agent-cause of the murder of Colonel Mustard even if Professor Plum's device renders her incapable of choosing to do otherwise. The incompatibilist's most fundamental claim is that moral responsibility requires that one's choice and action not result from a deterministic causal process that traces back to factors beyond one's control. An argument of the sort that Frankfurt advances cannot dislodge this claim. This incompatibilist premise does not entail the proposition that moral responsibility requires that one be able to choose to do otherwise, and this proposition, for the reasons Frankfurt has advanced, is best rejected.[19]

III

Let us now consider the libertarians, who claim that we have a capacity for indeterministically free action, and that we are thereby morally responsible. According to one libertarian view, what makes actions free is just their being constituted (partially) of indeterministic natural events. Lucretius, for example, maintains that actions are free just in virtue of being made up partially of random swerves in the downward paths of

18. Fischer, "Responsibility and Control," pp. 182–5.

19. Given this view, the incompatibilist would still be right to claim that one is not morally responsible for an action if one could not have done otherwise due to the action's resulting from a deterministic causal process that traces back to factors beyond one's control.

atoms.[20] These swerves, and the actions they underlie, are random (at least) in the sense that they are not determined by any prior state of the universe. If quantum theory is true, the position and momentum of microparticles exhibit randomness in this same sense, and natural indeterminacy of this sort might also be conceived as the metaphysical foundation of indeterministically free action. But natural indeterminacies of these types cannot, by themselves, account for freedom of the sort required for moral responsibility. As has often been pointed out, such random physical events are no more within our control than are causally determined physical events, and thus, we can no more be morally responsible for them than, in the indeterminist opinion, we can be for events that are causally determined.[21]

Alternatively, many libertarians advocate the theory of agent causation, the view that freedom of action is accounted for not (simply) by randomly occurring events of the sort we have described, but by agents capable of causing their actions deliberately. In this view, an agent's causation of her action is not itself produced by processes beyond her control.[22] Positing such agent-causes, in my view, involves no internal incoherence. There is no internal incoherence in the idea of an agent having a non-Humean causal power to cause her actions deliberately in such a way that her causation of her actions is not itself produced by processes beyond her control. It is unclear, however, whether we have any reason to believe that such entities exist.[23]

20. Lucretius, *De Rerum Natura,* translated by W. H. D. Rouse, Loeb Classical Library (Cambridge: Harvard University Press, 1982), 2.216–93, " . . . but what keeps the mind itself from having necessity within it in all actions . . . is the minute swerving of the first beginnings at no fixed place and at no fixed time" (2.289–93).

21. See, for example, A. J. Ayer, "Freedom and Necessity," p. 18; Honderich, pp. 184ff, 332–4.

22. Cf. Randolph Clarke, "Toward a Credible Agent-Causal Account of Free Will," *Noûs* XXVII (June 1993), pp. 191–203, at p. 192. Theories of agent causation have been advanced by Roderick Chisholm, for example in "Human Freedom and the Self," in Gary Watson, ed. *Free Will,* pp. 24–35 [Selection 14 in this volume], and in *Person and Object,* (La Salle: Open Court, 1976), pp. 53–88, and by Richard Taylor, for instance in *Action and Purpose,* (Englewood Cliffs: Prentice-Hall, 1966), pp. 99–152, and in *Metaphysics,* pp. 33–50.

23. Clarke, in "Toward a Credible Agent-Causal Account of Free Will," provides an argument for agent causation and for libertarianism more generally at pp. 199–200; cf. Immanuel Kant, *Critique of Pure Reason,* Bxxix–xxxiii.

Furthermore, we have not encountered any divergences from the predictions of our physical theories. The libertarian could, of course, advocate a theory that embraces such divergences, but this, by itself, would provide a powerful reason to reject such a view. So let us focus on those theories that attempt to reconcile agent-causation with the predictions of our physical theories.

Suppose first that the physical world is a deterministic system. If this is so, then the physical component of any action—constituent events describable, for example, by neurophysiology, physiology, chemistry, physics—will be causally determined. As Kant argues, it is *possible* that undetermined, non-physical agents always make free choices for just those potential actions whose physical components are causally determined.[24] In Kant's view, this possibility is all we need for rational faith in indeterministic freedom. But is it credible that this possibility is actually realized? There would certainly be nothing incredible about an undetermined agent-cause making a free choice *on some particular occasion* for a possible action whose physical component was causally determined. However, it would be incredible if for any substantial period of human history all free choices made by agent-causes should be for just those possible actions whose physical components are causally determined to occur, and none of these choices should be for the alternatives. Independent of an idealistic theory according to which agents construct the physical world, the coincidences this view implies are too wild to believe.[25]

24. Immanuel Kant, *Critique of Pure Reason,* A538/B566–A558/B586. For a related view, focussed not on defending libertarianism but on interactionist concerns, see Tyler Burge, "Philosophy of Language and Mind: 1950–1990." *The Philosophical Review* CL (January 1992), pp. 3–51, at pp. 36–9.

25. One might attempt a nonreductive materialist defense of the compatibility of libertarian freedom with determinism at the physical level, by arguing that since psychological laws do not reduce to physical laws, everything's being causally determined at the physical level does not entail that events at the psychological level are causally determined. But although the existence of deterministic physical laws does not entail the existence of deterministic psychological laws, this argument fails. According to the nonreductive materialist view, although psychological laws do not reduce to physical laws, the fact that every token event is completely physically realized places restrictions on the genesis of token psychological events such as actions. For if the physical realization of every token event is causally determined, and an action (and everything implicated in its individuation) is completely physically realized, it must be that the action is also causally determined. Hence, if nonreductive materialism is true, and determinism is true at the

To try to solve this problem of wild coincidences, the libertarian might invoke indeterminacy in nature. Nevertheless, in ordinary cases, quantum indeterminacy only allows for an extremely small probability of counterfactual events at the scale of human actions.[26] Suppose, by analogy, that the soda can on the table remains where it is for the next minute. Given quantum indeterminacy, there is some probability that instead it would spontaneously move one inch to the left sometime during this minute. But for this event to occur, each of many quantum indeterminacies would have to be resolved in a specific alternative way, the probability of which is extremely small. The prospects for counterfactual human actions are similarly bad. Even if quantum indeterminacy results in the indeterminacy of certain neural events, like the firing of individual neurons, so that at certain times both the probability that the neural event will occur and that it will not are significant, the likelihood of physical components of counterfactual actions occurring is insignificant. The reason is that the making of a decision is an event of a much larger scale than is an event like the firing of a neuron. When a decision is made, a very large number of individual quantum and neural events are involved, and quantum indeterminacy would not undergird a significant probability for counterfactual events of this magnitude.

Let us assume that what determines an indeterministically free agent's choices is how she finally weighs the reasons. The weighing of each reason will be (partially) realized in a very large complex of neural and quantum events. But this complex will be too large for quantum indeterminacy to substantiate a significant probability of counterfactual actions. Suppose an agent actually makes a decision to perform action A rather than action B, and that the physical realization of her weighing of reasons is large-scale neural pattern of type X. Given quantum indeterminacy, there is some antecedent probability—the probability, let us say, just as the agent begins to weigh the reasons for action—that her brain should realize a very different neural pattern upon weighing the reasons, one of type Y, which is

---

physical level, then actions are no less determined than their physical realizations. For a characterization of nonreductive materialism, see Hilary Putnam, "Philosophy and Our Mental Life," *Readings in the Philosophy of Psychology*, v. 1, Ned Block, ed. (Cambridge, Mass.: Harvard University Press, 1980), pp. 134–43.

26. For an extensive discussion of the relation between freedom and quantum theory, see Honderich, pp. 304–36. See also Daniel Dennett, *Elbow Room: Varieties of Free Will Worth Wanting*, (Cambridge, Mass.: MIT Press, 1984), pp. 135–6.

correlated with performing action B. But for a pattern of type B to come about, each of many indeterminacies would have to be resolved in a specific alternative way, the antecedent probability of which is extremely small. More generally, the antecedent probability of the occurrence of the physical component of any counterfactual action is extremely small. And it would be too wildly coincidental to believe that for any substantial interval of human history all or even almost all indeterministically free choices made by agent-causes should be for just those possible actions the occurrence of whose physical components has the extremely high antecedent physical probability, and not for any of the alternatives. Thus the fact that quantum theory allows counterfactual actions to have non-zero antecedent probability fails to remedy the problem of wild coincidences posed by the attempt to reconcile libertarianism with strict determinism.

Now it might be objected that the problem of wild coincidences arises only if it turns out that, at the neurophysiological level, counterfactual events do not have significant antecedent probability. Yet there are examples, such as the moving of the needle on a Geiger counter, of microphysical indeterminacies that are magnified to significantly indeterminate events at the macrolevel. Perhaps similar magnifications occur in the brain.[27] Randolph Clarke suggests that a libertarian might take advantage of macrolevel natural indeterminacy of this sort by positing agent causes who have the power to make the difference as to which of a series of naturally possible actions is performed.[28] Might this picture not offer the libertarian a way out of the wild coincidences problem? No. Suppose that physical components of counterfactual actions do have a significant antecedent probability of occurring. Consider a class of possible actions each of which has a physical component whose antecedent probability of occurring is approximately 0.32. If indeterminist free action is to be compatible with what our physical theories predict to be overwhelmingly likely, then over a long enough period of time these possible actions would have to be freely chosen almost exactly 32 percent of the time. Yet their actually being freely chosen almost exactly 32 percent of the time would constitute a coincidence no less wild than the coincidence of possible actions whose physical components have an antecedent probability of about 0.99 being

27. Cranston Paull raised this issue in discussion of this article. See Peter van Inwagen, *An Essay on Free Will,* pp. 191–201.

28. Randolph Clarke, "Toward a Credible Agent-Causal Account of Free Will," p. 193.

freely chosen about 99 percent of the time. The problem of wild coincidences, therefore, is independent of the physical components of actions having any particular degree of antecedent probability.[29]

This point reveals the fundamental difficulty for libertarian agent causation. Whether the physical laws are deterministic or quantum indeterministic, the antecedent probabilities of the physical components of human actions are fixed. With deterministic laws, the antecedent probability of any such component is either 1 or 0. According to quantum theory, such probabilities will be different. But regardless of which view is true, it would be wildly coincidental, and hence too bizarre a scenario to believe, if for any substantial span of human history frequencies of indeterministically free choices should happen to dovetail with determinate physical probabilities.

Thus, barring revolutionary discoveries in neurophysiology or physics, it seems unlikely that libertarianism is true. Accordingly, let us focus our attention on the hard determinist version of incompatibilism. But first, our discussion of libertarianism reveals the need to revise our characterization of the wider issues: assuming the truth of our best scientific theories, determinism turns out to be false. However, the kinds of indeterminacies these theories posit provide us with no more control over our actions than we would have if determinism were true. Our actions may not result from deterministic causal processes that trace back to factors over which we have no control, but yet there are processes, either deterministic or indeterministic, over which we have no control, that produce our actions, and this is enough to rule out freedom of the sort required for moral responsibility. Hence the fundamental incompatibilist intuition turns out to be "responsibility only if her action is not produced by processes, either deterministic or indeterministic, beyond her control." For the sake of simplicity and meshing with the traditional discussion, however, I shall continue to describe the position I am defending as "hard determinism," with the understanding that this term is strictly speaking inaccurate,

29. Thanks to David Christensen for helping to formulate the argument of this paragraph. Clarke says that on his theory "there is no observational evidence that could tell us whether our world is an indeterministic world with agent causation or an indeterministic world without it . . . even highly improbable behavior could occur in a world without agent causation" (p. 199). But as we can now see, there is observational evidence that bears on the question. Only in the absence of agent causation should we, in the long run, *expect* observed frequencies to match the frequencies that our physical theories predict.

but not in a way that makes a difference to the issues we shall now explore.

IV

The alternative to soft determinism and libertarianism is hard determinism, the view that because determinism is true, we lack the freedom required for moral responsibility. Let us examine this option to ascertain whether it must be as unacceptable as it may initially seem.

One instinctive reaction to hard determinism is that if it were true, we would have no reason to attempt to accomplish anything—to try to improve our lives or the prospects of society—because our deliberations and choices could make no difference. This challenge has also been directed towards soft determinists, and they have responded persuasively. Ayer and Dennett, among others, have pointed out that the determination of our deliberations, choices, actions, and their consequences does not undermine their causal efficacy.[30] The hard determinist can legitimately appropriate this position. It is true that according to hard determinism we are not free in the sense required for moral responsibility, and therefore, what happens cannot be affected by choices that are free in this sense. But what happens may nevertheless be caused by the deliberations we engage in and the choices we make.

It is undeniable that we feel we have the ability to choose or do otherwise; for example, that you feel that it is now possible for you either to continue or to stop reading this article. In the hard determinist's judgment, this feeling of freedom is an illusion (and soft determinists of some types agree). This judgment would be challenged by those who believe that our introspective sense provides us with infallible beliefs about our own abilities. But it is a familiar fact that such an assessment of introspection is implausible. Kant, however, provides us with a different reason not to discount the feeling of freedom. He suggests that engaging in a process of deliberation requires that one suppose that more than one choice for action is causally possible.[31] This view seems compelling: could one deliberate about which roads to take if one believed that one was causally capable of choosing only one of them? But according to hard determinism,

30. A. J. Ayer, "Freedom and Necessity," p. 23; Daniel Dennett, *Elbow Room*, pp. 100–30.

31. Immanuel Kant, *Groundwork of the Metaphysics of Morals*, Part III, Ak IV, 448.

one cannot choose otherwise than the way one actually does. Thus, as van Inwagen argues, whenever one engages in a process of deliberation, one would be making a false supposition, and hence if one were a self-professed hard determinist, one would often have inconsistent beliefs; "anyone who denies the existence of free will must, inevitably, contradict himself with monotonous regularity."[32]

There are two replies available to the hard determinist. The first grants that when we deliberate, at the moment of choice we must indeed make the false and unjustified assumption that more than one course of action is open to us. But it is legitimate to assume this cognitive posture, because the practical gains of engaging in deliberation are significant enough to outweigh the losses of having false and unjustified beliefs. In this view, deliberation requires us to choose between theoretical and practical irrationality. One is irrational in the theoretical sense when, for example, one has a belief that has no justification, or a belief one knows to be false, and one is irrational in the practical sense if, for instance, one does something one knows will frustrate what one wants, all things considered. Hard determinism would seem to leave us with the following choice: either deliberate and have a belief that you know to be false whenever you do, or cease to deliberate. Practical rationality would appear to have the upper hand.

It is nevertheless disturbing to maintain that one must be theoretically irrational whenever one deliberates. There is, however, a more attractive alternative which does not require that one override the canons of theoretical rationality. The hard determinist might deny that at the moment of choice, one must assume that more than one option is causally possible. One might instead believe that one's actions are determined by way of one's choices, that one's choices are determined by means of one's deliberation, and that one does not know in advance of deliberation which action one will choose. As long as one's actions are determined by deliberation and choice, and one does not know beforehand what the result of one's deliberation will be, there will be no interference with the deliberative process. Indeed, the deliberative process might be jeopardized if one had previous knowledge of the choice that would result. Perhaps it is even incoherent to suppose that one might know in advance of deliberation which of two roads one will choose, for in such a situation genuine deliberation would be undermined. But given that one cannot know the results of one's deliberation in advance, the process can go on unimpeded.

32. Peter van Inwagen, *An Essay on Free Will*, pp. 153–61, the quote is on p. 160; see also Richard Taylor, *Metaphysics*, pp. 46–7.

V

A very prominent feature of our ordinary conception of morality that would be undermined if hard determinism were true is our belief that people deserve credit and praise when they deliberately perform morally exemplary actions, and that they deserve blame when they deliberately perform wrongful actions. To deserve blame is to be morally liable to blame by deliberately choosing to do the wrong thing. Hard determinism rules out one's ever deserving blame for deliberately choosing to act wrongly, for such choices are always produced by processes that are beyond one's control.

Someone might argue that even if no one ever deserves blame, it would nevertheless be best for us to think and act as if people sometimes do, because thinking and acting this way is a superb method for promoting moral reform and education. More generally, even if no one is ever really morally responsible, it would still be best sometimes to *hold* people morally responsible. Such a view might be justified on practical grounds, were we confident, for example, that thinking and acting as if people sometimes deserve blame is often necessary for effectively promoting moral reform and education. But this option would have the hard determinist thinking that someone deserves blame when she also believes him not to, which is an instance of theoretical irrationality, and would have her blaming someone when he does not deserve to be blamed, which would seem to be morally wrong.

There is, however, an alternative practice for promoting moral reform and education which would suffer neither from irrationality nor apparent immorality. Instead of blaming people, the determinist might appeal to the practice of moral admonishment and encouragement. One might, for example, explain to an offender that what he did was wrong, and then encourage him to refrain from performing similar actions in the future. One need not, in addition, blame him for what he has done. The hard determinist can maintain that by admonishing and encouraging a wrongdoer one might communicate a sense of what is right, and a respect for persons, and that these attitudes can lead to salutary change.[33] Hence, one

33. I have, so far, avoided discussion of punishment. One current theory of punishment that would be undermined by hard determinism is the retribution theory, since it justifies punishment by way of desert. But hard determinism provides no special reason to reject any other current view about the justification of punishment, for example, the deterrence, self-defense, or moral education theories. For a thorough discussion of the relation between determinism and

need not hold the wrongdoer morally responsible for what he has done, but rather consider him responsive to moral admonishment and encouragement. Likewise, although one could not justifiably think of one's own wrongful actions as deserving of blame, one could legitimately regard them as wrongful, and thereby admonish oneself, and resolve to refrain from similar actions in the future. But like blame of others, blame of self, and more generally, holding oneself morally responsible, would be best avoided.

But what of the character who regularly and deliberately does wrong, and refuses to make a commitment to doing what is right? Doesn't the hard determinist have little to say to such a person? While the hard determinist can only admonish, the advocate of moral responsibility can also blame. But having recourse to blame in such circumstances is not clearly a significant practical advantage. One might argue that hard determinism is a threat to moral practice because the character we have described might offer determinism as an excuse for his behavior. Certainly, the hard determinist would have to accept his excuse, whereas the proponent of moral responsibility would not. But the practical advantages from this point on do not favor either side. Both face the task of moral education and imparting a respect for persons, and it is not obvious that the hard determinist has fewer resources for this project than those available to her opposition.

The hard determinist position implies that the appalling actions of persons are much more similar to earthquakes and epidemics than they are according to views that hold persons morally responsible. The justification we assume for regarding especially wrongful actions of persons as deeply different from natural disasters is that persons are typically responsible for their actions. But according to hard determinism, because a person's actions are the result of processes over which he has no control, we cannot consider him responsible for them, just as we cannot hold earthquakes or epidemics responsible for their effects. One still might legitimately have a feeling of moral concern about what persons do, or about what persons who are reasons-responsive do, which would differ from one's attitudes to earthquakes and epidemics. This feeling would be legitimate supposing it has no cognitive component that conflicts with hard determinism. But as I shall soon argue in further detail, the various attitudes that presuppose the cognitive component that persons are morally responsible would be unjustified.

---

punishment practices see Honderich, pp. 541–613.

Honderich contends rightly, I believe, that in the face of determinism we must eschew retribution, but he also argues that

> we can persist in certain responses to the desires and intentions of others, and hence to them. There is no obstacle to my abhorrence of the desires and intentions of the treacherous husband foreseeing his divorce, or, more important, to my abhorrence of him, a man whose personality and character are consistent with these desires and intentions, and support them.[34]

But the determinist must be more abstemious here. Abhorrence of a person because of the actions he has performed at least typically involves blaming him for those actions, which, in turn, presupposes that his actions and character did not result from processes beyond his control. If one were to discover that an especially wrongful "action" was caused by some non-psychological, physiological reaction in the person, one's abhorrence would tend to vanish, and this would suggest that one's abhorrence was founded in blame. It is legitimate to feel moral concern in response to a wrongful action, and to be deeply saddened that there are persons with immoral characters, but at least most often one's response of abhorrence, because it involves blaming someone, is unjustified.[35]

Perhaps one can learn to abhor people because of the wrongful actions they perform without blaming them, just as one might abhor soggy corn flakes because of their sogginess without blaming them. But it is doubtful that developing such an attitude towards people could be justified on moral grounds if determinism is true. One might be able to abhor people for their wrongful actions without being theoretically irrational, but it seems unlikely that one would advance the good by fostering this attitude, by contrast, for example, with attitudes such as moral concern or sadness.

Susan Wolf has argued that whereas deserved blame cannot be justified if determinism is true, deserved praise does not collapse along with it.[36] As she puts it, she is "committed to the curious claim that being psychologically determined to perform good actions is compatible with deserving praise for them, but that being psychologically determined to perform bad

34. Honderich, p. 533.

35. Thanks to Rachel Wertheimer for convincing me to make this point.

36. Susan Wolf, *Freedom within Reason,* (Oxford: Oxford University Press, 1990), pp. 79–85; see also her "Asymmetrical Freedom," *Journal of Philosophy* 77 (March 1980), pp. 151–66 [Selection 18 in this volume].

actions is not compatible with deserving blame."[37] Wolf, in effect, endorses the hard determinist's view about deserved blame, but not about deserved praise. She cites the following example in support of her view:

> Two persons, of equal swimming ability, stand on equally uncrowded beaches. Each sees an unknown child struggling in the water in the distance. Each thinks "The child needs my help" and directly swims out to save him. In each case, we assume that the agent reasons correctly—the child *does* need her help—and that, in swimming out to save him, the agent does the right thing. We further assume that in one of these cases, the agent has the ability to do otherwise, and in the other case not.[38]

Wolf says that whereas according to the libertarian only the first of these agents is responsible, "there seems to be nothing of value that the first agent has but the second agent lacks." Perhaps the second agent does not have the ability to do otherwise because "her understanding of the situation is so good and her moral commitment so strong." Wolf concludes that the fact that the second agent is determined to do the right thing for the right reasons does not make her any less deserving of praise than the first agent.

First of all, Wolf's argument is susceptible to an objection inspired by the point Fischer raises in connection with Frankfurt's case. Given the way Wolf presents her lifesaver case, the reader might yet presuppose that the swimmer who cannot do otherwise is not causally determined to deliberate and act as she does. If it were specified that her action results from a deterministic causal process that traces back to factors she could not have produced, altered, or prevented—perhaps by adding that she is controlled by neuroscientists—the intuition that she deserves praise might well vanish. Wolf's case may indicate that an agent might deserve praise even if she could not have done otherwise, but it fails to show that an agent deserves praise even if her action results from a deterministic causal process that traces back to factors beyond her control.

But suppose that the intuition that the second swimmer deserves praise persists even if it is specified that she is causally determined. The hard determinist can now argue that while according to ordinary intuitions both swimmers deserve praise, the second swimmer really does not. Ordinarily,

37. *Freedom within Reason,* p. 79.

38. *Freedom within Reason,* pp. 81–2.

we consider persons praiseworthy for their great intelligence, good looks, or native athletic ability, even though these qualities are not due to any agency of theirs, and hence, even though they in no sense really deserve praise for these qualities. Thus it comes as no surprise that we would ordinarily consider the second swimmer, who is determined to do the right thing for the right reasons, praiseworthy. She may be considered praiseworthy because she is a good person, and has acted in pursuit of the good, but as in the case of the person of great intelligence, we need not conclude that she is genuinely deserving of praise.

Sometimes it may well be a good thing to praise someone despite her not deserving it, perhaps because praise can at times simply be an expression of approbation or delight about the actions or accomplishments of another. By contrast, blaming someone who does not deserve it would seem always to be (at least prima facie) wrong. The reason for this (as Wolf notes) might be that because blaming typically causes pain, it must be wrong unless it is deserved, whereas since praise is far from painful, it can be appropriate beyond cases in which it is deserved. Whatever may be the case here, the intuition that the determined swimmer is praiseworthy fails to undermine the hard determinist view, that not only deserved blame but also deserved praise is incompatible with determinism.

VI

Another feature of our ordinary conception of morality that would be threatened if we accepted hard determinism is the belief that statements of the following form are sometimes true: 'Although you did not choose x, you ought, morally, to have chosen x.' There are different senses of the moral 'ought,' but the central senses might well be undermined in a hard determinist picture. It would seem that in all cases in which one could never have performed an action, it is never true that one ought to have performed the action.[39] Consequently, if because one is causally determined one can never choose otherwise than the way one actually does, then it is false that one ever morally ought to choose otherwise. And further, if it is never true that one ought to have chosen otherwise than the way one does, then what would be the point of a system of moral 'ought's? Hard determinism imperils this system, because it would seem that if 'A

39. For a discussion of issues of this sort, see Walter Sinnott-Armstrong, "'Ought' Conversationally Implies 'Can'." *The Philosophical Review* XCIII (April 1984), pp. 249–61, and "'Ought to Have' and 'Could Have'," *Analysis* 45 (1985), pp. 44–8.

ought to choose x' is true at all, it must be true not only when A comes to choose x, but also when A does not come to choose x.

But even if moral 'ought' statements are never true, moral judgments, such as 'it is morally right for A to do x,' or 'it is a morally good thing for A to do x,' still can be. Thus, even if one is causally determined to refrain from giving to charity, and even if it is therefore false that one ought to give to charity, it still might be the right thing or a good thing to do.[40] Cheating on one's taxes might be a wrong or a bad thing to do, even if one's act is causally determined, and hence, even if it is false that one ought not to do so. These alternative moral judgments would indeed lack the deontic implications they are typically assumed to have, but nevertheless, they can be retained when moral 'ought' statements are undermined. In addition, the various benefits of the system of moral 'ought's can be recouped. For instance, when one is encouraging moral action, one can replace occurrences of 'you ought to do x' with 'it would be right for you to do x,' or with 'it would be a good thing for you to do x.' Discouragement of wrongful action could be revised analogously.

One might argue that if moral 'ought' statements were never true, we could have no reason to do what is right. But this view is mistaken. Although it is false that one ought to eat boiled rather than poached eggs, one might still have reason to choose one over the other, perhaps in virtue of one's preference for boiled eggs, or even because one thinks that one type is objectively better than the other, and one has resolved to aspire to excellence. Similarly, one might treat others with respect because one prefers to do so, or because one has resolved to do what is right, even if it is not the case that one ought to do so. If one has resolved to do what is right, by whatever motivation, one thereby has reason to act in accordance with this resolution.

It may seem that relinquishing the moral 'ought' together with deserved praise and blame restricts hard determinism to a consequentialist position in ethics. One might be tempted by the claim that although rejection of the moral 'ought' is consistent with the goodness of certain consequences and, derivatively, with the goodness of actions that bring about such consequences, abandoning the moral 'ought' does rule out principles of right that are based on nonconsequentialist considerations. But this claim seems

40. Honderich argues (pp. 525–30) that although determinism is incompatible with retributive attitudes, since these attitudes presuppose that agents causally originate actions, it is not incompatible with judgements of right and wrong, goodness and badness. The picture I am developing here is close to his, although the way I prefer to articulate and argue for my view is somewhat different.

mistaken for the reason that insofar as they have been developed, the metaphysical bases for nonconsequentialist positions do not clearly involve an essential appeal to a notion of freedom unavailable to the hard determinist. One might argue that the hard determinist is restricted to consequentialism because her rejection of deserved praise and blame confines her to forward-looking ethical views, and such forward-looking views are consequentialist. But although the hard determinist may not look to the past to assess praise and blame, she can legitimately make judgments about the rightness and wrongness of past actions. Furthermore, not all forward-looking ethical views are consequentialist. The Kantian principle, "Act only on that maxim which you can also will to be a universal law" is no less forward-looking than the utilitarian principle. "Act so as to maximize happiness." The hard determinist seems free to accept nonconsequentialist ethical views.

VII

If hard determinism is true, how would it be best to regard our reactive attitudes, for example, our resentment and anger upon being betrayed, or our gratitude upon receiving help in trouble? In the face of a deterministic universe, the Stoics urge self-discipline aimed at eradicating at least the negative reactive attitudes. David Hume and P. F. Strawson, on the other hand, advance the psychological thesis that our reactive attitudes cannot be affected by a general belief in determinism, or by any such abstract metaphysical view, and that therefore the project of altering or eliminating our reactive attitudes by a determinist conviction would be ineffectual.[41]

Let us address two issues: first, whether the reactive attitudes really are immune from alteration by a belief in determinism, and second, whether it would be good for them to be altered by such a belief (if they could be). On the first issue, Gary Watson provides a compelling example, the case of Robert Harris, who brutally murdered two teenage boys in California in 1978.[42] When we read an account of these murders "we respond to his

41. David Hume, *An Enquiry Concerning Human Understanding*, §8, part II; P. F. Strawson, "Freedom and Resentment," in *Free Will*, Gary Watson, ed., pp. 59–80 [Selection 13 in this volume]. For an important discussion of the reactive attitudes, see Jonathan Bennett, "Accountability," in *Philosophical Topics, Essays in Honor of P. F. Strawson*, Zak Van Straaten, ed. (Oxford: Oxford University Press, 1979), pp. 14–47.

42. Gary Watson, "Responsibility and the Limits of Evil," in *Responsibility, Character, and the Emotions*, Ferdinand Schoeman, ed. (Cambridge: Cambridge University Press, 1987), pp. 256–86.

heartlessness and viciousness with loathing."[43] But an account of the atrocious abuse he suffered as a child "gives pause to the reactive attitudes."[44] Upon absorbing such information, not everyone relinquishes his attitude of blame completely, but this attitude is at least typically tempered. It is not only that we are persuaded to feel pity for the criminal. In addition, our attitude of blame is mitigated by our coming to believe that the criminal was at least partially determined to behave as he did. One might claim that although belief in determinism about a particular situation can affect reactive attitudes, the general belief in determinism never can. But I can think of no reason to accept this view. Because particular cases of determinism can be vividly described, they can much more readily affect one's attitudes, but there is no reason to believe that the general conviction cannot have a similar effect.

It would be implausible to maintain that in every case the presence or the intensity of one's reactive attitudes can be affected by a belief in determinism. Sometimes a wrong committed might be too horrible for such a belief to have any effect on one's subsequent reaction. The Stoics maintained that we can always prevent or eradicate attitudes like grief and anger, regardless of their intensity, with the aid of a determinist conviction. But they might well have overestimated the extent of the control we have over our emotional lives. If someone were brutally to murder your family, it might well be psychologically impossible for you ever to eradicate feelings of intense anger toward the killer. This fails to show, however, that a determinist conviction cannot affect reactive attitudes, even in typical cases.

Let us suppose, therefore, that a determinist conviction can affect our reactive attitudes. Would it be a good thing if they were affected by this means? According to Strawson, human beings would stand to lose much if reactive attitudes were dislodged by a belief in determinism, for we would then be left with a certain "objectivity of attitude." A stance of this sort, Strawson believes, conflicts with the types of attitudes required for good interpersonal relationships:

> To adopt the objective attitude to another human being is to see him, perhaps, as an object of social policy; as a subject for what, in a wide range of sense, might be called treatment; as something certainly to be taken account, perhaps precautionary account, of; to be managed or

43. Watson, pp. 268–71.

44. Watson, pp. 272–74.

> handled or cured or trained; perhaps simply to be avoided. . . . The objective attitude may be emotionally toned in many ways: it may include repulsion or fear, it may include pity or love, though not all kinds of love. But it cannot include the range of reactive feelings and attitudes which belong to involvement or participation with others in interpersonal human relationships: it cannot include resentment, gratitude, forgiveness, anger, or the sort of love which two adults can sometimes be said to feel reciprocally, for each other.[45]

Strawson is right to believe that objectivity of attitude would destroy interpersonal relationships. But he is mistaken to think that objectivity of attitude would result or be appropriate if determinism were to undermine the reactive attitudes. As Honderich argues, a reasonable determinist attitude towards the moral life "recommends no such bloodlessly managerial an attitude toward others."[46]

In his analysis, Honderich points out that one's reactive attitudes presuppose certain beliefs about the persons to whom they are directed, and that these beliefs can sometimes be undermined by determinist convictions.[47] I agree, and I would develop the claim in this way. One's reactive attitudes presuppose beliefs of this sort, and when these presuppositions lack adequate justification, or when one believes them to be false, or when they have little or no justification and conflict with justified beliefs one holds, then maintaining attitudes that have such presuppositions is irrational in the theoretical sense. Suppose, for example, that you are angry with the guests because they are very late for dinner. Your anger presupposes the belief that they reasonably could have been on time. But you come to know that they are late because an airplane crashed on the freeway, and the resulting traffic jam trapped them for an hour. Given that your presupposition no longer has justification, and since it conflicts with a justified belief you hold, it is theoretically irrational for you to maintain your anger, and you would therefore have to give up your anger to escape irrationality.

Now suppose that you have a justified belief that hard determinism is true, and that you are angry with a friend because he has betrayed a confidence. Your anger presupposes the belief that he deserves blame and that his betrayal was not produced by processes beyond his control. You

45. P. F. Strawson, "Freedom and Resentment," p. 66.

46. Honderich, pp. 532–3.

47. Honderich, pp. 400–9.

have no justification for this presupposition, let us suppose, and it conflicts with your justified belief that his action was produced by processes beyond his control. Consequently, your anger is irrational in the theoretical sense, and in order to escape this irrationality, you must give up your anger.

Someone might point out, however, that such anger may not be practically irrational, and since practical and theoretical rationality may conflict, an issue may arise about which sort it would then be best to secure. If one's anger is practically rational in virtue of playing a part in a system of attitudes required for interpersonal relationships, but it is nevertheless theoretically irrational because of its presuppositions, how would it be best to act? For Hume and Strawson, the issue would happily be resolved by facts about human psychology, since we would be psychologically incapable of theoretical rationality in such situations. But since their psychological claim is implausible, the issue again becomes live.

If the hard determinist were to acknowledge that a determinist conviction could affect the reactive attitudes, but that adopting an objectivity of attitude would be practically irrational in virtue of being destructive to human relationships, she might well override theoretical rationality by retaining her normal reactive attitudes. If she acted in this way, however, she would be reduced to the uncomfortable position of maintaining attitudes that are theoretically irrational. But the hard determinist is not clearly forced into such a difficult situation. For first, although many ordinary reactive attitudes might be irrational, these reactive attitudes are not obviously required for good interpersonal relationships. Some reactive attitudes, like certain kinds of anger and resentment, may well not be good for relationships at all. And secondly, the reactive attitudes one would want to retain have analogues that do not have false presuppositions. Such analogues by no means amount to Strawson's objectivity of attitude, and they are sufficient to sustain good interpersonal relationships.

In Strawson's view, some of the attitudes most important for interpersonal relationships are resentment, anger, forgiveness, gratitude, and mature love. As I have suggested, a certain measure of resentment and anger is likely to be beyond our power to affect, and thus even supposing that one is committed to doing what is right and rational, one would still not be able to eradicate all of one's resentment and anger. As hard determinists, we might expect these attitudes to occur in certain situations, and we might regard them as inevitable and exempt from blame when they do. But we sometimes have the ability to prevent, alter, or eliminate resentment and anger, and given a belief in hard determinism, we might well do so for the sake of morality and rationality. Modification of anger and resentment, aided by a determinist conviction, could well be a good thing for relationships (supposing that no unhealthy repression is induced). At very least, the claim that it would be harmful requires further argument.

The attitude of forgiveness seems to presuppose that the person being forgiven deserves blame, and therefore, forgiveness is indeed imperiled by hard determinism. But there are certain features of forgiveness that are not threatened by hard determinism, and these features can adequately take the place this attitude usually has in relationships. Suppose your companion has wronged you in similar fashion a number of times, and you find yourself unhappy, angry, and resolved to loosen the ties of your relationship. Subsequently, however, he apologizes to you, which, consistent with hard determinism, signifies his recognition of the wrongness of his behavior, his wish that he had not wronged you, and his genuine commitment to improvement. As a result, you change your mind and decide to continue the relationship. In this case, the feature of forgiveness that is consistent with hard determinism is the willingness to cease to regard past wrongful behavior as a reason to weaken or dissolve one's relationship. In another type of case, you might, independently of the offender's repentance, simply choose to disregard the wrong as a reason to alter the character of your relationship. This attitude is in no sense undermined by hard determinism. The sole aspect of forgiveness that is jeopardized by a hard determinist conviction is the willingness to overlook deserved blame or punishment. But if one has given up belief in deserved blame and punishment, then the willingness to overlook them is no longer needed for relationships.

Gratitude would seem to require the supposition that the person to whom one is grateful is morally responsible for an other-regarding act, and therefore hard determinism might well undermine gratitude.[48] But certain aspects of this attitude would be left untouched, aspects that can play the role gratitude commonly has in interpersonal relationships. No feature of the hard determinist position conflicts with one's being joyful and expressing joy when people are especially considerate, generous, or courageous in one's behalf. Such expression of joy can produce the sense of mutual well-being and respect frequently brought about by gratitude. Moreover, just as in the case of gratitude, when one expresses joy for what another person has done, one can do so with the intention of developing a human relationship.

48. See Honderich's discussion of gratitude, pp. 518–19.

Finally, the thesis that love between mature persons would be subverted if hard determinism were true requires much more thorough argument than has been provided. One might note, first of all, that parents love their children rarely, if ever, because these children possess the freedom required for moral responsibility, or because they freely (in this sense) choose the good, or because they deserve to be loved. But moreover, when adults love each other, it is also seldom, if at all, for these kinds of reasons. Explanations for love are complex. Besides moral character and action, factors such as appearance, manner, intelligence, and affinities with persons or events in one's history all have a part. But suppose we agree that moral character and action are of paramount importance in producing and maintaining love. Even then, it is unlikely that one's love would be undermined if one were to believe that moral character and action do not come about through free and morally responsible choice. Love of another involves, most fundamentally, wishing well for the other, taking on many of the aims and desires of the other as one's own, and a desire to be together with the other. Hard determinism threatens none of this.

While certain reactive attitudes might well be irrational because of the presuppositions these attitudes have, turning to analogues of the sort we have described is in no sense irrational, and it is far from assuming the objectivity of attitude so destructive to interpersonal relationships. Furthermore, nothing about hard determinism recommends assuming an objectivity of attitude. The specter of this outlook arises from the sense that the hard determinist is constrained to view other persons as mere mechanical devices, to be used and not respected. The hard determinist, however, is not forced to view persons in this way. She is not compelled to deny that human beings are rational and responsive to reasons, and no feature of her view threatens the appropriateness of respecting persons for their rational capacities.

Accordingly, someone's thinking and acting in harmony with her hard determinist conviction would not endanger her interpersonal relationships. She would resist anger, blame, and resentment, but she would not be exempt from pain and unhappiness upon being wronged. She might, if wronged, admonish, disregard the wrongdoing, or terminate the relationship. Although she would avoid gratitude, she could enjoy and express joy about other persons' efforts in her behalf. No obstacle would be posed to her loving others. Only if, in addition, she had an unappealing tendency to control another, would she see him "as an object of social policy; as a subject for what, in a wide range of sense, might be called treatment; as something certainly to be taken account, perhaps precautionary account, of; to be managed or handled or cured or trained; perhaps simply to be avoided. . . . "[49] But taking on such an objectivity of attitude would not be justified by her hard determinist conviction.

VIII

Given that free will of some sort is required for moral responsibility, then libertarianism, soft determinism, and hard determinism, as typically conceived, are jointly exhaustive positions (if we allow the "deterministic" positions the view that events may result from indeterministic processes of the sort described by quantum mechanics). Yet each has a consequence that is difficult to accept. If libertarianism were true, then we would expect events to occur that are incompatible with what our physical theories predict to be overwhelmingly likely. If soft determinism were true, then agents would deserve blame for their wrongdoing even though their actions were produced by processes beyond their control. If hard determinism were true, agents would not be morally responsible—agents would never deserve blame for even the most cold-blooded and calmly executed evil actions. I have argued that hard determinism could be the easiest view to accept. Hard determinism need not be of the hardest sort. It need not subvert the commitment to doing what is right, and although it does undermine some of our reactive attitudes, secure analogues of these attitudes are all one requires for good interpersonal relationships. Consequently, of the three positions, hard determinism might well be the most attractive, and it is surely worthy of more serious consideration than it has been accorded.[50]

49. Strawson, p. 66.

50. This article benefitted greatly from suggestions for revision by Marilyn Adams, Robert Adams, Lynne Rudder Baker, Randolph Clarke, Keith De Rose, Emily Fleschner, Bernard Gert, Hilary Kornblith, Arthur Kuflik, Isaac Levi, Don Loeb, William Mann, Michael Otsuka, Cranston Paull, Seana Schiffren, George Sher, Walter Sinnott-Armstrong, Rachel Wertheimer and the referees for *Noûs.* The philosophers at Dartmouth College provided a stimulating and useful discussion of an earlier draft. I wish to thank David Christensen for especially thorough, careful and incisive commentary.

23

Randolph Clarke, from "Agent Causation and Event Causation in the Production of Free Action"

Randolph Clarke is a professor of philosophy at Florida State University and an advocate of a new variety of agent-causal libertarianism, which he presents in this selection. Clarke's view departs from more traditional versions in several respects, and he argues that his position provides solutions to important problems that have been raised for this kind of libertarianism.

Agent-causal accounts of free will maintain that when an agent acts with free will, the agent is a cause of her action (or of some event involved in the action). This alone is not enough to distinguish these views; for on any causal theory of action, an agent may be said to cause her behavior. However, on most, the behavior's being so caused is said to consist wholly in its being caused by certain events involving the agent. In contrast, agent causalists deny that causation by the agent is reducible to or consists in event causation; the agent is held to be a substance, and agent causation is held to be the causation of an event by a substance. Since a substance is not the sort of entity that can itself be a causal effect,[1] on agent causal views, when an agent acts freely, she is in a strict and literal sense an originator of her action. To many philosophers, it has seemed that only an account committed to agent causation (understood in this way) can capture what free will is supposed to be.

This is an abbreviated version of a paper by the same title that appeared in *Philosophical Topics* 24 (1996). Reprinted by permission of *Philosophical Topics* and Randolph Clarke. In the present version, some sections and parts of sections have been omitted and some have been resequenced. Some introductory and transitional passages have been reworded to accommodate these changes.

1. Proponents of agent-causal views often regard the agent (the person) as a living human organism, understood to be a physical substance. Certainly events involving that organism—its conception, its birth, and perhaps its entire life—are causal effects. However, the organism itself is held to be an individual substance, not an event, and for that reason not a causal effect. (Of course, it is controversial whether a person is a living organism; I shall not deal with this issue here.)

The chief burden of a proponent of an agent-causal account is, of course, to render intelligible and plausible the claim that an agent—a substance—can cause an event. I shall address this issue in section 2.1 of this paper. However, the traditional agent-causal view encounters several other serious difficulties, stemming from the view's requirement that some event involved in a free action have no event-cause. Perhaps the most important of these difficulties are the related problems of allowing for an account of free action that is performed for a certain reason and allowing for an account of the rational explanation of free action. In section 2.2 I describe an agent-causal view that departs from the tradition in that it rejects the indicated requirement. In the remainder of the paper, I argue that this alternative agent-causal account retains what seemed desirable in the traditional agent-causal view, and I examine some of the advantages that accrue to the alternative account because of its rejection of the requirement in question.

1. The Traditional Account

What I shall call the traditional agent-causal view is in fact a family of views, and there are important differences between members of the family.[2] I shall note these differences as I proceed, but my target will be a feature common to all family members.

All versions of the traditional view take agent causation to be a different kind of causation from event causation. Agent causation is sometimes

2. See Roderick M. Chisholm, "Freedom and Action," in Keith Lehrer, ed., *Freedom and Determinism* (New York: Random House, 1966), "Reflections on Human Agency," *Idealistic Studies* 1 (1971), pp. 36–46, "The Agent as Cause," in Myles Brand and Douglas Walton, eds., *Action Theory* (Dordrecht: D. Reidel, 1976), *Person and Object* (La Salle: Open Court, 1976), and "Comments and Replies," *Philosophia* 7 (1978), pp. 597–636; Alan Donagan, *Choice: The Essential Element in Human Action* (London: Routledge & Kegan Paul, 1987); Timothy O'Connor, "Agent Causation," in Timothy O'Connor, ed., *Agents, Causes, and Events: Essays on Indeterminism and Free Will* (Oxford: Oxford University Press, 1995); Thomas Reid, *Essays on the Active Powers of the Human Mind*, in *The Works of Thomas Reid, D.D.*, Third Edition, Sir William Hamilton, ed. (Edinburgh: Maclachlan and Stewart, 1852); William L. Rowe, *Thomas Reid on Freedom and Morality* (Ithaca: Cornell University Press, 1991); Richard Taylor, *Action and Purpose* (Englewood Cliffs: Prentice-Hall, 1966), and *Metaphysics*, Fourth Edition (Englewood Cliffs: Prentice-Hall, 1992); John Thorp, *Free Will: A Defence Against Neurophysiological Determinism* (London: Routledge & Kegan Paul, 1980); and Michael J. Zimmerman, *An Essay on Human Action* (New York: Peter Lang, 1984).

regarded as the only true causation,[3] sometimes as something that is exercised at will rather than exerted in virtue of an object's nature,[4] sometimes as unanalyzable,[5] sometimes as analyzable in terms of a primitive notion of endeavoring or undertaking,[6] sometimes as so different from event causation that the two should not both be called causation,[7] and sometimes (even by proponents) as strange or even mysterious.[8] In all versions, though, when an agent acts with free will, that agent, person, or human being causes an event to occur, and causation by the agent does not consist at all in causation by an event.

Versions of the traditional view differ with regard to what is directly caused by the agent when she performs some overt action. On some versions, what is directly caused, in cases of overt behavior, is a bodily movement;[9] on others, the event that is directly caused is a brain event,[10] the agent's endeavoring or undertaking something,[11] an intention,[12] a choice,[13] or a volition.[14] Sometimes the event that is directly caused by the agent is regarded as the action, or an event that begins the action, while in

3. In Essay I of *Essays on the Active Powers of the Human Mind,* Reid treats agent causation as the only kind of causation. However, elsewhere (*The Works of Thomas Reid, D.D.*, p. 67) he distinguishes between a cause in the "proper and strict sense," which he regards as an intelligent agent, and a cause in the "physical" sense, which may be an inanimate physical object or a physical event. For discussion of Reid's views on causation, see Rowe, *Thomas Reid on Freedom and Morality,* esp. ch. 4.

4. Donagan, *Choice,* e.g., p. 168; and O'Connor, "Agent Causation," pp. 175–80.

5. Taylor, *Action and Purpose,* e.g., p. 12. Donagan (*Choice,* p. 173) seems to regard the notion of agent causation as not in need of analysis. That notion, he says, is not invoked to *explain* what action is, but rather as a summary of the theory of action.

6. Chisholm, "The Agent as Cause," *Person and Object,* and "Comments and Replies."

7. Taylor, *Action and Purpose,* p. 262, and *Metaphysics,* p. 52.

8. Taylor, *Metaphysics,* p. 53; and Thorp, *Free Will,* p. 106.

9. Taylor, *Action and Purpose,* passim.

10. Chisholm, "Freedom and Action," p. 43.

11. Chisholm, "The Agent as Cause," *Person and Object,* and "Comments and Replies."

12. O'Connor, "Agent Causation," p. 181.

13. Donagan, *Choice.*

14. Reid, *Essays on the Active Powers of the Human Mind,* Essays II and IV; and Rowe, *Thomas Reid on Freedom and Morality.*

other cases the agent's causing this event is considered the action.[15] One version holds that the event that the agent directly causes is identical with the agent's causing that very event.[16]

All versions of the traditional view maintain that, when an agent acts with free will, the event that is directly agent-caused has no event cause.[17] Only if there is such an absence of event causation, it is said, can there be two or more courses of action that are genuinely open to the agent; only then can it be assured that when an agent acts, it is genuinely up to the agent what she does.

Here I aim to establish two points. First, the absence of event causation is unnecessary. Even taking for granted the incompatibility of determinism and free will, what is of crucial importance in agent-causal accounts may be retained even if it is held that prior events cause the event that, in acting freely, the agent directly causes. Second, allowing for unbroken chains of event causation removes some grave difficulties faced by the traditional view. We are left with a more tenable account of acting with free will if we locate agent causation within an event-causal account of action.

15. Taylor (*Action and Purpose*) holds that (in cases of overt behavior) it is a bodily movement that is directly caused, and he writes sometimes as though he regards the resulting movement as the action, and sometimes as though he regards the agent's causing that movement as the action. O'Connor ("Agent Causation") regard's the agent's causing a certain event (or sequence of events) as the action.

16. Thorp, *Free Will*, pp. 102–3.

17. Chisholm ("Reflections on Human Agency," p. 45, and "Comments and Replies," pp. 628–30) does allow that in some cases of free action, some prior event may "contribute causally" to the event that is directly agent-caused. However, the notions of "contributing causally" that he employs differ from that of probabilistic causation. (In "Reflections on Human Agency," he maintains that when there is no sufficient causal condition for E, event C causally contributes to E just in case: E occurs; C occurs together with certain other events D; and D together with the nonoccurrence of C would constitute a sufficient causal condition for the nonoccurrence of E. In his "Comments and Replies," a reason is said to causally contribute to a free action if that reason is part of a sufficient causal condition for the agent's performing some action of a general type, such as jumping off a pedestal, while there is no sufficient causal condition for the agent's performing some action of a more specific type, such as jumping to the east off the pedestal rather than to the north.) Moreover, elsewhere ("Freedom and Action," "The Agent as Cause," and *Person and Object*) Chisholm appears not to allow that one event may causally contribute to another unless there is a sufficient causal condition for the second.

2. An Alternative Agent-Causal Account[18]

The alternative that I wish to propose agrees with the traditional view in regarding agent causation as not reducible to and not consisting at all in causation by events. As I mentioned earlier, all versions of the traditional view treat agent causation as in one way or another quite different from event causation. Critics commonly object that agent causation is left unintelligible, or at best mysterious; and I am inclined to agree. Although the characterization of agent causation itself is not my main concern here, the argument of this paper would be of little importance if that notion were plainly unacceptable. Hence I shall make some prefatory suggestions about how agent causation might be explicated. I must acknowledge, however, that I am able to offer no more than a sketch.

2.1. Causation by an Agent

If there is, in any possible world, such a thing as agent causation, the fundamental difference between it and event causation, as I see it, is just that with the former, the first relatum of the causal relation is a substance, while with the latter, the first relatum is an event. Unlike proponents of the traditional view, I would not maintain that there are any further fundamental differences between agent causation and event causation (although, as I shall discuss below, the fact that the first relatum of the causal relation is a different kind of entity may itself imply certain other differences). Rather, on the view I favor, the relation that obtains between cause and effect in an instance of agent causation is the very same relation that obtains between cause and effect in an instance of event causation.

Of course, the relation involved in agent causation cannot be the same one that is involved in event causation if the right account of the latter is some sort of reduction in terms of constant conjunction or counterfactual dependence. The view of agent causation that I have suggested assumes that, on the contrary, the right account of event causation is some sort of realist or nonreductive view. Quite apart from any considerations concerning free will, there are strong reasons to favor a realist account of event

18. In an earlier paper, I briefly set out a view very similar to the one that I shall describe here. See "Toward a Credible Agent-Causal Account of Free Will," *Noûs* 27 (1993), pp. 191–203, reprinted in O'Connor, ed., *Agents, Causes, and Events.* However, I have changed my mind on a few points, and consequently some of the details differ.

causation.[19] I do not make a case for such an account here; my aim is the more modest one of making intelligible, within the context of such an account, the claim that a substance can be a cause.

Causal realists take the relation of causation to be among the basic constituents of the universe, and hence not reducible to noncausal and nonnomological properties and relations. The fundamental notion of causation, we may say, is that of producing, bringing about, or making happen. Whether and how this fundamental notion can be elucidated are points on which different causal realists give quite different answers. I shall focus here on just one type of realist account, one that treats causation as a theoretical relation that can be specified using a technique developed by Ramsey and refined by Lewis to provide nonreductive definitions of theoretical terms.[20] My intention is simply to illustrate how some type of realist account might be extended to cover agent causation; I do not intend an endorsement of this particular sort of realist view.

On the account in question, causation is held to be that first-order relation (one that obtains between particulars) that is connected in a specified way to causal laws. A causal law is understood as a contingent, second-order relation between properties (where properties are construed as universals). Such a law governs causal relations between event particulars consisting in the exemplifying of the first of the properties related by the law and event particulars consisting in the exemplifying of the second of the properties. In the case of deterministic causation, the governing law consists in the contingent fact that a certain property causally necessitates a certain other property. In the case of nondeterministic causation, the relation involved in the governing law is that of causal probabilification (to a certain degree).[21]

19. For an overview of the issue here, see the Introduction to Ernest Sosa and Michael Tooley, eds., *Causation* (Oxford: Oxford University Press, 1993). One source of arguments against reductionist views of causation is Tooley's "Causation: Reductionism versus Realism," *Philosophy and Phenomenological Research* 50 (1990), pp. 215–36, reprinted in Sosa and Tooley, eds., *Causation.*

20. See David Lewis, "How to Define Theoretical Terms," *Journal of Philosophy* 67 (1970), pp. 427–46, reprinted in his *Philosophical Papers,* Volume 1 (New York: Oxford University Press, 1983).

21. Accounts of causation and laws of nature along these lines are advanced in D. M. Armstrong, *What Is a Law of Nature?* (Cambridge: Cambridge University Press, 1983); and Michael Tooley, *Causation: A Realist Approach* (Oxford: Clarendon Press, 1987). A similar account of laws is defended in Fred Dretske, "Laws of

The task of identifying causation is that of specifying the several (*n*) relations—causation, causal necessitation, and causal probabilification to various degrees—to which the account appeals. If the arguments against reductionism are correct, the terms designating these relations cannot be reductively defined. It may nevertheless be possible to offer a set of postulates that specify these relations nonreductively—nonreductively because the postulates use the very terms that are being defined. Such postulates could indicate the relations in question by specifying the role that each relation necessarily (if it exists) occupies within the domain of events and properties. The postulates should be formulated so that all of the terms being defined are names; we then replace each of these names with its own variable, leaving a theory that employs only antecedently understood, noncausal and nonnomological vocabulary. Finally, we add that the relations of causation, causal necessitation, etc. are the components of the unique ordered *n*-tuple that satisfies the open formula of the theory.[22]

If such a strategy succeeds in specifying a real, irreducible relation of

---

Nature," *Philosophy of Science* 44 (1977), pp. 248–68. Here I gloss over details and differences between these various views that do not affect the issues of central concern in this paper.

Difficulties for this type of view have been raised by Bas C. Van Fraassen, *Laws and Symmetry* (Oxford: Clarendon Press, 1989), ch. 5; Theodore R. Sider, "Tooley's Solution to the Inference Problem," *Philosophical Studies* 67 (1992), pp. 261–75; and John W. Carroll, *Laws of Nature* (Cambridge: Cambridge University Press, 1994), appendix A. A reply to some of these objections appears in D. M. Armstrong, "The Identification Problem and the Inference Problem," *Philosophy and Phenomenological Research* 53 (1993), pp. 421–22. The problems raised in these works concern the conception of laws of nature as relations among universals; they do not directly affect the broader strategy of treating causation as an irreducible theoretical relation.

22. Tooley (*Causation*, ch. 8) employs such a strategy, though he takes the relata of causal relations to be state-of-affairs particulars rather than events. On his view, "what is absolutely fundamental to the concept of causation is the idea that the [logical] probability of a given state of affairs is a function of the probabilities of states of affairs upon which it is causally dependent, in a way in which it is *not* a function of the probabilities of states of affairs that are causally dependent upon it, either directly or indirectly" (p. 256). As I mention in the text below, someone who wants to explicate agent causation in the way I am suggesting can agree with the idea that "determining the direction of the logical transmission of probabilities" is what causation necessarily does among states of affairs (or events) but may need to deny that this idea is what is *fundamental* to the concept of causation.

causation that obtains between event particulars, then we have an account of the causal relation to which we may appeal in explicating agent causation. The claim that a substance causes an event, we should say, simply states that the relation specified by those postulates, the very relation that occupies the indicated role in the domain of events and properties, obtains between that substance and that event.

This approach provides a clear response to a challenge that Chisholm raised for his own agent-causal view. He asked: "What is the difference between saying, of an event A, that A just happened and saying that someone caused A to happen?"[23] On the suggested view, the difference is that the second statement, but not the first, asserts that a certain non-reductively specifiable relation obtained between the agent and the event, the very same relation that obtains between one event and another when the first causes the second.

Now, presumably, the causal relation would not occupy the very same role among *substances*, events, and properties that it occupies among events and properties. (Our theory might be supplemented to accommodate any differences.) If we took the original theory as stating what was fundamental to the concept of causation, then perhaps we could make no sense of the claim that a substance might be a cause. However, arguably what is most fundamental (even if not, in itself, very informative) is just that causing is producing, bringing about, or making happen. We can get a grip on what this (producing, bringing about, making happen) is by figuring out what causation would necessarily do in the domain of events and properties. But (the idea of) what causation necessarily does in that domain need not be, and arguably is not what is basic to our concept of causation. Causation, in other words, need not reduce to what our theory tells us that it does among events and properties. Having understood this, we would seem to be in a position to make sense of the application of causal notions to things other than events. In particular, we should be able to find intelligible the assertion that the relation that necessarily does a certain something when it takes as both of its relata events can sometimes have as its first relatum a substance. (The point here is just that such an assertion can be rendered intelligible. Whether it is true, or even possibly true is, of course, another matter; I shall turn to this issue shortly.)

Event causation, on the above view, is governed by laws of nature. Can

23. Chisholm, "Freedom and Action," p. 21. Chisholm's reply was that the challenge is no more easily met in the case of causation by events. My suggestion is that the challenge may be met in one and the same way in both cases.

agent causation also be seen as so governed? I think that it can, though in a somewhat different and indirect manner. A causal law, it was said, relates one property to another and governs causal relations between particular events. In addition to causal laws, there are noncausal laws; such laws consist in, for example, simultaneous determination relations between properties. On an account like that above, such a law is held to consist in one property's standing in a contingent relation of (noncausal) nomological necessitation to another. (Relations such as nomological necessitation that are involved in noncausal laws may be defined in the same manner as that indicated above.) A law governing agent causation might relate the property of having a certain mental capacity, such as a capacity to direct one's behavior by reflective practical reasoning, to the property of having that variety of control that is free will. The law would consist in the contingent fact that the first of these properties nomologically necessitates the second. Now, agent causalists maintain that it is a necessary truth that if an agent acts with free will, then she (the agent, the person) causes the action that she performs. Supposing that to be so, it will be necessarily true that if the indicated noncausal law holds, then whenever an agent acts with the capacity for effective, self-conscious practical reasoning, she brings about, by agent-causing, the action that she performs. Such a law would govern agent causation without precluding freedom. For although it will be necessary that, given the law, any agent who acts with the indicated rational capacity is a cause of her action, it may nevertheless be the case (and on the account I shall describe, when an agent acts freely it will be the case) that conditions at any moment prior to the action leave it open which specific type of action the agent will cause. (As I shall explain in the next section, on the view I am proposing, which specific type of action the agent performs freely will be governed by causal laws, but by nondeterministic rather than deterministic laws.)

On the suggested account, whenever an agent has the relevant rational capacity, she has the variety of control that is free will. When she acts, she (the agent) stands in the first-order relation of causation to the specific action that is performed with the indicated rational capacity. If the agent's standing in that relation to that action is itself an event, that event occurs at the same time as the action. But this is not a case of simultaneous causation; the cause of the action is the agent, a substance, not the event that consists of the agent's causing that action. (I address in section 2.3 the question what, if anything, causes this event.) Nor is this a case of a nomological or causal loop. One property nomologically necessitates another, and a substance causes an event. Nor do we have here a temporal loop. The action does not occur until it is caused by the agent, and it is not caused by the agent until it occurs; but if its being caused by the agent is an event, that event is simultaneous with the action.

Even if an account like the one sketched here succeeds in rendering intelligible the claim that a substance can be a cause, the most difficult challenge in developing a workable notion of agent causation remains. For it will no doubt be objected that what the account now intelligibly asserts is something that is plainly false; given such an understanding of a cause, it may be said, a substance simply cannot be a cause.

However, the causal realm is the realm of concrete particulars (or perhaps more specifically of spatiotemporal concrete particulars). And a physical substance, like an event involving such a substance, is a (spatiotemporal) concrete particular. If one type of concrete particular can be a cause while another cannot, there must be some reason for this difference. It is no good to claim here that the impossibility is self-evident. If something like the realist view of event causation sketched here is correct, the objection that a substance cannot be a cause requires some argument.

Certainly there are differences in the respects in which a physical substance and an event involving that substance are "in" space and time.[24] Perhaps what the issue comes down to is whether and how these differences might make for a difference with respect to which of these entities can be a cause. Regrettably, there has been almost no exploration of this issue in the literature on agent causation. To my knowledge, only one argument against the possibility of agent causation appeals to such a difference. . . . that the alternative agent-causal view presented here can meet it. That seems to leave unresolved the question of the possibility of causation by a substance. I propose that we take an agnostic position on this issue until further arguments are provided. That, at any rate, is my position, and it is from that position that the main argument of this paper is offered.

2.2. *Agent Causation, Event Causation, and Agent-Control*

My primary concern in this paper is how, in an adequate agent-causal account, causation by events and causation by the agent should be said to be involved in the production of free action. Whereas the traditional view maintains that the event that is directly caused by the agent when she acts

24. These differences are discussed in Lawrence Brian Lombard, *Events: A Metaphysical Study* (London: Routledge & Kegan Paul, 1986), pp. 69–70.

freely has no event cause, on the alternative view that I favor, this event is nondeterministically caused by prior events.

The account may be illustrated as follows. Suppose that, as may well be the case, many or all of our decisions and overt actions are probabilistically rather than deterministically caused by prior events. (Whatever causal laws are, the laws governing these event-causal relations are nondeterministic.) For example, suppose that on some occasion, there is a nonzero probability that a prior event R1 consisting in an agent's having (or acquiring) certain beliefs and desires will nondeterministically cause event A1, a certain action performed by the agent; and suppose that there is, as well, a nonzero probability that a prior event R2 consisting in the agent's having (or acquiring) certain other beliefs and desires will cause event A2, a certain alternative action, instead. Then, given all prior conditions, it is genuinely open to the agent to perform action A1 and genuinely open to her to perform the alternative action A2. Now suppose that, in the circumstances, whichever of the available actions the agent performs, that action will be performed, and it will be caused by the reasons that favor it, only if the agent causes that action. Finally, suppose that, as it happens, the agent performs action A1. Her action is caused by her, and it is nondeterministically caused by R1. On the view I propose, the agent's acting with free will consists (crucially but not wholly) in her action's being caused, in this way, by her and by her reasons.[25]

The basic conception of free will on which this alternative view is founded runs as follows. Free will is held to be a certain valuable variety of control, and the variety of control possessed by an agent on some occasion when she acts is held to be fundamentally a matter of what causally produces (and in what manner it causally produces) her action. It appears that proponents of the traditional agent-causal view would agree with this conception. In any case, on the basis of this conception, the alternative view agrees with the traditional view in maintaining that if the agent is not herself an effect of other causes, if she causally produces her making a certain decision or performing a certain overt action, and if her causing that decision or action is not itself causally determined by events over which she has never had any control, then her causal production of the action contributes to her control over what she does on that occasion.

Given such a conception, in a case like the one described above, which-

25. I say 'not wholly' because the agent must also act with a capacity for effective, self-conscious practical reasoning. I address this point in the present section of the paper.

ever of the available actions the agent performs, she exercises a certain variety of control (call it bare actional control) in virtue of the fact that her action is causally brought about (in the right way) by, and hence motivated and guided by, certain of her reasons. If, additionally, the agent possesses, at the time of her action, a capacity to reflect rationally on her alternatives and on the reasons favoring each, and to govern rationally her behavior on the basis of such reflection, we may say that she acts with a more desirable variety of control (call it rational control). Finally, given this conception of agent-control, in a case like the one described, the agent exercises a yet more desirable variety of control if, additionally, she (the agent) causes her action. For the agent is not herself an effect of prior causes, she causes her performing a certain action, and her causing that action is not causally determined by any events over which she has never had any control. In thus causing the action, the agent is in a strict and literal sense an originator of her action.

Bare actional control and rational control could be possessed if all the causes of an action were events, even if those events deterministically caused the action. Compatibilists are right, then, that certain varieties of control are compatible with determinism. However, since an agent may have a capacity for rational self-governance and yet not determine, herself, whether or how she exercises that capacity, there is good reason to think that even rational control does not suffice for free will.

Yet, it does not appear that any more desirable variety of control could be possessed by an agent if her actions were nondeterministically caused by events and not caused by anything else. When such an indeterministic agent acts, she actually performs a certain action with a certain variety of control, and there may have been a chance that she would perform a different action with that same variety of control. But the variety of control that is *actually* exercised here is just the same variety that a deterministic counterpart might exercise.[26] It is either bare actional control, or, at most, rational control. Only the presence of the *chance* of acting differently while still exercising that same variety of control distinguishes the indeterministic agent from her deterministic counterpart. And the presence of such a chance does not by itself constitute the agent's acting

26. It is sometimes held that if the causal relations between the reasons and the action are nondeterministic, then the agent exercises *less* control than she would have if those causal relations had been deterministic. I argue against such a view in "Indeterminism and Control," *American Philosophical Quarterly* 32 (1995), pp. 125–38.

with a variety of *control* that her deterministic counterpart lacks. Chance may *leave room for* additional control, but it does not by itself *constitute* additional control. To have some further variety of control, the indeterministic agent would have to have some further causal power, some further power to causally influence which of the actions she might actually perform she will actually perform. Since this further causal power would be a power to causally influence which of the alternative actions left open by prior events will actually be performed, an agent's possessing such an additional causal power does not appear to be possible as long as all the causes of an agent's actions are events.

Causation of the action by the agent does appear to make some further variety of control possible (and, so far as I can tell, it is the only thing that will do so). For the agent's causing a certain action is not identical with, and it does not consist even partly in, the causation of that action by events. (The agent's causing a certain action consists simply in the causation of an event by a substance.) In agent-causing a certain action, then, the agent exercises a power—one distinct from the causal power of any events involving the agent—to causally influence which of the alternative actions left open by prior events will actually be performed. And that is precisely what seemed needed if some further variety of control was to be possible.

2.3. Additional Control

This alternative agent-causal view (call it the causal agent-causal view, since it incorporates a causal theory of action) mixes event causation and agent causation in its account of the production of free action. This feature of the account raises the question whether, in such a context, agent causation would really contribute anything to the agent's control over what she does. And even if causation by the agent contributes something, the question arises whether the control provided by the causal agent-causal view suffices for free will, or whether, alternatively, what the traditional view provided that was of crucial importance has been lost.

It seems to me that the answer to the first of these questions is affirmative. In the case described above, the action, A1, is caused by the agent and caused by the event R1. The causation of the action by the agent is not identical with, and it does not consist even partly in, the causation of the action by that event. And the causation by that event is nondeterministic; given the laws and the occurrence of R1 (as well as all other prior conditions), it was not inevitable that the agent perform action A1. The causation by the agent is thus not redundant, and there seems to be no reason to say that the causation by the agent is irrelevant to the question what really causes the agent to perform action A1.

If we use the term *determinant* to designate any entity that is a cause of an event, whether that entity is a deterministic cause or not, both R1 and the agent are determinants of the action. Whereas on the traditional agent-causal view, the agent is the sole determinant of the event that she directly causes, here the agent is not the sole determinant but instead one determinant among others. (The event causes will presumably include more than just R1; but it will not lead us astray to focus only on R1.) But it is one thing to be one determinant among others, and another thing to be no determinant at all. As one determinant among others, the agent exercises real causal influence—and influence distinct from that exercised by any event—over which of the actions open to her she will actually perform. And that is what seemed needed to cause the agent to act with greater control than that available without agent causation.

Now, it is often held that, in addition to A1, there would also occur, in a case such as this, a complex event consisting of the agent's causing A1. The question then arises what, if anything, should be held to cause this complex event, given the causal agent-causal view.

Presumably, in the case at hand, if there is an event consisting of the agent's causing A1, then there is also an event consisting of R1's causing A1. With this latter complex event, R1 (the agent's having [or acquiring] certain reasons) is itself caused by prior events; and it seems that whatever causes R1 may properly be said to cause R1's causing A1, even if, as we are supposing, R1 nondeterministically causes A1. When we turn to the agent's causing A1, however, the first relatum is uncaused. Hence nothing causes the agent's causing A1 by causing the agent.

It has been argued that the only way in which one entity's causing a certain event can be caused is by causing the first entity, and hence that it is impossible for there to be any cause of an agent's causing an event.[27] This claim may be correct. But it would be a mistake to conclude from it that nothing can influence, by the exercise of causal power, whether the agent's causing a certain action will occur. For, supposing that there is such an event as the agent's causing A1, it seems plainly the case that the agent, in causing A1, influences, by exercising a causal power, whether that complex event will occur. For it occurs just in case the agent causes A1.

27. See O'Connor, "Agent Causation," pp. 184–7.

Indeed, on the causal agent-causal view, it appears that any entity that causes A1 thereby influences, by exercising a causal power, whether the agent's causing A1 will occur (supposing there is such a complex event). For, first, it is not causally determined by any prior events that either A1 or the agent's causing A1 will occur. Second, the agent's causing A1 occurs, it seems, precisely when A1 occurs. And third, A1 occurs in circumstances in which, we may suppose, it is nomologically necessary that if A1 occurs, it is caused by the agent. On the characterization of agent causation sketched above, if there is a noncausal law relating possession of an effective capacity for practical reflection to having free will, then whenever an agent acts with that capacity, she is an agent cause of her action. Hence, on the suppositions that the law holds and that the agent possesses the indicated capacity when she acts, A1 occurs only if the agent causes A1. Hence any event that causes A1 thereby influences, by the exercise of a causal power, whether the agent's causing A1 will occur. Such an event exercises that influence not by causing the agent, and perhaps not by *causing* the agent's causing A1. It does so by causing A1, in the circumstances just described.

However, again, since R1 nondeterministically causes A1, the occurrence of R1, together with other conditions present prior to the action, does not make it inevitable that the agent's causing A1 occur. (These prior events and conditions might make it inevitable that *some* agent-causal event occur; but, in the case at hand, that event might be the agent's causing A1, and it might instead be the agent's causing A2. And, as we have seen, the agent influences, by an exercise of causal power, which of these events will occur.) Again there is no reason to say that causation by the agent is irrelevant to the question what really influences, by the exercise of causal power, whether the agent's causing A1 will occur. Allowing that a "determinant" may be any entity that influences, by the exercise of causal power, whether a certain event will occur, either by causing that event or by causing another, the agent and R1 are both determinants of the agent's causing A1. Again, the influence exercised by the agent here is not identical with, and it does not consist even partly in, the influence exercised by the event. The agent is one determinant among others, but she is not no determinant at all. On the causal agent-causal view, then, the agent exercises real influence over which complex event—her causing A1 or her causing A2—left open by prior events will actually occur.

As far as the issue of control is concerned, it does not appear to matter whether we say that the agent and R1 bring about the agent's causing her action by causing that complex event, or instead say that the agent and R1 influence whether that complex event will occur just by causing A1.[28] (The latter view seems to me better justified.) Agent causation contributes something to control if the agent exercises some real causal influence over what happens. In exercising such influence on the occurrence of A1, the agent thereby exercises real influence on the occurrence of the agent's causing A1, and does so as genuinely as does R1. The agent is a codeterminant of both A1 and the agent's causing A1. Hence, despite the fact that, on the causal agent-causal view, agent causation and event causation are combined in the account of the production of free action, agent causation still contributes to the agent's control over what she does.

One might raise the following objection to this argument. On the account given, R1 and other events prior to the action cause the agent's performing a certain specific action with the indicated rational capacity. It is supposedly necessary that, given a certain noncausal law, if an agent performs any action with that capacity, then she is an agent cause of that action. Hence it is supposedly necessary that, given that law, if the agent performs *that* specific action with that capacity, then the agent causes that specific action. Thus, whether the agent causes a certain specific action is entirely due to the prior events that cause that specific action. The agent's causing that specific action, then, is entirely at the mercy of prior events, and since that is so, agent causation contributes nothing to control.

Where the objection goes wrong, I think, is in overlooking the fact that, on the causal agent-causal view, whether the agent's performing a certain specific action with the indicated rational capacity occurs in the first place is not entirely due to prior events. Prior events may render it inevitable that the agent act and that the agent act with that rational capacity. But in the range of cases in question, prior events do not render inevitable the agent's performing a certain specific action with that capacity. The agent

28. Agent causalists have wrestled hard with the question what causes an agent's causing a certain event when the agent acts with free will. The question appears to pose a trilemma. If nothing causes this event, then it would seem to be entirely random, and it would seem that agent causation does not then ground the agent's control over her behavior. If prior events cause this event, then it seems we are no better off with an agent-causal account than we are with determinism. And if the agent causes this event, then presumably the agent causes her causing this event, and we are off on an infinite regress.

We can, I think, adopt the first of these alternatives without incurring the alleged cost. The agent exercises real influence over whether her causing a certain action occurs in virtue of the fact that she is a real determinant of that action.

is an additional causal influence on her performing that specific action with that capacity. And by exercising causal influence on whether she performs that specific action, she thereby influences, by the exercise of causal power, whether her causing that specific action will occur. The agent's causing that specific action, then, is not entirely at the mercy of prior events. Agent causation does indeed contribute something to control.

2.4. Enough for Free Will?

I have argued that integrating agent causation within universal event causation still allows for a variety of control that is greater than any available in a deterministic world, or in an indeterministic world in which only events are causes. However, it may now be objected that even if, on the alternative view, agent causation contributes something to control, it does not contribute enough. On the traditional view, when an agent acts with free will, there is no event cause at all of the action, nor of the agent's causing the action; on the traditional view, the agent is the *sole* determinant of her free action. And only an account on which the agent is the sole determinant, it may be said, gives us the variety of control that is free will. The alternative view gives us less in the way of control than does the traditional view, and what is left out is of crucial importance for free will.

The difference between the two views comes down to this: on the causal agent-causal view, the agent is a codeterminant, but not the sole determinant, of her action and of her causing her action, whereas on the traditional view, the agent is the sole determinant of both. Is there any reason to think that free will requires the latter?

The following may be thought to provide such a reason. It is widely held that any adequate incompatibilist account of free will must maintain that, if any event causes a certain action, the agent acts with free will only if she controls the occurrence of that event.[29] Such a requirement would seem to imply that in acting with free will, an agent is ultimately the sole determinant of her action, even if she brings her action about by causing some events that in turn cause the action. But we do not in general control our acquisition or possession of reasons for action, and hence the causal agent-causal view fails to fulfill this requirement.

29. Galen Strawson relies on a requirement of this sort to argue that free will is impossible; see his *Freedom and Belief* (Oxford: Clarendon Press, 1986), ch. 2. I respond to his argument in "On the Possibility of Rational Free Action," *Philosophical Studies* 88 (1997), pp. 37–57.

However, I submit that the alleged requirement is mistaken. It is plausible if we think of event causation as only deterministic causation. For it appears to be a basic tenet of incompatibilism that if an agent does not control her acquisition or possession of a certain reason, and if the event that is her acquisition or possession of that reason causally determines her action, then the agent does not act with the control that constitutes free will. However, once we recognize that event causation may be nondeterministic, the possibility arises that an agent may act with free will even if her action is caused by some event over which she does not have any control, if, that is, the agent exercises a causal power that influences whether that event is followed by a certain action.[30] And this last condition is provided for on the causal agent-causal account. For on that view, the agent is a real determinant of her action. She exercises real causal influence over which action she performs. And in so doing, she exercises real causal influence over whether a certain prior event, her having or acquiring a certain reason, will be followed by a certain action. Thus, although she does not (in general) influence whether she acquires or possesses that reason, in virtue of agent-causing her action, she influences whether it will be the case that given that she has that reason, she will perform a certain action. Hence she genuinely influences which action she will perform, despite the fact that her action is nondeterministically caused by events the occurrence of which she does not control.

The original objection may be restated here, with only minor alteration. On the causal agent-causal view, the agent is not the only entity that influences whether a certain prior event will be followed by a certain action; prior events exercise such influence as well. And in order to act with the control that constitutes free will, it may be said, the agent must be the sole entity exercising influence over whether prior events will be followed by a certain action.

30. Peter van Inwagen defends a positive incompatibilist view along these lines; see *An Essay on Free Will* (Oxford: Clarendon Press, 1983), esp. pp. 147–50. Van Inwagen argues for incompatibilism on the basis of a principle according to which, if (1) an agent does not control the fact that a certain event occurs, and (2) the agent does not control the fact that if that event occurs, then the agent performs a certain action, then (3) the agent does not control the fact that she performs that action. However, he argues that an agent may act with control (act freely) if (2) is false. Van Inwagen proposes that (2) might be false if the action is nondeterministically caused by events and not caused by anything else, though he confesses that he does not see how this state of affairs could render (2) false. I think that it could not. We must add agent causation to the picture to get that result.

Is there any argument that can be given to support the objection at this point? I cannot think of any. Nor do I think that we have a sufficiently clear grasp of free will that we can see, as directly evident, that the objection is correct.

Moreover, a proponent of the objection faces the following challenge. It appears evident that, in our world, prior events influence what we do. This fact alone is not sufficient to show that we lack free will. Thus, free will seems to allow for the influence of entities other than the agent on what the agent does, and on whether certain prior events are followed by a certain action. Indeed, versions of the traditional agent-causal view seek in one way or another to capture this fact.[31] Prior events that exert such influence would, it seems, establish probability structures leaving some actions more likely than others, even if those prior events do not then cause the action that is actually performed. The only objection from a proponent of such a view could be that such influence must not be held to be causal. Now, a strong case can be made that there is no adequate noncausal construal of such influence.[32] However, the point here is a different one: even if there is some adequate noncausal construal of the influence of prior conditions on which action is performed freely, still, on an account that allows such influence, the agent is not the sole entity that influences what she does. If the other entities exercise genuine influence, what difference does it make, for the issue of control, whether that influence is properly characterized as causal or not? Is not genuine noncausal influence by entities other than the agent just as destructive of free will as causal influence by such factors is? Or, rather, is not causal influence by such factors just as consistent with free will as genuine noncausal influence by such factors is, so long as in both cases, the influence is probabilistic rather than deterministic? The answer to the latter question, it seems to me, is yes.

A second, quite different reason for objecting that the control characterized by the causal agent-causal account does not suffice for free will remains to be considered. I mentioned above (Section 2.1) that, in contrast with proponents of the traditional view, I would not insist that agent

31. Some of these attempts are discussed in Section 3.1 below. The longer version of this paper includes a discussion of some additional efforts by proponents of the traditional view to account for the influence of circumstances on what an agent does freely.

32. This case is made in Section 3.1 below and more fully in the longer version of this paper.

causation is fundamentally different from event causation, except with regard to the ontological category of the cause. And a proponent of the traditional view may claim that it is precisely in order to ground the agent's control over which action she performs that agent causation must be said to be to a greater extent different.

I doubt that this claim is correct, though it would take another paper to argue the point. However, for present purposes we should note that the point of difference from the traditional view under discussion right now is independent from the point of difference that is the main subject of this paper. We may keep the traditional understanding of what causation by an agent amounts to and still integrate agent causation into a nexus of unbroken event-causal chains. And if we do, then the advantages that I describe below are still ours.

3. Some Advantages of the Causal Agent-Causal View

On conceptual grounds, there are a number of reasons to find the alternative account more appealing than the traditional view. The causal agent-causal view allows us to draw in a more plausible way the distinction between free and unfree action; it provides for a better account of the way in which an agent's past experience, her current condition, and her surroundings can influence even her free actions; it leaves us with superior accounts of acting on certain reasons and of action explanation; and it softens a popular objection to the notion of agent causation. Here, in the interest of brevity, I discuss only the last two of these considerations.[33]

3.1. Acting on Reasons and Explaining Free Action

According to causal theories of action, an event counts as an action only in virtue of its event-causal history. Clearly, if such a view is correct, then the traditional agent-causal view of free will cannot be right. Now, I do believe that causal theorists (of action) have won the debate against their opponents. But I do not try to make a case for that claim here. Instead, I focus on an issue that is, I think, more easily decided in favor of causalism, namely, what it is for an agent to act on or for certain reasons.

It would be hard to overemphasize the advantage provided by causal theories of action when it comes to saying what an agent's acting on or for certain reasons in particular comprises. Causal theorists maintain that an

33. The other considerations are discussed in the longer version of this paper.

agent acts on or for a certain reason only if the associated reason-state is a cause of the agent's action. Only given such a causal relation, it is argued, can we adequately distinguish between reasons that an agent *has* to perform a certain action and reasons that she acts on. The challenge that must be met by any noncausal theory of action is to account for the *because* in such statements as, "Sam went to Seattle because he wanted to see the Space Needle."[34] No noncausal theory of action has met the challenge.

Causal theories of action, then, have a distinct advantage over noncausal theories when it comes to giving an account of acting for reasons. Since the causal agent-causal account of free will accepts that reason-states cause actions, such an account inherits this advantage. Traditional agent-causal accounts are at a serious disadvantage on this score.

Many versions of the traditional view offer no account of acting on or for certain reasons. Some versions, such as Taylor's, offer an intelligibility account, according to which the reasons on which an agent acts on a given occasion are those of her reasons that render her behavior intelligible.[35] Such an account will not do. An agent may have several different reasons each of which render her behavior intelligible, and yet she may act on some of those reasons but not on others. Nor will it do to say that those reasons that an agent has that render her behavior *most* intelligible are the reasons on which she acts. For we sometimes act less intelligibly than we might, for example when we act contrary to our better reasons.

Another version of the traditional view holds that the reasons on which an agent acts are those that she intends her action to realize or satisfy. For example, suppose that Cate wants to cheer up Dave, and she believes that if she tells him a joke, that will cheer him up. She then tells Dave a joke. According to O'Connor, the following make it the case that Cate told the joke in order to carry out her desire to cheer up Dave:

(i) prior to her telling the joke, Cate had a desire to cheer up Dave, and she believed that by telling the joke she would satisfy (or contribute to satisfying) that desire; and

(ii) Cate's telling the joke was initiated (in part) by her own self-determining causal activity (her behavior was agent-caused); and

34. See Donald Davidson, "Actions, Reasons, and Causes," *Journal of Philosophy* 60 (1963), pp. 685–700, reprinted in his *Essays on Actions and Events* (Oxford: Clarendon Press, 1980).

35. See, e.g., Taylor, *Action and Purpose*, ch. 14.

(iii) concurrent with her telling the joke, Cate remembered that prior desire and intended of her telling the joke that it satisfy (or contribute to satisfying) that desire.[36]

It is not part of this account that the agent's intending that her action satisfy a certain desire is a cause of the action. On the contrary, since the intention is held to refer directly to the action, it appears that the intention would have to be caused by the action, or by some part of the action.[37] If this is so, then whether the agent acted on a certain reason depends on something causally downstream from the action; it depends on whether the action, or some part of it, actually has (not just whether it is intended to have) a certain causal result, namely, a certain concurrent intention. But it is implausible that whether an agent acts on a certain reason depends on what actually causally results from the action.

We are, I think, far more strongly inclined to judge that whether an agent really acts on a certain reason depends on what actually causes the action. To see this, imagine that Cate has, besides the desire to cheer up Dave, a desire to annoy Emma and a belief that telling a joke will cause Emma to be annoyed. When Cate tells the joke, she is thinking of both desires and intending of her action that it satisfy both; her action, or some part of it, causes this concurrent intention. But suppose that the first desire is not at all causally related to the action, and that only the second is a cause of Cate's telling the joke.[38] Then, although conditions (i)–(iii) are

36. O'Connor, "Agent Causation," p. 192. His account is intended as an account of reason's explanation of action; but an explanation is a true reasons-explanation only if it cites reasons on which the agent acted. Zimmerman (*An Essay on Human Action,* p. 240) suggests a similar account, though the intentions to which he appeals are not said to refer directly to the action.

37. O'Connor's view of reasons-explanation is modeled after Ginet's, though Ginet's account does not involve agent causation. See Carl Ginet, *On Action* (Cambridge: Cambridge University Press, 1990). Ginet (p. 140) maintains that there is "a causal connection between the action and the intention required for the latter to refer directly to the former," a connection "from explained action to explaining intention rather than the other way around." This feature renders the view implausible when it is considered as an account of explanation. For the concurrent intention is supposed to explain the action, and yet, since the intention is caused by the action (or some part of it), the intention can presumably be explained by the action (or some part of it). We have, then, an explanatory relation that is symmetrical. But nothing, it seems, is explained by what it explains.

38. O'Connor ("Agent Causation") holds that a free action such as Cate's telling

satisfied, we will want to say, I think, that Cate did not really tell the joke to cheer up Dave; she did not act on her desire to cheer him up. If she thought that she was motivated in part by that desire, she was mistaken, perhaps having deceived herself that at least one of her effective motives was laudable. Alternatively, suppose that when Cate tells the joke, she is thinking of only the first desire and intending of the action that it satisfy that desire, but both desires cause, in the appropriate way, her action. Then again, I think, our judgment of which desires Cate acted on conflicts with the account in question, for in this last version of the case, we will judge that Cate knew only part of what she was aiming to do in telling the joke. (Again, she may have deceived herself in order to preserve her high opinion of herself.) The intention-in-action account of acting on reasons, then, fails.[39]

It might be objected that in both of the cases just described, the agent fails to act with free will precisely because she is partly mistaken about or not fully aware of what her purpose in acting is. Hence the examples would not count against the intention-in-action account, since that account aims to say in what consists an agent's acting *freely* on certain reasons.[40] However, the objection places too strong a requirement of self-understanding on acting freely. Even when we act with free will, we may be less than fully aware of, or somewhat mistaken about, what we are aiming to do. Perhaps the appropriate requirement of self-understanding is that when an agent acts with free will, she is *capable* of understanding her motives and aims in acting. She may, however, sometimes fail to exercise such a capacity.

Rowe, following Reid, suggests yet another way in which reasons or motives might influence free action without causing it; an action positively

---

the joke consists in the agent's causing some event or sequence of events, and that it is impossible for there to be a cause of an agent's causing an event or sequence of events. I am unsure about the truth of this second claim. However, the present objection may be restated in a way that sidesteps this issue. Call the event or sequence of events the agent's causing of which is said to be the action the "issue" of the action. The objection is then that there may be a difference between which desires Cate intends her action to satisfy and which desires cause the issue of her action. When there is such a difference, we will judge that the desires on which Cate really acted are those that were causes of the issue of her action.

39. Compare the arguments presented by Mele against noncausal accounts of action explanation; see Alfred R. Mele, *Springs of Action: Understanding Intentional Behavior* (New York: Oxford University Press, 1992), ch. 13.

40. The objection was suggested to me by O'Connor in conversation.

influenced by a given reason would, it seems, be performed for that reason. Animal motives—appetites, desires, natural affections—are said to give an impulse to the will, a force that, unless resisted by the agent, impels her to act in accord with such motives. In contrast, rational motives—judgments about duty or one's long-range good—are held to persuade or convince.[41]

However, both sorts of influence would seem to be causal. Suppose that an agent freely acts on an animal motive. Then, even though that motive did not deterministically cause her action, it would seem that the motive was a cause of the action. How else can we understand the motive's "giving an impulse to the will" or "impelling the agent to act"? And suppose that an agent freely acts on a rational motive. Even this sort of "persuasive" influence on the will would seem to be causal. No other account of it has been offered.

Insofar as some noncausal construal *can* be given to these kinds of influence, it seems that this view in fact amounts to a version of the intelligibility account. A motive may be present and felt as a force on the will, and yet the agent may not act on that motive; for she may act contrary to it. Hence the idea would seem to be that an agent acts on a motive if it has one of these sorts of influence and she acts in accord with it; the motive on which she acts is the one in light of which her action makes sense. But we have seen that such an account is inadequate; an agent may act in accord with a motive that she encounters as advice or feels as a force, and yet she may not be acting on that motive.

Finally, consider a proposal by Chisholm concerning the way in which a reason may "incline without necessitating." An agent's desire, say, for money may be said to incline without necessitating her toward accepting a bribe if it leaves her able to refrain from seeking a bribe but unable to resist if a bribe is offered.[42] Clearly the proposal will not do as a general account of inclination, since the agent's desire might incline even if she retains the ability to resist if a bribe is offered.

Causal theories have, and noncausal theories lack, a viable account of acting on reasons. Along with such an account comes an account of action explanation. If Cate acted (only) on her desire to annoy Emma, then we provide a true explanation of Cate's telling the joke by saying that she wanted to annoy Emma. Saying that Cate wanted to cheer up Dave may

41. Rowe, *Thomas Reid on Freedom and Morality,* pp. 172–80.

42. Chisholm, "Freedom and Action," pp. 25–8, and *Person and Object,* p. 69.

make her action intelligible, and it may tell us something that she had in mind when acting, but considered as an explanation it is just plain false.

An agent-causal account of free will that is combined with a causal theory of action inherits these accounts of acting on reasons and action explanation. Since Cate's freely telling the joke was an action, it was caused by certain of her reason-states. The causal relations between those states (or her acquisition of them) and her action are what make it the case that she acted on a certain desire. We explain what Cate did by citing some event(s) in the event-causal chain leading to and including her action.

Noting that Cate is also a cause of her action indicates a further cause, and it indicates that a necessary condition of Cate's having acted with a certain variety of control is met. It is unclear whether so noting contributes to an explanation of the action. It does not help answer *why* Cate told the joke; the reasons-explanation that cites event-causes of the action does that. Perhaps citing the agent, or citing causation by the agent, helps answer not a why-question but a how-actually-question: how did it come about that Cate told the joke?[43] But in any case, agent causation does not interfere with the event-causal explanation of the action, for agent causation does not interrupt or divert the ordinary causal route from reasons to action. The explanation that cites the agent's reasons is in no way false or incomplete as a rational explanation, even if it does not tell the entire story about what causally produced the action, and even if it does not reveal that a certain necessary condition of the agent's having acted with a certain variety of control was fulfilled.

Action explanation, on the causal agent-causal view, is in an important respect like the explanation of other events in nature. We may cite prior events as causes, and if we know more, we may articulate the laws governing such causal relations, and even the fundamental laws from which these first laws are derived. The alternative account is thus considerably more naturalistic than its traditional counterpart. Given the causal agent-causal view, it may be false to say, as some proponents of the traditional view say, that if we act with free will, then there can be no scientific explanation of human behavior.[44]

43. If citing the agent does not contribute in any way to an explanation of the action, does that show that the agent is not a cause of the action? It would if causation were analyzable in terms of explanation, but causation is certainly not so analyzable. Hence some defense of the principle that every cause is explanatory would be needed. I do not see what the defense would be.

44. Chisholm ("Freedom and Action," pp. 24–5) says that "there can be no

3.2. Softening an Objection

Although the credibility of the notion of agent causation itself is not my main concern here, I shall discuss one respect in which the causal agent-causal view contributes to the acceptability of that notion. A frequently repeated objection to the possibility of agent causation is the claim that if an event is caused, then some part of that event's total cause must be an occurrence at a particular time; otherwise, it is said, there would be no way to account for the effect's occurring when it did.[45] If an agent directly causes an event, then, the objection goes, there must be something the agent does, or some change the agent undergoes, that causes that event.[46]

Since the traditional view denies that the event that is directly caused by the agent has any event causes, proponents of that view have to meet this objection head-on.[47] In contrast, although a proponent of the causal agent-causal view will still have an objection to meet, some of the force will be taken out of it first.

The causal agent-causal view maintains that, when an agent directly causes an event, part of the total cause of that event *is* an occurrence at a particular time, something that the agent undergoes, namely, the acquisition (or perhaps the continued possession) of certain reasons.[48] Some part of the total cause of the effect *does*, then, account for the effect's occurring

---

complete science of man." Taylor (*Action and Purpose*, p. 224) claims that human behavior "can never be understood in terms of the concepts of physical science." There may be some reason having nothing to do with freedom why nothing that is an action can be given a scientific explanation. I doubt that there is; but my point here is that *freedom* should not be seen as preventing scientific explanation.

45. See, e.g., C. D. Broad, *Ethics and the History of Philosophy* (London: Routledge & Kegan Paul, 1952), p. 215; and Ginet, *On Action*, pp. 13–14.

46. Rowe puts the objection this way; see his remarks on p. 371 of "Two Criticisms of the Agency Theory," *Philosophical Studies* 42 (1982), pp. 363–78.

47. Rowe (*Thomas Reid on Freedom and Morality*, pp. 156–9) maintains that an agent can directly cause an event only by exerting her active power to bring about that event. Thus, on his view, the agent *must* do something in order to produce an event. However, Rowe argues that the agent's exerting her active power does *not* cause the event that the agent directly causes, so we are still left with an event that has no event among its causes.

48. The reasons may or may not be reasons to perform the action at a particular time. What is important here is that the acquisition or possession of the reasons is an event that occurs at a particular time.

at a certain time. A proponent of the causal agent-causal view can grant the claims made in the objection, for they do not bear on that view.

This observation helps meet the objection, even if it does not do away with it. For on the causal agent-causal view, the causation by the agent is held itself not to consist even in part in causation by an occurrence or by something the agent does or undergoes. Thus, the objection may be modified to claim that *any* part of a total cause must be an occurrence at a particular time.

However, this modified objection is simply the assertion, without argument, that agent causation is impossible; and as I argued in section 2.1, this claim requires some argument to back it up. The original objection here had an argument to support it, and a plausible one at that. But that argument cannot support the modified objection. I do not claim that the needed argument cannot be provided, nor that the modified objection can be adequately met. But an agent causalist has made progress, I think, by moving the debate from the original objection to the modified version.

4. Conclusion

I have argued that an agent-causal account of free will that integrates causation by agents into an event-causal theory of action loses nothing that is crucial in the traditional agent-causal view. Such an alternative is preferable in that it provides a more naturalistic view of free action, and it evades several serious difficulties encountered by the traditional account.

Of course, a fully adequate agent-causal account must successfully defend the notion of agent causation itself. Such a defense would need to render intelligible the claim that some substances sometimes cause certain events, and it would need to establish that this claim could possibly be true (that there are worlds in which it is true). In section 2.1, I briefly indicated how, in my view, the first of these tasks may be accomplished. And in section 3.2, I addressed what is, so far as I know, the only argument that has ever been offered for the impossibility of agent causation; the causal agent-causal view provides a reply to that argument. Still, causation by a substance seems to many to be plainly impossible. However, if it is possible for one kind of concrete particular, an event, to cause an event, but impossible for another kind of concrete particular, a substance, to cause an event, then there must be some reason, stemming from differences between particulars of these two kinds, why something of the first kind can be a cause but something of the second kind cannot. Certainly there are differences; but it remains to be shown whether those differences provide the sort of reason in question. There is a need for careful exploration of what arguments there might be one way or the other on this issue. Until we have conducted such an exploration, we are warranted neither in reflexive dismissal nor in complacent acceptance of any agent-causal account.[49]

49. I wish to thank Carl Ginet, Alfred Mele, Timothy O'Connor, David Robb, Alex Rosenberg, William Rowe, and Michael Zimmerman for their comments on earlier versions of this paper. Work on this paper was supported by a grant from the University of Georgia Research Foundation.

24

Timothy O'Connor, "Agent-Causal Power"

Timothy O'Connor is a professor of philosophy at Indiana University. In this article, he develops a characterization of agent-causal power and defends a conception of human beings as possessing this power against a series of recurring objections.

Our universe is populated, at bottom, by a vast number of partless particulars of a few basic kinds. Each of these particulars instantiates some of a small range of primitive qualities and stands in primitive relations with other particulars. We may conceive of qualities as immanent universals that are numerically identical in their instances, along the lines championed by David Armstrong (1978), or as "tropes" that are non-identical but exactly resembling in their instances, following C. B. Martin (1997). (Nothing of what follows hangs on which alternative one prefers.) In calling these qualities "primitive," we are contending that they are real existents whose being does not consist, even in part, in the existence or instantiation of other entities. The nature of these qualities is irreducibly dispositional: they are tendencies to interact with other qualities in producing some effect, or some range of possible effects. (Or, in certain cases—as we shall consider below—they may instead confer upon their possessor a tendency towards, or power to produce, some such effects.) It *may* be that the dispositional profile of a quality does not exhaust its nature, so that it has a further "qualitative character," or quiddity. Here again, we may be neutral on this question for present purposes.[1]

The formal character of a feature's dispositionality may be variable. For a couple of centuries after Newton, it was usual to conceive dispositions deterministically: given the right circumstances, causes strictly necessitate their effects. But fundamental physics since the early twentieth century encourages the thought that dispositions may be probabilistic, such that

1. For discussion, see especially Molnar 2003; Heil and Martin 1999; and Hawthorne 2001.

'there are objective probabilities less than one that a cause will produce its characteristic effect on a given occasion. On this view, deterministic propensities are simply a limiting case of probabilistic ones. What is more, it seems possible to conceive pure, unstructured tendencies, ones that are nondeterministic and yet have no particular probability of being manifested on a given occasion.

The qualities of composite particulars (if we do not here embrace eliminativism) are typically structural, consisting in the instantiation of qualities of and relations between the composite's fundamental parts.[2] Very often, the terms we use to refer to features of composites do not pick out such structural properties, since they are insensitive to minor variation in the composite's exact underlying state. (A water molecule's being in a structured arrangement of hydrogen and oxygen atoms persists through small-scale changes in its microphysical composition and state. Of course, there are also much more dramatic cases of underlying variation across instances consistent with applicability of the same macroscopic term, with functional terms providing obvious examples.) Here, we should say that the *concept* is satisfied in different cases in virtue of the instantiation of different structural qualities. Despite superficial ways of speaking, there is no distinctive causal power attached to the satisfaction of such a concept, as that would require the causal powers theorist to accept an objectionable form of double counting of causes, one for the macroscopic structural property (itself nothing over and above the instantiation of microscopic properties and relations) and one for the putative multiply-realized functional "property."

Such are some central elements of a causal powers metaphysic. There are many disputes of detail among its adherents—to the disputed matters already noted, we should add the nature of primitive external relations and the substantiality of space or spacetime.[3] Such disputes aside, the causal powers metaphysics stands opposed both to the neo-Humean vision that

2. David Armstrong has been the key contemporary figure in developing the idea of structural properties as part of a "sparse" ontology. Nonetheless, he waffles a bit in his understanding of their reducibility. He speaks of them as something subtly "extra"—distinct from the underlying instances of properties and relations but strongly supervening upon them (Armstrong 1997: 37). But this is hard to square with his adamant contention that they are an "ontological free lunch." (See his discussion on pp. 34–45.)

3. On the nature of fundamental external relations, see Molnar 2003: ch. 10; Ellis 2001; and the skeptical discussion in Armstrong's contribution to Armstrong, Martin, and Place 1996.

David Lewis (1983) popularized and the second-order Humean metaphysic of causal realism without causal powers defended in recent years by David Armstrong (1997) and Michael Tooley (1987).[4]

In what follows, I shall presuppose the ecumenical core of the causal powers metaphysics. The argument of this paper concerns what may appear at first to be a wholly unrelated matter, the metaphysics of free will. However, an adequate account of freedom requires, in my judgment, a notion of a distinctive variety of causal power, one which tradition dubs "agent-causal power." I will first develop this notion and clarify its relationship to other notions. I will then respond to a number of objections either to the possibility of a power so explicated or to its sufficiency for grounding an adequate account of human freedom.

7.1 The Problem of Freedom and Agent-Causal Power

Central to the notion of metaphysical freedom of action, or free will, is the thought that what I do freely is something that is "up to me," as Aristotle says. A familiar, disputed line of reasoning, which turns upon the principle that where certain truths that are not up to an agent logically (and so unavoidably) entail some further truth, the latter truth is itself not up to the agent, concludes that nothing of what we do would be up to us were our actions to be embedded within a strictly deterministic universe.[5] But if determinism would threaten our freedom, so would the complete absence of any intelligible causation of our actions. So one might steer a middle course by supposing that the world is governed throughout by unfolding causal processes, just not deterministic ones. In particular, one might suppose that our free actions are caused by our own reasons-bearing states at the time of the action. An action's being "up to me," on this view, consists in the nondeterministic causal efficacy of certain of my reasons: I might have performed a different action in identical circumstances

4. I characterize the Armstrong-Tooley view as a gratuitously complicated kind of Humeanism because, despite their intentions, second-order relational structure to the world (their *N*(*F,G*) necessitation relation) cannot *explain* first-order facts (instances of *G* regularly following instances of *F*), since the second-order relations presuppose the supposed explananda. Were God to construct a Tooley-Armstrong world, determining the distribution of first-order *F* and *G* facts must precede decisions about *N*(*F,G*) facts.

5. Peter van Inwagen has heavily influenced discussion of this argument over the last thirty years by his careful formulation of the argument. See van Inwagen 1983 and O'Connor 2000 for a friendly amendment.

because there was a non-zero (and perhaps pronounced) chance that other reasons-bearing states had been efficacious in producing the action which they indicated.[6] However, according to many critics (myself among them), indeterminist event-causal approaches falter just here, in the fact that the free control they posit is secured by an *absence,* a removal of a condition (causal determination) suggested by the manifestly inadequate varieties of compatibilism. If there is no means by which I can take advantage of this looser connectivity in the flow of events, its presence can't confer a greater kind of control, one that *inter alia* grounds moral responsibility for the action and its consequences.[7] Given the causal indeterminist view, if I am faced with a choice between selfish and generous courses of action, each of which has some significant chance of being chosen, it would seem to be a matter of luck, good or bad, whichever way I choose, since I have no means directly to settle which of the indeterministic propensities gets manifested.

The familiar considerations just sketched lead certain philosophers to conclude that the kind of control necessary for freedom of action involves an ontologically primitive capacity of the agent directly to determine which of several alternative courses of action is realized. In these instances of *agent causation,* the cause of an event is not a state of, or event within, the agent; rather, it is the agent himself, an enduring substance.

I will not defend the claim that any actual agents have such a capacity. The philosophical claim is that agents must exercise such a capacity if they are to have metaphysical freedom, but it is an empirical claim whether human agents do exercise such a capacity (and thus do in fact act freely). Our concern is what such an agent-causal power would be, and, given the analysis, whether any agents *could* possibly have it, given fairly modest assumptions about the agents and their embeddedness within an environment.

We begin by considering what the notion of agent causation requires us to assume concerning the nature of the agent having such a power. It is commonly supposed that the notion requires a commitment to agents as partless and nonphysical entities. A radically distinct kind of power, the thought goes, requires a radically distinct kind of substance. And this seems further encouraged by my earlier contention that the causal powers metaphysics pushes one to regard typical "high-level" features as

6. The most prominent advocate of this view of freedom has been Robert Kane. Kane has developed his view in a number of writings, culminating in *The Significance of Free Will.*

7. A few preceding sentences are borrowed from O'Connor and Churchill 2004.

structural properties wholly composed of microphysical properties arranged in a certain way.

But there is more to be said. While the tidiness of substance dualism has its appeal, it is in fact optional for the metaphysician who believes that human beings have ontologically fundamental powers (whether of freedom or consciousness or intentionality). For we may suppose that such powers are *emergent* in the following sense: (*i*) They are ontologically basic properties (token-distinct from any structural properties of the organism); (*ii*) As basic properties, they confer causal powers on the systems that have them, powers that non-redundantly contribute to the system's collective causal power, which is otherwise determined by the aggregations of, and relations between, the properties of the system's microphysical parts. Such non-redundant causal power necessarily means a difference even at the microphysical level of the system's unfolding behavior. (This is not a violation of the laws of particle physics but it is a supplement to them, since it involves the presence of a large-scale property that interacts with the properties of small-scale systems.) In respects (*i*) and (*ii*), emergent powers are no less basic ontologically than unit negative charge is taken to be by current physics. However, emergent and microphysical powers differ in that (*iii*) the appearance of emergent powers is caused (*not* "realized") by the joint efficacy of the qualities and relations of some of the system's fundamental parts and it persists if and only if the overall system maintains the right kind of hierarchically-organized complexity, a kind which must be determined empirically but is insensitive to continuous small-scale dynamical changes at the microphysical level.[8] One cannot give uncontroversial examples of emergent properties. Though there are ever so many macroscopic phenomena that seem to be governed by principles of organization highly insensitive to microphysical dynamics, it remains an open question whether such behavior is nonetheless wholly determined, in the final analysis, by ordinary particle dynamics of microphysical structures in and around the system in question.[9] Given the intractable diffi-

8. Concepts of emergence have a long history—one need only consider Aristotle's notion of irreducible substantial forms. Their coherence is also a matter of controversy. For an attempt to sort out the different ideas that have carried this label, see O'Connor and Wong 2002. And for a detailed exposition and defense of the notion I rely on in the text, see O'Connor and Wong 2005.

9. For numerous examples of such phenomena, see Laughlin, Pines, Schmalian, Stojkovic, and Wolynes 2000.

culties of trying to compute values for the extremely large number of particles in any medium-sized system (as well as the compounding error of innumerable applications of approximation techniques used even in measuring small-scale systems), it may well forever be impossible in practice to attempt to directly test for the presence or absence of a truly (ontologically) emergent feature in a macroscopic system. Furthermore, it is difficult to try to spell out in any detail the impact of such a property using a realistic (even if hypothetical) example, since plausible candidates (e.g., phase state transitions or superconductivity in solid state physics, protein functionality in biology, animal consciousness) would likely involve the simultaneous emergence of multiple, interacting powers. Suffice it to say that if, for example, the multiple powers of a particular protein molecule were emergent, then the unfolding dynamics of that molecule *at a microscopic level* would diverge in specifiable ways from what an ideal particle physicist (lacking computational and precision limitations) would expect by extrapolating from a complete understanding of the dynamics of small-scale particle systems. The nature and degree of divergence would provide a basis for capturing the distinctive contribution of the emergent features of the molecule.

As sketchy as the foregoing has been, we must return to our main topic. I have suggested that we can make sense of the idea of ontologically emergent powers, ones that are at once causally dependent on microphysically-based structural states and yet ontologically primitive, and so apt to confer ontologically primitive causal power. If this is correct, then the fact that agent causal power would be fundamental, or nonderivative, does not imply that the agent that deploys it be anything other than a mature human organism. It is simply an empirical question whether or not the dispositions of the ultimate particles of our universe include the disposition to causally generate and sustain agent-causal power within suitably organized conscious and intelligent agents.

One important feature of agent-causal power is that it is not directed to any particular effects. Instead, it confers upon an agent a power to cause a certain type of event within the agent: the coming to be of a state of intention to carry out some act, thereby resolving a state of uncertainty about which action to undertake. (For ease of exposition, I shall hereafter speak of "causing an intention," which is to be understood as shorthand for "causing an event which is the coming to be of a state of intention.") This power is multi-valent, capable of being exercised towards any of a plurality of options that are in view for the agent. We may call the causing of this intentional state a "decision" and suppose that in the usual case it is a triggering event, initiating the chain of events constituting a wider observable action.

Following agent causalists of tradition (such as Thomas Reid), I conceive agent-causal power as *inherently* goal-directed. It is the power of an agent to cause an intention in order to satisfy some desire or to achieve some aim. How should we understand this goal-directedness?

One way is a variation on a familiar view in action theory, the causal theory of action. The rough idea behind developed versions of the causal theory is that the agent's having a potential reason *R* actually motivated action A (and so contributes to its explanation) just in case *R* is a salient element in the set of causes that "nondeviantly" produce A. (*R* might be, e.g., a belief–desire pair or a prior intention.) In line with this, one might be tempted to say that *R* actually motivated *an agent's causing of intention i* just in case *R* is among the set of causes that nondeviantly produce it.

However, it is not clear that anything *could* (in strict truth) produce a causally-complex event of the form *an agent's causing of intention i.* On the causal powers theory, causation consists in the manifestation of a single disposition (limiting case) or the mutual manifestation of a plurality of properties that are, in C. B. Martin's term, "reciprocal dispositional partners" (typical case). We sometimes speak of an external event's "triggering" a disposition to act (as when the lighting of the fuse is said to trigger the dynamite's disposition to explode). And this way of speaking might tempt one to assert, in more explicit terms, that the lighting of the fuse directly caused the causally-complex event, *the dynamite's emitting a large quantity of hot gas caused the rapid dislocation of matter in its immediate vicinity.* But neither of these statements can be taken at face value when it comes to the metaphysics of causation. The unstable chemical properties of the dynamite's active substance (nitroglycerin) would be involved in any number of effects relative to an appropriate wider circumstance. However, in each case, a variety of conditions C are exercising a *joint* disposition towards the particular effect, E. And nothing directly *produces their producing* of the effect, as this could only mean that the conditions C did not, after all, include all the factors involved in producing E. Granted, there is a perfectly good sense in which a prior event that produces one or more of C's elements may be said to *indirectly* cause C's causing E, in virtue of causing part of C itself to obtain. (So, the lighting of the fuse did lead more or less directly to the rapid burning process of the chemical substance, which event caused the production of the hot gas, which in turn caused the surrounding matter to be rapidly pressed outward.) But this indirect causing of a causal chain by virtue of causing the chain's first element cannot apply to instances of agent causation, for the simple reason that here the first element within the causal chain is not an event or condition, but a substance. It is not the event of the agent's existing at t that causes the coming to be of a state of intention—something that *could* have a cause—but the agent himself. The notion of *causing a substance,* qua substance, has no clear sense.[10]

Thus, we cannot coherently suppose that the obtaining of a reason in the agent may be said to be among the factors that causally *produce* the agent's causing an intention. But perhaps we can sensibly stop a little short of this supposition by supposing instead that the obtaining of the reason appropriately affects (in the typical case, by increasing) an *objective propensity of the agent* to cause the intention. On this latter suggestion, while nothing produces an instance of agent causation, the possible occurrence of this event has a continuously evolving, objective likelihood. Expressed differently, agent causal power is a structured propensity towards a class of effects (the formings of executive intentions), such that at any given time, for each causally possible, specific agent-causal event-type, there is a definite objective probability of its occurrence within the range (0, 1), and this probability varies continuously as the agent is impacted by internal and external influences. To emphasize: events that alter this propensity do *not* thereby tend toward the production of the agent's causing the coming to be of an intention (in the sense that they potentially contribute to the *causing* of this latter event). Even where the event promoted occurs, the effect of the influencing events is exhausted by their alteration of the relative likelihood of an outcome, which they accomplish by affecting the propensities of the agent-causal capacity itself. Where reasons confer probabilities in this manner, I will say that the reasons *causally structure* the agent-causal capacity.

It will perhaps be helpful to clarify what I have and have not just said. I am at this point taking it as provisionally given that we have a decent grasp on the very idea of agent causal power. I argued in the penultimate paragraph that we cannot coherently suppose reasons to constrain agent-causal power in one familiar way, that of tending to produce agent-causal events. I then tried to explicate another (albeit less familiar) way, that of structuring a propensity of an agent to produce an event *without thereby tending toward the production of* the agent's producing said event. However, I have in no way suggested that one could not coherently jettison the idea of

10. See O'Connor 2000: 52–5, for further discussion.

agent causation in favor of an event-causal theory of action on which the having of reasons does indeed tend directly towards the production of one's executive intentions to act. This is the guiding idea of causal theories of action and, unlike some agent causationists such as Richard Taylor, I do not maintain that it is impossible to give a satisfactory theory of action along these lines. I would only insist that such a theory cannot capture the more ambitious notion of *freedom of action.* Here, I maintain, purely event-causal theories (whether deterministic or not) will inevitably fail. Thus, I am committed to supposing that there is more than one broad sort of way that the having of reasons might influence an intentional action. As with other propensities, the effect of events constituted by the having of reasons to act depends on surrounding circumstances. The agent-causal account I am advancing suggests that the presence of agent-causal power is one very important determinant on such effects. In the presence of such a power, the causal contribution of the having of reasons is exhausted by the alteration of the probability of a corresponding agent-causal event.

With this idea in hand, we can specify *one* way in which agent causal events are inherently purposive. Necessarily, when an agent causes an intention *i* to occur at time t_1, he does so in the presence of a motivational state whose onset began at a time $t_0 < t_1$ and which had an appreciable influence on the probability between t_0 and t_1 of his causing of *i.* Let us say that when a reason *R* satisfies this description, the agent freely acted *on R.*[11]

The controverted metaphysics of agent causation aside, this sufficient condition for acting on a reason is quite minimal. Some would contend that it is objectionably weak because it allows that I may act on a reason of which I am entirely unconscious. In such a case, it will be claimed, the reason is exerting a brutely causal influence, and not a rational influence.[12] In my view, this objection mistakenly seeks to assimilate all cases of reasons-guided activity into a single framework. I agree that *some* free actions manifest a heightened degree of conscious control and I try to capture what this might consist in immediately below. But we need to recognize that not even all free actions are created equal—freedom itself comes in degrees. If a reason inclines me to undertake an action but its content is unknown to me (if, say, I am aware merely that I have an inclination to undertake the action), the latter fact diminished my free-

11. I first developed the distinction in the text between *acting on* and *acting for* a reason in O'Connor 2005.

12. Nikolaj Nottelmann raised this objection to me in discussion.

dom, since I am thereby unable to subject my motivation to rational scrutiny. Nonetheless, if it remains open to me to undertake the action or not, I exhibit the goal-driven self-determination that is the core element of freedom of the will.[13] Agents who act freely to any degree, then, directly produce the intentions that initiate and guide their actions, acting on an inclination that is the causal product of certain reasons they acquired (and subsequently retained) at some point prior to this causal activity. But sometimes, it would appear, there is more to be said about the way that reasons motivate freely undertaken actions. Often enough, not only am I conscious of certain reasons that favor the course of action I am choosing, I expressly choose the action for the purpose of achieving the goal to which those reasons point. This goal enters into the content of the intention I bring into being. In such cases, I cause the intention to *A for the sake of G,* where *G* is the goal of a prior desire or intention that, together with the belief that *A*-ing is likely to promote *G,* constitutes the consciously-grasped reason *for* which I act. Now, since I freely and consciously bring the intention into being and thus give it just this purposive content, that purpose cannot but be one for which I am acting. What is more, a further explanatory connection between that reason and the choice is forged beyond the reason's influence on the choice's prior probability. This connection consists in the conjunction of the external relation of prior causal influence and the purely internal relation of sameness of content (the goal *G*). There may be several reasons that increase the likelihood that I would cause the intention to *A*. In the event that I do so, each of these reasons are ones *on* which I act. But if I am conscious of a particular reason, *R,* that promotes a goal *G* (and no other reason promotes that goal), and I cause the intention to *A* for the sake of *G,* then *R* plays a distinctive explanatory role, as shown by the fact that it alone can explain the goal-directed aspect of the intention's content. It alone is one *for* which I act.

It is commonly objected to nondeterministic accounts of human freedom that, despite what I've just said, undetermined actions cannot be explained by the agent's reasons since those reasons cannot account for why the agent performed action *A* rather than *B,* one of the alternatives that were also causally possible in the circumstances. This objection fails to appreciate that explanation need not always be contrastive. If there are truly indeterministic quantum mechanical systems capable of generating any of a plurality of outcomes, whatever results is not absolutely inexplicable. A perfectly good explanation may be given by citing the system and its

13. For further discussion of the idea of degrees of freedom, see O'Connor 2005.

relevant capacities that in fact produced the outcome, even if there is no explanation at all of why that outcome occurred rather than any of the others that might have. Similarly, if an agent is capable of causing any of a range of intentions that would result in different corresponding actions, the reason(s) that inclined the agent to do what he in fact does serve to explain it even though there may be no explanation of why he did that rather than any of the alternatives.

7.2 Arguments for the Impossibility of Agent-Causal Power

The possibility of agent causation has been widely doubted, especially in recent philosophy. Sometimes, the claim is that it is absolutely, or metaphysically, impossible insofar as it posits conditions that contradict certain necessary truths about certain ontological categories, such as that of event or substance. Other times, the form of impossibility is epistemic: agent causation, it is held, is incompatible with what we have excellent reason to believe are basic truths concerning the physics of our world; or with the relationship between the physics and any high-level processes to which basic physics gives rise; or with a general sort of ontological economy that obtains in our world (no superfluous explanatory features). I will now consider four reasons that some have put forward as grounds for doubting the coherence of agent causation, either absolutely, or with respect to some such general feature of our world.

7.2.1 From the Timing of Actions

C. D. Broad's oft-cited objection to the possibility of agent causation runs thus:

> I see no *prima facie* objection to there being events that are not completely determined. But, in so far as an event *is* determined, an essential factor in its total cause must be other *events*. How can an event possibly be determined to happen at a certain date if its total cause contained no factor to which the notion of date has any application? And how can the notion of date have any application to anything that is not an event? (1952: 215)

Broad's objection, or something like it, would have considerable force against an agent-causal view that maintained that nothing about the agent at the time of his action was explanatorily relevant to its performance.

Such an "action" would indeed seem freakish, or inexplicable in any significant way. But no agent causationist imagines such a scenario. On the version of the view advanced here, the agent's capacity to cause action-triggering events is causally structured by the agent's internal state, involving the having of reasons and other factors, before and up to the time of the action. These events within the agent suffice to explanatorily ground the agent's causing the event to happen "at a certain date" without collapsing the view into one on which those events themselves produce the action.

Randy Clarke, an erstwhile defender of an agent-causal account of freedom, has recently claimed that a modified version of Broad's objection has some force.[14] Events, but not substances, are "directly" in time in that their times are constituents of the events. By contrast, he maintains, "a substance is in time only in that events involving it . . . are directly in time." (This is supposed to be directly parallel to a reverse contention with respect to space, on which substances occupy space directly whereas events in their careers occupy a location only via its constituent object.) From this, he suggests, one can argue that the fact that effects are caused to occur at times "can be so only if their causes likewise occur at times—only, that is, if their causes are directly in time in the way in which events are but substances are not" (2003: 201).

The contention that drives this argument is obscure. It can easily be taken to suggest that events are ontologically more fundamental than objects, a contentious claim that any agent causationist will reject out of hand. But if this is not being claimed—as the reverse contention regarding occupation of space confirms—the point is unclear. What does it mean, exactly, to say that an object exists at a time "only in that" events it undergoes exist at that time? It cannot be the claim that the object's existing at that time metaphysically depends on the event's existing, as the object might have undergone another event at that time instead. If we weaken the claim to the plausible observation that, necessarily, an object exists at time t only if there is some event or other involving it that occurs at t, the dependence is no longer asymmetrical: for any event occurring at t that involves an object, O, necessarily, *that* event exists at t only if O exists

14. 2003: 201–2. Clarke does not claim that this argument is individually decisive. Instead, he presents several considerations, including some that I present below, that he believes to tell against the possibility of agent causation and that cumulatively make the impossibility of agent causation more likely than not. I will argue to the contrary that none of the main considerations he adduces has significant force.

at t. Since I can think of no other way of explicating the "exists only in that" relation, I do not see here a promising basis for Broad's assertion that the cause of an event can only be another "datable" entity.

7.2.2 From the Uniformity of Causal Power

A second objection on which Clarke puts a great deal of weight begins with the following observation. If there is such a thing as agent causation, then there is a property or set of properties whose dispositional profile is precisely to confer on the agent a capacity to cause an intention to act. Notice how this contrasts with other causal powers in a very basic respect: the obtaining of properties that constitute "event-causal" powers themselves tend towards certain effects (conditional on other circumstances). Hence,

> *Event-causal powers* are tendencies towards effects, i.e., the powers themselves are disposed to produce effects.
>
> *Agent-causal power* confers a capacity upon agents to produce effects, i.e., the power is not disposed to produce anything, it merely confers on its possessor a generic disposition to cause effects.

The uniformity objection to the thesis of agent causation is simply that it is doubtful that there can be any such property that fundamentally "works differently" (by conferring a power on its possessor to cause an effect) (2003: 192–3). If true, "causation would then be a radically disunified phenomenon" (2003: 208), and this is evidently a bad thing. We may read this objection as making the claim that the ontological category of *property* has an abstract functional essence that includes the tendency in the presence of other properties towards the direct, joint production of certain effects. Is there reason to think that this is so? One reason to doubt it stems from the variety of property theories philosophers have advanced: transcendent vs. immanent universals vs. tropes; pure powers vs. Humean non-dispositional qualities vs. a "dual-aspect" combination of the two. In the face of serious commitment to and elaboration of such diverse positions, one might think that the range of possibility is correspondingly broad. However, this sort of reason for rejecting the uniform dispositional essence thesis is not compelling. Nearly all philosophers holding one or another of the competing theories of properties just noted believes the truth of their favored theory to be necessary, with the other alleged entities judged to be impossibilities. And that seems the right thing to say, whatever one's view. In particular, if one rejects Humean qualities in favor of either the pure powers or dual-aspect theory, then one should hold that, whatever the variation across possibility space when it comes to the specific kinds of properties there are, they all conform to the general features of one's property.[15]

Thus, one who maintains the uniformity thesis may allow that figuring out the right conception of properties is difficult while contending that, once we have embraced a general approach (here presumed to include irreducible dispositionality), we should presume an absolute unity of nature at a suitable level of abstraction. But at *what* level of abstraction should the thesis be applied? Consider that, in the advent of statistical laws in fundamental physics, many metaphysicians are now comfortable with the notion that there are nondeterministic dispositions varying in strength along a continuum, with deterministic potentialities merely being a limiting case. Consider further that, while properties typically work in tandem towards effects, a natural way of interpreting the phenomenon of radioactive particle decay is as an entirely self-contained process whose timing is radically undetermined by any sort of stimulus event. Finally, some adhere to the truth of (and still others to the possibility of) a view that all or many conscious mental properties are intrinsically intentional while this is true of no physical properties. None of these claims concern free will, and yet all posit a kind of variability in the nature of dispositional properties that warrants classifying them into different basic types. Given these examples, it is hard to see why there may not be a further partition of types of the sort envisioned by the agent causationist. Doubtless there is a unity across these divisions at *some* level of abstraction. But assuming the agent causationist's position is otherwise motivated, he may reasonably contend that it must be sufficiently abstract as to encompass the division his theory requires. Indeed, why may not the unity of *basic* dispositional properties simply consist in their making a net addition to the pool of causal powers?

15. A complication here is that one version of the causal powers theory maintains that there are two fundamental kinds of properties and relations: those whose nature is dispositional and certain "framework" relations such as spatio-temporal relations. (See Ellis 2001.) Suppose this is correct. Even so, one may argue for the abstract functional uniformity of all properties falling on the powers side of this division.

7.2.3 From the Connection between Causation and Probability-Raising

A third consideration for doubting the possibility of agent causation (also given by Clarke 2003) takes as its point of departure that causation is somehow bound up with probability raising. As Clarke notes, it is difficult if not impossible to state a very precise thesis here. In most cases of indeterministic event causation, the obtaining of a causally relevant feature to some degree *raised* the probability of the effect in question—but not, or at least not obviously, in all cases. Given the fact that the obtaining of potential causes may screen off other factors that would otherwise potentially influence an outcome, we can readily imagine cases where something that actually contributed to an effect nonetheless rendered it either no more or even *less* likely than it would have been had that factor not obtained.[16] Still, he contends, there is "considerable plausibility" to the claim that a cause must be the sort of entity that can *antecedently affect the probability* of their effects. But an agent, as such, is not this sort of entity—clearly, only an event or enduring state could be. So the thesis of agent causation runs contrary to a plausible constraint on indeterministic causation by positing agents who are indeterministic causes of certain effects while necessarily not having a direct influence on the prior probability of those effects (2003).

In reply, I suggest that Clarke's proposed constraint on admissible causes is at best a rough, first pass at capturing a conceptual connection between causal factors and probability transmission. And to the extent that there is a plausible intuition underlying it, my structured tendency account of agent causation conforms to it. On this account, agent causation is not something wholly disassociated from the evolving chain of probabilistic causes constituting the world's history. Agent causes act on the basis of prior factors that confer a positive objective probability on their occurrence. This should suffice to conform to any independently plausible, refined thesis that is intended to capture the vague intuition that probability transmission is a fundamental feature of causation. We may grant that, if one *already* believes on independent grounds that agent causation is impossible, then Clarke's more specific claim is a reasonable way to express the intuition. But in the present context, it seems to me a gratuitous strengthening of a general intuition in a way that arbitrarily precludes the possibility of agent causation.

16. Clarke cites (2003) putative illustrations in Dowe 2000: 33–40; Salmon 1984: 192–202; and Ehring 1997: 36. For a deft and thorough development of a theory of indeterministic event causal-powers, see Hiddleston 2005a.

7.2.4 From the Superfluity/Unknowability of Agent Causing That Is Probabilistically Constrained

By constructing a picture on which agent causal power is causally structured by reasons and other factors, I have tried to integrate the view of human freedom it anchors into a view of the wider world as an evolving network of interacting powers. Critics of traditional, less constrained versions of the view have understandably complained that it depicts a godlike transcendence of natural forces. The present project suggests that the objectionable aspect is inessential, since it is possible to give freedom a human face.[17]

To other critics, however, that merely opens up other vulnerabilities. Eric Hiddleston charges that the view of agent causation as probabilistically structured renders it superfluous for explanatory purposes (2005b: 552–3). Any event that one might explain as caused by an agent whose power was probabilistically structured by reasons R1 and R2 might equally well and more economically be explained by the direct causal efficacy of R1 and R2, acting nondeterministically. Furthermore, the agent causal theorist practically invites such an alternative explanation when he allows that in some cases, reasons do in fact bring about actions (though these would not be directly *free* actions).

An initial reply simply notes that the agent causationist will expect that cases where reasons directly bring about actions differ in detectable ways from those in which agent causal power is at work. Viewed from another direction, there is no reason to suppose that an agent whose agent-causal power was rendered inoperative with all else being left untouched would simply carry on exactly as before.

But Hiddleston, I believe, would wish to persist as follows: why would we have reason to posit agent causal power in the first place instead of a causal theory of action on which reasons are productive? It seems that nothing in the observable pattern of events could, even in principle, require us to ascribe certain events to agents as causes.[18]

In reply, I first question the premise that there are no distinctive features of agent-causal processes as against possible cases in which reasons

17. Another recent effort along these lines is O'Connor 2005. Randolph Clarke 2003 is similarly an attempt to give a recognizably human version of the agent causal account of freedom. John Churchill and I give reasons for rejecting Clarke's approach in our 2004.

18. Clarke (2003: 206) endorses the undetectability claim while denying that it gives reason to reject the possibility of agent causation.

nondeterministically produce actions. First, just given the way highly deliberate and unpressured choices seem to us to unfold, it seems doubtful that our reasons fix a probability for the precise timing of the action which they promote. At most, there is an interval of time in which a possible choice is likely to occur, with the likelihood being subject to fluctuation as the agent deliberates. It seems, on some occasions, that I am capable of putting off decisions or continuing to search for reasons pro and con various courses of action, and that there are not fixed probabilities of my ceasing to dither at particular moments. (This is consistent with assuming that there is a high conditional probability for the agent's causing intention *i* at t_1 on *i*'s occurring at t_1.) One might construct a model analogous to the way physicists model particle decay, on which a sample of a radioactive substance of a given mass has an associated probability distribution that measures the likelihood for each moment over an interval of its having lost half its mass by that time. But any such model generally applied to the case of freely making a choice would seem contrived.

Second, the agent causationist can plausibly suppose that while there is a probability of an agent's causing an intention to *A*, there is no particular probability of that intention's having a further goal-directed content in the sense I spoke of as acting *for*, and not just *on*, a reason. That is, there may be a probability of 0.6 that an agent will, within a specified interval of time, cause an intention to *A*, but no probabilities to its having the precise content of simply *A*, *A-for-the-sake-of-G1*, or *A-for-the-sake-of-G2*.

I put forward these two suggestions with some diffidence, as they are grounded in vague intuitions concerning how actions seem to us to unfold. A more firmly-grounded response to the "no evidence" objection is that, even if there weren't these differences from possible cases of indeterministic causation by reasons, we have a general explanatory reason to accept that agents are sometimes causes. The thesis that agents are sometimes causes, in my view, best reflects the phenomenology of many of our actions and it is required by our (related) native belief that most human adults are free and morally responsible agents.

In general respects, the explanatory appeal to agent causation is similar to the appeal to causal realism. The skeptical Humean insists that all we need are the observable patterns among events, (allegedly) conceived non-dispositionally. According to the realist, we must go deeper, explaining the patterns themselves in terms of the structured propensities of the world's basic features. Humean complaints that primitive causation is an "occult" metaphysical relation are just so much throwing dust in the air and complaining that one cannot see. We have an intuitive grasp—albeit one that is highly general, needing elucidation—on the idea of causal power and it is fundamental to our naïve conception of the world around us. Now, Hiddleston himself is no Humean. As it happens, however, he endorses Nancy Cartwright's (1989) idiosyncratic claim to provide a purely *empirical,* neutral case for the existence of event-causal dispositions, a case that turns on the nature of successful scientific practice in isolating causal influences. (And so he thinks there is a principled asymmetry concerning the possibility of evidence for event and agent causal dispositions.) Here, I can only join hands with many others in confessing not to understand exactly how Cartwright's argument is supposed to go—how it is that the convinced Humean cannot give an alternate interpretation (however perverse to my realist eyes on non-empirical grounds) of what is observed and the empirical inferences and theorizing based upon it.

Many philosophers (including Hiddleston) dispute the claim that our experience of acting in any way supports the thesis that human agents are sometimes (literally) causes. Randy Clarke writes:

> I do not find it a credible claim that ordinary human agents have any experience, or any belief arising directly from experience, the content of which is correctly characterized in terms of agent causation . . . . Ordinary human agents, it seems plain, lack the concept of substance causation. A representation of free action as substance-caused (or as consisting on the substance causation of some event internal to the action) is a sophisticated philosophical construction. (2003: 206–7)

Now, something in the neighborhood of Clarke's remarks is surely correct. It takes philosophical reflection to attain a clear grasp on the idea of agents qua substance as causes, as distinct from either events internal to the agent as causes or the bogus Humean surrogate of patterns of (actual or counterfactual) regularity among events internal to the agent. But, for all that, it may be (and I contend, *is*) the case that (a) the content of the experience-in-acting of ordinary human agents involves a fairly inchoate sense of themselves as bringing about their actions and that (b) the reflective account that best captures this inchoate content is the agent-causal account. I observe that this position on the ordinary *experience* of agency is supported by Daniel Wegner, a prominent cognitive psychologist who goes on to argue that our experience of agency is deeply illusory.[19]

19. See Wegner 2002, chapter 1. I criticize Wegner's case for the illusory character of what he terms "conscious willing" in my 2005: 220–6.

7.2.5 From the Insufficiency (for Freedom) of Agent Causing That Is Probabilistically Constrained

Recall that an apparent difficulty facing an alternative, causal indeterminist account of human freedom—an account that eschews agent causation in favor of a nondeterministic causation of choices by one's reasons—is that it appears to be a matter of luck which of the undetermined possibilities is realized in a particular case. Given the presence of desires and intentions of varying strength, making certain outcomes more likely than others, the agent possesses no further power to determine which outcome in fact is brought about. The determination is a product of the propensities of the agent's states, and the agent doesn't seem to directly control which propensity will "fire." If we imagine two identical agents in identical circumstances, with one agent nondeterministically choosing alternative *A* and the other choosing *B*, it seems a matter of luck from the standpoint of the agents themselves which alternative occurs in which person.

Supposing there is a power of agent causation has the virtue that it seems to avoid this "problem of luck" facing other indeterministic accounts.[20] Agent causation is precisely the power to directly determine which of several causal possibilities is realized on a given occasion. However, Derk Pereboom has recently argued that this is so only if agent causation does not conform to pre-given indeterministic tendencies.[21] He writes:

> . . . to answer the luck objection, the causal power exercised by the agent must be of a different sort from that of the events that shape the agent-causal power, and on the occasion of a free decision, the exercise of these causal powers must be token-distinct from the exercise of the causal powers of the events. Given this requirement, we would expect the decisions of the agent-cause to diverge, in the long run, from the frequency of choices that would be extremely likely on the basis of the

20. In addition to causal indeterminist and agent causal theories of freedom, there is noncausal indeterminism, on which control is an intrinsic, noncausal feature of free choices or actions. For versions of this view, see Goetz 1988; Ginet 1990; McCann 1998; and Pink 2004.

21. Others have recently argued that agent causation does not necessarily avoid the problem of luck (or, as it is sometimes put, the "problem of control"). See Haji 2004; Widerker 2005; and Mele 2006. I will not here address their ways of pressing the issue, though I find their arguments even less compelling than the one by Pereboom that I discuss in the text. Pereboom (2005: 243–4) also rejects the arguments of Mele and Haji.

> events alone. If we nevertheless found conformity, we would have very good reason to believe that the agent-causal power was not of a different sort from the causal powers of the events after all, and that on the occasion of particular decisions, the exercise of these causal powers was not token-distinct. Or else, this conformity would be a wild coincidence. (2005: 246)

Though Pereboom expresses the matter in epistemological terms, I take it that he intends to be making a linked pair of metaphysical claims, as follows. If agent-causal power is to truly enable the agent directly to determine which causally-possible choice obtains, and so overcome the luck objection plaguing other accounts of freedom, then it must be a different sort of power from event-causal powers such as the propensities of one's reasons, such that its exercise is token-distinct from the exercise of any of these event-causal powers. And the latter condition can be met only if the outcomes of agent-causal events are not strictly governed by the propensities of any relevant set of obtaining event-causal powers.

The agent causationist readily endorses the first of these conditionals, on a straightforward reading of "different sort of power" and "token-distinct exercise." After all, the view posits a fundamental, irreducible power of agents to form intentions. But the second conditional directly rejects the viability of any account on which agent causal power is probabilistically structured by reasons. Why does Pereboom assert it? His thought seems to be that if the event of one's having certain reasons along with other prior events ensure that one's choices will fit a certain pattern—more accurately, make the pattern-fitting likely, given a sufficiently large number of cases—then one's supposed agent-causal power in choosing is at best a shadowy accompaniment to the event-causal power. In truth, it is no power at all, as it adds nothing to the mix of factors already in play. With no authority to act on its own, its presence makes no discernible difference to what occurs in the aggregate. If it would be a matter of luck, beyond my direct control, which of my indeterministic propensities happens to be realized on any given occasion, were the causal indeterminist account correct, then adding the ability to "directly determine" the outcome wouldn't help if I am ineluctably constrained by those very propensities.

It is easy to feel the pull of this thought, but it should be resisted. First, we insist upon the importance of the distinction between (the persisting state or event of one's having) reasons *structuring* one's agent-causal power in the sense of conferring objective tendencies towards particular actions and reasons *activating* that power by producing one's causing a specific intention. On the view I have described, nothing other than the agent himself activates the agent causal power in this way. To say that I have an objective probability of 0.8 to cause the intention to join my students at the local pub ensures nothing about what I will in fact do. I can resist this rather strong inclination just as well as act upon it. The probability simply measures relative likelihood and serves to predict a distribution of outcomes were I to be similarly inclined in similar circumstances many times over (which of course I never am in actual practice). The reason that the alternative, causal indeterminist view is subject to the luck objection is *not* that it posits objective probabilities to possible outcomes but that it fails to posit a kind of single-case form of control by means of which the agent can determine what happens in each case. After all, were the causal indeterminist picture modified so that agents' choices are caused but not determined by appropriate internal states whose propensities, while nondeterministic, lacked definite measure, the problem of luck or control would remain. Again, that problem concerns not prior influence but the ability to settle what occurs on the occasion of a causally undetermined outcome. The agent causationist's solution is to posit a basic capacity of just that sort, while allowing that the capacity is not situated within an indifferent agent, but one with evolving preferences and beliefs. Surely having preferences does not undermine control!

7.3 Conclusion

Causation is a primitive, yet fairly simple concept. Reflective theorizing, both philosophical and scientific, has yielded a variety of forms in which it can be coherently conceived. Absent convincing reason to think one of these imagined forms is defective in some unobvious way, we ought to deem it possible. It has been the aim of the present essay to specify a coherent way we might think about the idea of agent-causal power, an idea that has guided some who theorize about freedom of the will and that is even deemed intuitively attractive by some who resist it. It may be metaphysically impossible that there be such a thing, but I have yet to encounter a convincing argument for it.

Works Cited

Armstrong, D. 1978. *A Theory of Universals.* (Vol. 2 of *Universals and Scientific Realism.*) Cambridge: Cambridge University Press.

Armstrong, D. 1997. *A World of States of Affairs.* Cambridge: Cambridge University Press.

Armstrong, D., C. B. Martin, and U. T. Place. 1996. *Dispositions: A Debate.* London: Routledge Press.

Broad, C. D. 1952. "Determinism, Indeterminism, and Libertarianism." In his *Ethics and the History of Philosophy: Selected Essays.* New York: Humanities Press.

Cartwright, N. 1989. *Nature's Capacities and Their Measurement.* Oxford: Oxford University Press.

Clarke, R. 2003. *Libertarian Accounts of Free Will.* New York: Oxford University Press.

Dowe, P. 2000. *Physical Causation.* Cambridge: Cambridge University Press.

Ehring, D. 1997. *Causation and Persistence.* New York: Oxford University Press.

Ellis, B. 2001. *Scientific Essentialism.* Cambridge: Cambridge University Press.

Ginet, C. 1990. *On Action.* Cambridge: Cambridge University Press.

Goetz, S. 1988. "A Noncausal Theory of Agency." *Philosophy and Phenomenological Research* 49: 303–16.

Haji, I. 2004. "Active Control, Agent-Causation, and Free Action." *Philosophical Explorations* 7 (2): 131–48.

Hawthorne, J. 2001. "Causal Structuralism." *Philosophical Perspectives* 15: 361–78.

Heil, J., and C. B. Martin. 1999. "The Ontological Turn." *Midwest Studies in Philosophy* 23: 34–60.

Hiddleston, E. 2005a. "Causal Powers." *The British Journal for the Philosophy of Science* 56 (1): 27–59.

Hiddleston, E. 2005b. "Critical Notice: Timothy O'Connor, *Persons and Causes.*" *Noûs* 39 (3): 541–56.

Kane, R. 1996. *The Significance of Free Will.* New York: Oxford University Press.

Laughlin, R. B., D. Pines, J. Schmalian, B. Stojkovic, and P. Wolynes. 2000. "The Middle Way." *Proceedings of the National Academy of Sciences* 97 (Jan. 4): 32–7.

Lewis, D. 1983. *Philosophical Papers,* Vol. 1. New York: Oxford University Press.

Lowe, E. J. 2002. *A Survey of Metaphysics.* Oxford: Oxford University Press.

Martin, C. B. 1997. "On the Need for Properties: The Road to Pythagoreanism and Back." *Synthese* 112: 193–231.

McCann, H. 1998. *The Works of Agency.* Ithaca: Cornell University Press.

Mele, A. 2006. *Free Will and Luck.* New York: Oxford University Press.

Molnar, G. 2003. *Powers: A Study in Metaphysics.* Ed. by S. Mumford. Oxford: Oxford University Press.

O'Connor, T. 2000. *Persons and Causes: The Metaphysics of Free Will.* New York: Oxford University Press.

O'Connor, T. 2005. "Freedom with a Human Face." *Midwest Studies in Philosophy* 29: 207–27.

O'Connor, T., and J. Churchill. 2004. "Reasons Explanation and Agent Control: In Search of an Integrated Account." *Philosophical Topics* 32: 241–54.

O'Connor, T., and H. Y. Wong. 2002. "Emergent Properties." *Stanford Online Encyclopedia of Philosophy.* http://plato.stanford.edu/entries/properties-emergent/.

O'Connor, T., and H. Y. Wong. 2005. "The Metaphysics of Emergence." *Noûs* 39: 659–79.

Pereboom, D. 2005. "Defending Hard Incompatibilism." *Midwest Studies in Philosophy* 29: 228–47.

Pink, T. 2004. *Free Will: A Very Short Introduction.* Oxford: Oxford University Press.

Salmon, W. 1984. *Scientific Explanation and the Causal Structure of the World.* Princeton, NJ: Princeton University Press.

Tooley, M. 1987. *Causation: A Realist Approach.* Oxford: Clarendon Press.

Van Inwagen, P. 1983. *An Essay on Free Will.* Oxford: Clarendon Press.

Wegner, D. 2002. *The Illusion of Conscious Will.* Cambridge, MA: MIT Press.

Widerker, D. 2005. "Agent-Causation and Control." *Faith and Philosophy* 22 (1): 87–98.

Selected Bibliography

Books

Allison, Henry. *Kant's Theory of Freedom,* Cambridge: Cambridge University Press, 1990.

Arpaly, Nomy. *Merit, Meaning, and Bondage: An Essay on Free Will,* Princeton: Princeton University Press, 2006.

Berofsky, Bernard. *Freedom from Necessity: The Metaphysical Basis of Responsibility,* New York: Routledge and Kegan Paul, 1987.

Bok, Hilary. *Freedom and Responsibility,* Princeton: Princeton University Press, 1998.

Chisholm, Roderick. *Person and Object,* La Salle: Open Court, 1976.

Clarke, Randolph. *Libertarian Theories of Free Will,* New York: Oxford University Press, 2003.

Dennett, Daniel. *Elbow Room,* Cambridge, MA: MIT Press, 1984.

———. *Freedom Evolves,* New York: Viking, 2003.

Double, Richard. *Metaphilosophy and Free Will,* New York: Oxford University Press, 1996.

———. *The Non-Reality of Free Will,* New York: Oxford University Press, 1991.

Ekstrom, Laura W. *Free Will: A Philosophical Study,* Boulder: Westview, 2000.

Fischer, John Martin. *My Way,* New York: Oxford University Press, 2006.

———. *The Metaphysics of Free Will,* Oxford: Blackwell, 1994.

Fischer, John Martin, and Mark Ravizza. *Responsibility and Control: A Theory of Moral Responsibility,* New York: Cambridge University Press, 1998.

Fischer, John Martin, Robert Kane, Derk Pereboom, and Manuel Vargas. *Four Views on Free Will,* Oxford: Blackwell, 2007.

Ginet, Carl. *On Action,* Cambridge: Cambridge University Press, 1990.

Goetz, Stewart. *Freedom Teleology and Evil,* London: Continuum, 2008.

Haji, Ishtiyaque. *Deontic Morality and Control,* Cambridge: Cambridge University Press, 2003.

———. *Incompatibilism's Allure: Principal Arguments for Incompatibilism,* Calgary: Broadview Press, 2009.

———. *Moral Appraisability,* New York: Oxford University Press, 1998.

Harris, James A. *Of Liberty and Necessity: The Free Will Debate in Eighteenth-Century British Philosophy,* Oxford: Oxford University Press, 2005.

Honderich, Ted. *A Theory of Determinism,* Oxford: Oxford University Press, 1988.

Kane, Robert. *The Significance of Free Will,* New York: Oxford University Press, 1996.

McCann, Hugh. *The Works of Agency: On Human Action, Will, and Freedom,* Ithaca: Cornell University Press, 1998.

Mele, Alfred. *Autonomous Agents,* Oxford: Oxford University Press, 1995.

———. *Free Will and Luck,* Oxford: Oxford University Press, 2006.

Moya, Carlos. *Moral Responsibility: The Ways of Skepticism,* Oxford: Oxford University Press, 2006.

Nagel, Thomas. *The View from Nowhere,* Oxford: Oxford University Press, 1986.

O'Connor, Timothy. *Persons and Causes,* Oxford: Oxford University Press, 2000.

Pereboom, Derk. *Living without Free Will,* Cambridge: Cambridge University Press, 2001.

Priestly, Joseph. *The Doctrine of Philosophical Necessity Illustrated.* London: J. Johnson, 1777. Reprinted in Joseph Priestly, *Disquisitions Relating to Matter and Spirit and Philosophical Necessity Illustrated.* New York: Garland, 1976.

Pink, Thomas. *Free Will: A Very Short Introduction,* New York: Oxford University Press, 2004.

Rowe, William. *Thomas Reid on Freedom and Morality,* Ithaca: Cornell University Press, 1991.

Russell, Paul. *Freedom and Moral Sentiment: Hume's Way of Naturalizing Responsibility,* New York: Oxford University Press, 1995.

Scanlon, Thomas. *Moral Dimensions: Permissibility, Meaning, Blame,* Cambridge, MA: Harvard University Press, 2008.

Sher, George. *In Praise of Blame,* New York: Oxford University Press, 2006.

Smilansky, Saul. *Free Will and Illusion,* Oxford: Oxford University Press, 2000.

Strawson, Galen. *Freedom and Belief,* Oxford: Oxford University Press, 1986.

Stump, Eleonore. *Aquinas,* London: Routledge, 2003.

Taylor, Richard. *Action and Purpose,* Englewood Cliffs: Prentice-Hall, 1966.

Timpe, Kevin. *Free Will: Sourcehood and Its Alternatives,* London: Continuum, 2008.

Van Inwagen, Peter. *An Essay on Free Will,* Oxford: Oxford University Press, 1983.

Wallace, R. Jay. *Responsibility and the Moral Sentiments,* Cambridge, MA: Harvard University Press, 1994.

Waller, Bruce. *Freedom without Responsibility,* Philadelphia: Temple University Press, 1990.

Watson, Gary. *Agency and Answerability,* Oxford: Oxford University Press, 2004.

Wolf, Susan. *Freedom within Reason,* Oxford: Oxford University Press, 1990.

Yaffe, Gideon. *Liberty Worth the Name: Locke on Free Agency,* Princeton: Princeton University Press, 2000.

———. *Manifest Activity: Thomas Reid's Theory of Action,* Oxford: Oxford University Press, 2004.

Anthologies and Collections

Essays on Free Will and Moral Responsibility, Nick Trakakis and Daniel Cohen, eds., Newcastle: Cambridge Scholars Press, 2008.

Free Will, Robert Kane, ed., Oxford: Blackwell Publishers, 2001

Free Will, Second Edition, Gary Watson, ed., New York: Oxford University Press, 2003.

Freedom, Responsibility, and Agency: Essays on the Importance of Alternative Possibilities, Michael McKenna and David Widerker, eds., Aldershot: Ashgate, 2003.

The Oxford Handbook of Free Will, Robert Kane, ed., New York: Oxford University Press, 2002.

Responsibility, Character, and the Emotions, Ferdinand Schoeman, ed., Cambridge: Cambridge University Press, 1987.

Articles

Balaguer, Mark. "A Coherent, Naturalistic, and Plausible Formulation of Libertarian Free Will," *Noûs* 38 (2004), pp. 379–406.

Clarke, Randolph. "Dispositions, Abilities to Act, and Free Will," *Mind* 118 (2009), pp. 323–51.

Fara, Michael. "Masked Abilities and Compatibilism," *Mind* 117 (2008), pp. 848–65.

Fischer, John Martin. "Responsibility and Control," *Journal of Philsoophy* 79 (1982), pp. 24–40.

Ginet, Carl. "In Defense of the Principle of Alternative Possibilities: Why I Don't Find Frankfurt's Arguments Convincing," *Philosophical Perspectives* 10 (1996), pp. 403–17.

———. "Freedom, Responsibility, and Agency," *Journal of Ethics* 1 (1997), pp. 85–98.

Hobart, R. E. "Free Will as Involving Determinism and Impossible without It," *Mind* 43 (1934), pp. 1–27.

Hunt, David. "Moral Responsibility and Unavoidable Action," *Philosophical Studies* 97 (2000), pp. 195–227.

———. "Moral Responsibility and Buffered Alternatives," *Midwest Studies in Philosophy* 29 (2005), pp. 126–45.

James, William. "The Dilemma of Determinism," in *The Will to Believe and Other Essays,* New York, Longman, 1909. *Unitarian Review* 22 (1884), pp. 193–224.

Kapitan, Thomas. "Deliberation and the Presumption of Open Alternatives," *Philosophical Quarterly* 36 (1986), pp. 230–51.

Lewis, David. "Are We Free to Break the Laws?" *Theoria* 47 (2003), pp. 113–21.

McKenna, Michael. "Saying Good-Bye to the Direct Argument in the Right Way," *Philosophical Review* 117 (2008), pp. 349–83.

———. "Where Frankfurt and Strawson Meet," *Midwest Studies in Philosophy* 29 (2005), pp. 163–80.

Mele, Alfred, and David Robb. "Rescuing Frankfurt-Style Cases," *Philosophical Review* 107 (1998), pp. 97–112.

Nahmias, Eddy, Stephen Morris, Thomas Nadelhoffer, and Jason Turner. "Is Incompatibilism Intuitive?" *Philosophy and Phenomenological Research* 73 (2006), pp. 28–53.

Nelkin, Dana. "Deliberative Alternatives," *Philosophical Topics* 32 (2004), pp. 215–40.

Nelkin, Dana, "Responsibility and Rational Abilities: Defending an Asymmetrical View," *Pacific Philosophical Quarterly* 89 (2008), pp. 497–515.

Nichols, S., and J. Knobe, "Moral Responsibility and Determinism: The Cognitive Science of Folk Intuitions," *Noûs* 41 (2007), pp. 663–85.

Oshana, Marina. "Moral Accountability," *Philosophical Topics* 32 (2004), pp. 255–74.

Otsuka, Michael. "Incompatibilism and the Avoidability of Blame," *Ethics* 108 (1998), pp. 685–701.

Shabo, Seth. "Uncompromising Source Incompatibilism," *Philosophy and Phenomenological Research,* forthcoming.

Smart, J. J. C. "Free Will, Praise, and Blame," *Mind* 70 (1963), pp. 136–51.

Smith, Angela. "Conflicting Attitudes, Moral Agency, and Conceptions of the Self," *Philosophical Topics* 32 (2004), pp. 331–52.

Sommers, Tamler. "The Objective Attitude," *The Philosophical Quarterly* 57 (2007), pp. 321–41.

Speak, Daniel. "Toward an Axiological Defense of Libertarianism," *Philosophical Topics* 32 (2004), pp. 253–70.

Stump, Eleonore. "Libertarian Freedom and the Principle of Alternative Possibilities," in *Faith, Freedom, and Rationality,* Jeff Jordan and Daniel Howard Snyder, eds., Lanham, MD: Rowman and Littlefield, 1996, pp. 73–88.

Vihvelin, Kadri. "Freedom, Causation, and Counterfactuals," *Philosophical Studies* 64 (1991), pp. 161–84.

———. "Free Will Demystified: A Dispositional Account," *Philosophical Topics* 32 (2004), pp. 427–50.

Warfield, Ted. "Causal Determinism and Human Freedom Are Incompatible," *Philosophical Perspectives* 14 (2000), pp. 167–80.

Watson, Gary. "Free Agency," *Journal of Philosophy* 72 (1975), pp. 205–20.

———. "Responsibility and the Limits of Evil," in *Responsibility, Character, and the Emotions,* Ferdinand Schoeman, ed., Cambridge: Cambridge University Press, 1987, pp. 256–86.

Widerker, David. "Frankfurt's Attack on Alternative Possibilities," *Philosophical Perspectives* 14 (2000), pp. 181–201.

———. "Libertarianism and Frankfurt's Attack on the Principle of Alternative Possibilities," *Philosophical Review* 104 (1995), pp. 247–61.

Wyma, Keith D. "Moral Responsibility and Leeway for Action," *American Philosophical Quarterly* 34 (1997), pp. 57–70.